Corporate Compliance

NEW HORIZONS IN LAW AND ECONOMICS

Series editors: Gerrit De Geest, Washington University in St. Louis, USA; Roger Van den Bergh, Erasmus University Rotterdam, The Netherlands; and Thomas S. Ulen, University of Illinois at Urbana-Champaign, USA.

The application of economic ideas and theories to the law and the explanation of markets and public economics from a legal point of view is recognized as one of the most exciting developments in both economics and the law. This important series is designed to make a significant contribution to the development of law and economics.

The main emphasis is on the development and application of new ideas. The series provides a forum for original research in areas such as criminal law, civil law, labour law, corporate law, family law, regulation and privatization, tax, risk and insurance and competition law. International in its approach it includes some of the best theoretical and empirical work from both well-established researchers and the new generation of scholars.

Titles in the series include:

New Perspectives on Economic Crime
Edited by Hans Sjögren and Göran Skogh

Law, Economics and Cyberspace
The Effects of Cyberspace on the Economic Analysis of Law
Niva Elkin-Koren and Eli M. Salzberger

Games and Public Administration
The Law and Economics of Regulation and Licensing
Georg von Wangenheim

Law and the State
A Political Economy Approach
Edited by Alain Marciano and Jean-Michel Josselin

Democracy, Freedom and Coercion
A Law and Economics Approach
Edited by Alain Marciano and Jean-Michel Josselin

The Economics of Courts and Litigation
Francisco Cabrillo and Sean Fitzpatrick

Transport, Welfare and Externalities
Replacing the Polluter Pays Principle with the Cheapest Cost Avoider Principle
Dieter Schmidtchen, Christian Koboldt, Jenny Helstroffer, Birgit Will, Georg Haas and Stefan Witte

New Trends in Financing Civil Litigation in Europe
A Legal, Empirical, and Economic Analysis
Mark Tuil and Louis Visscher

Comparative Contract Law and Economics
Mitja Kovač

The Law and Economics of Class Actions in Europe
Lessons from America
Edited by Jürgen G. Backhaus, Alberto Cassone and Giovanni B. Ramello

Corporate Compliance
New Approaches to Regulatory Enforcement
Sharon Oded

Corporate Compliance

New Approaches to Regulatory Enforcement

Sharon Oded

Assistant Professor, Erasmus University Rotterdam, The Netherlands and Senior Associate, De Brauw Blackstone Westbroek, The Netherlands; formerly, Visiting Fellow, University of California, Berkeley, USA

NEW HORIZONS IN LAW AND ECONOMICS

Edward Elgar

Cheltenham, UK • Northampton, MA, USA

Published by
Edward Elgar Publishing Limited
The Lypiatts
15 Lansdown Road
Cheltenham
Glos GL50 2JA
UK

Edward Elgar Publishing, Inc.
William Pratt House
9 Dewey Court
Northampton
Massachusetts 01060
USA

A catalogue record for this book
is available from the British Library

Library of Congress Control Number: 2013936181

This book is available electronically in the ElgarOnline.com Law Subject Collection, E-ISBN 978 1 78195 475 1

ISBN 978 1 78195 474 4

Typeset by Servis Filmsetting Ltd, Stockport, Cheshire
Printed and bound in Great Britain by T.J. International Ltd, Padstow

To my beloved wife, Maya
Confidante, sweetheart, partner, friend

Contents

Acknowledgements

It is a pleasure to thank those who made this research endeavor possible. First and foremost, I owe my deepest gratitude to Michael G. Faure for his endless support and insightful advice, enthusiasm, and inspiration. I would like to extend my sincere gratitude to Robert Cooter and Daniel Rubinfeld for sponsoring me during my period as a visiting scholar at the University of California, Berkeley (2010–2011), and for offering their sage advice. I am also grateful to Robert A. Kagan, Jennifer H. Arlen, Anthony Ogus and Roger J. Van den Bergh for their helpful comments on previous drafts of my work. I am indebted to Alessio M. Pacces and Louis T. Visscher for their intellectual stimulation and generosity with their time. Lastly, I would like to thank my family, whose unconditional support I knew I could always rely on.

Tables and figures

TABLES

FIGURES

Abbreviations

ACCC	Australian Competition and Consumer Commission
CEO	Chief Executive Officer
CM	An Independent Corporate Monitoring Firm
DG	Directorate-General (department) at the European Commission
DOJ	U.S. Department of Justice
DPA	Deferred Prosecution Agreement
ECJ	European Court of Justice
EPA	U.S. Environmental Protection Agency
EU	European Union
FCPA	Foreign Corrupt Practices Act
FTC	U.S. Federal Trade Commission
GAO	U.S. Government Accountability Office
HHS	U.S. Department of Health and Safety
ICC	International Chamber of Commerce
NPA	Non-Prosecution Agreement
OFT	U.K. Office of Fair Trading
OIG	Office of Inspector General at the HHS
OSG	Organization Sentencing Guidelines
RICO	Racketeer Influenced and Corrupt Organizations Act
SEC	U.S. Securities and Exchange Commission
SOX	Sarbanes-Oxley Act of 2002
TFT	Tit-for-Tat
TPTM	Third-Party-Based Targeted Monitoring
USSC	U.S. Sentencing Commission

Prologue: the *President Coolidge*

The steamship "President Coolidge" arrived in the harbor of Honolulu August 26, 1937, and tied up at pier 8. At about the hour of 10 a.m. of that day, one Norman R. Arthur, a harbor patrol boatman under the United States District Engineer, was passing under the stern of the "President Coolidge" in a patrol boat, when a quantity of garbage, consisting of cabbage, orange peel, celery, tea leaves, and water, descended upon him, part thereof falling in the water . . . Immediately following his being drenched with the refuse, Arthur cleared his eyes, then looked and saw a person, apparently Chinese, walking away from the stern rail of the Coolidge, carrying a can or bucket . . . Arthur fastened his small boat to the pier, changed clothes and boarded the "President Coolidge" to make a search for the person responsible. He saw the chief mate and explained what had happened and the officer conducted an investigation, but no further information was secured.

There was testimony on behalf of the claimant that orders had been issued by the Company against throwing of refuse from the ship while in harbor; that signs were placed in conspicuous places written in English and Chinese, warning employees not to throw things overboard; that locks were placed upon the slop chutes to prevent their use while in harbor; that the officers of the ship had no knowledge of violation of the law or their orders in this respect and in this instance. . . .

Having committed his ship to the seas, an owner takes the risk of much which he cannot easily control. Any other construction would change the statute from one of prohibition to that requiring merely due care.

Affirmed.

With these words, on January 23rd, 1939, the Honorable Francis A. Garrecht, a senior ninth circuit court judge, affirmed the District Court of Hawaii's decree, which penalized the corporation that owned the steamship *President Coolidge*, for its employee's misconduct.[1] No questions were raised regarding what genuine efforts the corporation had made to prevent the violation. Nor were any additional arguments presented concerning other precautionary measures the corporation might have taken to prevent the violation. In fact, it was never argued that the corporation could have exercised more control over its employees or could have prevented their misconduct. Notwithstanding, the corporation was held strictly liable for the misconduct of its employee.

In the seven decades since the *President Coolidge* case, corporate

1 See *Dollar S.S. Co. v. United States* 101 F.2d 638 (9th Cir. 1939).

enforcement policies around the globe have gone through a sea of change. One major factor underlying contemporary policy developments is the recent acknowledgment that in many contexts corporations are able to control their employees more efficiently than public authorities.[2] It is not surprising, therefore, that current law enforcement measures perceive corporations as potential partners, rather than enemies, in the battle against law-breaking.[3] These contemporary perceptions, however, provide no single recipe for the structure of optimal enforcement policies. In some jurisdictions, such as with U.S. Federal law, the traditional, rigid approach, which disregards corporations' compliance efforts in determining corporate liability, has been replaced by a more conciliatory approach. Contemporary Federal laws in the U.S. recognize a given corporation's internal enforcement efforts as a relevant determinant of that corporation's liability.[4] By contrast, enforcement policies in other jurisdictions, such as in certain areas of EU law, have evolved through an alternative route, replacing the conciliatory approach, which accepted corporate

---

[2] See, for instance, Jennifer Arlen and Reinier Kraakman, "Controlling Corporate Misconduct: An Analysis of Corporate Liability Regimes," *NYU Law Review* 72(4) (1997), p. 700; Charles J. Walsh and Alissa Pyrich, "Corporate Compliance Programs as a Defense to Criminal Liability: Can a Corporation Save its Soul?" *Rutgers Law Review* 47 (1995), p. 678; Vikramaditya S. Khanna and Timothy L. Dickinson, "The Corporate Monitor: The New Corporate Czar," *Michigan Law Review* 105 (2007), pp. 1728–1729; Ben W. Heineman, Jr., "Caught in the Middle," *Corporate Counsel*, April 2007, p. 89; Reinier Kraakman, "Vicarious and Corporate Liability," in *Tort Law and Economics*, Michael Faure ed., 2nd. edn (Cheltenham, U.K. & Northampton, MA, U.S.A.: Edward Elgar, 2009), p. 671; Steven Shavell, *Economic Analysis of Accident Law* (Cambridge, MA: Harvard University Press, 1987), pp. 173–174; Jennifer Arlen, "The Potentially Perverse Effects of Corporate Criminal Liability," *Journal of Legal Studies* 23(2) (1994), 833–867; Kevin B. Huff, "The Role of Corporate Compliance Programs in Determining Corporate Criminal Liability: A Suggested Approach," *Columbia Law Review* 96 (1996), p. 1281; Vikramaditya S. Khanna, "Corporate Liability Standards: When Should Corporations be Held Criminally Liable?" *American Criminal Law Review* 37 (2002), p. 1245.

[3] See, for instance, Huff, "The Role of Corporate Compliance Programs in Determining Corporate Criminal Liability: A Suggested Approach," pp. 1263, 1295; Harvey L. Pitt and Karl A. Groskaufmanis, "Minimizing Corporate Civil and Criminal Liability: A Second Look at Corporate Codes of Conduct," *Georgetown Law Journal* 78 (1990), p. 1573; Walsh and Pyrich, "Corporate Compliance Programs as a Defense to Criminal Liability: Can a Corporation Save its Soul?," pp. 620–621, 636, 678; Steven Shavell, "The Optimal Level of Corporate Liability Given the Limited Ability of Corporations to Penalize their Employees," *International Review of Law and Economics* 17(2) (1997), 203–213.

[4] A detailed overview of policy developments in U.S. enforcement policies is provided in Chapter 5.

compliance efforts as a justification for liability mitigation, with a by-the-book approach, which harshly penalizes corporations for employee misconduct regardless of corporate efforts to secure compliance.[5] Despite their different approaches, all such policies share a similar goal; they seek not only to deter corporations from law-breaking, but also to induce them to ensure, proactively, compliance by those acting on their behalf. Such policies seek, for instance, to encourage corporations to act to prevent employee misconduct by providing employees with clear guidelines, manuals, and ethics codes directing their behavior. Moreover, such policies also encourage corporations to monitor the activity of their employees, to detect misconduct, and to take appropriate actions against detected misconduct, including sanctioning employees and reporting violations to the relevant enforcement authorities.

These different approaches raise a number of questions. How should a regulatory enforcement system be crafted to efficiently induce corporate proactive compliance? Should corporations be held liable for their employee misconduct? How should the role played by corporations in supporting, or combating employee misconduct affect corporate exposure to liability? Should enforcement measures apply, uniformly, in all cases? What if the violation was conducted by an employee against clear corporate policies and direct instructions, as was the case on board the *President Coolidge*? And, may enforcement authorities consider corporations' violation records when imposing corporate liability? These questions lie at the heart of this book.

---

[5] A comparative analysis of enforcement policies is provided in Chapter 5, Section 5.8.

1. Introduction

1.1 REGULATORY ENFORCEMENT AND CORPORATE COMPLIANCE

Most of the economic activity in modern societies is conducted through business corporations.[1] Given the profound impact of corporate activity on the entire society, corporate misconduct comprises a significant threat to social welfare. Imprudent or irresponsible corporate actions may harm a wide group of people, both economically and physically.[2] Hence, despite recent "free market" global trends, governments in modern societies hold a central position in directing and controlling corporate activity. In an attempt to promote societal goals, and broadly protect the interests of society, governments issue a wide range of regulations with the aim of establishing the necessary rules of conduct required to engender a socially desirable state of affairs.

The enforcement of regulations is a key aspect of every regulatory system. The social value of regulations is contingent, first and foremost, on the desirability of the standards of behavior dictated by them. Nevertheless, the promulgation of socially desirable standards of behavior does not guarantee their positive impact on society.[3] To attain socially desirable ends, regulations must be adequately enforced, while the particularities

---

1 The central role of business corporations in modern societies has been acknowledged by courts, see, for instance, *New York Cent. & Hudson River R.R. v. United States*, 212 U.S. 481, 495–496 (1909); see also, Roland Hefendehl, "Corporate Criminal Liability: Model Penal Code Section 2.07 and the Development in Western Legal Systems," *Buffalo Criminal Law Review* 4 (2000), p. 290.

2 See Law Reform Commission of New South Wales, "Sentencing: Corporate Offenders," Issues Paper 20 (2001); available at: http://www.lawlink.nsw.gov.au/lrc.nsf/pages/ip20chp01.

3 For a discussion of the particularities of regulatory enforcement see Anthony Ogus, "Criminal Law and Regulation," in *Criminal Law and Economics*, Nuno Garoupa ed., 2nd edn (Cheltenham, U.K. & Northampton, MA, U.S.A.: Edward Elgar Publishing, 2009), 90–110; Anthony Ogus, "Enforcing Regulation: Do We Need the Criminal Law?" in *New Perspectives on Economic Crime*, H. Sjogren and G. Skogh eds (Cheltenham, U.K. & Northampton, MA, U.S.A.: Edward Elgar Publishing, 2004), 42–55.

of the regulatory ecology are taken into consideration.[4] For instance, as opposed to the enforcement of traditional criminal law (*e.g.*, murder, burglary), the enforcement of regulations cannot be blind to potential *positive* externalities of regulated activities. If excessively enforced, regulatees may either avoid socially desirable activities or employ excessive (costly) precautions to the detriment of social welfare.[5] Therefore, rather than applying aggressive, uncompromising enforcement measures, regulators must find a creative way to induce regulatory compliance without generating excessive social costs.[6] Moreover, unlike traditional civil and criminal laws, regulations normally provide detailed standards of behavior; they are frequently updated to meet ever-changing market needs; and often require a certain level of expertise to be fully grasped and obeyed. Hence, an enforcement policy directed at inducing regulatory compliance must encourage regulatees to move from a "reactive" to a "proactive" compliance approach – that is, to take the required steps to learn and correctly implement regulatory requirements. Furthermore, regulations normally seek to overcome market failures that may hamper the proper functioning of market forces, thereby securing a particular social benefit.[7]

---

[4] From a social perspective, regulations are worthless if market agents do not comply with them. See Anthony G. Heyes, "Making Things Stick: Enforcement and Compliance," *Oxford Review of Economic Policy* 14 (1998), p. 61: "Regulations are only useful insofar as they are enforced – either fully or partially;" Paul Fenn and Cento G. Veljanovski, "A Positive Economic Theory of Regulatory Enforcement," *The Economic Journal* 98 (1988), p. 1055: "The enforcement of regulation and government controls is complex and to a large extent determines the effects of the law." See also, Robert Baldwin and Martin Cave, *Understanding Regulation: Theory, Strategy, and Practice* (New York: Oxford University Press, 1999), p. 96; John Armour, Henry Hansmann and Reinier Kraakman, "Agency Problems and Legal Strategies," in *The Anatomy of Corporate Law: A Comparative and Functional Approach*, Reinier Kraakman and others, eds (New York: Oxford University Press, 2009), p. 45.

[5] See Ogus, "Criminal Law and Regulation," 90–110; Ogus, "Enforcing Regulation: Do We Need the Criminal Law?," 42–55.

[6] The particular legal environment in which enforcement policies are employed is crucial to consider when crafting an enforcement policy. See, for instance, Robert D. Cooter, "Prices and Sanctions," *Columbia Law Review* 84 (1984), 1523–1560, who suggests that in legal areas, in which a certain behavior needs to be deterred, enforcement should employ punitive measures. In contrast, when the goal of an enforcement policy is to induce the internalization of the ramifications of certain actions, enforcement policies better employ a pricing mechanism. See also, Robert Cooter and Thomas Ulen, *Law and Economics*, 5th edn (Boston: Pearson Addison Wesley, 2007), p. 493.

[7] See Ogus, "Criminal Law and Regulation," 90–110; Ogus, "Enforcing Regulation: Do We Need the Criminal Law?," 42–55.

Accordingly, when crafting a regulatory enforcement policy, the expected social benefit of regulations should be juxtaposed against the social cost associated with the enforcement of such regulations. Hence, from a social welfare perspective, the employment of regulatory enforcement measures can be justified merely to the extent that the social marginal cost of misconduct reduction clears its social marginal benefit.[8] Additionally, where corporate regulatees are concerned, policymakers must be attentive to the regulatees' organizational settings, where various agents may act on the behalf of the corporation. This complex structure of corporate regulatees requires policymakers to consider certain challenges pertaining to the dispersion of responsibility and the control of agents' behavior, as well as to potential conflicts of interest that may arise within the corporate "black box." If regulatory enforcement policies are aimed at inducing, efficiently, corporate proactive compliance, then all such considerations should be factored in when tailoring a particular regulatory enforcement regime.

1.1.1 The Goal of the Book

The goal of this book is to identify a structure of enforcement policies that efficiently induces corporate proactive compliance. To this end, the book initially aims at exploring the major philosophies of law enforcement and analyzing their application within the regulatory enforcement ecology. It seeks to examine what, in fact, comprises each of these major schools of thought, and to identify the major promises and pitfalls of actual enforcement regimes developed based on these approaches. Provided that the traditional schools of thought regarding law enforcement do not generate an optimal enforcement regime, the book aims at examining whether a combination of different elements of the traditional schools of thought may generate an improved enforcement paradigm. Having analyzed the major approaches to law enforcement on a general level, the book seeks to look closely at the two key components of regulatory enforcement policies, *i.e.*, corporate liability regimes and regulatory monitoring. It aims to explore how each of these policy components should be structured to efficiently induce corporate proactive compliance, and how the two components may be integrated into a comprehensive, efficient regulatory enforcement policy.

---

[8] See Cooter and Ulen, *Law and Economics*, p. 511. See also, George J. Stigler, "The Optimum Enforcement of Laws," *The Journal of Political Economy* 78(3) (1970), p. 526; Mitchell A. Polinsky, "Punitive Damages: An Economic Analysis," *Harvard Law Review* 111(4) (1998), pp. 877–878.

1.1.2 Methodology

This book follows a multifaceted analytical approach. As a major methodology, it uses a law and economics approach to identify structures of enforcement regimes that may efficiently induce corporate proactive compliance. The point of departure of the analysis is the "Deterrence Theory," which has been accepted among the law and economics scholarly literature as the fundamental economic theorem of crime and punishment.[9] Applying the deterrence theory to the context of corporate regulatory compliance, the book examines various structures of enforcement policies according to the compliance incentive schemes they introduce to corporate regulatees, in order to enlist them as proactive players in the battle against law-breaking. Each enforcement regime is evaluated according to its impact on the total social welfare, taking into consideration both the costs and benefits associated with achieving misconduct reduction.

A key concept in the analysis is the notion of *efficiency*. This book follows the law and economics literature on corporate compliance and regulatory enforcement in perceiving the maximization of total social welfare as the goal of enforcement policies. The book analyzes alternative enforcement regimes according to their prospective impact on the wealth of the society as a whole, rather than according to the utility of individual players. Wealth distribution within a society is not taken into consideration. This analytical framework corresponds with the well-established Kaldor-Hicks measure of efficiency.[10] Accordingly, an optimal enforcement policy is taken to imply a policy that minimizes the sum of

---

[9] See Gary S. Becker, "Crime and Punishment: An Economic Approach," *The Journal of Political Economy* 76 (2) (1968), 169–217; Stigler, "The Optimum Enforcement of Laws," 526–536; Heyes, "Making Things Stick: Enforcement and Compliance," 50–63; Mitchell A. Polinsky and Steven Shavell, "The Economic Theory of Public Enforcement of Law," *Journal of Economic Literature, American Economic Association* 38(1) (2000), 45–76; David B. Spence, "The Shadow of the Rational Polluter: Rethinking the Role of Rational Actor Models in Environmental Law," *California Law Review* 89(4) (2001), p. 919. The deterrence theory and its policy applications are discussed in Chapter 2.

[10] The Kaldor-Hicks measure of economic efficiency is named after the economists Nicholas Kaldor (1908–1986) and John Hicks (1904–1989). Under this measure, changes in the evaluated system are perceived as efficient when the gains produced by them to some society members are larger than the losses caused to others. Kaldor-Hicks-efficiency is achieved when – *theoretically* – those members of society made better off by the change would fully compensate those members made worse off and still be better off. See Nicholas Kaldor, "Welfare Propositions of Economics and Interpersonal Comparisons of Utility," *The Economic Journal*

the social costs associated with corporate regulatory misconduct and its prevention.[11]

Notwithstanding, the book acknowledges the criticism voiced by many social scientists on a purely economic approach to law enforcement, and considers the alternative philosophy proposed by those scholars. The analysis reveals that the enforcement philosophy proposed by those scholars, known as the "Cooperative Enforcement" approach, is not flawless in itself. Therefore, rather than favoring either approach, the book seeks to identify enforcement policies that reconcile both schools of thought in a way that overcomes their pitfalls while sustaining their promises.

To identify a practical, socially beneficial reconciliation of deterrence-based and cooperative approaches to law enforcement, the book uses the wisdom of the game theoretic "prisoner's dilemma" and applies the Tit-for-Tat strategy to the regulatory ecology. In addition, the book relies on a legal analysis of existing enforcement policies, and explores policy development within civil and criminal areas of enforcement. Finally, the book relies on a comparative legal analysis of recent enforcement policy developments on both sides of the Atlantic Ocean.

1.2 THE STRUCTURE OF THE BOOK

The book is structured in three major parts. Part I, which follows the introductory chapter and is composed of Chapters 2 through 4, explores two major *philosophies regarding law enforcement* and the potential reconciliation thereof. Part II, composed of Chapters 5 and 6, focuses attention on *corporate liability regimes*, and aims at identifying a liability regime that efficiently induces corporate proactive compliance. Part III, composed of Chapters 7 and 8, addresses *regulatory monitoring policies* and aims at identifying a regulatory monitoring policy that efficiently induces corporate proactive compliance. The conclusions of this book are drawn in Chapter 9.

---

49 (1939), 549–552; John R. Hicks, "The Foundations of Welfare Economics," *The Economic Journal* 49 (1939), 696–712.

[11] See Cooter and Ulen, *Law and Economics*, pp. 511–512; see also, Stigler, "The Optimum Enforcement of Laws," p. 533; Arun S. Malik, "Avoidance, Screening and Optimum Enforcement," *RAND Journal of Economics* 21(3) (1990), p. 397.

1.2.1 Part I – Major Schools of Thought Regarding Law Enforcement

Chapters 2 and 3 explore two major schools of thought regarding law enforcement: the *deterrence-based enforcement* approach and the *cooperative enforcement* approach, respectively. Both schools share the same objective, *i.e.*, ensuring regulatory compliance in a socially desirable manner. Yet, each approach endorses different enforcement styles in achieving this objective. Chapters 2 and 3 present the building blocks of each school of thought, and describe the different structures of enforcement regimes endorsed by each of them. Furthermore, these chapters include an analysis of the different enforcement paradigms offered by the different schools of thought, according to their promises and pitfalls from a social welfare point of view. As a conclusion, Chapters 2 and 3 propose that neither of the "stand-alone" schools of thought is categorically superior to the other, and that each of them is fraught with various perils that may thwart their intended function.

Chapter 4 proposes that within the context of corporate regulatory compliance, policymakers are not necessarily required to follow a single enforcement paradigm. Given the heterogeneity of regulatees, social welfare maximization favors an inclusive approach that addresses all types of regulatees, while integrating deterrence-based and cooperative enforcement styles of enforcement. The main aim of this chapter is to explore "regulatory mixed regimes" that combine deterrence-based and cooperative enforcement strategies, while generating higher social welfare compared with the "stand-alone" enforcement regimes. Initially, the chapter explores the enforcement dilemma arising within the regulatory contexts in a realistic setting of a world with heterogeneous regulatees. Then, it presents the game theoretic wisdom of the well-known prisoner's dilemma and its potential application to the regulatory ecology. Next, the chapter presents various structures of "regulatory mixed regimes," which have been developed in the scholarly literature, and highlights the virtues of such mixed regimes from a social welfare standpoint. Eventually, the chapter points at the major pitfalls of these mixed regimes that have not received sufficient attention in the polemic literature, although they may hamper the efficient functioning of such regimes. Given such shortcomings, this chapter concludes that in order to overcome their pitfalls while sustaining their promises, the regulatory mixed regimes should be looked at afresh. This chapter, which closes the first part of the book, establishes the intellectual challenge for the ensuing parts of the book, in which more efficient regulatory mixed regimes are developed.

1.2.2 Part II – Corporate Liability and the Incentive Apparatus for Corporate Proactive Compliance

This part of the book aims at identifying a structure of corporate liability regimes that may efficiently induce corporate proactive compliance. Such a structure is sought to sustain the promises of the mixed enforcement regimes proposed by the existing literature while overcoming their pitfalls.

Chapter 5 provides a legal overview of major corporate liability regimes that are employed in practice to control corporate misconduct. This chapter mainly focuses on the U.S. legal system, which has gone through the most comprehensive transformation of perceptions regarding the optimal structure of corporate liability regimes. In addition to canvassing the alternative structures of liability regimes, the chapter identifies a clear tendency of recent U.S. corporate liability developments to depart from the traditional strict approaches to corporate liability. The chapter presents various policy-development channels through which corporate liability regimes – both civil and criminal – have been softened in recent years by accepting corporate internal enforcement efforts as a mitigating factor of – and sometimes even as a shield from – corporate liability. Furthermore, the analysis of the U.S. legal system is complemented by insights from other legal systems (the British, Canadian, and Australian systems) that have undergone similar developments, as well as by insights from another major system (the EU legal system), which has undergone a completely reverse transformation. This chapter exposes the reader to the great diversity of existing corporate liability regimes, and to diverse policy perspectives upheld on both sides of the Atlantic. This multiplicity of corporate liability structures emphasizes the complexity of this field. In conclusion, Chapter 5 calls for a systematic evaluation of the alternative regimes from a social welfare perspective. Such an evaluation, which is the central goal of the following chapter, may illuminate a socially desirable structure of corporate liability regimes.

Chapter 6 takes on the challenge of evaluating the alternative corporate liability regimes through law and economics lenses. Initially, the chapter presents the economic functions of corporate liability regimes and their particular roles from a social welfare perspective. Thereafter, each of the major types of liability regimes discussed in this chapter is evaluated according to its aptitude to achieve the social goals of corporate liability regimes. The comparative analysis concludes that neither of the existing regimes presents an optimal structure of corporate liability regimes for efficiently inducing corporate proactive compliance. Corresponding to the findings of Part I of this book, the analysis is attentive to the perils of both "stand-alone" approaches to law enforcement. Hence, rather than focusing on the choice between a "harsh" and a "conciliatory" corporate liability framework, the chapter conceives an innovative corporate liability regime, the "Compound Corporate Liability Regime," that may succeed where existing liability regimes fail. The proposed regime reconciles both stand-alone approaches to law enforcement in a socially desirable manner, and ensures an efficient inducement of corporate proactive compliance.

1.2.3 Part III – Corporate Monitors: Can "Swords" Turn into "Shields"?

This part of the book aims at identifying a structure of regulatory monitoring regimes that may efficiently induce corporate proactive compliance. The structure developed in this part utilizes corporate monitors as a signaling mechanism that facilitates the creation of a targeted monitoring system. This monitoring system is sought to sustain the promises of the mixed enforcement regimes discussed in Part I of the book, while overcoming their pitfalls.

Chapter 7 explores the unique enforcement instruments, known as Deferred Prosecution Agreements (DPAs) and Non-Prosecution Agreements (NPAs), which have been developed recently in the U.S. as an alternative enforcement measure against culpable corporations. An intriguing feature of the newly emerged DPAs and NPAs is the use of corporate monitors as "watchdogs" that seek to ensure compliance by culpable corporations. The book considers corporate monitors a valuable instrument that may facilitate the formation of an efficient regulatory monitoring system. Hence, the goal of this chapter is to expose the reader to the contemporary use of corporate monitors in a related enforcement context, and to the specific challenges arising when using this enforcement mechanism. Accordingly, this chapter looks closely at the evolution of corporate monitors as an enforcement instrument within the emerging policies of DPAs and NPAs, and explores the primary criticisms of such policies found in the scholarly literature. This exposition facilitates the analysis for the ensuing chapter, in which corporate monitors are utilized to establish an efficient regulatory monitoring policy.

Chapter 8 takes on the challenge of developing an innovative regulatory monitoring system that may efficiently facilitate corporate proactive compliance. This chapter begins by presenting the major challenge involved in the classification of corporate regulatees into differently monitored groups as part of a targeted monitoring system, and discusses the alternative classification criteria proposed by the existing literature. Thereafter, the chapter develops an innovative monitoring policy, the "Third-Party-Based Targeted Monitoring System," or the "TPTM system," which utilizes both liability threats and reputation concerns in inducing corporate proactive compliance. The proposed policy allows for a delegation of some enforcement powers to corporate monitors functioning both as third-party enforcers and as a signaling mechanism attesting to corporations' genuine normative commitment. Such corporate monitors are specifically designed to overcome the flaws of currently used molds of corporate monitors in DPAs and NPAs policies, as revealed in Chapter 7. The proposed monitoring system increases the private gains resulting from employing genuine internal enforcement efforts, and thereby efficiently strengthens the corporations' motivation to become proactive in ensuring compliance among their employees.

Chapter 9 refines the findings of the book and proposes a comprehensive structure of regulatory enforcement policy that may efficiently induce corporate proactive compliance.

1.3 CAVEATS

The book seeks to identify regulatory enforcement policies that may induce corporate proactive compliance. Accordingly, the book focuses attention on *regulatory violations*, rather than any other type of wrongdoing; and on *corporate regulatees*, rather than individual ones. Hence, broader theories and insights discussed in the book with respect to law enforcement, compliance motivations, and misconduct risks are analyzed and interpreted as applied within the context of corporate regulatory compliance.

The book does not deal with the question of the *desirability* of *governmental intervention* through *regulations*, or of particular standards of behavior set forth by regulations. The desirability of governmental regulation has been questioned in many contexts and heavily criticized in the scholarly literature. The opponents of regulatory intervention often identify with the neoclassical economic approach, which favors the ideas of economic liberalism and free markets rather than a central planner dictating behavioral standards.[12] In addition, a great deal of criticism addresses particular standards of behavior set by such regulations. Commentators often criticize regulations for being excessively ambiguous, inefficient,

---

[12] The leading neoclassical school of thought within the academic community of economists is identified with the Chicago School of Economics. For a discussion of the Chicago School of thought see Ross B. Emmett, ed., *The Elgar Companion to the Chicago School of Economics* (Cheltenham, U.K. & Northampton, MA, U.S.A.: Edward Elgar Publishing, 2010).

or at odds with other social ends.[13] The current analysis departs from the broader discussion of the desirability of regulation and focuses instead on the enforcement of such regulations provided that they include clear and valid regulatory standards.

The analysis in this book addresses regulatory enforcement systems that are based on *public* (criminal or administrative) *enforcement*. Private enforcement is indirectly considered merely as part of the discussion concerning potential policy implications of the deterrence-based school of thought in Chapter 2. The liability and monitoring regimes developed in Parts II and III of the book may apply to enforcement systems in which public enforcement is complemented by a private enforcement system. Nevertheless, in such cases the optimal sanction may differ, whereas when public and private enforcement mechanisms are used together, an optimal corporate liability regime should generate an expected liability that equals the total social cost of the misconduct minus the expected liability generated by the private enforcement mechanism.

Furthermore, the book does not address the well-established *principal–agent problem* between corporate management and shareholders, but rather focuses on a different agency problem; the one that exists between corporations (or the management thereof) and corporate employees undertaking corporate activity. Each of these agency problems has different causes and therefore requires a focused evaluation. As shown by the scholarly literature, the agency problem between managers and shareholders is caused by the separation of ownership and control within corporations, which often generates costs pertaining to potential conflicts of interest between those who run the corporation and those who own it.[14] Recent corporate scandals have propelled this agency problem to the front of the corporate governance debate, and spurred the re-evaluation

---

13 See for instance, John T. Scholz, "Cooperation, Deterrence, and the Ecology of Regulatory Enforcement," *Law and Society Review* 18 (1984), p. 183; John T. Scholz, "Voluntary Compliance and Regulatory Enforcement," *Law & Policy* 6(4) (1984), p. 386; John T. Scholz, "Enforcement Policy and Corporate Misconduct: The Changing Perspective of Deterrence Theory," *Law and Contemporary Problems* 60(3) (1997), 253–268; Eugene Bardach and Robert A. Kagan, *Going by the Book: The Problem of Regulatory Unreasonableness* (Philadelphia: Temple University Press, 1982), pp. 58–59; Scholz, "Enforcement Policy and Corporate Misconduct: The Changing Perspective of Deterrence Theory," p. 258. See also, Baldwin and Cave, *Understanding Regulation: Theory, Strategy, and Practice*, pp. 103–106.

14 For an overview of the agency problems between managers and shareholders see, for instance, John Armour, Henry Hansmann and Reinier Kraakman, "Agency Problems, Legal Strategies, and Enforcement," in *The Anatomy of*

of disciplinary mechanisms, such as internal monitoring schemes, market controls, and remuneration packages to corporate executives.[15] In contrast, despite its great importance, the agency problem between corporations and their employees undertaking corporate activity has received only scant attention in the scholarly literature. This agency problem, which results from the difficulties involved in controlling numerous employees working as an integrated group in undertaking corporate activity, is not solved by the disciplinary mechanisms mentioned above, and requires a closer look and a separate evaluation. This book pays close attention to the aptitude of enforcement policies to induce corporations to proactively ensure compliance among employees undertaking their activity.

Corporate Law: A Comparative and Functional Approach, Reinier Kraakman *et al.* eds (New York: Oxford University Press, 2009), 21–32.

[15] For an overview of disciplinary mechanisms of corporate management see Stephen G. Marks, "The Separation of Ownership and Control," in *Encyclopedia of Law and Economics*, Bouckaert, Boudewijn and De Geest, Gerrit eds, Vol. 5630 (available online: http://encyclo.findlaw.com/index.html: Edward Elgar and the University of Ghent, 1999), 692–724; George Bittlingmayer, "The Market for Corporate Control (Including Takeovers)," in *Encyclopedia of Law and Economics*, Bouckaert, Boudewijn and De Geest, Gerrit eds, Vol. 5640 (available online: http://encyclo.findlaw.com/index.html: Edward Elgar and the University of Ghent, 1999), 725–771.

PART I

Major schools of thought regarding law enforcement

2. Deterrence-based regulatory enforcement

2.1 INTRODUCTION

Corporations in modern societies are subject to an ever-growing array of regulations that standardize substantial aspects of their business activities. Such regulations, including environmental, health and safety, antitrust, employment, and securities regulations, are aimed at controlling and restricting corporate behavior in order to achieve desirable social ends. To be socially valuable, regulations must be obeyed.[1] Hence, from a social welfare perspective, the actual value of regulations is highly contingent upon the existence of a well-functioning enforcement policy that secures their implementation. Therefore, the key element of a socially desirable regulatory system is an appropriately crafted enforcement policy that optimally ensures the obedience of the regulatees.

Various philosophies have been developed throughout the years as to the optimal design of regulatory enforcement policies. In this chapter and the following one, I present the two major schools of thought regarding law enforcement: the *deterrence-based enforcement* approach and the *cooperative enforcement* approach. Both schools share the same objective, *i.e.*, ensuring compliance in a socially desirable manner. Yet, each approach endorses different strategies to achieve this objective. On the one hand, the *deterrence-based* approach coerces compliance through a confrontational enforcement style that is centered upon sanctioning violators. By contrast, *cooperative enforcement* fosters regulatory com-

[1] From a social perspective, regulations are worthless if market agents do not comply with them. See Heyes, "Making Things Stick: Enforcement and Compliance," p. 61: "regulations are only useful insofar as they are enforced – either fully or partially;" Fenn and Veljanovski, "A Positive Economic Theory of Regulatory Enforcement," p. 1055: "The enforcement of regulation and government controls is complex and to a large extent determines the effects of the law." See also, Baldwin and Cave, *Understanding Regulation: Theory, Strategy, and Practice*, p. 96; Armour, Hansmann and Kraakman, "Agency Problems and Legal Strategies," p. 45.

pliance through cooperative governance, bargaining, and persuasion methods. *What are the bedrocks of these different schools of thought? What are the pitfalls of each of them?* In what follows, I wish to shed some light on these fundamental questions. In this chapter, I present the deterrence-based enforcement approach as developed in the law and economics literature. The cooperative enforcement approach is presented in Chapter 3.

The deterrence-based enforcement approach originates in the economic literature that applies traditional economic tools in analyzing the behavioral decision-making processes. The roots of the economic analysis of law enforcement can be traced back to early works published in the eighteenth century by Montesquieu (1748), Beccaria (1767), and Bentham (1789).[2] Yet, a formalized version of the deterrence-based enforcement approach that applies the notion of the rational choice theory to the compliance and enforcement contexts first appeared in the seminal work by Gary S. Becker in 1968.[3] In what follows, I present the building blocks of the deterrence-based approach and describe its unique "recipe" of how to optimize regulatory enforcement in Section 2.2. I then examine in Section 2.3 some policy implications of the deterrence-based enforcement school of thought as it has been extensively discussed in the law and economics literature surrounding the choice between private and public enforcement of the law. In Section 2.4, I look at the major pitfalls of the deterrence-based approach. Finally, I offer a chapter summary and conclude in Section 2.5.

2.2 THE BUILDING BLOCKS

2.2.1 The Rational Choice Theory

The most dominant paradigm developed by economic scholars who analyze human and organizational behavior is the *rational choice theory*. At the heart of the rational choice theory rests the notion of *rationality*. As opposed to the vague colloquial meaning of the concept – usually explained as "reasonable" or "sane" – economists have narrowly stipu-

---

[2] See Montesquieu, Charles de Secondat (Baron de), *The Spirit of Laws*, Rept. Edn of 1977 (California: University of California Press, Berkeley, 1748); Cesare Beccaria, *On Crime and Punishment, and Other Writings*, Richard Bellamy, ed. Richard Davies, trans. 1995 edn (Cambridge & New York: Cambridge University Press, 1767); Jeremy Bentham, *An Introduction to the Principles of Morals and Legislation*, 1973 edn (Garden City, NY: Anchor Books, 1789).

[3] See Becker, "Crime and Punishment: An Economic Approach," 169–217.

lated rationality as an actors' propensity to juxtapose the expected costs and benefits of alternative behavioral choices and to opt for the behavior that maximizes their own objectives (utility).[4] Following this line of thinking, the fundamental idea of the rational choice theory is that actors' behavior in society reflects their conscious choices made to achieve their own greatest satisfaction.[5] The theory focuses on the decision-making process that produces actors' behavioral decisions, and suggests that when deciding upon a certain behavior, actors consider different courses of action according to their expected costs and benefits, and opt for the course of action that maximizes their own utility.

The rational choice theory hinges upon several core assumptions. *First*, each actor in the marketplace strives to maximize his/her own objectives (commonly referred to as the "Utility Maximization Assumption"). Such an objective/utility consists of personal goals, values, and aspirations, and thereby may differ from one actor to another. For instance, lay-persons may seek to maximize their well-being, happiness, or satisfaction; politicians may seek to maximize votes; celebrities may seek to maximize their popularity; and business corporations may seek to maximize shareholder value through profit maximization. *Second*, all alternative courses of action can be ranked in order of preference, but an actors' indifference between two or more courses of action is also possible (commonly referred to as the "Completeness Assumption").[6] According to this assumption, when faced with a finite set of choices, actors can always indicate whether they prefer A to B, B to A, or whether they are indifferent between A and B. *Third*, actors' choices are transitive, *i.e.*, if actors prefer A to B, and B to C, they necessarily prefer A to C (commonly referred to as the "Transitivity Assumption").[7]

Based on the assumptions above, the rational choice theory postulates that actors make decisions according to a cost–benefit analysis. More

---

[4] See Milton Friedman, *Essays in Positive Economics* (Chicago: The University of Chicago Press, 1953), 15–31.

[5] For a general overview of the rational choice theory see, for instance, Michael Allingham, *Rational Choice* (New York: St. Martin's Press Inc., 1999), p. 143; Margaret S. Archer and Jonathan Q. Tritter, *Rational Choice Theory: Resisting Colonization* (New York: Routledge, 2001), p. 257.

[6] See, for instance, Jonathan H. Turner, *The Structure of Sociological Theory*, 7th edn (Belmont, CA: Wadsworth Publishing Company, 2003).

[7] For an elaborated description of rationality assumptions see Fuad Aleskerov, Denis Bouyssou and Bernard Monjardet, *Utility Maximization, Choice and Preference*, 2nd edn (New York: Springer, 2007), p. 283; Richard A. Posner, *Economic Analysis of Law*, 6th edn (New York: Aspan Publications, 2003), pp. 361, 346; Cooter and Ulen, *Law and Economics*, p. 30.

particularly, actors commence by identifying the available alternative courses of action, for instance, buying a new car, buying a second-hand car, or buying no car at all. Next, actors estimate the benefits and the costs associated with each course of action and evaluate the net outcome thereof. Finally, actors juxtapose the net outcomes of the alternative courses of action and opt for the one that maximizes their utility.[8] This method of decision making is used by economists to explain and evaluate actors' day-to-day decisions, such as buying/renting/selling an asset, applying for a certain job, whether and where to relocate, as well as more complex business-oriented decisions, such as what and how much to produce, launching a joint venture or merging with another firm, etc. Normally, when the matter at hand is more complex or substantial, the cost–benefit analysis undertaken is more knowledgeable and explicit.

The rational choice theory can be applied even when actors are unable to determine the outcome of each alternative course of action with certainty. In such a case, actors are assumed to employ a probabilistic evaluation, under which they estimate the *expected outcomes* by estimating the plausible payoffs of each alternative course of action and discount them by the probability of their occurrence.[9] Yet, scholars have underscored the subjective nature of such a decision-making process, showing that evaluations may still be rooted in people's past perceptions, personal attitudes, and values.[10]

Before proceeding, it is worth noting that the rational choice theory has been the subject of a great deal of criticism, calling into question some of

---

[8] For a more elaborated presentation of the theory see Victor A. Thompson, *Decision Theory: Pure and Applied* (New York: General Learning Press, 1971); Gary S. Becker, *The Economic Approach to Human Behavior* (Chicago: University of Chicago Press, 1978), p. 320.

[9] For instance, action A may produce a \$100 net gain with a probability of .6, and a \$40 net loss, with a probability of .4. Hence the net expected outcome of action A is $100 \times .6 + (-)40 \times .4$, or \$44. For elaborations see Jack Hirshleifer and John G. Riley, "The Analytics of Uncertainty and Information – an Expository Survey," *Journal of Economic Literature* 17(4) (1979), p. 1377; Max H. Bazerman and Don A. Moore, *Judgment in Managerial Decision Making*, 7th edn (Hoboken, NJ: John Wiley & Sons, Inc., 2008), pp. 33–44; Allingham, *Rational Choice*, pp. 31–52; Thomas S. Ulen, "Rational Choice Theory in Law and Economics," in *Encyclopedia of Law and Economics*, Boudewijn Bouckaert and Gerrit De Geest eds., Vol. 0710 (available online: http://encyclo.findlaw.com/0710book.pdf: Edward Elgar and the University of Ghent, 1999), pp. 806–809.

[10] See Gary S. Becker, "Nobel Lecture: The Economic Way of Looking at Behavior," *The Journal of Political Economy* 101(3) (1993), p. 386. See also, the discussion of bounded rationality in Section 2.4.4 below.

its assumptions and behavioral predictions.[11] Some of this criticism is discussed in Section 2.4 below. Nevertheless, and for the sake of presenting the deterrence-based approach, the following sections in this chapter use the rational choice theory as an applicable paradigm for the analysis of both human and organizational behavioral decision making.

2.2.2 The Deterrence Theory

The deterrence theory, which comprises one of the bedrocks of the modern economic analysis of enforcement systems, emerged through an application of the rational choice theory into the compliance and enforcement context.[12] The first to formalize the deterrence hypothesis was Becker (1968), who analyzed offenders' behavioral choices as decisions made by rational agents weighing the costs and benefits of their actions when deciding whether to commit a crime.[13] Becker's deterrence hypothesis, according to which crime rates fall in the severity and in the probability of punishment, is based on the premise that actors are rational, "amoral calculators."

---

[11] See, for instance, Cooter and Ulen, *Law and Economics*, p. 16, and on webnote 2.1; and Mary Zey, *Rational Choice Theory and Organizational Theory: A Critique* (Thousand Oaks, CA: Sage Publications, Inc., 1998); Daniel Kahneman and Amos Tversky, "Prospect Theory: An Analysis of Decision Under Risk," *Econometrica* 47(2) (1978), 263–290. For an overview of critical literature see Ulen "Rational Choice Theory in Law and Economics," 790–818.

[12] See Becker, "Crime and Punishment: An Economic Approach," 169–217.

[13] See *ibid.*, See also, Janet A. Gilboy, "Compelled Third-Party Participation in the Regulatory Process: Legal Duties, Culture, and Noncompliance," *Law & Policy* 20(2) (1998), p. 136: "it is assumed [by the deterrence-based approach] that noncompliance is essentially the outgrowth of rational calculations regarding the risks of detection and potential penalties, and that violations can be understood in terms of the profitability of noncompliance with legal duties;" and Scholz, "Cooperation, Deterrence, and the Ecology of Regulatory Enforcement," p. 179. The perceptions of regulatees as "profit-maximizers," and "amoral calculators" are central elements of the deterrence theory. Some advocates of this theory even go further and argue that there is an inherent contradiction between profit-making and being socially responsible for the ramifications of corporate actions. Hence, as the argument goes, the only way to induce compliance is by empowering enforcers to coerce legal orders. See, for instance, Frank Pearce and Steve Tombs, "Ideology, Hegemony, and Empiricism: Compliance Theories of Regulation," *British Journal of Criminology* 30(4) (1990), 423–443; Frank Pearce and Steve Tombs, "Policing Corporate 'Skid Rows': A Reply to Keith Hawkins," *British Journal of Criminology* 31(4) (1991), p. 415. For a different view see, for instance, Keith Hawkins, "Compliance Strategy, Prosecution Policy, and Aunt Sally: A Comment on Pearce and Tombs," *British Journal of Criminology* 30(4) (1990), 444–466.

According to Becker, actors "carefully determine the means to achieve illegal ends, without restraint by guilt or internalized morality."[14] Such rational actors compare their expected compliance utility, *i.e.*, the payoffs expected to be obtained when they obey the law, with their expected violation utility, *i.e.*, the expected payoffs when they violate the law. Accordingly, actors commit crimes only when their expected violation utility is greater than their expected compliance utility.[15] Hence, according to Becker's contribution, punishment may efficiently deter actors from committing crimes by changing the cost of the crime.[16]

2.2.3 Optimal Deterrence

Becker's analytical apparatus has been recognized as a generic law and economics framework for the analysis of law enforcement in a wide range of contexts.[17] Scholars have relied on the deterrence theory in explaining

---

[14] See Cooter and Ulen, *Law and Economics*, p. 494. See also, Dorothy Thornton, Neil Gunningham and Robert A. Kagan, "General Deterrence and Corporate Environmental Behavior," *Law and Policy* 25(2) (2005), p. 263: "The basic theory of general deterrence rests on the notion that regulated business entities are profit-driven 'amoral calculators' . . . Thus, only fear of imminent legal penalties that exceed the cost of compliance can induce profit-seeking firms to invest in compliance with regulatory demands;" and Robert A. Kagan and John T. Scholz, "The 'Criminology of the Corporation' and Regulatory Enforcement Strategies," in *Enforcing Regulation*, Keith Hawkins and John M. Thomas eds (Boston; The Hague [etc.]: Kluwer-Nijhoff, 1984), 352–377.

[15] See Becker, "Crime and Punishment: An Economic Approach," 169–217; Stigler, "The Optimum Enforcement of Laws," 526–536; Heyes, "Making Things Stick: Enforcement and Compliance," 50–63; Polinsky and Shavell, "The Economic Theory of Public Enforcement of Law," 45–76; Spence, "The Shadow of the Rational Polluter: Rethinking the Role of Rational Actor Models in Environmental Law," p. 919.

[16] This hypothesis has been supported by psychology studies that have tested the effect of sanctions on behavior, and have shown that negative consequences that are imposed on a certain behavior reduce that particular behavior. See, for instance, William K. Estes, *An Experimental Study of Punishment* (Evanston, IL.: The American Psychological Association, Inc., 1944). See also, Albert Bandura, *Principles of Behavior Modification* (New York: Holt, Rinehart and Winston, 1969); Barry Schwartz, *Psychology of Learning and Behavior* (New York: Norton, 1989). For different empirical evidence see *infra* note 71.

[17] Becker himself has recognized that "one reason why the economic approach to crime became so influential is that the same analytic apparatus can be used to study enforcement of all laws." See Becker, "Nobel Lecture: The Economic Way of Looking at Behavior," p. 391. Becker's contribution has been elaborated by many others. See, for instance, Stigler, "The Optimum Enforcement of Laws," 526–536;

the social goal of enforcement policies. As the argument goes, provided that market players act rationally in deciding whether to obey the law, enforcement policies must deter market players from law-breaking by creating an incentive scheme that makes market players better off by obeying the law, rather than violating it.[18] The basic idea is that when would-be offenders know that law-breaking triggers sanctions, then they may be deterred from breaking the law.

When crafting regulatory enforcement policies, policymakers may control several important variables, through which the level of deterrence is determined. The first variable is the *kind of sanction imposed*. For the sake of simplifying the analysis, in this book I primarily consider sanctions as cash fines since these are the most common form of regulatory sanctions. Nevertheless, in reality, sanctions against regulatory violations may come in different forms, such as license revocation or suspension, confiscation, and even incapacitation. For those kinds of sanctions, the application of the analysis in this book requires a pre-evaluation of the sanctions' monetary value. The second variable is the *severity of the sanction*. Policymakers have to determine the severity of the sanction imposed, *e.g.*, the amount of cash-fines imposed against specific violations. The third variable is the *probability of violation detection and sanctioning* (hereafter referred to as the "probability of detection"). The probability of detection is normally described as a function of enforcement efforts exerted by enforcement authorities. For instance, the greater the monitoring efforts are, the greater (marginally diminishing) the probability of detection is.[19] The product of the last two variables determines the expected liability faced by regulatory subjects:

John R. Harris, "On the Economics of Law and Order," *The Journal of Political Economy* 78(1) (1970), 165–174; Isaac Ehrlich, "Participation in Illegitimate Activities: A Theoretical and Empirical Investigation," *The Journal of Political Economy* 81(3) (1973), 521; Isaac Ehrlich, "The Deterrent Effect of Capital Punishment: A Question of Life and Death," *The American Economic Review* 65(3) (1975), 397–417; Isaac Ehrlich and Mark Randall, "Fear of Deterrence: A Critical Evaluation of the 'Report of the Panel on Research on Deterrent and Incapacitative Effects'," *The Journal of Legal Studies* 6(2) (1977), 293–316; Isaac Ehrlich, "Crime, Punishment, and the Market for Offenses," *The Journal of Economic Perspectives* 10(1) (1996), 43–67.

[18] See Ogus, "Enforcing Regulation: Do We Need the Criminal Law?" 42–55.

[19] For instance, if the number of environmental inspections is increased, then the number of detected violations is expected to increase as well, even if the latter increase is marginally diminishing.

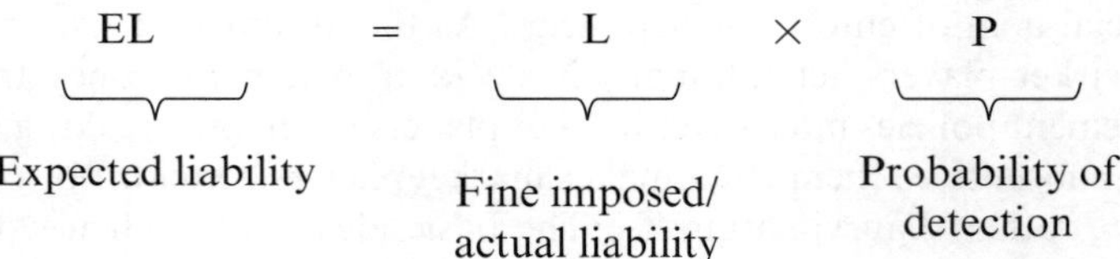

By determining the expected liability faced by market players, regulators determine the level of deterrence that is produced in society. From a social perspective it is crucial that the level of deterrence produced is optimal. The scholarly literature has shown that both under-deterrence and over-deterrence adversely affect the social welfare.[20] On the one hand, *under-deterrence* implies that regulatory subjects are insufficiently motivated to comply with regulatory orders, thereby imposing excessive social costs by departing from the socially desirable standard of behavior.[21] In that case the social welfare may increase with the deterrence level. On the other hand, *over-deterrence* may imply that some regulatees are induced to take over-precautions,[22] or are deterred from engaging in productive activities that could otherwise increase social welfare.[23] In order to maximize social

---

[20] See, for instance, Mitchell A. Polinsky, "Private Versus Public Enforcement of Fines," *The Journal of Legal Studies* 9(1) (1980), 105–127; Mitchell A. Polinsky and Steven Shavell, "Public Enforcement of Law," in *Criminal Law and Economics*, Nuno Garoupa ed., 2nd edn (Cheltenham, U.K. & Northampton, MA, U.S.A.: Edward Elgar Publishing, 2009), 1–59; Roger Bowles, Michael Faure and Nuno Garoupa, "The Scope of Criminal Law and Criminal Sanctions: An Economic View and Policy Implications," *Journal of Law and Society* 35(3) (2008), 389–416; Roger Van den Bergh, "Should Consumer Protection Law be Publicly Enforced? An Economic Perspective on EC Regulation 2006/2004 and its Implementation in the Consumer Protection Laws of the Member States," in *Collective Enforcement of Consumer Law: Securing Compliance in Europe through Private Group Action and Public Authority Intervention*, Willem van Boom and Marco Loos eds. (Groningen, the Netherlands: Europa Law Publishing, 2007), 177–203; Richard A. Bierschbach and Alex Stein, "Overenforcement," *The Georgetown Law Journal* 93 (2005), 1743–1781.

[21] This result is contingent upon the regulatory orders being socially optimal.

[22] See, for instance, Polinsky, "Punitive Damages: An Economic Analysis," p. 879: ". . . if damages exceed harm, firms might be led to take socially excessive precautions. A socially excessive precaution is one that costs more than the reduction of harm produced by it."

[23] The risk of over-deterrence is straightforward when regulatory violations are concerned, whereas unlike mainstream crime, regulatory violations may occur while the actor is engaged in productive activities. See, for instance, Ogus, "Criminal Law and Regulation," pp. 95–96: "Fourthly, excessively severe penalties can lead to over-deterrence . . . It may be the case that with mainstream crimes, such as theft, assault or arson, there is little or no social

welfare, regulatory enforcement should produce an *efficient* level of deterrence, that is, the level of deterrence that motivates regulatees to act in a socially desirable manner.

2.2.4 Efficient Sanctioning

The scholarly polemic is bifurcated into two competing approaches as to the determination of an "optimal sanction." One prevailing approach promotes a *gain-based sanction*, which forces the infringer to disgorge the gains achieved through the violation.[24] According to this approach the expected liability faced by market players should be set at the level of the offender's expected benefit from law-breaking. The underlying logic is that by clearing any expected gain from law-breaking, market players have no incentive to engage in law-breaking.[25] An alternative approach proposes the *harm-based sanction*, according to which the expected liability should be set at a level of the social harm created by the violation. That way, market players will internalize the social ramifications of their actions.[26] In this book, I follow the *harm-based sanction* determination of optimal sanctions for the following reasons:

(i) Unlike a gain-based sanction, a harm-based one induces regulatees to *internalize* the social ramifications of their activities, and thereby

---

utility in the behavior which constitutes the offence, but regulatory offences are different . . . The latter normally arise during the course of everyday activities, including industrial and commercial undertakings, which enhance social welfare. Of course, with insufficient precautions, those activities may generate harm which exceeds the social benefit, hence the regulatory control, but if the prospect of a severe penalty induces the firm either to reduce the amount of the activity or to invest in an excessive level of care, or both, social welfare losses are incurred."

[24] See, for instance, Becker, "Crime and Punishment: An Economic Approach," 169–217; Van den Bergh, "Should Consumer Protection Law be Publicly Enforced? An Economic Perspective on EC Regulation 2006/2004 and its Implementation in the Consumer Protection Laws of the Member States," p. 196.

[25] See, for instance, Cooter and Ulen, *Law and Economics*, p. 498.

[26] Stigler, "The Optimum Enforcement of Laws," 526–536; Cooter, "Prices and Sanctions," 1523–1560; Gary S. Becker, "Make Punishment Fit the Corporate Crime," *Business Week* March 13 (1989), 22; Michael K. Block, "Optimal Penalties, Criminal Law and the Control of Corporate Behavior," *Boston University Law Review* 71 (1991), 395–419; Heyes, "Making Things Stick: Enforcement and Compliance," 50–63; Polinsky and Shavell, "The Economic Theory of Public Enforcement of Law," 45–76.

efficiently determine the level of precautions,[27] as well as the level of activity.[28] This internalization goal is a common central objective of the enforcement of regulations, as opposed to the enforcement of traditional crimes, given the positive externalities that are involved in the regulated activities.[29]

(ii) Directly related to the first reason; a harm-based sanction allows for *efficient regulatory violations* to take place, *i.e.*, violations in which the private gain to the actor is greater than the social cost of the violation.[30]

(iii) As shown by Polinsky and Shavell (1994), when considering the possibility of courts' errors in estimating the gain and harm, harm-based liability may be superior to gain-based liability.[31] As the argument goes, when the sanctions are based on gains to the lawbreaker, there is a risk that if the court underestimates these gains, then the incentives provided to would-be lawbreakers are inadequate.

(iv) Another argument pertains to what was coined by Stigler (1970) as "marginal deterrence." As the argument goes, imposing similar sanctions against various violations that differ from each other in the

---

[27] See Polinsky, "Punitive Damages: An Economic Analysis," p. 879: "If damages equal harm, potential injurers will in theory have socially correct incentives to take precautions. Specifically, they will be induced to spend money on precautions if the expenditure is socially worthwhile in the sense that the expenditure reduces the harm by a greater amount."

[28] See *ibid.*, p. 882: "If damages equal harm, potential injurers have the socially correct incentives to engage in risky activities. In particular, they will engage in an activity if and only if the benefit they derive exceeds the additional harm caused by their decision to engage in it."

[29] See Ogus, "Criminal Law and Regulation," 90–110; Ogus, "Enforcing Regulation: Do We Need the Criminal Law?," 42–55.

[30] From a policy perspective, an efficient regulatory violation may occur when the standard set by the regulation is suboptimal and a violation may lead to a positive net social welfare.

[31] See Mitchell A. Polinsky and Steven Shavell, "Should Liability be Based on the Harm to the Victim Or the Gain to the Injurer?" *Journal of Law, Economics and Organization* 10(2) (1994), 427–437: "The problem with gain-based liability is that any underestimation of the gain will in principle lead an individual to commit an undesirable act, no matter how great the resulting harm may be. Suppose, for example, that an act would produce a gain of $1,000 for an individual and that the gain is slightly underestimated, say it is thought to be $950. Then the individual will be led to commit the act – he would profit by $50 – regardless of the harm, whether it is $2,000, $20,000, or $200,000. In contrast, under harm-based liability, the individual is not likely to commit the act when the harm greatly exceeds his gain of $1,000, because his liability is likely to exceed $1,000 even if the measurement of harm is subject to substantial error."

resulting social harm may distort would-be offenders' decisions and induce them to commit crimes that may result in greater social harm.[32] Unlike the gain-based sanction, the harm-based one is determined while factoring in the severity of the ramifications of violations.

(v) Lastly, a practical reason; the harm-based determination is broadly accepted by the literature on corporate misconduct and regulatory enforcement.[33] By adhering to the major analytical framework of the existing literature, I am better able to address my research questions while proposing a valuable contribution to the extensive body of studies.

Taken all together, an optimal level of deterrence may be reached when the expected liability faced by market-players (*i.e.*, P × L) is set at the level of the social harm created by the violation.

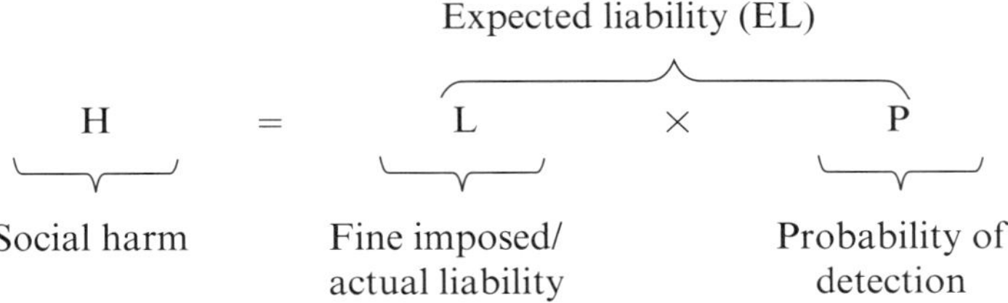

In that respect, two additional inquiries may require further attention: (1) *What is the optimal combination of the probability of detection (P) and the actual sanction (L) in obtaining a certain level of expected liability?* (2) *What is the social harm that needs to be factored in when determining the expected liability?* As for the first question the scholarly literature has shown that given that a higher probability of detection requires more enforcement expenditures, whereas a larger cash fine is not necessarily involved with higher collection costs, a socially efficient combination would be to allocate resources to make sanctions less certain (lower P), but

32 See Stigler, "The Optimum Enforcement of Laws," 526–536. See also, Steven Shavell, "A Note on Marginal Deterrence," *International Review of Law and Economics* 12(3) (1992), 345–355; Dilip Mookherjee and Ivan Paak-Liang Png, "Marginal Deterrence in Enforcement of Law," *Journal of Political Economy* 102(5) (1994), 1039–1066; David Friedman and William Sjostrom, "Hanged for a Sheep: The Economics of Marginal Deterrence," *The Journal of Legal Studies* 22(2) (1993), 345–366; Becker, "Crime and Punishment: An Economic Approach," 169–217.

33 See, for instance, Arlen and Kraakman, "Controlling Corporate Misconduct: An Analysis of Corporate Liability Regimes," 687–779.

more severe (higher L).[34] Yet, in reality, various considerations, such as the need to secure marginal deterrence, prevent policymakers from setting applicable sanctions for certain violations at the highest possible level. In such cases, the probability of detection may be set lower than the maximal possible level. This, of course, may imply that higher monitoring efforts are required to secure a sufficiently high probability of detection. As for the second question, the scholarly literature has shown that when determining the optimal sanction as a harm-based sanction, the *total social costs created by the misconduct* should be taken into account, including not only the direct harm created in the market (*e.g.*, the harm created to a neighboring population due to river pollution), but also *relevant enforcement costs*, which are the cost of enforcement actions associated with the specific misconduct.[35]

---

[34] See Becker, "Crime and Punishment: An Economic Approach," 169–217; Cooter and Ulen, *Law and Economics*, p. 513. See also, Becker, "Nobel Lecture: The Economic Way of Looking at Behavior," pp. 390–391: "Total public spending on fighting crime can be reduced, while keeping the mathematically expected punishment unchanged, by off-setting a cut in expenditures on catching criminals with a sufficient increase in the punishment to those convicted. However, risk-preferring individuals are more deterred from crime by a higher probability of conviction than by severe punishments. Therefore, optimal behavior by the state would balance the reduced spending on police and courts from lowering the probability of conviction against the preference of risk-preferring criminals for a lesser certainty of punishment. The state should also consider the likelihood of punishing innocent persons." According to Mitchell A. Polinsky and Steven Shavell, "The Optimal Tradeoff between the Probability and Magnitude of Fines," *The American Economic Review* 69(5) (1979), 880–891, a combination of minimal probability and a maximal fine may be optimal given the assumption of risk-neutral regulatory targets. However, when the regulatory targets are risk averse, an alternative combination may be preferable, namely, if the cost of detection is sufficiently small, the optimal probability equals one. Additionally, if it is optimal to control the activity at all, then, regardless of how costly it is to catch individuals, it may never be optimal to catch them with a very low probability and to fine them much more than the external costs. Other studies have shown under certain circumstances setting the penalties for violations below their maximal level may be compliance enhancing. See also, Anthony G. Heyes, "Cutting Environmental Penalties to Protect the Environment," *Journal of Public Economics* 60(2) (1996), 251–265; Winston Harrington, "Enforcement Leverage when Penalties are Restricted," *Journal of Public Economics* 37(1) (1988), 29–53.

[35] The importance of enforcement costs as part of the total social costs associated with misconduct was first introduced by George Stigler. Stigler has shown that the goal of the enforcement authority is to minimize the sum of the damages created by the misconduct and the enforcement cost; see Stigler, "The Optimum Enforcement of Laws," p. 533. See also, Malik, "Avoidance, Screening and Optimum Enforcement," p. 347.

2.2.5 Summing Up

The deterrence-based enforcement approach hinges upon the rationality of agents, thereby perceiving the role of enforcement systems as a mechanism ensuring that amoral regulatees find it in their best interests to obey the law.[36] This "by-the-book" approach seeks to coerce compliance through an optimal combination of detection and sanctioning that produces just the right level of deterrence.[37] As such, the deterrence-based enforcement approach endorses a confrontational style of enforcement, under which would-be violators may anticipate that they will be detected and sanctioned in a manner that makes law-breaking undesirable from a private perspective.[38]

2.3 POLICY IMPLICATIONS: PRIVATE AND PUBLIC ENFORCEMENT OF REGULATIONS

The optimal design of enforcement systems has been thoroughly analyzed in the polemic law and economics literature. Many studies have taken the deterrence-based enforcement approach as the generic analytical framework for the analysis of potential welfare impacts of various enforcement systems. Given the major interest of this book in controlling corporate misbehavior, I confine the discussion below to a brief overview of the major enforcement regimes that are normally being used for the enforcement of regulations, rather than other legal norms and contractual obligations.

2.3.1 Regulatory Enforcement

Regulations may be enforced through various enforcement channels. Table 2.1 presents the major enforcement channels through which regulations

---

[36] See, for instance, Scholz, "Cooperation, Deterrence, and the Ecology of Regulatory Enforcement," p. 179; Becker, "Nobel Lecture: The Economic Way of Looking at Behavior," p. 389.

[37] See, for instance, Richard Johnstone, "From Fiction to Fact – Rethinking OHS Enforcement," *National Research Center for Occupational Health and Safety Regulation* Working Paper 11 (2003), p. 10; Julia Black, "Managing Discretion," *ARLC Conference Papers. Penalties: Policy, Principles and Practice in Government Regulation* (available at: http://w.lse.ac.uk) (2001), p. 4.

[38] See, for instance, Block, "Optimal Penalties, Criminal Law and the Control of Corporate Behavior," 395–419; Neil Gunningham, *Mine Safety: Law, Regulation, Policy* (Sydney: The Federation Press, 2007), p. 117.

Table 2.1 Alternative legal regimes for the enforcement of regulations

	Private Enforcement		Public Enforcement	
	Civil-private Regime	Criminal Regime	Civil-public Regime	Administrative Regime
Prosecutor	Victim	Public prosecutor	Regulatory agency	Regulatory agency
Decision Maker	Court	Court	Court or tribunal	Regulatory agency
Sanctions	Damages Injunctions	Fine Confiscation Prison	Penalty Injunction License revocation/ suspension	Cessation order Fine

are normally enforced.[39] From right to left, the table moves from routine to less frequently used enforcement measures.

The most commonly used regulatory enforcement regime is the *administrative regime*. Under this regime regulatory violations are handled by a regulatory authority empowered to issue cessation orders and administrative fines.[40] In these cases, the regulatory authority that investigates the violation is the same authority that imposes the sanction. In many cases, sanctioned regulatees are entitled to challenge the regulatory decision to impose a fine before a higher regulatory authority or a court. An alternative enforcement regime is the *civil-public regime*, under which regulatory agencies seek penalties, injunctions, or license revocation/suspension through the court system or a specialized tribunal.[41] The use of public-civil regimes in the regulatory context is reserved for exceptional cases. For instance, public-civil regimes are used when regulatees fail to comply with the sanction imposed by the regulatory authority, or when severe regulatory violations are involved and the regulatory authority may (or is required to) bring those before the court.[42] A third enforcement channel that has gained importance in recent years, especially in the field of environmental regulations, is the

[39] Table 2.1 is based on the presentation of enforcement regimes by Ogus, "Enforcing Regulation: Do We Need the Criminal Law?," p. 44.

[40] See *ibid.*, p. 44

[41] See *ibid.*, p. 44

[42] See *ibid.*, p. 44

criminal regime.[43] Under this regime, the prosecution role is normally taken by a public prosecution agency, which seeks criminal penalties against violators before the court. Under the criminal regime, the regulatory authority is mainly responsible for the detection and investigation of regulatory violations. Once sufficient incriminating evidence is gathered, the regulatory authority passes on its recommendation to the prosecution agency, which decides whether to initiate a criminal prosecution. All the regimes discussed thus far belong to the public enforcement domain, whereas enforcement actions are initiated and mainly controlled by a public agency. The fourth enforcement channel is the *private-civil regime*, under which victims claim damages or an injunction before the court.[44] This channel of enforcement is used in particular regulatory contexts, such as in the field of competition law, and requires no (or minimal) involvement of the regulatory agency.

2.3.2 Private Enforcement of Regulations

The deterrence-based enforcement approach has been used by law and economics scholars to analyze major enforcement regimes, according to their aptitude to produce an optimal level of deterrence. Consider initially the private-civil regime. This regime is usually aimed at ensuring that victims are fully compensated for the losses suffered because of harmful actions by a tortfeasor. Empowering private parties to enforce regulatory obligations through damage claims is supported by the fact that in many settings these parties have better information concerning potential and actual law-breaking than the regulatory authorities have.[45] Given that the

---

43 See, for instance, Michael Faure, "Environmental Crimes," in *Criminal Law and Economics*, Nuno Garoupa ed., 2nd edn (Cheltenham, U.K. & Northampton, MA, U.S.A.: Edward Elgar Publishing, 2009), 320–345; Bowles, Faure and Garoupa, "The Scope of Criminal Law and Criminal Sanctions: An Economic View and Policy Implications," 389–416; Ogus, "Criminal Law and Regulation," 90–110; Ogus, "Enforcing Regulation: Do We Need the Criminal Law?," 42–55.

44 See, for instance, Thomas Eger and Peter Weise, "Limits to the Private Enforcement of Antitrust Law," *German Working Papers in Law and Economics* 2007(2) (2007); Commission of the European Communities, "Green Paper – Damages Actions for Breach of the EC Antitrust Rules," *Brussels, Commission of the European Communities* [19 December, 2005].

45 The private information superiority may exist both *ex ante*, information about potential violations, and *ex post*, information about the specific circumstances under which a violation has occurred. See Steven Shavell, "Liability for Harm Versus Regulation of Safety," *Journal of Legal Studies* 13 (1984), pp. 359–360.

acquisition of such information by public authorities may be costly and incomplete,[46] empowering private individuals to enforce regulations may generate an efficient utilization of knowledge.[47] From a deterrence point of view, the private-civil regime may generate an optimal level of deterrence, provided that the detection of regulatory violations is certain and that all the damages of the regulatory violations are actually paid for.[48] Under such circumstances, would-be wrongdoers are motivated to internalize the social ramifications of their actions, and thereby they are expected to behave in a socially desirable manner.[49] However, although at times private enforcement mechanisms may be preferable to alternative ones, under certain circumstances, private enforcement may fail to produce an optimal level of deterrence. I briefly discuss below some of the major arguments advanced in the literature against the use of private enforcement:

(i) Private information superiority is context-dependent; in many cases the relevant information is not obvious and its collection and evaluation require the exertion of efforts or special expertise.[50]
(ii) Regulatory enforcement actions often involve substantial costs associated with detection, evidence collection and complex legal proceedings. Private enforcers are motivated to undertake enforcement actions only to the extent that the expected (private) benefit of such

---

[46] See Friedrich A. Hayek, "The Use of Knowledge in Society," *The American Economic Review* 35(4) (1945), 519–530. Hayek explores the advantages of the market system over a centrally planned economy, based on the utilization of individuals' knowledge about specific circumstances of time and place, which cannot be communicated to the central authority.

[47] See Ilya R. Segal and Michael D. Whinston, "Public vs. Private Enforcement of Antitrust Law: A Survey," *European Competition Law Review* 28(5) (2007), p. 310.

[48] For the sake of simplicity, the analysis disregards the possibility of punitive damages.

[49] See, for instance, William M. Landes and Richard A. Posner, "The Private Enforcement of Law," *Journal of Legal Studies* 4(1) (1975), 1–46; Polinsky and Shavell, "The Economic Theory of Public Enforcement of Law," 45–76; Steven Shavell, "The Optimal Structure of Law Enforcement," *Journal of Law & Economics* 36(1) (1993), 255–278; Polinsky, "Private Versus Public Enforcement of Fines," 105–127; Eger and Weise, "Limits to the Private Enforcement of Antitrust Law;" Segal and Whinston, "Public Vs. Private Enforcement of Antitrust Law: A Survey," 306–315.

[50] See Shavell, "Liability for Harm Versus Regulation of Safety," p. 360; see also, Van den Bergh, "Should Consumer Protection Law be Publicly Enforced? An Economic Perspective on EC Regulation 2006/2004 and its Implementation in the Consumer Protection Laws of the Member States," pp. 183–187.

actions exceeds their costs. Therefore, the high enforcement costs associated with regulatory enforcement may produce a "rational apathy" among private parties, making them reluctant to enforce.[51] In such cases, the level of enforcement is expected to be insufficient.[52]

(iii) Private parties are driven to act in accordance with the expected private consequences of their actions. These private agents may not capture the entire social effect of their actions, and hence may depart from a socially desirable level of enforcement.[53]

(iv) Under certain circumstances, the full payment for damages may not be feasible due to the limited wealth of the offender. If the damages awarded to the victim exceed the value of the violator's assets, the deterrence effect of the private enforcement system is insufficient (commonly referred to as "the judgment proof problem").[54] In such cases, alternative sanctions that are normally unavailable within the private-civil regime, such as incapacitation, may be required.

(v) Some commentators have argued that privately-held enforcement powers may be improper when enforcement requires the use of force. As the argument goes, states may prefer to solely maintain the right to use force as an enforcement measure.[55]

---

[51] Common examples for the "rational apathy" problem are the enforcement of violations that result in trifle damages (too little benefit); violations that are difficult to assess (uncertain benefit); and enforcement against insolvent infringer (unexpected benefit). See Van den Bergh, "Should Consumer Protection Law be Publicly Enforced? An Economic Perspective on EC Regulation 2006/2004 and its Implementation in the Consumer Protection Laws of the Member States," p. 185; and Posner, *Economic Analysis of Law*.

[52] See Shavell, "Liability for Harm Versus Regulation of Safety," p. 360.

[53] See Van den Bergh, "Should Consumer Protection Law be Publicly Enforced? An Economic Perspective on EC Regulation 2006/2004 and its Implementation in the Consumer Protection Laws of the Member States," p. 187; Posner, *Economic Analysis of Law*; Polinsky and Shavell, "The Economic Theory of Public Enforcement of Law," p. 3; Steven Shavell, "The Social Versus the Private Incentive to Bring Suit in a Costly Legal System," *The Journal of Legal Studies* 11(2) (1982), 333–339.

[54] See Steven Shavell, "The Judgment Proof Problem," *International Review of Law and Economics* 6(1) (1986), 45–58; Heyes, "Making Things Stick: Enforcement and Compliance," p. 50; Steven Shavell, "Criminal Law and the Optimal use of Nonmonetary Sanctions as a Deterrent," *Columbia Law Review* 85(6) (1985), 1232–1262.

[55] See Polinsky and Shavell, "The Economic Theory of Public Enforcement of Law," p. 47. Using power in enforcement can reduce the costs of acquiring information, *e.g.*, by the threat of jail, searches conducted by the police, seizures of evidence. See Segal and Whinston, "Public vs. Private Enforcement of Antitrust Law: A Survey," p. 311.

2.3.3 Public Enforcement of Regulations

Public enforcement, in which public agents are primarily the initiators and controllers of enforcement activity, may – to a certain extent – alleviate the weaknesses of the private scheme. As described above, public enforcement of regulations may be undertaken through three major regimes: administrative, public-civil, and the criminal regime. The scholarly literature has pointed out various advantages of public enforcement that are relevant to the regulatory context:

(i) Public authorities are sometimes more qualified to acquire and analyze relevant information, particularly when vast amounts of information are involved, or when the collection or analysis of information requires special expertise.[56]
(ii) Unlike private enforcers, public servants are appointed to pursue social goals dictated by public policy, rather than private objectives.[57] In this respect, planned and coordinated public enforcement actions are presumed to reflect socially desirable actions, while avoiding duplication of expenditures associated with the private scheme.[58]
(iii) An enforcement process that is led or supported by a professional regulatory authority may facilitate a desirable regulatory development through professional and consistent clarification of the regulation.[59]
(iv) Public enforcement regimes provide public agencies with a wider array of detection and means of investigation, as well as alternative sanctioning possibilities, including incapacitation, which under

---

[56] See Van den Bergh, "Should Consumer Protection Law be Publicly Enforced? An Economic Perspective on EC Regulation 2006/2004 and its Implementation in the Consumer Protection Laws of the Member States," 177–203; Segal and Whinston, "Public vs. Private Enforcement of Antitrust Law: A Survey," 306–315.

[57] This is, of course, subject to the possibility of bribes and collusion among public servants. See Gary S. Becker and George J. Stigler, "Law Enforcement, Malfeasance, and Compensation of Enforcers," *The Journal of Legal Studies* 3(1) (1974), 1–18; Van den Bergh, "Should Consumer Protection Law be Publicly Enforced? An Economic Perspective on EC Regulation 2006/2004 and its Implementation in the Consumer Protection Laws of the Member States," p. 201.

[58] See Shavell, "The Optimal Structure of Law Enforcement," p. 265; Polinsky, "Private Versus Public Enforcement of Fines," p. 107.

[59] For a general assessment see Wouter P. J. Wils, "The Relationship Between Public Antitrust Enforcement and Private Actions for Damages," *World Competition* 32(1) (2009), 3–26.

certain circumstances, may be required to provide an optimal level of deterrence.

Yet, public enforcement regimes are not always able to produce an optimal level of deterrence. Various drawbacks imbedded in the public enforcement system may hinder its functioning. For instance:

(i) The assumption of socially-committed public servants is not always accurate. Public servants' judgment may be distorted by (conflicting) private incentives. In this case, their actions may depart from socially desirable goals.[60]
(ii) A major flaw of public enforcement regimes pertains to its social costs. At the outset, public agencies are normally involved with substantial administrative and bureaucracy costs. Those agencies tend to be less efficient than private firms.[61] On top of that, public authorities are regularly financed through taxes. Considering the deadweight loss created as a side effect of tax collection, this way of funding is, by itself, socially costly.[62]

2.3.4 The Choice between Private and Public Enforcement

When evaluated through the deterrence-based enforcement approach, neither private nor public enforcement regimes are able to guarantee an optimal level of deterrence at all times. In an attempt to identify the optimal structure of an enforcement policy, law and economics scholars suggested different determinants for the choice between private and public enforcement. The criteria used by these scholars to determine which enforcement scheme should be used in each case rely on the comparative advantages of each enforcement scheme under specific sets

---

60 See Posner, *Economic Analysis of Law*; See also, Becker and Stigler, "Law Enforcement, Malfeasance, and Compensation of Enforcers," 1–18.

61 Private enforcers are often more susceptive to the cost of enforcement and, hence, other things being equal, they are more efficient in carrying out their activities. See Segal and Whinston, "Public vs. Private Enforcement of Antitrust Law: A Survey," p. 311; Posner, *Economic Analysis of Law*. However, as mentioned above, public enforcement is usually coordinated, and hence, in certain cases the avoidance of the duplication of investigating costs makes public enforcement's costs lower than the total private enforcement costs. See Polinsky, "Private Versus Public Enforcement of Fines," p. 108.

62 See Segal and Whinston, "Public vs. Private Enforcement of Antitrust Law: A Survey," 306–315; Polinsky, "Private Versus Public Enforcement of Fines," 105–127.

of circumstances. For instance, Shavell in a 1993 article suggests that the enforcement scheme to be used should be selected according to the capability of the enforcer to supply the required information.[63] Further, Shavell argues, in two articles published in 1984, that the choice of the enforcement scheme should be based on available information, administrative costs, insolvency problems, and the risk of escaping suits.[64] Polinsky (1980) links the choice of an optimal enforcement regime to the costs of each method, as well as the magnitude of external damages which may result from the violation.[65] Van den Bergh (2007) suggests allocating enforcement powers according to the availability of relevant information and the need to achieve an efficient level of law enforcement.[66] He further argues that when under both schemes there is a risk of suboptimal enforcement, it might be preferable to opt for a combination of private and public enforcement so that they can then mitigate each others' disadvantages.[67]

---

[63] Shavell, "The Optimal Structure of Law Enforcement," pp. 266–267. According to this view, private individuals should be empowered to enforce the law whenever they possess superior information regarding the identity of injurers. However, when efforts must be exerted to identify injurers, a state authority should enforce the law.

[64] See, firstly, Shavell, "Liability for Harm Versus Regulation of Safety," 357–374. The author suggests that information and administration costs considerations generally favor private enforcement (tort liability). However, when insolvency problems are involved (because of the limited wealth of the violators and/or large harm caused), and when there is high risk of escaping liability (*e.g.* because of widely dispersed harm, a long time gap between the violation and the detection of harm, etc.), public enforcement is preferable. Secondly, in Steven Shavell, "A Model of the Optimal use of Liability and Safety Regulations," *RAND Journal of Economics* 15(2) (1984), 271–280, a similar idea is applied to the choice between (*ex-post*) liability and (*ex-ante*) safety regulations. According to this study, safety regulations are preferable when (1) the level of violators' assets is low; (2) the probability of a suit is low (easy to escape legal suits); and (3) the variability in potential harm among potential injurers is sufficiently small.

[65] See Polinsky, "Private Versus Public Enforcement of Fines," 105–127. According to this study, when external damages are high, then a public enforcement system is superior. When external damages are intermediate or low, then a competitive or monopolistic private enforcement is superior, respectively.

[66] In Van den Bergh, "Should Consumer Protection Law be Publicly Enforced? An Economic Perspective on EC Regulation 2006/2004 and its Implementation in the Consumer Protection Laws of the Member States," 177–203, the author argues that the case for public enforcement will be stronger the more serious the information asymmetries are and the higher the risk of over/under deterrence.

[67] See *ibid.*, pp. 183, 201.

2.3.5 Summing Up

The discussion of alternative enforcement schemes in the law and economics literature demonstrates the practical application of the deterrence-based enforcement approach to policy making. As shown above, each of the alterative enforcement schemes is evaluated according to its aptitude to establish an enforcement policy that produces an optimal level of deterrence at the lowest cost. Obviously, the choice of a particular enforcement scheme in specific regulatory contexts may be a challenging one. Nevertheless, the deterrence-based enforcement approach provides a conceptual analytical framework that allows a systematic and comparative analysis of the choice between alternative enforcement schemes.

2.4 THE PITFALLS OF DETERRENCE-BASED ENFORCEMENT

Advocates of the deterrence-based enforcement approach underscore the high levels of certainty and of credibility that are produced by a deterrence-based enforcement system. Commentators have argued that enforcement systems that are based on the deterrence approach adequately link the "goals of the enforcement system" with the "means of attainment."[68] Others have argued that deterrence-based enforcement systems reduce the risk of arbitrariness by avoiding an over-reliance on the discretion of public servants and provide a sense of neutrality to enforcement activities.[69] In addition, it has been argued that deterrence-based enforcement systems enhance social pressure to comply by reinforcing social sentiments of disapproval and identifying errant conduct as unacceptable.[70] Nevertheless, throughout the last decades, the deterrence-based enforcement approach has been subject to growing criticism – some of which has been supported empirically.[71] In what follows, I survey the major lines of criticism of the deterrence-based enforcement approach.

---

68 See, for instance, Neal Shover, Donald Clelland and John Lynxwiler, *Enforcement Or Negotiation: Constructing a Regulatory Bureaucracy* (Albany, NY: State University of New York Press, 1986), p. 128.

69 See, for instance, Faure, "Environmental Crimes," p. 336; Bardach and Kagan, *Going by the Book: The Problem of Regulatory Unreasonableness*, pp. 35–36.

70 See, for instance, Baldwin and Cave, *Understanding Regulation: Theory, Strategy, and Practice*, p. 98.

71 The empirical analysis of the deterrence hypothesis started in the 1970s. See, for instance, Philip J. Cook, "Research in Criminal Deterrence: Laying

2.4.1 Regulatory "Cat-and-Mouse" Game

One of the most powerful critiques of the deterrence-based enforcement approach pertains to the high social costs involved in its application. Since the deterrence-based approach seeks to coerce compliance through sanctioning regulatory violations, it is confrontational by nature. As such, the deterrence approach endorses a regulatory "cat-and-mouse" game between law enforcers and regulatory targets. Enforcers invest their resources in pursuing potential wrongdoers, while the wrongdoers invest in minimizing their expected liability. This unique framework produces substantial social costs, which in turn, reduce the social welfare.[72] Here are some examples of the costs involved in the "cat-and-mouse" game associated with a deterrence-based enforcement approach:

(i) *Administrative costs* – The administrative costs of the public enforcement system are enormous. Among these costs we may include the

---

the Groundwork for the Second Decade," *Crime and Justice* 2 (1980), 211–268; Jack P. Gibbs, *Crime, Punishment, and Deterrence* (New York: Elsevier, 1975), p. 249; Franklin E. Zimring and Gordon Hawkins, *Deterrence: The Legal Threat in Crime Control* (Chicago: University of Chicago Press, 1973). Empirical evidence concerning the deterrence hypothesis is ambiguous. Some studies have supported the deterrence hypothesis. See, for instance, Ehrlich, "Participation in Illegitimate Activities: A Theoretical and Empirical Investigation," p. 521; Ehrlich, "The Deterrent Effect of Capital Punishment: A Question of Life and Death," p. 397; Roy A. Carr-Hill and Nicholas H. Stern, "An Econometric Model of the Supply and Control of Recorded Offences in England and Wales," *Journal of Public Economics* 2(4) (1973), 289–318; Llad Phillips and Harold L. Votey Jr., "Crime Control in California," *The Journal of Legal Studies* 4(2) (1975), 327–349; Kenneth I. Wolpin, "An Economic Analysis of Crime and Punishment in England and Wales," *The Journal of Political Economy* 86(5) (1978), 815–840; Kenneth I. Wolpin, "Capital Punishment and Homicide in England: A Summary of Results," *The American Economic Review* 68(2) (1978), 422–427; Jiang Yu and Allen E. Liska, "The Certainty of Punishment: A Reference Group Effect and its Functional Form," *Criminology* (Beverly Hills) 31(3) (1993), 447–464; Jiang Yu, "Punishment Certainty and Severity: Testing a Specific Deterrence Model on Drunk Driving Recidivism," *Journal of Criminal Justice* 22(4) (1994), 355–366. Other studies have denied the deterrence hypothesis. See, for instance, Alfred Blumstein, Jacqueline Cohen and Daniel Nagin, *Deterrence and Incapacitation: Estimating the Effects of Criminal Sanctions on Crime Rates* (Washington DC: National Academy of Sciences, 1978); Kenneth L. Avio, "Capital Punishment in Canada: A Time-Series Analysis of the Deterrent Hypothesis," *The Canadian Journal of Economics* 12(4) (1979), 647–676.

[72] See Tom R. Tyler, *Why People Obey the Law* (Princeton, NJ: Princeton University Press, 2006), pp. 22–23.

costs of prosecution agencies, the legal defense of the defendants, a court system, police, execution bureaus and prisons.[73]

(ii) *Litigation costs* – The litigation process, which is a central feature of a deterrence-based enforcement approach, often involves substantial procedural costs, including the costs of collecting evidence or obtaining expert opinions and witness testimonies.[74]

(iii) *Error costs* – Beside the direct institutional and procedural costs, prosecution and sanctioning may involve error costs of both types; prosecuting or convicting an innocent person (type I error) or discharging a culpable one (type II error). Although evidence and procedural laws often employ various measures to reduce the probability of errors (such as standards of proof and evidence admissibility rules), error costs are unavoidable by-products of prosecutors' and courts' decisions.[75]

(iv) *Evasion costs* – Given the "cat-and-mouse" game generated by the deterrence approach, violators may find it worthwhile to commit violations (and gain the benefits associated thereby), while bearing some additional expenditures to cover their tracks and thereby reduce their expected liability.[76]

---

[73] See Scholz, "Cooperation, Deterrence, and the Ecology of Regulatory Enforcement," p. 207.

[74] See Anthony Ogus and Carolyn Abbot, "Pollution and Penalties," in *An Introduction to the Law and Economics of Environmental Policy: Issues in Institutional Design*, Book Series: Research in Law and Economics, Timothy Swanson ed., Vol. 20 (Bingley, U.K.: Emerald Group Publishing Limited, 2002), p. 505.

[75] See Heyes, "Making Things Stick: Enforcement and Compliance," p. 55; Polinsky and Shavell, "The Economic Theory of Public Enforcement of Law," p. 23.

[76] See Malik, "Avoidance, Screening and Optimum Enforcement," p. 18; Heyes, "Making Things Stick: Enforcement and Compliance," 50–63; Robert Innes, "Violator Avoidance Activities and Self-Reporting in Optimal Law Enforcement," *Journal of Law, Economics and Organization* 17(1) (2001), 239–256. See also, Scholz, "Cooperation, Deterrence, and the Ecology of Regulatory Enforcement," p. 207, according to which a deterrence style which leads to confrontation might motivate corporations to evade, whereas by doing so they minimize their regulatory costs; and Pinaki Bose, "Regulatory Errors, Optimal Fines and the Level of Compliance," *Journal of Public Economics* 56(3) (1995), 475–484, which develops a model, according to which high penalties may lead to regulators' efforts to obstruct the enforcement process, including greater incentives to challenge the regulatory sanction in court.

2.4.2 Alienation of Regulatory Subjects

Another line of criticism of the deterrence-based enforcement approach is related to the impact of rigorous enforcement routines on a subject's mind-set and attitude. This criticism relies on the *Cognitive Evaluation Theory*, according to which people's self-perception of their competence and autonomy is vital for their motivation to undertake voluntary activities. The theory posits that actors need to feel competent and autonomous to be intrinsically motivated to act.[77] Accordingly, the theory suggests that factors that promote subjects' sense of competence and autonomy, such as positive feedback, may strengthen subjects' intrinsic motivation to act.[78] By contrast, factors that undermine these feelings, such as negative feedback, tend to weaken subjects' intrinsic motivation.[79] Furthermore, testing the Cognitive Evaluation Theory, scholars have shown that extrinsic motivators may, under certain circumstances, hinder feelings of autonomy and therefore hamper intrinsic motivations.[80]

---

[77] See Marylène Gagné and Edward L. Deci, "Self-Determination Theory and Work Motivation," *Journal of Organizational Behavior* 26 (2005), p. 332. Explaining people's behavioral motivations, the theory draws an important distinction between intrinsic and extrinsic incentives for actors' behavior. *Intrinsic incentives* are referred to as involving subjects who engage in a certain activity and derive spontaneous satisfaction from the activity itself, rather than from exogenous sources. *Extrinsic incentives*, on the other hand, encompass a variety of instruments, such as tangible and verbal rewards that are expected as a natural consequence of the activity, and thereby provide the actor with satisfaction. See Lyman W. Porter and Edward E. Lawler, *Marginal Attitudes and Performance* (Homewood, IL: Dorsey Press, 1968), p. 163. When such extrinsic motivations exist, actors' satisfaction springs from these external rewards and *not* from the activity as such. See Gagné and Deci, "Self-Determination Theory and Work Motivation," p. 331.

[78] See, for instance, Edward L. Deci, "Effects of Externally Mediated Rewards on Intrinsic Motivation," *Journal of Personality and Social Psychology* 18 (1971), 105–115.

[79] See, for instance, Cynthia D. Fisher, "The Effects of Personal Control, Competence, and Extrinsic Reward Systems on Intrinsic Motivation," *Organizational Behavior & Human Performance* 21(3) (1978), 273–288.

[80] See, for instance, Teresa M. Amabile, William DeJong and Mark R. Lepper, "Effects of Externally Imposed Deadlines on Subsequent Intrinsic Motivation." *Journal of Personality and Social Psychology* 34(1) (1976), 92–98; Mark Lepper and David Greene, "Turning Play into Work: Effects of Adult Surveillance and Extrinsic Rewards on Children's Intrinsic Motivation," *Journal of Personality and Social Psychology* 31(3) (1975), 479–486. It should be noted that some studies have evaluated the impact of different sorts of extrinsic

When applying the idea of the cognitive evaluation theory to the regulatory enforcement ecology, scholars show that rigorous enforcement activities may undermine regulatory subjects' sense of competence and autonomy, and in turn, weaken their intrinsic motivations to comply with regulations.[81] As a result, commentators argue that a strict and intransigent enforcement system may cause laws to lose their perceived legitimacy.[82] In that case, an enforcement system is likely to produce the opposite behavior from that which is sought.[83] Specifically, it may generate resistance and antagonism among regulatory targets and undermine their willingness to comply.[84] Consequently, market actors may either not comply with the law or strive to defy the spirit of the law.[85] They

---

motivators, showing that while positive verbal feedback may enhance intrinsic motivation, tangible rewards are more likely to reduce intrinsic motivation. See Deci, "Effects of Externally Mediated Rewards on Intrinsic Motivation," 105–115; Gagné and Deci, "Self-Determination Theory and Work Motivation," 331–362.

[81] See John Braithwaite and Ian Ayres, *Responsive Regulation: Transcending the Deregulation Debate* (New York: Oxford University Press, Inc., 1992), 205; Marsha Blumenthal, Charles Christian and Joel Slemrod, "The Determinants of Income Tax Compliance: Evidence from a Controlled Experiment in Minnesota," *National Bureau of Economic Research Working Papers no. 6575* (1998); Kagan and Scholz, "The 'Criminology of the Corporation' and Regulatory Enforcement Strategies," pp. 72–73; John Braithwaite, *Restorative Justice & Responsive Regulation* (New York [etc.]: Oxford University Press, 2002), p. 35.

[82] See Tom R. Tyler, "The Psychology of Legitimacy: A Relational Perspective on Voluntary Deference to Authorities," *Personality and Social Psychology Review* 1(4) (1997), 323–345. For instance, Tyler has shown that a poor treatment by authorities affects the subjects' perception about the overall legitimacy of these authorities. Moreover, Jonathan D. Casper, Tom R. Tyler and Bonnie Fisher, "Procedural Justice in Felony Cases," *Law & Society Review* 22(3) (1988), 483–507 have shown that subjects' concerns about fairness remain crucial even when the actual outcomes are important.

[83] See Sharon S. Brehm and Jack Williams Brehm, *Psychological Reactance: A Theory of Freedom and Control* (New York: Academic Press, 1981).

[84] See Blumenthal, Christian and Slemrod, "The Determinants of Income Tax Compliance: Evidence from a Controlled Experiment in Minnesota;" Valerie Braithwaite and John Braithwaite, "An Evolving Compliance Model for Tax Enforcement," in *Crimes of Privilege*, N. Shover and J. P. Wright eds. (Oxford: Oxford University Press, 2001); Kristina Murphy, "'Trust Me, I'm the Taxman': The Role of Trust in Nurturing Compliance," *Centre for Tax System Integrity Working Paper no. 43* (2002); Brehm and Brehm, *Psychological Reactance: A Theory of Freedom and Control*; Kagan and Scholz, "The 'Criminology of the Corporation' and Regulatory Enforcement Strategies," pp. 73, 112–116; Baldwin and Cave, *Understanding Regulation: Theory, Strategy, and Practice*, p. 98

[85] See Bardach and Kagan, *Going by the Book: The Problem of Regulatory Unreasonableness*, p. 123. Empirical studies have shown that a general belief in

may exploit loopholes in the law by contravening the intent of the law without technically breaking it.[86] As Bardach and Kagan (1982) point out: "[L]egalistic enforcement strategies that are indifferent to the insights and attitudes of key personnel in regulated enterprises destroy rather than build cooperation and thereby undercut the potential effectiveness of regulatory program. . . . Resentment and hostility from those who are regulated are direct effects of legalism and its attendant unreasonableness."[87]

The adverse effect of irreconcilable enforcement policies might raise even greater concerns when the possibility of innocent law violations is concerned.[88] Regulations are ever-changing and can sometimes be too ambiguous.[89] In some cases the regulatory requirements are very technical and difficult to understand. Therefore, regulatory violations may sometimes result from an innocent mistake, wrong interpretation, or ignorance.[90] Under such circumstances, the adverse psychological impacts of a harsh enforcement style may be even more powerful. If one has exerted special efforts to do what one believes is the right thing, but is

---

the legitimacy of regulatory requirements was found to be an element which induces compliance. Neil Gunningham, Dorothy Thornton and Robert A. Kagan, "Motivating Management: Corporate Compliance in Environmental Protection," *Law & Policy* 27(2) (2004), 289–316.

[86] See Karyl Kinsey, "Deterrence and Alienation Effects of IRS Enforcement: An Analysis of Survey Data," in *Why People Pay Taxes: Tax Compliance and Enforcement*, Joel Slemrod ed. (Ann Arbor: University of Michigan Press, 1992), p. 259. Kinsey argues that "the fear of getting caught and the severity of sanctions motivate taxpayers to comply with the law. However, the retroactive, confrontational, and coercive aspects of a deterrence approach to law enforcement also have an indirect, negative effect by alienating taxpayers and lowering their willingness to comply voluntarily with the law." See also, Baldwin and Cave, *Understanding Regulation: Theory, Strategy, and Practice*, pp. 102–103, who discuss practices of what they label "creative compliance," whereby regulatees avoid law-breaking by circumventing the scope of a rule while still breaching the spirit of the rule; and Bardach and Kagan, *Going by the Book: The Problem of Regulatory Unreasonableness*, p. 117.

[87] Bardach and Kagan, *Going by the Book: The Problem of Regulatory Unreasonableness*, pp. 102, 104.

[88] See *ibid.*, p. 63.

[89] See Spence, "The Shadow of the Rational Polluter: Rethinking the Role of Rational Actor Models in Environmental Law," pp. 931–936. For instance, Spence examines the complexity of environmental regulations and shows that they are often numerous, difficult to understand, dynamic and sometimes even hard to find. Therefore, the compliance task is often unreasonably difficult, and noncompliance often stems from misunderstanding surrounding environmental laws.

[90] See Reinier Kraakman, "Corporate Liability Strategies and the Costs of Legal Controls," *Yale Law Journal* 93 (1984), p. 864; Baldwin and Cave, *Understanding Regulation: Theory, Strategy, and Practice*, p. 101.

eventually treated by the enforcement system as a transgressor, then one may be willing to sidestep the regulation in the future.[91] Summing up, rigid enforcement practices may foster frustration among the regulatees and reduce compliance levels. Such strict and formal enforcement practices may hinder the achievement of regulatory goals.[92]

2.4.3 Impracticable Optimal Expected Liability

A central element of the deterrence theory is the *expected liability* faced by potential perpetrators, that is, the product of the *probability of detection* and the *actual sanction*.[93] As discussed above, according to the deterrence-based enforcement approach, when an expected liability equals the social cost of misconduct, potential perpetrators internalize the social consequences of their conduct.[94] Theoretically, when setting the expected liability for a certain regulatory violation, regulators face a wide variety of possible combinations of actual sanctions and probabilities of detection.[95] However, in reality each of these variables may be subject to various constraints, and therefore the scope of the regulatory discretion is often somewhat limited. Consider first, the constraints faced by policymakers when setting *actual sanctions*. At the outset, actual sanctions are constrained by the limited wealth of the regulatees. As mentioned earlier, if the actual fine exceeds the value of their net assets, it provides no deterrence effect since regulatees are not deterred by facing an obligation to pay more than they actually have.[96] In addition, if stern sanctions are applied for every violation, the marginal deterrence of sanctions is eroded, and thereby potential perpetrators may be encouraged to commit more

---

91 See Bardach and Kagan, *Going by the Book: The Problem of Regulatory Unreasonableness*, pp. 106–107.

92 See Braithwaite and Ayres, *Responsive Regulation: Transcending the Deregulation Debate*, pp. 47–49. See also, Kagan and Scholz, "The 'Criminology of the Corporation' and Regulatory Enforcement Strategies," pp. 67–68, according to which corporations' regulatory violations can be explained by three different explanations: corporations being "amoral calculators" or "political citizens," or "organizational incompetence." According to the authors, most corporations have a primary commitment to act in a socially responsible manner, and at most times, they do not act as amoral calculators. Therefore, harsh punishment may not produce a deterrence effect. For a similar approach see Keith Hawkins, *Environment and Enforcement: Regulation and the Social Definition of Pollution* (Oxford: Clarendon Press, 1984), p. 110.

93 See Section 2.2.3.

94 See Section 2.2.3.

95 See *supra* note 34 and the related main text.

96 See *supra* note 54 and the related main text.

serious violations.[97] Additionally, high sanctions may encourage risk-averse regulatory subjects to behave over-protectively.[98] On top of that, severe sanctions imposed on culpable corporations may ultimately fall on innocent parties, such as stockholders, bondholders, employees, and consumers, and thereby create another source of inefficiency (often referred to as "collateral effects").[99]

Similarly, the choice of the *probability of detection* may be subject to some constraints that stem from the direct costs involved in monitoring actions. Hypothetically, if monitoring is costless, an optimal probability of detection goes to unity.[100] However, in reality there is a limit to what enforcement authorities can detect.[101] Detection of misconduct is often costly, and enforcement resources are seldom adequate to inspect more than a fraction of potential perpetrators.[102] Furthermore, from a social perspective, enforcement actions are desirable only to the extent that their costs are not higher than the social harm caused by the misconduct.[103]

---

[97] See *supra* note 32 and the related main text. According to the marginal deterrence consideration, the greater the severity of the social costs caused by the misconduct, the greater the sanction for such misconduct should be. The rationale behind this is that if would-be wrongdoers face the same sanction for a less and a more severe violation, they may be motivated to commit the more severe wrong. See *supra* note 32 and the related main text.

[98] See Polinsky and Shavell, "The Optimal Tradeoff between the Probability and Magnitude of Fines," 880–891.

[99] See John C. Coffee Jr., "No Soul to Damn: No Body to Kick: An Unscandalized Inquiry into the Problem of Corporate Punishment," *Michigan Law Review* 79(3) (1981), pp. 402–407. See also, Baldwin and Cave, *Understanding Regulation: Theory, Strategy, and Practice*, p. 98: "A further criticism of strict enforcement is that it may produce undesired side-effects (e.g. driving certain firms out of business and causing unemployment) . . ."

[100] See Becker, "Crime and Punishment: An Economic Approach," 169–217; Polinsky and Shavell, "The Optimal Tradeoff between the Probability and Magnitude of Fines," 880–891; Segal and Whinston, "Public Vs. Private Enforcement of Antitrust Law: A Survey," 306–315.

[101] See Bardach and Kagan, *Going by the Book: The Problem of Regulatory Unreasonableness*, pp. 101–102. See also, Harrington, "Enforcement Leverage when Penalties are Restricted," pp. 32–33.

[102] See Becker, "Crime and Punishment: An Economic Approach," 169–217; Stigler, "The Optimum Enforcement of Laws," p. 527; Polinsky and Shavell, "The Optimal Tradeoff between the Probability and Magnitude of Fines," 880–891; Scholz, "Voluntary Compliance and Regulatory Enforcement," 385–404; Segal and Whinston, "Public vs. Private Enforcement of Antitrust Law: A Survey," 306–315; Gilboy, "Compelled Third-Party Participation in the Regulatory Process: Legal Duties, Culture, and Noncompliance," p. 140.

[103] See Becker, "Crime and Punishment: An Economic Approach," 169–217. See also, Chapter 1, Section 1.1; Baldwin and Cave, *Understanding Regulation:*

As long as an optimal combination of the probability of detection and actual sanctions can be reached in reality, the deterrence-based approach may achieve its goal of combating misconduct. However, in many cases the optimal combination of sanctions and probabilities of detection is impracticable. In these cases, a deterrence-based enforcement regime may fail to achieve its social goals.

2.4.4 Bounded Rationality

Critics of the deterrence-based approach question the rationality assumption that lies at the heart of this enforcement approach. Commentators argue that in many cases people's behavioral choices may deviate from what is predicted as a rational choice.[104] As the argument goes, people essentially have "bounded rationality" which reflects the limited ability of human beings to satisfactorily adapt to the complexity of the world and the ambiguity involved in decision making.[105] Given this bounded rationality, it is often the case that people make decisions that do not maximize their own utility.[106] Under such circumstances, the deterrence-based approach might fail to achieve its social goals.[107]

Although there is no consensus regarding the exact causes of an agent's deviation from the rational calculus, there has been no shortage of hypotheses seeking to explain this phenomenon. One central line of research

---

Theory, Strategy, and Practice, p. 110: "It is not sensible for regulators to aim for perfect compliance or the complete elimination of hazard. This is because enforcement costs tend to rise alongside increases in levels of compliance and a point will arrive where the costs of further enforcement are not justified by the gains."

[104] For a clear exposition of this topic see Michael Faure, *The Impact of Behavioral Law and Economics on Accident Law* (The Hague, NL: Boom Juridische Uitgevers, 2009). See also, Cass R. Sunstein, ed., *Behavioral Law and Economics* (Cambridge & New York: Cambridge University Press, 2000); Russell B. Korobkin and Thomas S. Ulen, "Law and Behavioral Science: Removing the Rationality Assumption from Law and Economics," *California Law Review* 88 (2000), 1051–1144.

[105] See Herbert A. Simon, "A Behavioral Model of Rational Choice," *The Quarterly Journal of Economics* 69(1) (1955), 99–118; Herbert A. Simon, "Rational Decision Making in Business Organizations," *The American Economic Review* 69(4) (1979), 493–513.

[106] See Korobkin and Ulen, "Law and Behavioral Science: Removing the Rationality Assumption from Law and Economics," 1051–1144.

[107] See Reinier Kraakman,"Gatekeepers: The Anatomy of a Third-Party Enforcement Strategy," *Journal of Law, Economics, and Organization* 2(1) (1986), p. 56: "it [deterrence strategy] may fail because wrongdoers lack the capacity or information to make self-interested compliance decisions."

focuses, for instance, on individuals' limited ability to think rationally when potential outcomes involve *uncertainty*. According to the literature, decision makers tend to make behavioral choices in a way that allows them to avoid uncertainty. This phenomenon, commonly referred to as "*probability neglect*," implies that when choosing between alternatives, decision makers tend to focus their attention on the *absolute* outcomes and neglect the probability that such outcomes are actually obtained.[108] Such findings have inspired a follow-up research on a related phenomenon, known as "*ambiguity avoidance*." As suggested by the literature, when making behavioral choices, people tend to discount the importance of ambiguous information, and therefore such information has little, if any, effect on their final decision.[109] As a result, when behavioral decisions involve a consequential evaluation (*i.e.*, require the evaluation of alternative anticipated outcomes and their perceived likelihood), individuals are likely to deviate from the predictions of the rational choice theory.[110] Since people often do not take into account the probability of each outcome or tend to ignore ambiguous information, improbable outcomes may be overestimated while probable ones may be underestimated.[111]

A related cognitive bias, known as "*availability heuristic*," suggests that people tend to predict the probability of an event based on how easily an

---

[108] See Faure, *The Impact of Behavioral Law and Economics on Accident Law*, pp. 23–24.

[109] See, for instance, Eric Van Dijk and Marcel Zeelenberg, "The Discounting of Ambiguous Information in Economic Decision Making," *Journal of Behavioral Decision Making* 16(5) (2003), 341–352. The study includes three experiments which tested the responses of decision makers to ambiguous information. The collective results of the experiments suggest that decision makers discount ambiguous information. See also, Shawn P. Curley, Frank J. Yates and Richard A. Abrams, "Psychological Sources of Ambiguity Avoidance," *Organizational Behavior and Human Decision Processes* 38(2) (1986), 230–256; Colin Camerer and Martin Weber, "Recent Developments in Modeling Preferences: Uncertainty and Ambiguity," *Journal of Risk and Uncertainty* 5(4) (1992), 325–370; Gideon Keren and Léonie E. M. Gerritsen, "On the Robustness and Possible Accounts of Ambiguity Aversion," *Acta Psychologica* 103(1–2) (1999), 149–172.

[110] See, for instance, Eldar Shafir and Amos Tversky, "Thinking through Uncertainty: Nonconsequential Reasoning and Choice," *Cognitive Psychology* 24(4) (1992), 449–474. The authors refer to the deviation from the rational choice which occurs under uncertainty as a *disjunction effect*: such effect occurs when people prefer x over y when they know that event A obtains, and they also prefer x over y when they know that event A does not obtain, but they prefer y over x when it is unknown whether or not A obtains.

[111] See Faure, *The Impact of Behavioral Law and Economics on Accident Law*, pp. 23–24.

example can be brought to their mind.[112] For instance, one may argue that smoking is not harmful because his Uncle Sam smoked 50 cigarettes a day and lived to 93.[113] Of course, Uncle Sam is not a representative case of smoking risks, but given that his case is readily available in one's memory, it is used for an evaluation of the probability of outcomes.[114] This example may be explained by another cognitive bias identified in the literature, according to which people tend to take decisions with a "*selective optimism and over-confidence*." This bias is supported by a considerable number of empirical studies showing that individuals tend to perceive positive outcomes as more probable than negative ones, especially when they have a certain level of control over actions associated with the outcome.[115] Thus, according to these findings, a rational probabilistic method of decision making, under which alternative outcomes are weighted according to the probability of their occurrence, is often replaced by a non-systematic evaluation, which relies on one's personal memory or groundless optimism.

The psychology and behavioral economics literature on possible biases in decision making is extensive, and the list of explanations offered by the literature is a lengthy one. Yet, in spite of the variance of plausible explanations, the large body of literature agrees on the basic fact that an agent's cognition may be influenced by various biases and thus people may behave differently than predicted on the basis of the utility maximization hypothesis. Given this conclusion, one may argue that a regulatory enforcement system that rests entirely on an agent's rationality may not always be able to produce socially optimal incentives for the regulated subjects. In order to guarantee its efficient application in policy making, the deterrence-based enforcement approach should somehow be adjusted to the cognitive biases of regulatory subjects. However, such an adjustment may turn out to be an extremely complex exercise: *first*, it is highly questionable whether all potential biases can be recognized *ex-ante* for every possible setting; *second*, the actual effect of each bias may greatly differ from one decision maker to another; and *third*, although in many cases the direction in which each of the biases affects decision makers' choices is predictable

---

112 See Amos Tversky and Daniel Kahneman, "Judgment Under Uncertainty: Heuristics and Biases," *Science* 185 (1974), 1124–1131.

113 See Anthony Esgate, David Groome and Kevin Baker, *An Introduction to Applied Cognitive Psychology* (New York: Psychology Press, 2004), p. 201.

114 See Faure, *The Impact of Behavioral Law and Economics on Accident Law*, p. 24.

115 See Christine Jolls, "Behavioral Economics Analysis of Redistributive Legal Rules," *Vanderbilt Law Review* 51(6) (1998), pp. 1658–1663; Faure, *The Impact of Behavioral Law and Economics on Accident Law*, pp. 26–28.

(*e.g.*, towards less uncertain outcomes, or towards choices associated with less ambiguous information), the net impact of all relevant biases on final compliance choices is not always clear.[116]

That said, two important clarifications are worthy of attention: *first*, although the literature on bounded rationality and behavioral biases underscores the risk of over-reliance on the rationality of agents, this literature does *not* imply that *bounded rationality* is *irrationality*; regulatees' compliance decisions should not be deemed irrational just because they fail to accord with a purely rational maximization of utility.[117] Therefore, the behavioral insights discussed above should not be interpreted as suggesting that no systematic enforcement scheme can achieve compliance goals. As we shall see in what follows, the behavioral stream of research led to the development of an alternative approach to law enforcement, which seeks to be responsive to the intrinsic motivations of actors. *Second*, given the focus of this book on corporate regulatees, it is important to clarify that the bounded rationality critique is somewhat less powerful when *corporations* rather than *individuals* are concerned. Although, in fact, corporate behavior is decided and executed by "flesh and blood agents," corporations themselves are often assumed to come closer to the "*rational agent*" or the "*economic man*" than most individuals.[118] When corporations are concerned, the goal of maximizing pecuniary gains is rather explicit, and usually executed with the support of accountancy departments and professional advisors.[119] Therefore, where regulated firms are concerned,

---

[116] See *ibid.*, pp. 28–31.

[117] See Reinhard Selten, "What is Bounded Rationality?" in *Bounded Rationality: The Adaptive Toolbox*, Gerd Gigerenzer and Reinhard Selten eds. (Cambridge, MA: MIT Press, 2002), p. 15.

[118] See, for instance, Bary M. Staw, "Dressing Up Like an Organization: When Psychological Theories can Explain Organizational Action," *Journal of Management* 17(4) (1991), 805–819, which discusses the application of psychological models to the organizational level where individual behaviors influence organizational action. For arguments regarding the defective rationality of corporate agents see Steven Croley, "Vicarious Liability in Tort: On the Sources and Limits of Employee Reasonableness," *Southern California Law Review* 69 (1995), 1705–1738; Gary T. Schwartz, "The Hidden and Fundamental Issue of Employer Vicarious Liability," *Southern California Law Review* 69 (1995), 1739–1767. For the rationality of business organizations see Edwin H. Sutherland, *White Collar Crime: The Uncut Version* (New Haven: Yale University Press, 1983).

[119] See, for instance, Walsh and Pyrich, "Corporate Compliance Programs as a Defense to Criminal Liability: Can a Corporation Save its Soul?," p. 633: "Corporations are typically viewed as calculating actors. Because corporations presumably act in their economic best interests, they are more likely than individuals to weigh costs and benefits before undertaking an action. Therefore,

the critique regarding individuals' bounded rationality should not be overestimated.

2.5 SUMMARY AND CONCLUDING REMARKS

The deterrence-based enforcement approach provides an economic analytical framework for the analysis of law enforcement. Based on agents' rationality, this school of thought perceives the role of enforcement systems as deterring would-be wrongdoers from law-breaking. As such, the deterrence-based approach adopts a strict, confrontational style of enforcement, which coerces compliance through an optimal combination of detection and sanctioning. As revealed in this chapter, a practical implication of the deterrence-based enforcement approach in policy making requires a prudent evaluation of its weaknesses. Such weaknesses include: the high costs of enforcement associated with the regulatory "cat-and-mouse" game endorsed by this approach; the potential alienation of regulatees; challenges involved in determining the optimal probability of detection and sanctions; and the inability to cope with the bounded rationality of regulatees.

The inherent flaws of the deterrence-based approach have led various scholars to the conclusion that an enforcement system cannot achieve its end-goals merely by manipulating subjects' expected payoffs. A socially desirable enforcement framework must move beyond the rational calculus of the deterrence-based enforcement approach and account for some intrinsic motivations of regulatees, which may play a crucial role in inducing regulatory compliance. The search for an improved regulatory framework has led scholars to develop an alternative approach that seeks to address the weaknesses of the deterrence-based enforcement approach. The following chapter describes the cooperative-enforcement school of thought developed by behavioral scholars as an alternative for the deterrence-based enforcement paradigm.

---

corporations are more likely than individuals to be deterred from criminal acts by the possibility of incurring fines or other penalties" (references omitted). See also, Pearce and Tombs, "Ideology, Hegemony, and Empiricism: Compliance Theories of Regulation," p. 425; Sutherland, *White Collar Crime: The Uncut Version*, pp. 236–238.

3. Cooperative enforcement

3.1 INTRODUCTION

Having sketched the layout of the deterrence-based enforcement school of thought in Chapter 2, this chapter focuses on an alternative approach to law enforcement – commonly referred to as *cooperative enforcement*. The cooperative approach was developed by behavioral scholars as an alternative paradigm to the deterrence-based one. In discussing this alternative approach, I start by presenting its fundamental premises (Section 3.2), while paying particular attention to a key element of this approach, *i.e.*, regulatory cooperation (Section 3.3). I then explore some policy implications of the cooperative enforcement approach by discussing various regulatory enforcement regimes developed based on the cooperative enforcement philosophy (Section 3.4). Having explored various cooperative enforcement regimes, I go on in the following section to discuss the pitfalls of the cooperative enforcement approach (Section 3.5). Finally, I summarize and conclude this chapter in Section 3.6.

3.2 COOPERATIVE ENFORCEMENT: THE BUILDING BLOCKS

Cooperative enforcement comprises an alternative approach to the economically-oriented, deterrence-based approach discussed in Chapter 2. The cooperative enforcement approach has been developed by opponents of the deterrence-based school of thought, pointing at shortcomings of the economically-oriented analytical framework. As discussed below, the cooperative enforcement approach hinges upon major insights from behavioral sciences in tackling the regulatory enforcement riddle.

3.2.1 Regulatees' Normative Commitment

Regulatees' motivations to comply with legal orders have been thoroughly studied by behavioral scholars.[1] Commentators have questioned the aptitude of pure economic calculus to explain regulatees' behavioral choices.

To support their doubts, scholars have pointed at a puzzling phenomenon, according to which under various circumstances people tend to comply with the law even when a rational calculus would predict differently.[2] These scholars base their criticism on empirical evidence, according to which in certain contexts regulatees tend to obey the law even when the threat of sanctions is significantly low.[3] Consequently, behavioral scholars

---

[1] See, for instance, David Easton, "The Perception of Authority and Political Change," in *Authority*, Carl J. Friedrich ed. (Cambridge, MA: Harvard University Press, 1958); John R. French Jr. and Bertram Raven, "The Bases of Social Power," in *Studies in Social Power*, Dorwin Cartwright ed. (Ann Arbor, MI: University of Michigan, 1959); Tom R. Tyler and E. Allan Lind, "A Relational Model of Authority in Groups," in *Advances in Experimental Social Psychology*, Mark P. Zanna ed., Vol. 25 (New York: Academic Press, 1992), 115–191; Tyler, "The Psychology of Legitimacy: A Relational Perspective on Voluntary Deference to Authorities," 323–345; Tyler, *Why People Obey the Law*.

[2] See, for instance, Hugh L. Ross, *Deterring the Drinking Driver: Legal Policy and Social Control*, Reviewed and updated ed. (Lexington, Mass.: Lexington Books, 1984), who shows how public campaigns against drunk drivers lessen law infringements although they have marginal (if any) influence on expected sanctions. See also, Tom R. Tyler, "Justice and Leadership Endorsement," in *Political Cognition*, Richard Lau and David Sears eds. (Hillsdale, NJ: Lawrence Erlbaum and Associates, 1986), 257–278, who examines people's choice to comply with laws that impose burdens such as tax duties, and shows that in spite of the very low probability of being caught for tax-law infringements, people tend to obey the law. For further discussion see Tyler, *Why People Obey the Law*, p. 22.

[3] The law and economics scholarship is not a stranger to this phenomenon. In fact, this phenomenon was recognized in the late 1980s by Winston Harrington, and labeled after him ("the *Harrington Paradox*"); see Harrington, "Enforcement Leverage when Penalties are Restricted," 29–53. Harrington refers to empirical evidence on environmental compliance to show that a considerable proportion of the time, subjects tend to comply with the law, although in reality the expected liability is often much lower than the costs of compliance. In his study, Harrington notes the following paradox: "In the United States, empirical studies of the enforcement of continuous compliance with environmental regulations, especially air and water pollution regulations, have repeatedly demonstrated the following: (i) For most sources the frequency of surveillance is quite low. (ii) Even when violations are discovered, fines or other penalties are rarely assessed in most states. (iii) Sources are, nonetheless, thought to be in compliance a large part of the time." *Ibid.*, p. 29. See also, Clifford S. Russell, "Game Models for Structuring Monitoring and Enforcement Systems," *Natural Resource Modeling* 4(2) (1990), pp. 145–146. Note, the paradox itself has been questioned later on by the scholarly literature which provided contradicting evidence supporting the standard deterrence theory predictions. See Karine Nyborg and Kjetil Telle, "Firms' Compliance to Environmental Regulation: Is There Really a Paradox?" *Environmental & Resource Economics* 35(1) (2006), 1–18. This study used the empirical data of the Norwegian Pollution Control Authority (NPCA) to show that Harrington's presentation of 'stylized facts' may be perceived differently if looked at from

have suggested that actors' compliance decisions should not be evaluated merely according to their fear of punishment.[4] Instead, personal attitudes and moral obligations must be taken into account when elucidating behavioral choices.[5]

The cooperative enforcement approach departs from the deterrence-based presumption of actors' rationality. Instead, this approach hinges upon regulatees' nature as law-abiding creatures. As the argument goes, most regulatees have a *law-abiding nature* that powerfully motivates them to obey the law even in the absence of significant threats of punishment.[6] Advocates of the cooperative enforcement approach argue that regulatees are concerned to do what is right, and to be faithful to their sense of responsibility. They often comply with the law merely because they believe it is the right thing to do – *just because it is the law*;[7] they voluntarily presume their obligation to obey the law and feel personally committed to comply with regulatory requirements, regardless of the risk of being sanc-

---

another angle. The authors show that in the case of the NPCA, a closer look at the data reveals that the "enforcement of minor violations is lax, but such violations do flourish; serious violations, on the other hand, are subject to credible threats of harsh punishment, and such violations are more uncommon" which is just as predicted by the standard deterrence theory. See also, Anthony G. Heyes and Neil Rickman, "Regulatory Dealing – Revisiting the Harrington Paradox," *Journal of Public Economics* 72(3) (1999), pp. 361–362.

[4] See Kagan and Scholz, "The 'Criminology of the Corporation' and Regulatory Enforcement Strategies," pp. 67–68; Hawkins, *Environment and Enforcement: Regulation and the Social Definition of Pollution*, p. 110.

[5] See Braithwaite, *Restorative Justice & Responsive Regulation*; Kagan and Scholz, "The 'Criminology of the Corporation' and Regulatory Enforcement Strategies," 352–377.

[6] See, for instance, Hawkins, "Compliance Strategy, Prosecution Policy, and Aunt Sally: A Comment on Pearce and Tombs," 444–466; Kagan and Scholz, "The 'Criminology of the Corporation' and Regulatory Enforcement Strategies," 352–377; Bardach and Kagan, *Going by the Book: The Problem of Regulatory Unreasonableness*. For empirical evidence supporting this perception see, for instance, Raymond Paternoster and Sally Simpson, "Sanction Threats and Appeals to Morality: Testing a Rational Choice Model of Corporate Crime," *Law and Society Review* 30(3) (1996), 549–583 who have investigated MBA candidates' intent to commit corporate crime and have shown that "where moral inhibition [was] high, considerations of the cost and benefit of corporate crime were virtually superfluous," *i.e.* when people hold personal moral codes, these codes may be more influential on their behavior than the rational calculus of the expected costs and benefits of regulatory violations. See also, John Braithwaite, *To Punish or Persuade: Enforcement of Coal Mine Safety* (Albany, NY: State University of New York Press, 1985).

[7] See Braithwaite and Ayres, *Responsive Regulation: Transcending the Deregulation Debate*, p. 22.

tioned for non-compliance.[8] Scholars further stipulate that regulatees' normative commitment is generated by two important factors: *personal morality*, *i.e.*, people wish to behave in a way that coincides with what they perceive as morally right; and *legitimacy*, *i.e.*, people tend to align their behavior with orders coming from an authority when they view this authority as legitimate.[9]

Note, advocates of the cooperative enforcement school of thought are not blind to the fact that business corporations may sometimes succumb to the temptation of misbehavior when encountered with an opportunity of gain.[10] Nevertheless, their approach rests on the presumption that most regulatees are "good apples," whose inclination to comply with the law increases when they perceive themselves fairly treated by a reasonable enforcement policy.[11] Accordingly, the cooperative enforcement approach posits that regulatory violations need not be explained by an amoral calculus undertaken by rational actors. A more plausible explanation, it is argued, is that these violations result from organizational incompetence, the misinterpretation of fluid and ambiguous laws, or simply from ignorance.[12]

---

8 See Tyler and Lind, "A Relational Model of Authority in Groups," 115–191; Tyler, "The Psychology of Legitimacy: A Relational Perspective on Voluntary Deference to Authorities," 323–345; Tyler, *Why People Obey the Law*; Kristina Murphy, "Procedural Justice and Tax Compliance," *Australian Journal of Social Issues* 38(3) (2003), 379–407.

9 See Tyler, *Why People Obey the Law*, p. 25.

10 See Kagan and Scholz, "The 'Criminology of the Corporation' and Regulatory Enforcement Strategies," p. 71.

11 See Bardach and Kagan, *Going by the Book: The Problem of Regulatory Unreasonableness*, pp. 59–61, 66; William Ker Muir Jr., *Police: Streetcorner Politicians* (Chicago: University of Chicago Press, 1977), p. 306; Braithwaite and Ayres, *Responsive Regulation: Transcending the Deregulation Debate*, pp. 23–34; Kagan and Scholz, "The 'Criminology of the Corporation' and Regulatory Enforcement Strategies," pp. 67–68; Hawkins, *Environment and Enforcement: Regulation and the Social Definition of Pollution*, p. 110. See also, Keith Hawkins, "Bargain and Bluff: Compliance Strategy and Deterrence in the Enforcement of Regulation," *Law and Policy Quarterly* 5(1) (1983), p. 44. Most polluters are described here as "responsible or public-spirited people" and "... field-staff believe that serious pollution that is the result of negligence or deliberate misconduct does not now occur regularly or on a large scale."

12 See Bardach and Kagan, *Going by the Book: The Problem of Regulatory Unreasonableness*, p. 63; Kagan and Scholz, "The 'Criminology of the Corporation' and Regulatory Enforcement Strategies," pp. 67–68; Hawkins, *Environment and Enforcement: Regulation and the Social Definition of Pollution*, p. 110.

3.2.2 From Compulsion to Cooperation

The cooperative enforcement approach departs from the penal, accusatory, and adversarial style of the deterrence-based one. This approach seeks to facilitate regulatory cooperation by favoring conciliation and compromising attitudes to law enforcement.[13] According to the cooperative approach, enforcement systems should chiefly play advisory and educative roles.[14] As the arguments goes, compliance can best be achieved through persuasion rather than through a threat of sanctions. Therefore, enforcement policies should accentuate *cooperation*, rather than confrontation, and *conciliation*, rather than coercion.[15] Practically, enforcement authorities should account for the particular circumstances of the observed violation; corporations should be initially given the benefit of doubt; insignificant violations should be ignored; and reasonable considerations for non-compliance should be accepted; more serious violations should be granted generous abatement periods; and acceptable correction and restoration efforts should forestall prosecution.[16]

The dichotomy between the deterrence-based and the cooperative enforcement approaches has been portrayed by Keith Hawkins as follows:

> A conciliatory style is remedial, a method of "social repair and maintenance, assistance for people in trouble," concerned with "what is necessary to ameliorate a bad situation." Penal control, on the other hand, "prohibits certain conduct, and it enforces its prohibitions with punishment". Its

[13] See Shover, Clelland and Lynxwiler, *Enforcement Or Negotiation: Constructing a Regulatory Bureaucracy*, pp. 127–129. As explained by Keith Hawkins in his pioneering book, *Environment and Enforcement: Regulation and the Social Definition of Pollution*: "[Cooperative enforcement] seeks to prevent harm rather than punish an evil. Its conception of enforcement centers upon the attainment of the broad aims of legislation, rather than sanctioning its breach. . . . [Cooperative enforcement] is concerned with repair and results, not retribution. . . . If prevention of future misconduct occurs, it does so as a result of negotiation rather than the deterrence which (presumably) inhibits future rule-breaking in a sanctioning system."

[14] See Hawkins, "Bargain and Bluff: Compliance Strategy and Deterrence in the Enforcement of Regulation," p. 36: "[I]f repair is the primary objective in a compliance system, in a sanctioning system it is retribution."

[15] See Hawkins, *Environment and Enforcement: Regulation and the Social Definition of Pollution*, p. 8; Gunningham, *Mine Safety: Law, Regulation, Policy*, p. 116.

[16] See Scholz, "Cooperation, Deterrence, and the Ecology of Regulatory Enforcement," pp. 180–183.

nature is accusatory, its outcome binary: "all or nothing – punishment or nothing."[17]

3.2.3 The Residual Role of Coercion

The cooperative enforcement approach does not belittle the value of punishment threats.[18] It acknowledges that at times, internal motivations alone cannot be trusted to provide sufficient motivations for compliance.[19] Thus, the threat of formal enforcement measures, although thrust behind the scenes, still plays a subtle but important role.[20] Enforcement authorities' efforts to achieve compliance should not blind them to the possibility that regulatees may act opportunistically and try to escape reasonable laws. Therefore, when persuasion and negotiation fail, coercive practices can still be used to ensure compliance.[21] Yet, commentators point out that such practices should be used sparingly, and as far as possible, should be left as a matter of last resort.[22]

3.3 THE VIRTUES OF REGULATORY COOPERATION

As discussed above, regulatory cooperation is a central objective of the cooperative enforcement school of thought. In what follows, I explore the virtues of regulatory cooperation from a social welfare standpoint. The basic idea conveyed in this section is that the social welfare is generally higher if genuine compliance is achieved through cooperation between

---

[17] See Hawkins, *Environment and Enforcement: Regulation and the Social Definition of Pollution*, p. 4 (references omitted).

[18] See Braithwaite, *Restorative Justice & Responsive Regulation*, p. 34.

[19] See Bardach and Kagan, *Going by the Book: The Problem of Regulatory Unreasonableness*, p. 62, 102.

[20] See, for instance, Hawkins, "Bargain and Bluff: Compliance Strategy and Deterrence in the Enforcement of Regulation," pp. 35, 39; John T. Scholz, "Can Government Facilitate Cooperation? An Informational Model of OSHA Enforcement," *American Journal of Political Science* 41(3) (1997), 693–717; Braithwaite, *To Punish or Persuade: Enforcement of Coal Mine Safety*; Peter J. May and Soren Winter, "Regulatory Enforcement and Compliance: Examining Danish Agro-Environmental Policy," *Journal of Policy Analysis and Management* 18(4) (1999), 625–651.

[21] See Bardach and Kagan, *Going by the Book: The Problem of Regulatory Unreasonableness*, p. 124.

[22] See Gunningham, *Mine Safety: Law, Regulation, Policy*, p. 117.

regulators and regulatees, rather than through a deterrence-based enforcement regime.[23]

3.3.1 Cost-Effectiveness

The first virtue of well-functioning cooperative enforcement regimes is their cost-effectiveness.[24] A genuine regulatory cooperation may relinquish some of the costs associated with the regulatory "cat-and-mouse" game, typically endorsed by the deterrence-based enforcement approach, including, litigation, error, and avoidance (defying) costs.[25] When both enforcement authorities and regulatees are truly committed to regulatory cooperation, both parties invest in securing meaningful, socially desirable compliant behavior, that is, behavior that promotes the spirit of regulations and their social objectives, rather than behavior that leads to costly legal battles over the "black letter" of regulations.

3.3.2 Compliance

Advocates of the cooperative enforcement approach maintain that a cooperative enforcement policy strengthens regulatees' moral obligation to obey the law, and thereby, if compared with the deterrence-based approach, it generates a higher level of regulatory compliance.[26] Scholars argue that the

---

[23] See Scholz, "Voluntary Compliance and Regulatory Enforcement," pp. 386, 392. See also, Scholz, "Cooperation, Deterrence, and the Ecology of Regulatory Enforcement," p. 179; Braithwaite and Ayres, *Responsive Regulation: Transcending the Deregulation Debate*, p. 205.

[24] See, for instance, Scholz, "Voluntary Compliance and Regulatory Enforcement," pp. 385–386.

[25] For the discussion of the regulatory "cat-and-mouse" game associated with the deterrence-based enforcement approach see Chapter 2, Section 2.4.1. See also, Scholz, "Cooperation, Deterrence, and the Ecology of Regulatory Enforcement," p. 184; Baldwin and Cave, *Understanding Regulation: Theory, Strategy, and Practice*, p. 98; Braithwaite and Ayres, *Responsive Regulation: Transcending the Deregulation Debate*, p. 19; Tyler, *Why People Obey the Law*, pp. 22–23; Baldwin and Cave, *Understanding Regulation: Theory, Strategy, and Practice*, p. 98.

[26] See Braithwaite, *Restorative Justice & Responsive Regulation*, pp. 78–79; Tom R. Tyler and Peter Degoey, "Trust in Organizational Authorities: The Influence of Motive Attributions on Willingness to Accept Decisions," in *Trust in Organizations*, Roderick M. Kramer and Tom R. Tyler, eds. (Thousand Oaks, CA: Sage Publications, Inc., 1996); Tyler, *Why People Obey the Law*. See also, Bardach and Kagan, *Going by the Book: The Problem of Regulatory Unreasonableness*, p. 100; Tyler and Lind, "A Relational Model of Authority in Groups," 115–191; Tyler, "The Psychology of Legitimacy: A Relational Perspective on Voluntary

alienation generated by a policy of deterrence-based enforcement may be alleviated when enforcement authorities follow a cooperative approach.[27] This line of argument is supported by empirical evidence, according to which compliance levels are significantly higher when regulatees perceive inspectors as treating them with respect and trust.[28]

On the theoretical frontier, commentators refer to the well-established *Procedural Justice Theory* to support the cooperative enforcement approach. According to the theory, people's behavioral choices are directly linked to their views about the level of fairness involved in decision making and in the execution of decisions.[29] Empirical evidence shows that people's trust in an organization is higher when they perceive themselves

---

Deference to Authorities," 323–345; Murphy, "Procedural Justice and Tax Compliance," 379–407.

[27] See, for instance, Baldwin and Cave, *Understanding Regulation: Theory, Strategy, and Practice*, p. 98.

[28] See John Braithwaite and Toni Makkai, "Trust and Compliance," *Policing and Society* 4(1) (1994), 1–12. See also, Kazumasu Aoki, Lee Axelrad and Robert A. Kagan, "Industrial Effluent Control in the United States and Japan," in *Regulatory Encounters*, Robert A. Kagan and Lee Axelrad eds. (Berkeley, Los Angeles, London: University of California Press, 2000), who compare compliance motivations under two approaches of regulations, showing that a more legalistic and stringent regulatory system does not lead to superior environmental performance. Compare with, Michael Wenzel, "The Impact of Outcome Orientation and Justice Concerns on Tax Compliance: The Role of Taxpayers' Identity," *Journal of Applied Psychology* 87(4) (2002), 629–645, which explores the effect of perceived procedural justice on tax-compliance behavior. The author shows that subjects tend to comply (filing tax-reports) when they perceive themselves as fairly treated by the tax authority. Likewise, Michael Wenzel, "Principles of Procedural Fairness in Reminder Letters: A Field-Experiment," *Center for Tax System Integrity Working Paper no. 42* (2002), examines the different impact of various remainder letters which were sent to those who had not filed their statement on time for their compliance. The author finds that remainder letters that corresponded with fairness principles generated a higher compliance than the standard letters used by the authorities. See also, Murphy, "Procedural Justice and Tax Compliance," 379–407.

[29] See Tom R. Tyler and Heather J. Smith, "Social Justice and Social Movements," in *The Handbook of Social Psychology*, D. G. Gilbert, S. T. Fiske and G. Lindzey eds., 4th edn, Vol. II (New York: Oxford University Press, 1998), 595–629. This approach of the Procedural Justice Theory is commonly referred to as "the normative approach." Another strand of the theory, commonly referred to as "the instrumental approach" suggests that people do not concentrate on the outcomes of processes influencing their life, but instead they are concerned about their ability to influence the decision. See, for instance, John Walter Thibaut and Laurens Walker, *Procedural Justice: A Psychological Analysis* (Hillsdale, NJ: Erlbaum, 1975). See also, Edgar A. Lind and Tom R. Tyler, *The Social Psychology of Procedural Justice* (New York: Plenum, 1988); Tom R. Tyler and Steven L.

as fairly treated by this organization. Consequently, people get more cooperative and tend to follow the organization's decisions even when those do not coincide with personal wishes.[30] By contrast, when people perceive themselves as unfairly treated, they tend to confront decisions and act uncooperatively.[31] Applying the procedural justice theory to the regulatory ecology, scholars show that when an authority is perceived as being highly trustworthy then this strengthens the beliefs of regulatees regarding the legitimacy of the authority and its entitlement to be obeyed.[32] Consequently, regulatees believe that they ought to obey regulations irrespective of the likelihood or severity of the sanction that may follow from violations.[33]

3.3.3 Law Deficiencies

Proponents of the cooperative enforcement approach stipulate that cooperative enforcement strategies may become particularly invaluable when those allow enforcement authorities and regulatees to efficiently overcome

---

Blader, *Cooperation in Groups: Procedural Justice, Social Identity, and Behavioral Engagement* (Philadelphia: Psychology Press, 2000).

[30] See Tyler, "The Psychology of Legitimacy: A Relational Perspective on Voluntary Deference to Authorities," 323–345. Other studies were slightly more skeptical about the balance between the importance of perceived procedural fairness and the favorability of outcome. For an overview see Murphy, "Procedural Justice and Tax Compliance," 379–407.

[31] See Tyler and Smith, "Social Justice and Social Movements," 595–629; Tyler and Degoey, "Trust in Organizational Authorities: The Influence of Motive Attributions on Willingness to Accept Decisions," p. 331; Murphy, "'Trust Me, I'm the Taxman': The Role of Trust in Nurturing Compliance."

[32] See Tyler and Lind, "A Relational Model of Authority in Groups," 115–191; Tyler, "The Psychology of Legitimacy: A Relational Perspective on Voluntary Deference to Authorities," 323–345; Murphy, "Procedural Justice and Tax Compliance," 379–407; Tyler, *Why People Obey the Law*.

[33] Scholars have shown that regulatees tend to evaluate the regulatory authority's trustworthiness, while relying on their personal experience along with other factors, such as whether the authority is neutral and consistent; whether their needs are adequately considered by the authority; whether they were treated politely and respectfully by the authority; and whether the authority has willingly considered their arguments. See Tyler, "The Psychology of Legitimacy: A Relational Perspective on Voluntary Deference to Authorities," 323–345; Tyler and Smith, "Social Justice and Social Movements," 595–629; Murphy, "Procedural Justice and Tax Compliance," 379–407; Braithwaite, *Restorative Justice & Responsive Regulation*; Tyler and Degoey, "Trust in Organizational Authorities: The Influence of Motive Attributions on Willingness to Accept Decisions;" Tyler and Lind, "A Relational Model of Authority in Groups," 115–191.

deficiencies embedded in ambiguous or inefficient regulations.[34] Regulatory cooperation may, for instance, allow enforcement authorities and regulatees to reach agreed arrangements that cope with over- or under-inclusive regulations.[35] Hence, it is argued, under a cooperative enforcement setting, both enforcement authorities and regulatees may concentrate their efforts and resources on achieving the fundamental objectives of regulations rather than focusing on meeting "black-letter" requirements.[36]

3.3.4 Information Sharing

Cooperative enforcement regimes facilitate information sharing among regulators, enforcement authorities, and regulatees. Consequently, regulatees may gain access to cumulative information gathered and processed by public authorities, while these authorities may gain better access to industry-related information.[37] This flow of information regarding emerging technology, expected risks, and methods to avoid such risks, may facilitate better regulations, improve regulatees' performance, and strengthen future regulatory cooperation, while increasing the trust between public authorities and regulatees.

3.4 POLICY IMPLICATIONS

For some readers, the idea of cooperation between enforcement authorities and regulatees does not fit into the typical role of regulatory enforcement

---

[34] See Scholz, "Cooperation, Deterrence, and the Ecology of Regulatory Enforcement," pp. 183–184; Bardach and Kagan, *Going by the Book: The Problem of Regulatory Unreasonableness*, p. 100.

[35] See, for instance, Scholz, "Voluntary Compliance and Regulatory Enforcement;" Scholz, "Cooperation, Deterrence, and the Ecology of Regulatory Enforcement," p. 183; Scholz, "Enforcement Policy and Corporate Misconduct: The Changing Perspective of Deterrence Theory," p. 258.

[36] See Braithwaite and Ayres, *Responsive Regulation: Transcending the Deregulation Debate*, p. 60.

[37] See Bardach and Kagan, *Going by the Book: The Problem of Regulatory Unreasonableness*, pp. 131, 139. The authors argue that the more information flows to enforcement authorities, the more easily they can monitor compliance and create a data set that can be useful for future compliance. See also, Scholz, "Cooperation, Deterrence, and the Ecology of Regulatory Enforcement," p. 184. Scholz argues that regulatory cooperation is likely to induce regulatees to share information on "newly discovered problems not covered by regulations if agencies are likely to help solve the problem rather than promulgate simple rules and enforce them legalistically."

systems, which is traditionally taken to imply some coercive treatment and uncompromising attitudes towards violators. In fact, the cooperative enforcement approach has served as a prolific ideological ground for the development of several enforcement regimes embracing the idea of regulatory cooperation. I survey the major cooperative enforcement regimes developed in the scholarly literature below.

3.4.1 Compromising Enforcement

Compromising enforcement comprises a regulatory enforcement regime that focuses on *social goals* underlying regulations, rather than on particular procedures and technical requirements specified by regulations.[38] Under this regime regulations are not enforced in situations where their enforcement does not promote intended social goals; technical violations that do not involve substantial risks are overlooked; regulatees are treated with patience and tolerance; voluntary measures adopted by subjects are accepted, even if they do not comprise literal compliance, but if they are proved to achieve regulatory goals. Accordingly, a compromising enforcement regime grants enforcement authorities wide discretion, and allows them to "selectively negate, modify, or delay the enforcement of regulations when their literal application to a particular violation would be unreasonable or of secondary importance."[39] A central feature of a compromising enforcement regime is *responsiveness*.[40] Under this regime, enforcement authorities allow regulatees a fair hearing, in which their arguments are willingly considered before resorting to any "formal" enforcement procedures. When regulatees' arguments cannot justify a flexible treatment, enforcement authorities explain their adherence to the literal regulatory requirement and reasonably allow subjects to restore their compliance before employing non-cooperative procedures.[41]

The compromising enforcement regime underscores public authorities' *guidance* and *persuasion* roles. Under this regime, public authorities are encouraged to engage in a problem-solving dialogue with industry players, in order to identify potential failures and regulatory risks.[42] In the same vein, after a particular violation is detected, enforcement authorities draw

---

[38] See Scholz, "Cooperation, Deterrence, and the Ecology of Regulatory Enforcement," p. 180.

[39] See Bardach and Kagan, *Going by the Book: The Problem of Regulatory Unreasonableness*, pp. 130–131.

[40] See *ibid.*, pp. 130–131.

[41] See *ibid.*, p. 124.

[42] See *ibid.*, p. 145.

the attention of relevant regulatees to such violations, provide them with their own evaluation as to the causes of the violations, and advise them on appropriate ways to avoid reoccurrence.[43] Furthermore, when appropriate, enforcement authorities may encourage regulatory compliance by communicating the social necessity and the objectives of certain regulations to regulatees. The authorities' goal, under this regime, is to persuade regulatees to comply with regulations as a matter of good practice, rather than as an outlet of escaping penalties.[44]

3.4.2 Negotiated Compliance

The negotiated compliance regime was developed in Fenn and Veljanovski (1988).[45] This regime utilizes regulatory bargaining to encourage the obedience of regulatees. The authors acknowledge that in a world with a limited enforcement budget, enforcement authorities are unable to detect all violations and prosecute all violators, and therefore propose that a regulatory bargaining between enforcement authorities and violators may be socially beneficial. More particularly, it is suggested that enforcement authorities may agree to avoid prosecution of past violations in return for regulatees' commitment for future compliance.[46] Under the suggested setting, enforcement authorities may concentrate their limited resources mainly on detecting more violations. Once a violation is detected, these authorities may offer violators the choice between: (1) being subject to prosecution for the detected violation; and (2) committing themselves to future compliance, and thereby avoiding prosecution for the detected violation.[47] As the argument goes, regulatees that choose to enter with enforcement authorities into agreements that require future compliance

---

[43] See *ibid.*, p. 146.

[44] See *ibid.*, p. 133.

[45] Fenn and Veljanovski, "A Positive Economic Theory of Regulatory Enforcement," 1055–1070.

[46] See *ibid.*, p. 1057. The negotiated compliance regime is applied, *de facto*, in many regulatory areas through 'consent decrees,' according to which enforcement authorities agree to avoid formal litigation in return for the regulatees' commitment to undertake compliance-oriented activities. See Bardach and Kagan, *Going by the Book: The Problem of Regulatory Unreasonableness*, pp. 141–142. A similar setting is adopted in the recently developed policy of Deferred Prosecution Agreements (DPAs) where the prosecution is deferred in return for culpable corporations' commitment to follow the conditions specified by the DPA. For a detailed discussion of the DPA policies see Chapter 7.

[47] See Fenn and Veljanovski, "A Positive Economic Theory of Regulatory Enforcement," p. 1059.

are aware that they are more closely scrutinized, and thereby face a greater probability of being detected if they violate the regulations again. Hence, such regulatees have a greater incentive to comply with regulations.[48]

The negotiated compliance regime corresponds with the philosophy of the cooperative enforcement paradigm. This regime allows enforcement authorities to assume that regulatory violations may result from honest mistakes, accidents, or from the misinterpretation of regulations. Accordingly, before resorting to sanctioning measures, this regime allows regulatees to take the necessary precautions to avoid the reoccurrence of violations, and commit themselves to future compliance.[49]

3.4.3 Regulatory Dealing

The regulatory dealing regime was developed in Heyes and Rickman (1999), and was inspired by the cooperative enforcement school of thought.[50] This regime resembles the idea of the negotiated compliance regime, and applies it across different regulatory domains. The pivotal assumption of this regime is that the regulatory authority interacts with regulatees in more than one enforcement context or domain. For instance, an enforcement authority may enforce a specific law at two or more geographical areas where a certain regulatee operates. Alternatively, an

---

[48] The negotiated compliance regime follows the economic logic of plea-bargaining, where the prosecutor 'trades' a reduced penalty for a guilty plea. In both contexts, the mutual consent between regulators and regulatees saves everyone the costs associated with full-scale litigation, and facilitates rehabilitation and the re-establishment of cooperation. See Ogus and Abbot, "Pollution and Penalties," p. 504. See also, Bardach and Kagan, *Going by the Book: The Problem of Regulatory Unreasonableness*, p. 140.

[49] Note that although this regime corresponds with the cooperative enforcement school of thought, while developing this regime, the authors stay adherent to the economic-oriented analytical framework, showing that the negotiated compliance regime may provide optimal compliance incentives also to regulatees who are 'amoral calculators'. Specifically, the success of the negotiated compliance regime is contingent upon two crucial elements. The first is a repeated relationship between enforcement authorities and regulatees. Where the regulatory interaction comprises a single game, negotiated governance may lead to a "non-prosecution – non-compliance" outcome. See Fenn and Veljanovski, "A Positive Economic Theory of Regulatory Enforcement," p. 1064. Secondly, regulatees must be subject to a credible threat of prosecution and sanctions in the case of the "second bite of the cherry." Such a threat shall motivate regulatees to follow their commitment to future compliance. See Ogus and Abbot, "Pollution and Penalties," p. 504.

[50] Heyes and Rickman, "Regulatory Dealing – Revisiting the Harrington Paradox," pp. 361–378.

enforcement authority may enforce different regulations (*e.g.*, air pollution, and soil pollution) at a single location.[51] Under this setting, the authors show that when compliance levels are suboptimal, an efficiency improvement may be achieved if enforcement authorities adopt a method of *regulatory dealing*, according to which the authority agrees not to prosecute violators for a violation in one domain, in return for regulatees' commitment to comply in another domain.[52] Similar to the motivations produced by the negotiated compliance regime discussed above, under a regulatory dealing regime regulatees may have a strong motivation to comply with the law, given that every compliance/violation decision has a magnified impact on an additional domain.[53]

3.4.4 Responsive Regulation

The responsive regulation regime was developed in Braithwaite and Ayres (1992).[54] Based on the assumption that most regulatees have a law-abiding nature, the responsive regulation regime promotes the use of persuasion and advisory measures as initial enforcement measures that should be used before more intrusive measures come into play.[55] The responsive regulation regime warrants a *gradual* escalation of regulatory intervention against resisting regulatees.[56] At the heart of the responsive regulation regime lies an "Enforcement Pyramid," depicted in Figure 3.1.[57] The enforcement pyramid is composed of the least intrusive interventions at the bottom; moderate administrative measures at the middle; and harsh

---

[51] See *ibid.*, p. 363.

[52] See *ibid.*, p. 364.

[53] See *ibid.*, pp. 365–366.

[54] Braithwaite and Ayres, *Responsive Regulation: Transcending the Deregulation Debate*. See also, Braithwaite, *Restorative Justice & Responsive Regulation*, p. 29.

[55] See Braithwaite and Ayres, *Responsive Regulation: Transcending the Deregulation Debate*, pp. 21–27; Braithwaite, *Restorative Justice & Responsive Regulation*, p. 29.

[56] Under the responsive regulation regime, the determination of monitoring levels and actual enforcement measures is treated as a single choice. See, for instance, Braithwaite and Ayres, *Responsive Regulation: Transcending the Deregulation Debate*, p. 38: "[F]irms that resist initial compliance will be pushed up the enforcement pyramid. Not only escalating penalties, but also escalating frequency of inspection and tripartite monitoring by trade unions . . . can then negate the returns to delayed compliance."

[57] The argument that an enforcement pyramid may induce higher levels of compliance was first made in Braithwaite, *To Punish or Persuade: Enforcement of Coal Mine Safety*. The scheme for Figure 3.1 is adopted from Haines, *Corporate Regulation: Beyond 'Punish and Persuade'*, p. 35.

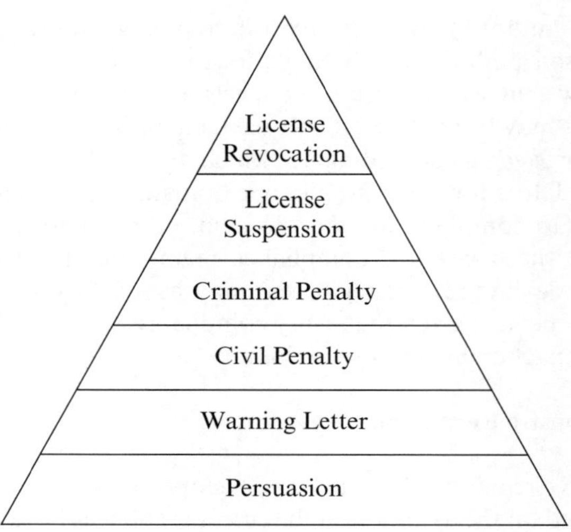

Figure 3.1 Enforcement pyramid

penalties at the top, with incapacitation sanction at the apex.[58] According to the responsive regulation regime, when encountering regulatory violations, enforcement authorities are required to start by utilizing the least intrusive measures at the bottom of the pyramid before resorting to any higher measure. Only when these measures fail to produce compliance, enforcement authorities may shift to a series of methods that gradually increase pressure on the wrongdoers, starting from soft practices (such as warnings), and gradually escalating to administrative sanctions, and eventually to harsh penalties.[59] According to the responsive regulation

[58] The specific measures placed in the different layers are illustrative only and can be replaced by other measures which: (1) are gradually structured in their gravity; and (2) headed by a credible peak measure which is sufficiently powerful to deter the most flagrant regulatory subject; the greater the gravity of the pinnacle sanction, the greater its capacity to induce regulatees' compliance using persuasive measures at the bottom of the pyramid. See Braithwaite and Ayres, *Responsive Regulation: Transcending the Deregulation Debate*, pp. 35–6; Braithwaite, *Restorative Justice & Responsive Regulation*, p. 30; Gunningham, *Mine Safety: Law, Regulation, Policy*, p. 123.

[59] See Braithwaite and Ayres, *Responsive Regulation: Transcending the Deregulation Debate*, pp. 35–38; Braithwaite, *Restorative Justice & Responsive Regulation*, pp. 30–31. Note, an escalation of enforcement responses under the responsive regulation regime includes both escalations of sanctions and of the

regime, the escalation of measures should be responsive to the degree of uncooperativeness of the firm.[60]

The shape of the pyramid, it is suggested, captures the anticipated proportional use of each layer of the pyramid.[61] Most offenses are likely to be treated at the base level, through persuasion. Fewer violations will face tougher measures, and only a small minority of violations – the most notorious ones – will face the apex-level sanction.[62]

3.4.5 Self-Regulation

Another enforcement regime that corresponds with the cooperative enforcement school of thought is self-regulation. In many regulatory contexts governments wishing to regulate particular industries promulgate 'Command and Control' regulations that specify detailed regulatory orders backed by the threat of criminal penalties.[63] An alternative way in which governments may promote the regulation of specific industries is through *self-regulation*. Self-regulation comprises a great variety of arrangements established by private organizations to regulate professional services and trading activities.[64] Under a self-regulation regime, a state's law-making powers are deliberately delegated to a non-governmental organization, composed of corporations whose activities are being regulated.[65] This organization establishes a set of rules and enforces them against its members.[66]

---

level of regulatory scrutiny. See Braithwaite and Ayres, *Responsive Regulation: Transcending the Deregulation Debate*, p. 38.

[60] See Fiona Haines, *Corporate Regulation: Beyond 'Punish and Persuade'* (Oxford: Clarendon Press, 1997), pp. 119–120. Haines has drawn attention to the possible side-effects of sanction escalation. According to Haines, as a response to sanction escalation corporations' attitude may shift "from cooperation and trust, to deterrence and mistrust." This implies that when escalating sanctions one should consider the possible adverse effect which may be produced.

[61] See Braithwaite and Ayres, *Responsive Regulation: Transcending the Deregulation Debate*, p. 41.

[62] See *ibid.*, p. 41.

[63] For a survey of regulatory techniques, see Baldwin and Cave, *Understanding Regulation: Theory, Strategy, and Practice*, pp. 34–62.

[64] See Anthony Ogus, "Self-Regulation," in *Encyclopedia of Law and Economics*, Bouckaert, Boudewijn and Gerrit De Geest, eds., Vol. 9400 (available online: http://encyclo.findlaw.com/index.html: Edward Elgar and the University of Ghent, 1999), p. 590.

[65] See *ibid.*, p. 590.

[66] See Baldwin and Cave, *Understanding Regulation: Theory, Strategy, and Practice*, p. 39. The notion of self-regulation has developed to include a multitude

A self-regulation regime broadens the scope of regulatory cooperation beyond the enforcement context to the context of standard-setting. This regime facilitates a unique governance mechanism in which regulatees – and organizations acting on their behalf – enforce self-established standards of behavior. In that respect, self-regulation may be seen as a type of tacit regulatory cooperation, under which market players are motivated to enforce self-set regulations, in order to avoid or diminish government intervention. In other words, under a self-regulation setting, market players volunteer to restrict their behavior by accepting certain norms, codes, and best practices established in a cooperative manner, in order to avoid legalistic regulations coerced by the regulator.[67]

3.4.6 Summing Up

This section surveyed several enforcement regimes that are based on the cooperative enforcement approach. As revealed, cooperative enforcement regimes may come in different guises, all of which depart from the "cat-and-mouse" regulatory game endorsed by the deterrence-based enforcement school of thought, and center upon cooperation between enforcement authorities and regulatees. Having discussed various implications of the cooperative enforcement approach and their virtues from a social welfare standpoint, in the following section I discuss the major pitfalls of cooperative enforcement regimes.

---

of institutional arrangements which differ from each other according to the degree of government intervention in two areas. *First*, the autonomy involved in standard-setting; some self-regulations are entirely private and independent while others may be created in association with the public authority or be subject to approval of the public authority. *Second*, the degree of legal potency: self-imposed behavioral standards may be a non-binding system of private ordering; they may be deemed as soft norms that apply as a default standard unless alternative behavior can be proven to meet the regulatory goals; or, enforceable norms that may be subject to civil or public enforcement. The latter are known as 'enforced self-regulation' or 'self-administered Command & Control regulation.' For a comprehensive overview of self-regulation see Ogus, "Self-Regulation;" John Braithwaite, "Enforced Self-Regulation: A New Strategy for Corporate Crime Control," *Michigan Law Review* 80(7) (1982), 1466–1507; Braithwaite and Ayres, *Responsive Regulation: Transcending the Deregulation Debate*, pp. 101–132; Baldwin and Cave, *Understanding Regulation: Theory, Strategy, and Practice*, p. 39.

[67] See Braithwaite, "Enforced Self-Regulation: A New Strategy for Corporate Crime Control," p. 1467.

3.5 THE PITFALLS OF COOPERATIVE ENFORCEMENT

As shown above, enforcement regimes that are based on the cooperative enforcement school of thought may cope with some of the major pitfalls of deterrence-based regimes. Yet, as suggested below, these regimes cannot ensure an optimal social outcome at all times. Under certain circumstances cooperative enforcement regimes may be abused by opportunistic regulatees, and thereby produce a suboptimal social outcome. In this section, I discuss the major pitfalls of the cooperative enforcement school of thought. As shown below, most lines of criticism challenge, directly and indirectly, the perception underlying the cooperative enforcement approach, *i.e.*, the law-abiding nature of regulatees.

3.5.1 Credulousness

The cooperative enforcement approach presumes regulatees' law-abiding nature.[68] This reliance on intrinsic motivations to comply with the law presents a serious risk of *credulousness*, that is, one's tendency to believe too readily, and therefore to be easily deceived. More particularly, as Braithwaite and Ayres (1992) point out:

> [t]he problem with the persuasion model, however, based as it is on a typification of people as basically good – reasonable, of good faith, motivated to abide by the law – is that it fails to recognize that there are some who are not good, and who will take advantage of being presumed to be so.[69]

Hence, enforcement policies that mostly avoid the use of coercive means of enforcement may simply "degenerate into intolerable laxity and fail to deter those who have no interest in complying voluntarily."[70]

---

[68] See Section 3.2.1 above.

[69] Braithwaite and Ayres, *Responsive Regulation: Transcending the Deregulation Debate*, p. 25. See also, Gunningham, *Mine Safety: Law, Regulation, Policy*, p. 123. In fact, even prominent proponents of the compliance approach acknowledge that not all regulatory subjects can be considered 'responsible or public-spirited' subjects. See, for instance, Muir, *Police: Streetcorner Politicians*; Bardach and Kagan, *Going by the Book: The Problem of Regulatory Unreasonableness*, pp. 59–61, 66; Hawkins, "Bargain and Bluff: Compliance Strategy and Deterrence in the Enforcement of Regulation," p. 44; Kagan and Scholz, "The 'Criminology of the Corporation' and Regulatory Enforcement Strategies," pp. 67–68; Hawkins, *Environment and Enforcement: Regulation and the Social Definition of Pollution*, p. 110.

[70] Gunningham, *Mine Safety: Law, Regulation, Policy*, p. 121.

3.5.2 Superfluous Tolerance and Regulatory Capture

Even when accepting the idea that most regulatees have a law-abiding nature, there is a wide agreement among scholars that under certain circumstances, uncompromising enforcement attitudes may be required to induce significant changes in corporate management.[71] Empirical evidence shows that a pure "guidance and advice" approach may not always suffice to induce compliance.[72] Therefore, indeed, the cooperative enforcement school of thought does not completely abandon the use of coercive enforcement measures. Instead, it acknowledges the potential use of coercive measures when cooperative attempts are proven to be ineffective.[73] Yet, in reality, the shift from cooperative to non-cooperative enforcement attitudes may be fairly challenging. Cooperation between enforcement authorities and regulatees may yield a strong bond between the individuals involved overtime, making the alternating between enforcement styles extremely difficult or unlikely.[74] In extreme cases, the ongoing relations between enforcement authorities and regulatees may generate "*regulatory capture*," whereby authorities act in the interests of those whom they are supposed to be monitoring, rather than in the general public interest.[75] In

---

71 See Bardach and Kagan, *Going by the Book: The Problem of Regulatory Unreasonableness*, p. 95.

72 See, for instance, James Baggs, Barbara Silverstein and Michael Foley, "Workplace Health and Safety Regulations: Impact of Enforcement and Consultation on Workers' Compensation Claims Rates in Washington State," *American Journal of Industrial Medicine* 43(5) (2003), 483–494. The authors empirically tested the impact of a purely conciliatory approach where inspectors act as consultants, providing guidance and advice, against a deterrence approach where inspectors act as enforcers. The authors found negligible impact of the conciliatory enforcement on compliance rates, whereas inspectoral interventions with an enforcement component were found to correlate with a 20–25% improvement in compliance rates.

73 See the discussion in Section 3.2.3 above.

74 See, for instance, Faure, "Environmental Crimes," p. 337: "when cooperative strategy has failed and the administrative agency has to change its position to a deterrence style, the cooperation and strong links between polluter and the agency may have made it difficult or even impossible to change to a deterrence approach when necessary." See also, Bardach and Kagan, *Going by the Book: The Problem of Regulatory Unreasonableness*, p. 111; Scholz, "Voluntary Compliance and Regulatory Enforcement," p. 401, according to which repeated cooperative interactions between controllers and those who are supposed to be the controlees, may lead to "undue laxness in monitoring compliance, uncritical acceptance of excuses for willful violations, and unwillingness to control managers even when compliance problems become evident."

75 See Baldwin and Cave, *Understanding Regulation: Theory, Strategy, and Practice*, p. 98. In the public choice theory literature, the risk of regulatory capture

such cases, it is argued, "the practice of backing away from legal conflict can sometimes become a habit so that the inspectorate loses all thirst for aggressive enforcement, even when it is badly needed, and loses enforcement know-how."[76] Therefore, cooperative enforcement regimes are sometimes criticized for being too "accommodative toward industry."[77]

---

is commonly underscored with respect to law-making and standard setting. In that respect, it is commonly argued that where powerful subjects with high-stakes interests in the outcome of the regulatory process may be motivated to exert efforts and resources in influencing law-makers' perceptions on the subject matter, other members of the public, having slight interest in the outcome, tend to ignore it altogether. See, for instance, Samuel P. Huntington, "The Marasmus of the ICC: The Commission, the Railroads, and the Public Interest," *The Yale Law Journal* 61(4) (1952), 467–509; George J. Stigler, "The Theory of Economic Regulation," *Bell Journal of Economics and Management Science* (3) (1971), 3–18; p. 3; Michael E. Levine and Jennifer L. Forrence, "Regulatory Capture, Public Interest, and the Public Agenda: Toward a Synthesis," *Journal of Law, Economics, & Organization* 6(1) (1990), 167–198; Jean-Jacques Laffont and Jean Tirole, "The Politics of Government Decision-Making: A Theory of Regulatory Capture," *The Quarterly Journal of Economics* 106(4) (1991), 1089–1127. Beside this traditional view of regulatory capture, cooperative enforcement strategies may generate some concerns about capture with respect to the enforcement phase as well. For empirical evidence of the potential involvement of capture in cooperative enforcement see, for instance, May and Winter, "Regulatory Enforcement and Compliance: Examining Danish Agro-Environmental Policy," 625–651.

[76] Bardach and Kagan, *Going by the Book: The Problem of Regulatory Unreasonableness*, p. 43. The superfluous tolerance of 'cooperating regulators' has been illustrated in Neil Gunningham, "Negotiated Non-Compliance: A Case Study of Regulatory Failure," *Law & Policy* 9(1) (1978), 69–96, who studied the enforcement routines followed by the New South Wales Mines Inspectorate in enforcing asbestos regulations. The study shows that the regulatory inspectorate was so reluctant to prosecute violators of the asbestos regulations, that when evidence of a serious violation was detected, the inspectorate used to warn the mine managers of prospective inspections, allowing them to restore and/or conceal their misconduct. Accordingly, the authors label such methods as "negotiated non-compliance," whereas it reflects "a toothless, passive, and acquiescent approach which, however attractive to the regulatory agency and to the regulated industry, has tragic consequences for those whom the legislation is ostensibly intended to protect." As a result, "strategies that stress consultation and conciliation typically end up with agencies endorsing the industry's own evaluation of what is reasonable and usually allow companies to negotiate their way out of penalties for violating even these agreements." See Pearce and Tombs, "Policing Corporate 'Skid Rows': A Reply to Keith Hawkins," p. 419.

[77] Shover, Clelland and Lynxwiler, *Enforcement or Negotiation: Constructing a Regulatory Bureaucracy*, p. 128.

3.5.3 Corruption

The slope between legitimate regulatory bargaining and corruption may be rather slippery. Long-lasting and continuous regulatory cooperation may create an environment for interested regulatees to entice enforcement agents into a superfluously lenient approach by means of personal incentives, such as bribes, gifts, and implicit promises for future employment.[78] Obviously, corruption among enforcement representatives presents a serious risk of distorting the incentives of those accountable for regulatory enforcement.[79] Hence, regulatory cooperation which is overwhelmingly embraced by both the parties involved should ring warning bells indicating a potential impending problem of collusion or corruption.[80]

3.5.4 The Discouraging Effect of the Conciliatory Strategy

Critics of the cooperative enforcement school of thought assert that "bad-apples" are not the only ones that may abuse cooperative enforcement regimes; "even good firms can take advantage of lesser security in order to delay or avoid compliance costs."[81] Empirical evidence suggests that a conciliatory style of enforcement, which allows law-infringers to go unpunished, might discourage compliance by those considered "good

---

[78] See Scholz, "Voluntary Compliance and Regulatory Enforcement," pp. 388, 401. See also, Michael A. Perino, "SEC Enforcement of Attorney Up-the-Ladder Reporting Rules: An Analysis of Institutional Constraints, Norms and Biases," *Villanova Law Review* 49(4) (2004), 851–866, who suggests that SEC attorneys are wary of filing suits against the type of firms they hope to join in the future.

[79] See Joseph Greenberg, "Avoiding Tax Avoidance: A (Repeated) Game-Theoretic Approach," *Journal of Economic Theory* 32(1) (1984), 1–13. See also, Roger Bowles and Nuno Garoupa, "Casual Police Corruption and the Economics of Crime," *International Review of Law and Economics* 17(1) (1997), 75–87; Sugata Marjit and He-Ling Shi, "On Controlling Crime with Corrupt Officials," *Journal of Economic Behavior & Organization* 34(1) (1998), 163–172; Juin-jen Chang, Ching-chong Lai and C. C. Yang, "Casual Police Corruption and the Economics of Crime: Further Results," *International Review of Law and Economics* 20(1) (2000), 35–51; Mitchell A. Polinsky and Steven Shavell, "Corruption and Optimal Law Enforcement," *Journal of Public Economics* 81 (2001), 1–24; Nuno Garoupa and Daniel Klerman, "Corruption and the Optimal Use of Nonmonetary Sanctions," *International Review of Law and Economics* 24(2) (2004), 219–225.

[80] See, for instance, Becker and Stigler, "Law Enforcement, Malfeasance, and Compensation of Enforcers," 1–18.

[81] Scholz, "Cooperation, Deterrence, and the Ecology of Regulatory Enforcement," p. 185.

apples." Such regulatees, who normally invest resources in compliance, may perceive themselves as being in a disadvantaged position given that others are simply getting away with it.[82]

3.5.5 Erosion of General Deterrence

A cooperative enforcement regime may erode the "general deterrence" among regulatees.[83] Knowing that enforcement authorities first exhaust all conciliatory techniques before turning to coercive measures, regulatees may adopt a "wait and see" approach, and delay compliance to a stage after which they were already addressed by the authorities.[84] As argued in Langbein and Krewin, "firms may avoid immediate compliance if they believe that it is likely to be cheaper to negotiate a compliance agreement with the enforcement agency."[85]

3.6 SUMMARY AND CONCLUDING REMARKS

The cooperative enforcement school of thought discussed in this chapter comprises an alternative ideological framework for the analysis of enforcement systems. This approach denies the central presumption of the deterrence-based approach, and instead of regarding regulatees as "amoral calculators," it perceives regulatees as socially committed, law-abiding actors. This different point of departure leads proponents of the cooperative enforcement school to embrace advisory, educative, and conciliatory enforcement tools, rather than the traditional, coercive ones.

The conciliatory style of cooperative enforcement regimes allows them to overcome some of the central flaws of deterrence-based enforcement regimes discussed in the previous chapter, such as the high cost of the regulatory "cat-and-mouse" game, and the risk of alienating regulatees.

---

[82] See Sidney A. Shapiro and Randy S. Rabinowitz, "Punishment Versus Cooperation in Regulatory Enforcement: A Case Study of OSHA," *Administrative Law Review* 49(3) (1997), 713–762: "Cooperative methods alone will not ensure voluntary compliance because non-compliers put compliers at a competitive disadvantage in their businesses."

[83] See Fenn and Veljanovski, "A Positive Economic Theory of Regulatory Enforcement," p. 1059.

[84] See *ibid.*, p. 1059.

[85] Laura Langbein and Cornelius M. Kerwin, "Implementation, Negotiation and Compliance in Environmental and Safety Regulation," *The Journal of Politics* 47(3) (1985), p. 854.

Yet a closer look at cooperative enforcement regimes reveals that they are subject to serious pitfalls, such as credulousness, superfluous tolerance, regulatory capture, corruption, as well as having a discouraging effect and eroding general deterrence – all of which should be juxtaposed against the virtues of regulatory cooperation in every context.

4. The reconciliation of deterrence-based and cooperative enforcement

4.1 INTRODUCTION

Although aiming at the same final goal of regulatory compliance, the deterrence-based and the cooperative enforcement approaches endorse distinctive enforcement strategies: the *deterrence-based enforcement approach* endorses "by-the-book," legalistic enforcement strategies, while the *cooperative enforcement approach* endorses cooperative, conciliatory ones. In the previous chapters, I showed that each of these distinctive schools of thought is fraught with various perils that may thwart its efficient functioning. This chapter proposes that within the context of corporate regulatory compliance, policymakers are not necessarily required to follow a single enforcement paradigm. Given the heterogeneity of regulatees and their changing preferences, the goal of social welfare maximization favors an *inclusive* enforcement approach that addresses all types of regulatees, while integrating deterrence-based and cooperative enforcement measures. The main aim of this chapter, then, is to explore regulatory mixed enforcement regimes that accommodate deterrence-based and cooperative enforcement strategies ("mixed regimes").

This chapter is structured as follows: I explore in Section 4.2 the enforcement dilemma in a realistic setting in a world with heterogeneous regulatees. In Section 4.3, I present an analytical framework that applies the game theoretic wisdom to the regulatory compliance context. This analytical framework is, then, used to portray and analyze the major regulatory mixed regimes proposed thus far in the scholarly polemic. In Section 4.4, I discuss the virtues of regulatory mixed regimes from a social standpoint, and in Section 4.5, I flag two major pitfalls of such regulatory mixed regimes that should be considered before these regimes are implemented in particular regulatory contexts. Finally, I summarize and conclude in Section 4.6.

4.2 THE ENFORCEMENT DILEMMA AND REGULATEE HETEROGENEITY

The ideological roots of the deterrence-based and the cooperative enforcement approaches can be seen as the Archimedean point from which the dichotomy between these two approaches is best observed. The deterrence-based approach perceives regulatees as "*rational, amoral calculators*," who are willing to comply with the law only when – and to the extent in which – it coincides with profit-maximization goals.[1] By contrast, the cooperative enforcement approach perceives regulatees as "*law-abiding creatures*," who are motivated to obey the law based on a sense of social responsibility.[2] These distinct perceptions of man's nature lie at the heart of the different enforcement approaches and may explain the polarity between the different enforcement strategies embraced by each of them.[3] Hence, when crafting an enforcement policy that aims at controlling corporate misbehavior, policymakers face a challenging enforcement dilemma: *which of the schools of thought – the deterrence-based or the cooperative enforcement approaches – should be employed when crafting a regulatory enforcement system?*

As one can expect, different answers to the enforcement dilemma were provided by different scholars. Commentators from both schools have indulged in lengthy polemics on the enforcement dilemma without reaching a consensus over a single superior paradigm. The tension between the two schools – and sometimes even between proponents of each one of them[4] – has eventually spurred the development of a third approach, which advocates the integration of both schools of thought into a mixed paradigm. As the argument goes, "to reject punitive regulation [the deterrence-based approach] is naive; to be totally committed to it is to lead a charge of the light brigade. The trick of successful regulation is to establish a synergy between punishment and persuasion."[5] The idea of

---

1 See Chapter 2, Section 2.2.

2 See Chapter 3, Section 3.2.1.

3 See, for instance, Faure, "Environmental Crimes," pp. 336–340.

4 See, for instance, the series of articles published in the *British Journal of Criminology*: Pearce and Tombs, "Ideology, Hegemony, and Empiricism: Compliance Theories of Regulation," 423–443; Hawkins, "Compliance Strategy, Prosecution Policy, and Aunt Sally: A Comment on Pearce and Tombs," 444–466; Pearce and Tombs, "Policing Corporate 'Skid Rows': A Reply to Keith Hawkins," 415–426; Keith Hawkins, "Enforcing Regulation: More of the Same from Pearce and Tombs," *British Journal of Criminology* 31(4) (1991), 427–430

5 See Braithwaite and Ayres, *Responsive Regulation: Transcending the Deregulation Debate*, p. 25.

the latter approach is that neither school of thought is entirely correct or categorically mistaken, whereas in actuality, regulatees comprise a heterogeneous population encompassed of both amoral calculators and law-abiding players.[6] Hence, any scholarly approach that ultimately assumes the homogeneity of a regulatee population is unlikely to address all regulatees.[7] Hence, a socially desirable enforcement regime must factor in the diversity of regulatees and address each type of regulatee with an appropriate regulatory response.[8] The plausible structures of such mixed regimes are the main focus of this chapter.

4.3 REGULATORY MIXED REGIMES

In this section, I explore regulatory mixed regimes that reconcile deterrence-based and cooperative enforcement responses in the regulatory context. The analysis rests on the game theoretical wisdom of the well-known prisoner's dilemma game, and applies the Tit-for-Tat strategy in exploring various

---

[6] See, for instance, Bardach and Kagan, *Going by the Book: The Problem of Regulatory Unreasonableness*, pp. 60, 64.

[7] See Braithwaite and Ayres, *Responsive Regulation: Transcending the Deregulation Debate*, p. 24. See also, Gunningham, *Mine Safety: Law, Regulation, Policy*, p. 123; Scholz, "Voluntary Compliance and Regulatory Enforcement," p. 387: "stringent enforcement against well-meaning firms may be as counterproductive as lenient enforcement with recalcitrant evaders."

[8] The arguments favoring the integration between deterrence-based and cooperative enforcement strategies are supported by empirical evidence showing that in reality both sanction threats and moral obligations play a central role in motivating compliance. See Paternoster and Simpson, "Sanction Threats and Appeals to Morality: Testing a Rational Choice Model of Corporate Crime," 549–583. The authors have tested the impact of sanction threats (the deterrence-based enforcement approach) and moral obligations (the cooperative enforcement approach) on corporate motivations to commit four types of crimes. The study shows that when moral inhibitions were relatively weak, deterrence was produced by the formal and informal sanction threats. However, when moral inhibitions were high, an economic calculus of expected cost and benefit was virtually superfluous; that is, normatively committed subjects tended to restrain their behavior regardless of the external sanction of threats. See also, May and Winter, "Regulatory Enforcement and Compliance: Examining Danish Agro-Environmental Policy," 625–651. This empirical study suggests that coercion may be required up to a certain level, after which it may become counterproductive; *ibid.*, p. 640: ". . . the threats of coercion can backfire once a certain threshold in formalism has been reached. But, below that threshold, coercion is helpful in bringing about better compliance." See also, Scholz, "Can Government Facilitate Cooperation? An Informational Model of OSHA Enforcement," 693–717.

Table 4.1 Payoffs in a classic prisoner's dilemma game

		Player A	
		Cooperate	Defect
Player B	Cooperate	(150, 150)	(40, 250)
	Defect	(250, 40)	(100, 100)

forms of regulatory mixed regimes. Before discussing these regimes, it may be useful to briefly describe the relevant analytical framework.

4.3.1 The Analytical Framework: Prisoner's Dilemma

In its simplest form, the prisoner's dilemma involves two players, each of which has a binary choice, either to "cooperate" or to "defect."[9] Players' decisions are made simultaneously and the parties cannot coordinate their choices. According to the settings of the game, if both players choose "cooperation" both gain the maximal payoff; if only one player chooses "cooperation," the other one, which opts for "defection," gains more; and if both choose "defection," both gain very little, but still more than the cooperator who was "defected" by his counter party. An example for the standard prisoner's dilemma payoffs matrix is described in Table 4.1, where the numbers at the left and the right parts of the parentheses represent Player A's and Player B's payoffs, respectively.

As demonstrated in Table 4.1, players A and B can maximize their joint payoff through mutual cooperation. However, given that the parties cannot coordinate their choices, it is expected that each player suspects that the counter player is going to succumb to the temptation of "defection," and therefore both players end up defecting. Hence, the simplest form of a one-shot game in the prisoner's dilemma anticipates that although mutual cooperation yields the highest total payoff, each player has an incentive to defect, irrespective of what the counter player does.

A totally different outcome of the prisoner's dilemma game is expected

[9] The prisoner's dilemma was originally framed by Merrill Flood and Melvin Dresher in 1953, and formalized later on by William Poundstone into a scene where two suspects are arrested by the police, each one has to choose to confess and testify against the other or not to confess. If both confess, each receive a five-year sentence; if one testifies against the other and the other chooses not to confess, the former goes unpunished and the latter receives a ten-year sentence; if both do not confess, each receives a minor sentence of six months. See William Poundstone, *Prisoner's Dilemma* (New York: Doubleday, 1992).

when the game is played repeatedly. In his innovative studies Robert Axelrod has shown that under the repeated prisoner's dilemma game, a stable cooperation may emerge if a reciprocal strategy, commonly referred to as the "*Tit-for-Tat*" (or TFT) strategy, is followed.[10] The TFT strategy involves cooperative play during the first round and echoes the other player's previous move in the following rounds.[11] As shown by Axelrod, when a game is played between repeated players for an infinite or an unknown period of time, sustainable cooperation may be reached if one player starts by cooperating, and sticks to cooperation unless provoked by his/her counterpart's defection. If provoked, the player retaliates in the next round of the game by defecting. In any case, the player is fast to forgive and will reciprocate the cooperation by cooperating.[12] Given that the game is played for an infinite period of time (or with an unknown end), the TFT strategy is superior to a variety of alternative strategies, and therefore, in spite of the adversarial nature of the game, the parties are expected to reach sustainable cooperation.

4.3.2 Tit-for-Tat Regulatory Enforcement

The game theoretic prisoner's dilemma and the TFT strategy have been embraced by law and economics scholars to help analyze compliance incentive schemes in various contractual contexts. Principally, the literature shows that in repeated game contexts, the use of a reactive strategy, the particular responses of which are determined by the behavioral choices of the counterparty, may sustain desirable cooperative contractual relations. More particularly, if A's cooperative behavior is reciprocated by B's cooperation, or if A's defection is reciprocated by B's defection, then in a

---

[10] See Robert Axelrod, "Effective Choice in the Prisoner's Dilemma," *The Journal of Conflict Resolution* 24(1) (1980), 3–25; Robert Axelrod, "More Effective Choice in the Prisoner's Dilemma," *The Journal of Conflict Resolution* 24(3) (1980), 379–403; Robert Axelrod, "The Emergence of Cooperation among Egoists," *The American Political Science Review* 75(2) (1981), 306–318; Robert Axelrod, *The Evolution of Cooperation* (New York: Basic Books, 1984).

[11] This condition assumes that although the players play simultaneously, after it is too late to change their choice, each player learns what the other player has chosen and both know the costs and benefits imposed on them in each round of the game.

[12] It should be noted that according to Robert Axelrod, *The Evolution of Cooperation* (New York: Basic Books, 1984), both players are required to be concerned enough about the future payoffs and thereby abstain from succumbing to the temptation to defect in a single game. See also, Scholz, "Cooperation, Deterrence, and the Ecology of Regulatory Enforcement," p. 191.

repeated game setting A and B may reach sustainable, mutually favorable cooperation. This analytical framework has been used, for instance, in analyzing the motivation for compliance with contractual obligations in close-knit industries, such as the diamond, cotton, and the whaling industries.[13] A similar framework has been used in analyzing nation states' motivations to comply with international treaties in spite of the lack of a central coercive enforcement mechanism.[14]

The logic of the prisoner's dilemma game is not limited to the horizontal, contractual setting. In a series of fascinating studies initiated in the early 1980s, John Scholz applied Axelrod's TFT strategy to the regulatory context, showing that enforcement authorities are not necessarily required to adhere to a single enforcement school of thought.[15] Instead,

---

[13] See Robert C. Ellickson, "A Hypothesis of Wealth-Maximizing Norms: Evidence from the Whaling Industry," *Journal of Law, Economics and Organization* 5(1) (1989), 83–97; Lisa Bernstein, "Private Commercial Law in the Cotton Industry: Creating Cooperation through Rules, Norms, and Institutions," *Michigan Law Review* 99(7) (2001), 1724–1790; Lisa Bernstein, "Opting Out of the Legal System: Extralegal Contractual Relations in the Diamond Industry," *Journal of Legal Studies* 21(1) (1992), 115–157.

[14] The scholarly literature investigating states' compliance motivations within international treaties points at a unique combination of deterrence-based and cooperative enforcement measures employed by states to motivate their counterparties to comply with their own obligations. See George W. Downs, "Reputation, Compliance, and International Law," *The Journal of Legal Studies* 31(s1) (2002), pp. 95–96. See also, Robert O. Keohane, *After Hegemony: Cooperation and Discord in the World Political Economy* (Princeton, NJ: Princeton University Press, 1984); Andrew T. Guzman, *How International Law Works: A Rational Choice Theory* (New York: Oxford University Press, 2008). For a legal overview of states' compliance with international agreements see, for instance, Abram Chayes and Antonia H. Chayes, "On Compliance," *International Organization* 47(2) (1993), 175–205; Thomas M. Franck, *Fairness in International Law and Institutions* (New York: Oxford University Press, 1995). States' compliance motivations with international treaties were also discussed by other social scientists. See, for instance, John J. Mearsheimer, "The False Promise of International Institutions," *International Security* 19(3) (1994), 5–49; George W. Downs, David M. Rocke and Peter N. Barsoom, "Is the Good News about Compliance Good News about Cooperation?" *International Organization* 50(3) (1996), 379–406. For an interdisciplinary approach see, for instance, Jack L. Goldsmith and Eric A. Posner, "A Theory of Customary International Law," *The University of Chicago Law Review* 66(4) (1999), 1113–1177; Alan O. Sykes, "The Economics of Public International Law," *Unpublished Manuscript, John M. Olin Law & Economics Working Paper, no. 216* (2004); Edward T. Swaine, "Rational Custom," *Duke Law Journal* 52(3) (2002), 559–627.

[15] See Scholz, "Cooperation, Deterrence, and the Ecology of Regulatory Enforcement," p. 179; Scholz, "Voluntary Compliance and Regulatory

these authorities may reach and sustain socially desirable cooperation with regulatees if they use mixed enforcement strategies that are responsive to regulatee performance. Such mixed regimes empower enforcement authorities to choose between using a deterrence-based response and a cooperative response in every particular case, while the choice between the different responses is based on regulatee past performance. As described by Scholz:[16]

> *The good firm*, like the good citizen in court, is subjected only to *reasonable enforcement* and given the benefit of any doubt about suspected wrongdoing. Regulatory inspectors come infrequently and work unobtrusively. Technical violations are overlooked if trivial or simply pointed out to the firm. More serious violations are noted, but reasonable explanations and a promise to correct them are accepted in lieu of prosecution. When prosecution is necessary, supervisors and courts alike seek minimal fines. *The bad firm*, on the other hand, is subjected to *harsher and more legalistic enforcement* appropriate for hardened criminals. Inspectors keep a closer watch on these firms. They thoroughly investigate any suspicious signs and meticulously gather evidence. Supervisors seek immediate prosecution even for trivial technical violations, and courts grant maximum penalties.

The consequences of a regulatory TFT enforcement regime are demonstrated in Scholz (1984a) using a simple example, in which an enforcement authority that enforces pollution regulations chooses between employing a deterrence-based and a cooperative enforcement style.[17] The study assumes that when choosing between enforcement styles, the regulatory authority is concerned with maximizing the net social benefit for society, *i.e.*, maximizing regulatory compliance at the lowest cost.[18] Given the

---

Enforcement," 385–404; John T. Scholz, "Cooperative Regulatory Enforcement and the Politics of Administrative Effectiveness," *The American Political Science Review* 85(1) (1991), 115–136; Scholz, "Can Government Facilitate Cooperation? An Informational Model of OSHA Enforcement," 693–717; Scholz, "Enforcement Policy and Corporate Misconduct: The Changing Perspective of Deterrence Theory," 253–268.

[16] See Scholz, "Voluntary Compliance and Regulatory Enforcement," pp. 387–388 (emphasis added). See also, Scholz, "Cooperation, Deterrence, and the Ecology of Regulatory Enforcement," pp. 182–183.

[17] Scholz, "Voluntary Compliance and Regulatory Enforcement," pp. 387–388.

[18] See, for instance, Scholz, "Cooperation, Deterrence, and the Ecology of Regulatory Enforcement," p. 193: "we will assume that the agency is solely concerned with maximizing net compliance benefits for society, or benefits minus enforcement costs." See also, Scholz, "Voluntary Compliance and Regulatory Enforcement," p. 400: "it is clear that symbols of legitimacy and accepted norms of enforcement (e.g., due process and equal treatment) must guide the choice of

		Agency's Enforcement Options	
		Cooperative (goal-oriented)	Deterrence (rule-oriented)
Firm's Initial Compliance Options	Comply	R = 100 tons Voluntary Compliance r = –$2 million	T = 125 tons Harassment s = –$4 million
	Evade	S = 50 tons Opportunism t = –$1 million	P = 75 tons Legalistic Battles p = –$3 million

– Agency payoffs (capital letters) represent the expected amount of pollution reduced annually.
– Firm payoffs (small letters) represent the total expected annual costs of compliance and sanctions.
– Cell labels reflect the situation as seen from the firm's perspective.
– The dilemma defined: T > R > P > S and t > r > p > s; 2R > S + T and 2r > s + t

Source: Adopted from John T. Scholz, "Cooperation, Deterrence, and the Ecology of Regulatory Enforcement," p. 186.

Figure 4.1 Alternative payoffs in an enforcement dilemma game

choices made by enforcement authorities, regulatees choose between complying and evading regulations. In this example, each player makes his/her choice without knowing the choice made by the other. After the round of the play is over, both players know what the other player has chosen and what the costs and benefits of this choice are.[19] The parties' expected payoff are described in Figure 4.1.

As in the standard prisoner's dilemma game, an optimal outcome may be reached if both parties to the regulatory game cooperate.[20] Yet, if the

cooperative and deterrence tactics, and that social acceptability limits agency manipulations of enforcement payoffs facing firms." And Scholz, "Enforcement Policy and Corporate Misconduct: The Changing Perspective of Deterrence Theory," pp. 265–267.

[19] See Scholz, "Cooperation, Deterrence, and the Ecology of Regulatory Enforcement," pp. 193–194. Note that in this study regulatees are not assumed to be normatively committed. Instead, they are deemed as affected by rational expectations, striving to minimize regulation-related cost, *i.e.*, compliance costs and sanctions.

[20] In that case, both parties obtain their reward outcome: the enforcement authority reaches an annual reduction in emissions of 100 tons; and the regulatee's annual costs of pollution-saving technology, including planning, implementation, and maintenance expenses, is only $2 million. Scholz shows that all alternative sce-

parties mainly consider the short-term consequences of their behavioral choices, then each party prefers defection to cooperation. In that case, the game generates an inefficient equilibrium (*i.e.*, the *Evade and Deterrence* cell).[21] However, given the repeated nature of the regulatory game, both parties are expected to determine cooperation as their dominant strategy (*i.e.*, *Comply and Cooperative* cell).[22] Therefore, in line with the general predictions of the prisoner's dilemma game, if enforcement authorities adopt a TFT strategy and reciprocate regulatees' behavioral choices, then their choices may generate mutually beneficial regulatory cooperation.[23]

Scholz's TFT regulatory enforcement regime has a direct policy implication. According to Scholz's findings, enforcement authorities may set a minimal level of compliance, below which regulatees' actions are deemed "defection." Regulatees that meet this minimum level are subject to a cooperative response by the enforcement authority. By

---

narios are suboptimal in their outcomes: First, the *Evade and Deterrence* option – the legal battles are expected to hinder the firm's modernization initiatives. Under these circumstances the corporation will employ expensive legally mandated measures and will be able to reach, at best, 75 tons emission reduction. Additionally, the regulatory costs incurred by the regulatee now include litigation expenses and fines and amount to $3 million. Second, the *Evade and Cooperative* option, the regulatee takes advantage of the compromising enforcement attitude and misleads the enforcement authority about its capabilities in emission reduction. In this case, the enforcement authority unknowingly endorses a non-appealing 50 tons emission reduction (sacker's (S) payoff), and the regulatee incurs the most tempting (t) regulatory costs of $1 million. And finally, the *Compliance and Deterrence* option, where the regulatee invests in developing innovative technology, but the enforcement authority insists on the implementation of a legally mandated measure as well. From the regulatee viewpoint, this is harassment, whereas in addition to the costs of technology development, it incurs also the costs of the mandated measures, say $4 million (sacker's (s) payoff), while the enforcement authority benefits from an additional source of emission reduction, and gain 125 tons of reduction (tempting (T) payoffs). See *ibid.*, pp. 186–187.

[21] When concentrating on short-run considerations, if the enforcement authority opts for a cooperative strategy, the corporation will choose to evade the regulation and earn the temptation payoff (t). Likewise, if the enforcement authority expects the corporation to cooperate, it may act opportunistically by requiring a literal compliance with the black letter of the law, regardless of the fact that all regulatory goals were achieved through voluntary compliance. See *ibid.*, p. 187.

[22] As in Axelrod's context (see *supra* note 12), here as well, a stable cooperation is contingent upon the discount parameter being high enough. The discount parameter is the product of the standard discount rate used to determine the current value of future payoffs, and the perceived probability in any given round that there will be another round. See *ibid.*, p. 189.

[23] See *ibid*; Scholz, "Cooperative Regulatory Enforcement and the Politics of Administrative Effectiveness," p. 118.

contrast, those not meeting the basic level of compliance incur a rigorous, deterrence-based enforcement response.[24] This regime maximizes the difference between compliance (cooperation) and evasion (non-cooperation) payoffs. Therefore, it elevates the benefit for compliant corporations (*e.g.*, by reducing compliance costs and expected sanctions), while increasing these costs for flagrant regulatees.[25] Consequently, it is argued, regulatees are likely to opt for compliance, and the regulatory game is likely to reach a cooperative equilibrium.

Before proceeding, it is worth noting that Scholz's TFT enforcement regime alternates enforcement responses with respect to both *monitoring efforts* and the *enforcement measures imposed*. Hence, according to this regime, corporations that have been identified as compliant are subject to a reduced scrutiny *ex ante*, as well as to more lenient enforcement measures *ex post*.[26] On the contrary, corporations that have been identified as recalcitrant are watched more closely and incur harsh sanctions.

4.3.3 Extension: State-Dependent Enforcement

The TFT regulatory enforcement regime has been extended to various structures of regulatory mixed regimes, collectively known as *State-Dependent Enforcement*.[27] Following the logic of the TFT strategy,

---

[24] See Scholz, "Voluntary Compliance and Regulatory Enforcement," p. 393.

[25] See *ibid.*, p. 395.

[26] See Braithwaite and Ayres, *Responsive Regulation: Transcending the Deregulation Debate*, p. 60.

[27] The mathematical model of a state-dependent enforcement regime was first demonstrated in Michael Landsberger and Isaac Meilijson, "Incentive Generating State Dependent Penalty System: The Case of Income Tax Evasion," *Journal of Public Economics* 19(3) (1982), 333–352. This model was extended later on in a wide range of studies, including Greenberg, "Avoiding Tax Avoidance: A (Repeated) Game-Theoretic Approach," 1–13; Harrington, "Enforcement Leverage when Penalties are Restricted," 29–53; Russell, "Game Models for Structuring Monitoring and Enforcement Systems," 143–173; Jon D. Harford and Winston Harrington, "A Reconsideration of Enforcement Leverage when Penalties are Restricted," *Journal of Public Economics* 45(3) (1991), 391–395; Jon D. Harford, "Measurement Error and State-Dependent Pollution Control Enforcement," *Journal of Environmental Economics and Management* 21(1) (1991), 67–81; Jon D. Harford, "Improving on the Steady State in the State-Dependent Enforcement of Pollution Control," *Journal of Environmental Economics and Management* 24(2) (1993), 133–138; Mark Raymond, "Enforcement Leverage when Penalties are Restricted: A Reconsideration Under Asymmetric Information," *Journal of Public Economics* 73(2) (1999), 289–295; Lana L. Friesen, "Targeting Enforcement to Improve Compliance with Environmental Regulations," *Journal of Environmental Economics and Management* 46(1) (2003), 72–85.

state-dependent enforcement regimes rely on differentiated enforcement responses, determined by the regulatees' past performance in the repeated regulatory game. In the simplest form of the state-dependent regime, the authority classifies subjects into two groups based on their past performance, *i.e.*, '*group V*' was composed of regulatees that were found violating the law in the recent inspection, and '*group C*' was composed of those who were not previously audited or audited and found compliant in the last inspection. According to state-dependent enforcement regimes, when a group-C regulatee is found in violation, then it is reclassified into group V, without bearing any additional sanction. By contrast, when a group-V regulatee is discovered to be violating the law, then it remains in group V and bears the maximum possible sanction.[28]

Under state-dependent enforcement regimes, regulatees take into account not only the direct sanction that would be levied by the enforcement system if they violate the regulation, but also the broader consequences of their (re)classification within the (non)compliant group. Namely, a group-V regulatee considers the benefit which may result from a certain violation against the total adverse consequences of violation detection, *i.e.* harsh punishment and frequent inspections, coupled with the present value of the loss of lenient treatment in the future, which could have been achieved had the corporation chosen to comply. Similarly, a group-C regulatee compares the potential benefits of the considered violation with the present value of exposure to harsh penalties and frequent inspections in the future.[29] Hence, the scholarly literature analyzing state-dependent enforcement regimes points out that such regimes provide regulatees with a powerful compliance incentive by using "penalty leverage."[30]

---

[28] The simplest form is based on Harrington, "Enforcement Leverage when Penalties are Restricted," 391–395, where the dynamic-state dependency is introduced with a *sanction* which varies across different groups of regulatees. An alternative form of a state-dependent enforcement regime may make individuals subject to varying *probabilities of detection*. See, for instance, Landsberger and Meilijson, "Incentive Generating State Dependent Penalty System: The Case of Income Tax Evasion," 333–352; Greenberg, "Avoiding Tax Avoidance: A (Repeated) Game-Theoretic Approach," 1–13; Harrington's model was extended in Russell, "Game Models for Structuring Monitoring and Enforcement Systems" to a three-group model, showing that even when monitoring errors are taken into account, a multiple-group strategy provides greater deterrence compared with the standard unified enforcement strategy.

[29] See Guido Suurmond, *Enforcing Fire Safety in the Catering Industry: An Economic Analysis* (Netherlands: Leiden University Press, 2008), p. 91.

[30] Harrington refers to "*leverage*" as the property of a firm having "an incentive to comply with regulation even though its cost of compliance [in] each period exceeds the expected penalties for violation, or even the maximum penalty that can

4.3.4 Summing Up

The game theoretic prisoner's dilemma comprises a robust analytical framework for the reconciliation of deterrence-based and cooperative enforcement strategies. Following the logic of the TFT strategy it becomes apparent that enforcement authorities are not required to adhere to a single enforcement approach. Instead, enforcement authorities may simply follow a mixed approach that endorses the use of either deterrence-based or cooperative enforcement measures, according to the particular circumstances at hand. The mixed regimes acknowledge that preferences, mind-set, and compliance motivations may differ across regulatees, and over time. Hence, these regimes do not rely on any inherent nature or intrinsic propensities of regulatees. Accordingly, the mixed regimes do not seek to *adjust* to any presumed nature of regulatees. Instead, they seek to *induce* regulatee compliance by using responsive motivating mechanisms.

While concerned with responsiveness, the regulatory mixed regimes discussed above focus attention on *regulatee past performance*.[31] More specifically, enforcement responses – both with respect to the level of monitoring and the style of measures employed – are determined by paying attention to regulatees' *violation records*.[32] Regulatees whose records are clean are subject to relatively infrequent inspections and are guided and persuaded to comply with the regulations. By contrast, regulatees with a history of regulatory violations are monitored closely and subject to strict, punitive measures.

Before proceeding it should be noted that mixed enforcement regimes are not purely theoretic. Such regimes are used in actuality in many regulatory contexts. Studies have shown that enforcement authorities often determine their regulatory responses according to regulatees' past performance, even without announcing these policies explicitly. Gray and Deily, for instance,

---

be levied in any period." See Harrington, "Enforcement Leverage when Penalties are Restricted," p. 32.

[31] See, for instance, Scholz, "Cooperation, Deterrence, and the Ecology of Regulatory Enforcement," p. 198; Scholz, "Voluntary Compliance and Regulatory Enforcement," pp. 393–397; Russell, "Game Models for Structuring Monitoring and Enforcement Systems," p. 146.

[32] The studies discussing the regulatory mixed regimes often treat monitoring levels and the choice of actual enforcement measures as a single choice. See Scholz, "Cooperation, Deterrence, and the Ecology of Regulatory Enforcement," p. 195; Scholz, "Voluntary Compliance and Regulatory Enforcement," pp. 387–388. With respect to state-dependent regimes see, for instance, Landsberger and Meilijson, "Incentive Generating State Dependent Penalty System: The Case of Income Tax Evasion," p. 335: "Dynamic state dependencies can be introduced through both the penalties function or the method of detection."

use data on individual steel plants to show the link between enforcement actions against pollution violations and plants' past levels of compliance. The study shows that steel plants that were considered compliant faced fewer enforcement attempts.[33] In the same vein, Russell (1990) refers to the U.S. Internal Revenue Service as an authority that uses data from past audits to define the probability of current year audits.[34]

4.4 THE VIRTUES OF REGULATORY MIXED REGIMES

Regulatory mixed enforcement regimes present important improvements to both deterrence-based and cooperative enforcement regimes. In fact, the mixed regimes sustain the major virtues of each of the "stand alone" regimes, while coping with their major pitfalls. First, corresponding to deterrence-based regimes, mixed regimes convey to regulatees a clear message that law-breaking is intolerable. Such regimes even magnify the impact of each regulatee compliance decision by linking the choice of enforcement responses to regulatee past performance.[35] At the same time, regulatory mixed regimes restrict the regulatory "cat-and-mouse" game

---

[33] See Wayne B. Gray and Mary E. Deily, "Compliance and Enforcement: Air Pollution Regulation in the U.S. Steel Industry," *Journal of Environmental Economics and Management* 31(1) (1996), 96–111. For similar results, see Heather Eckert, "Inspections, Warnings, and Compliance: The Case of Petroleum Storage Regulation," *Journal of Environmental Economics and Management* 47(2) (2004), 232–259, who investigated the use of inspections and warnings for environmental violations, showing that warnings are used to classify Canadian petroleum storage sites according to their past performance of compliance. See also, Sandra S. Rousseau, "Timing of Environmental Inspections: Survival of the Compliant," *Journal of Regulatory Economics* 32(1) (2007), 17–36; Sarah L. Stafford, "The Effect of Punishment on Firm Compliance with Hazardous Waste Regulations," *Journal of Environmental Economics and Management* 44(2) (2002), 290–308; Hawkins, *Environment and Enforcement: Regulation and the Social Definition of Pollution*; Bardach and Kagan, *Going by the Book: The Problem of Regulatory Unreasonableness*; Scholz, "Cooperation, Deterrence, and the Ecology of Regulatory Enforcement," p. 184; and May and Winter, "Regulatory Enforcement and Compliance: Examining Danish Agro-Environmental Policy," 625–651, according to which a monitoring system that determines the frequency of inspections based on regulatees' past behavior is more efficient than a system where the frequency of audits is picked randomly.

[34] See Russell, "Game Models for Structuring Monitoring and Enforcement Systems," p. 153.

[35] Under the mixed regimes current compliance decisions may affect the regulatory strategy to which regulatees are exposed in the following period. See *supra* note 30 and the related main text.

associated with deterrence-based regimes to circumstances in which it is truly warranted.[36] Second, corresponding to cooperative regimes, regulatory mixed regimes promote cooperation, avoid regulatee alienation, and save substantial social costs, while promoting voluntary compliance. At the same time, the mixed regimes are less prone to credulousness and to opportunistic abuse by regulatees than pure cooperative regimes.[37] Such merits may be attributed to two major virtues of regulatory mixed regimes: *inclusiveness* and *targeting attitudes*.

4.4.1 Inclusiveness

By departing from any *a priori* presumption regarding regulatees' nature, regulatory mixed regimes acknowledge the diversity of regulatees and the dynamics of their preferences and motivations. Given this point of departure, the mixed regimes follow an inclusive approach, which allows them to address all types of regulatees, while adjusting enforcement responses to the particular circumstances at hand. Once regulatory responses are well-adjusted, regulatees are expected to find that "cooperation" is their dominant strategy, and thereby regulatory cooperation becomes stable and sustainable.[38]

4.4.2 Targeting Attitudes

Targeting attitudes refers to the inclination of regulatory mixed regimes to address regulatees who have different motivations with a more tailored enforcement response. Under the mixed regimes enforcement expenditures are not used haphazardly or randomly against all enforcement targets. Instead, the allocation of resources is determined by considerations of their effectiveness.[39] Regulatory mixed regimes maximize the benefit extracted from regulatory enforcement resources. Specifically, when cooperative, compliant corporations are concerned, regulatory mixed regimes

---

[36] For a discussion of the adverse consequences of the deterrence-based regulatory "cat-and-mouse" game see Chapter 2, Section 2.4.1.

[37] For the virtues and pitfalls of cooperative enforcement regimes see Chapter 3, Sections 3.3 and 3.5.

[38] See Scholz, "Cooperation, Deterrence, and the Ecology of Regulatory Enforcement," p. 179.

[39] The targeted enforcement method was initially discussed in Harrington, "Enforcement Leverage when Penalties are Restricted," 29–53 as a plausible explanation for the Harrington Paradox. Various extensions of the theory have been developed later on by many scholars. See, for instance, *supra* note 27.

utilize cooperative enforcement measures, which are often less costly than deterrence-based ones.[40] The latter type of measures is reserved as the regulatory "weapon" in the battle against resistant, recalcitrant regulatees.[41] Hence, regulatory mixed regimes allow enforcement authorities to concentrate scarce resources on more problematic cases, where less costly conciliatory routines may not suffice.

4.5 THE PITFALLS OF THE REGULATORY MIXED REGIMES

Before glorifying the regulatory mixed regimes discussed thus far in the scholarly literature, it is important to point out that these regimes are also subject to pitfalls, which have not received sufficient attention in the literature. I examine below two major pitfalls that raise doubts regarding the social desirability of the regulatory mixed regimes discussed above: *information asymmetry* and *arbitrariness*.

4.5.1 Information Asymmetry

A central assumption of the game theoretic TFT strategy, on which regulatory mixed regimes are based, is that although players to the prisoner's dilemma game play simultaneously and cannot coordinate their choices, after each round of the game, each player *knows* what the other player has chosen.[42] This implies that credible information regarding the counterparty's choices is accessible to each player at the end of each round of the game. This crucial assumption has been upheld by the scholarly literature developing the regulatory mixed regimes.[43] These regimes are based on the

---

[40] Cooperative enforcement routines, such as guidance, information sharing, and persuasion, often do not require extensive agency resources. See, for instance, Scholz, "Voluntary Compliance and Regulatory Enforcement," pp. 385–386; Braithwaite and Ayres, *Responsive Regulation: Transcending the Deregulation Debate*, p. 60; Baldwin and Cave, *Understanding Regulation: Theory, Strategy, and Practice*, p. 98. On the contrary, deterrence-based methods often involve substantive costs associated with intrusive inspections, investigation and evidence collection, strict prosecution, and the imposition of sanctions. See, for instance, Tyler, *Why People Obey the Law*, pp. 22–23; Ogus and Abbot, "Pollution and Penalties," p. 505.

[41] See, for instance, Scholz, "Cooperation, Deterrence, and the Ecology of Regulatory Enforcement," p. 179.

[42] See *supra* note 11.

[43] See, for instance, the description of the game by Scholz, "Cooperation, Deterrence, and the Ecology of Regulatory Enforcement," p. 194: "[C]onsider the

assumption that regulatees and enforcement authorities possess credible information over the decisions made by each other in the previous rounds of the regulatory game.[44]

Indeed, under certain circumstances information regarding past performance is more likely to exist. That, for instance, would be the case within relatively small groups (*e.g.*, a close-knit industry). However, when an ordinary industry is concerned, credible information regarding the past behavior of every single player is not necessarily available to enforcement authorities.[45] In ordinary industries, which are monitored and controlled by enforcement authorities with a limited budget, it is fairly unlikely that the authority can be certain about the level of past compliance of every single regulatee.[46] Hence, when a regulatory ecology is concerned, regu-

---

simple two-person game between one firm and one enforcement agency. In each (arbitrarily defined) time period, the firm chooses some level of compliance activity and the agency assigns some level of enforcement to the firm. Each player must choose without knowing what choice the other is making, *although by the end of the period, after it is too late to change the current round's choice, both know what the other has chosen and both know the costs and benefits imposed on them during that period*" (emphasis added). See also, Harrington, "Enforcement Leverage when Penalties are Restricted," p. 34. And Johnstone, "From Fiction to Fact – Rethinking OHS Enforcement," p. 18: "the regulator needs to be able to identify the kind of firm it is dealing with, and the firm needs to know how to interpret the regulators' use of regulatory tools, and how to respond to them." Black, "Managing Discretion," p. 20; Gunningham, *Mine Safety: Law, Regulation, Policy*, p. 127.

44 See *ibid.*

45 See Scholz, "Cooperation, Deterrence, and the Ecology of Regulatory Enforcement," p. 211: ". . . the large jurisdictions of these newer agencies hamper cooperation by increasing uncertainty in the firm–agency relationship." See also, Gunningham, *Mine Safety: Law, Regulation, Policy*, p. 127, who discusses the information problem with respect to the enforcement pyramid of the responsive regulation model: ". . . where regulators make only occasional visits to mines (as may be the case with small companies, and in relation to contractors and sub-contractors in some circumstances), and where the reach of the state is seriously constrained, then the pyramid has more limited application." And Black, "Managing Discretion," p. 20: "Tailoring the enforcement response to individual firms is also highly resource intensive; it demands skill, time and other resources that are likely to be in short supply. The strategy also requires certain structural conditions: at the least that the firm and the regulator are in a long term relationship that will enable the regulator to observe and assess the firm's actions over a period of time." See also Russell, "Game Models for Structuring Monitoring and Enforcement Systems," p. 167, who shows that when the monitoring method available to the public enforcement authority is more precise, then the advantages of a mixed enforcement strategy are greater.

46 See, for instance, Gunningham, *Mine Safety: Law, Regulation, Policy*, pp. 112–113: "good regulation means invoking different responsive enforcement

latee *violation records* are usually taken as a proxy for their past level of compliance.[47]

The reliance on regulatee violation records may, indeed, provide enforcement authorities with an initial indication of the nature of past interactions between enforcement authorities and a particular regulatee. Nevertheless, such a proxy may not always be *credible* in reflecting regulatees' past levels of compliance. At the outset, violation records include only information on *violations*, rather than on compliance levels. Such information is centered upon *detected violations*, rather than on the overall level of law-breaking. Therefore, regulatees whose violations are harder to detect are wrongly perceived as compliant. In addition, violation records fail to reflect the heterogeneity of regulatees in terms of their level of activity; their risk exposure to regulatory violations; the significance of the detected violations to their overall compliance activity; the compliance technology they use; and the difficulties involved in detection.[48]

To illustrate the information asymmetry pitfall embedded in the mixed regimes, consider a simple TFT enforcement regime that treats compliant regulatees with cooperative enforcement measures, while treating recalcitrant ones with deterrence-oriented measures. As discussed earlier, the TFT enforcement regime determines the type of regulatees based on their past performance. For instance, suppose that regulatees whose violation records include fewer than four violations in the previous period are deemed compliant, and that those with more than four violations are deemed recalcitrant. Recall that, according to the regulatory mixed regimes

---

strategies depending upon whether one is dealing with leaders, reluctant compliers, the recalcitrant or the incompetent. However, the dilemma for regulators is that it is rarely possible to be confident in advance as to motivation of a regulated firm."

[47] Put crudely, to estimate future compliance motivations of regulatees, enforcement authorities rely on the violations records of regulatees in previous periods; hence, regulatees with fewer violations than a certain threshold are deemed compliant agents, while those exceeding the threshold are treated as recalcitrant. See Scholz, "Cooperation, Deterrence, and the Ecology of Regulatory Enforcement," p. 212; Scholz, "Cooperative Regulatory Enforcement and the Politics of Administrative Effectiveness," p. 119. See *supra* note 32 and the related main text.

[48] Suppose for instance, that two plants present the same risk of air pollution due to a toxic gas that may be emitted as a side effect of their production process. The sole difference between the plants is that the gas emitted by one of them is dark and highly visible, while the gas emitted by the other is completely transparent. Other things being equal, it is likely that the violation record of the latter is much brighter than the one of the former, although as stated above, both present a similar risk of creating social harm. Given the above, reliance on violation records may be misleading, and therefore must be used prudently.

Table 4.2 Violation records over subsequent periods

Firm's Actual Type	Period $t-1$	Period t
	Detected Violations / Total Violations	Detected Violations / Total Violations
Recalcitrant Regulatees	6/20	4/5
Evading Regulatees	2/20	2/25
Compliant Regulatees	1/3	2/10

suggested in the literature, the determination of monitoring efforts and actual enforcement measures (*i.e.*, persuasion/sanctioning) are treated as a single choice.[49] Therefore, corporations deemed compliant are watched less closely *ex ante* and face lenient enforcement measures *ex post*, while those deemed recalcitrant are watched more closely *ex ante*, and incur harsh sanctions *ex post*.[50] Table 4.2 presents the violation records and actual violations of three different types of regulatees in two subsequent periods.[51]

As illustrated, the industry in this example includes *recalcitrant regulatees*, *i.e.*, corporations that were insufficiently motivated to comply with regulations and therefore engaged in 20 violations in period *t-1*, six of which were actually detected; *compliant regulatees*, *i.e.*, corporations that were highly motivated to comply with regulations and therefore were accidently involved in only three violations in the period *t-1*, one of which was detected; and *evading regulatees*, *i.e.*, corporations that in period *t-1* were engaged in an equivalent number of violations as recalcitrant regulatees (20 violations), of which only two were detected.[52] The strategic enforcement response employed in period *t* is determined based on the violation records (*i.e.*, detected violations) in period *t-1*. The same applies for the subsequent period *t+1*, where strategic responses are determined relying on the records established in period *t*.

Table 4.3 presents the enforcement authority's perceptions of the different types of regulatees and the regulatory responses determined accordingly.

---

49 See *supra* notes 26 and 32 and the related main texts.

50 See *ibid*.

51 For simplification reasons it is assumed that the level of activity of all regulatees is similar, as well as the severity of all regulatory violations from a social perspective.

52 Due to avoidance activities that were aimed at reducing the probability of detection, or to other difficulties embedded in the detection of evading corporations, these corporations were subject to a lower probability of detection ($p^{evading} = 0.2$), compared with recalcitrant and compliance corporations ($p^{default} = 0.3$).

Table 4.3 Regulatory strategic responses determined by violation records evaluation

Firm's Actual Type	Authorities' Perception and Strategic Response					
	(Period T)			(Period $t+1$)		
	Perceived by the authorities as: (relying on period t–1)		Chosen strategy		Perceived by the authorities as: (relying on period t)	Chosen strategy
Recalcitrant Regulatees	Recalcitrant →	Deterrence (Close monitoring & sanctions)	→	Recalcitrant	→	Deterrence* (Close monitoring & sanctions)
Evading Regulatees	Compliant →	Cooperation (Soft monitoring & persuasion)	→	Compliant	→	Cooperation** (Soft monitoring & persuasion)
Compliant Regulatees	Compliant →	Cooperation (Soft monitoring & persuasion)	→	Compliant	→	Cooperation*** (Soft monitoring & persuasion)

Notes: * Although regulatees changed their attitude and became more committed to regulatory compliance; ** although regulatees stick to recalcitrant attitude; *** although regulatees changed their attitude and loosen up their commitment to compliance.

As shown in Table 4.3, according to the regulatory mixed regime, once regulatees have been classified as recalcitrant based on their performance in period $t-1$, in period t they face deterrence-oriented responses, including closer monitoring and sanctioning measures. Given their close monitoring in that period, there is a greater probability that these regulatees will be classified as recalcitrant in the next period, because they are now facing a higher probability of detection. In the example above, regulatees classified as recalcitrant substantially reduced the number of violations they engaged in from 20 in period $t-1$ to 5 in period t (see Table 4.2). Yet, given the closer monitoring of these regulatees in period t, four out of the total of five violations were detected (see Table 4.2). Hence, although in period t these corporations have implemented genuine measures to secure compliance and substantially improved their performance, in period $t+1$ they are still treated harshly by the enforcement authority and may be discouraged from further improving their performance.[53]

Let us now turn to the impact of the regulatory mixed regimes discussed above on compliant and evading regulatees. As illustrated above, given that in period $t-1$ compliant and evading regulatees had fewer than four detected violations (see Table 4.2), in period t they are addressed with cooperative responses, which imply soft monitoring (*e.g.*, less frequent inspections) and conciliatory measures rather than sanctions (see Table 4.3). Such a regulatory response may produce undesired ends, whereas the less intensive and the less frequent the monitoring becomes, the less information the enforcement authority is able to gather as to the past levels of compliance, and the less credible become authorities' evaluations over regulatees' compliance motivations.[54] Under such circumstances, lenient enforcement and infrequent inspections may turn even a *compliant* firm into an *evasive* one: "if cooperative enforcement is so lax that evasive actions are seldom discovered, cooperative firms will have little incentive to avoid cheating."[55] In addition, such a regime may motivate *evading* regulatees to engage in more violations, while benefiting from conciliatory regulatory responses. As it appears in Table 4.2, in period t both "compliant" and "evading" regulatees are engaged in a higher number of violations (ten and 25 respectively, while "recalcitrant" regulatees engage in only five violations), and they still benefit from lenient treatment by enforcement authorities.

---

[53] For the alienation effect of deterrence-based enforcement measures see Chapter 2, Section 2.4.2.

[54] See Johnstone, "From Fiction to Fact – Rethinking OHS Enforcement," p. 18; Gunningham, *Mine Safety: Law, Regulation, Policy*, p. 127.

[55] See Scholz, "Voluntary Compliance and Regulatory Enforcement," p. 397.

A partial solution to the uncertainty involved with the evaluation of past performance has been offered by the literature in the form of setting *optimal periods* of the regulatory game, the length of which is long enough to allow enforcement authorities to gather sufficient information required to identify regulatees' commitment to compliance at some level of certainty.[56] Indeed, longer periods may improve enforcement authorities' evaluations by providing cumulative information regarding past performance. However, it is doubtful whether such a solution may adequately cope with the deficiencies described above. Even when the determined periods of the game are long, regulatees may find it beneficial to "keep away from trouble" in a certain period, and by that gain lenient treatment in the following ones. Under such circumstances, regulatees may delay serious violations to future periods, in which the probability of detection is mitigated.

Other proposals made in the scholarly literature as ways to overcome the information asymmetry pitfall pertain to the classification of regulatees into groups. Russell (1990), for instance, explores the possibility of dealing with monitoring errors by establishing a regulatory mixed regime, under which deterrence-based regulatory responses are triggered only after regulatees pass a number of audits in a row.[57] According to the suggested regime, policymakers may increase the threshold of regulatee classification by requiring a higher number of violations recorded or the number of periods in which the corporation has to be found in violation.[58] In the same vein, Stafford (2008) examines a regulatory model in which regulatory responses are determined by the self-reporting of violations.[59]

---

[56] See Scholz, "Cooperation, Deterrence, and the Ecology of Regulatory Enforcement," p. 212: "one way of introducing the problem of uncertainty into the model is to equate the game's enforcement period with the length of time required for the agency to know the firm's choice at some predetermined level of certainty." See also, Scholz, "Voluntary Compliance and Regulatory Enforcement," p. 398.

[57] See Russell, "Game Models for Structuring Monitoring and Enforcement Systems," p. 159.

[58] When considering the state-dependent enforcement model, for instance, only if the corporation has been found violating regulations in a number of inspections (or in a number of periods) in a row, will it be reclassified as a group-V corporation. Compare also with Vibeke L. Nielsen, "Are Regulators Responsive?" *Law and Policy* 28(3) (2006), pp. 397–398; Braithwaite and Ayres, *Responsive Regulation: Transcending the Deregulation Debate*, p. 19, argue that judgments made of regulatee types on a narrow basis, or a single action, should be avoided and that a wider perspective of regulatees should be adopted instead.

[59] See Sarah L. Stafford, "Self-Policing in a Targeted Enforcement Regime," *Southern Economic Journal* 74 (2008), 934–951. Note that this study uses the term 'self-policing' to describe situations in which corporations inform the authorities about their own regulatory violations.

Stafford points out that by "rewarding facilities that disclose with lower penalties and more lenient future enforcement [an enforcement policy] increases the incentives to both audit and disclose."[60]

Although the proposals above may alleviate the information problem embedded in regulatory mixed regimes, it is doubtful whether they are able to sufficiently overcome this problem. Even when the "multiple-play" approach or the "self-reporting-based" approach are implemented, enforcement authorities may still fail to accurately determine regulatees' type, simply because none of these techniques ensures information alignment between enforcement authorities and regulatees, for instance, with respect to the different levels of activity of regulatees. In addition, both alternative methods are embedded with the risk of strategic behavior by regulatees: in the "multi-play" framework, regulatees may start by engaging in the most profitable violations, followed by compliant behavior, knowing that a non-cooperative regulatory response is only expected after a series of various violations. Similarly, if the "self-reporting-based" approach is upheld, firms may manipulate the enforcement authority by self-reporting minor violations, and thereby "earning" a reduced probability of detection for the more profitable ones.[61]

4.5.2 Arbitrariness

Regulatory mixed regimes are imbedded with a serious pitfall of arbitrariness, which may play out in various manners, namely, *misuse of regulatory discretion*, *regulatory inconsistency*, and *misperceived regulatory responses*. Let me elaborate on each of these aspects.

4.5.2.1 Misuse of regulatory discretion

A serious source of concern of regulatory mixed regimes pertains to the presumption of the benevolence of enforcement authorities. As mentioned earlier, mixed regimes assume that enforcement authorities are committed to the goal of social welfare maximization.[62] This assumption is often taken to imply that enforcement authorities are diligent agencies, which

---

60 See *ibid.*, p. 250.

61 See, for instance, Alexander A. Pfaff and William Sanchirico, "Big Field, Small Potatoes: An Empirical Assessment of EPA's Self-Audit Policy," *Journal of Policy Analysis and Management* 23(3) (2004), 415–432, who criticize the EPA's audit policy, by arguing that such a policy has led mainly to reports of minor violations.

62 See *supra* note 18 and the related main text.

act in a professional manner and possess reasonable capabilities to undertake their enforcement roles.[63] Given this assumption, the mixed regimes grant enforcement authorities wide discretion in undertaking enforcement duties.[64] This discretion, which is used by enforcement authorities in determining the appropriate regulatory response for each regulatee, is argued to be indispensible for the efficient functioning of mixed enforcement regimes. As the argument goes, narrowing down enforcement authorities' discretion may result in a "rulebook-oriented" regulatory system that thwarts the search for the most efficient regulatory response.[65]

A unique aspect of the regulatory discretion conferred upon enforcement authorities by the mixed regimes pertains to the fact that under these regimes regulatory discretion is pushed downward from the supervisory level to the field-workers' level of enforcement authorities.[66] As described by Bardach and Kagan (1982):[67]

> Inspectors meet representatives of regulated enterprises face-to-face; they look directly at particular production processes, the risks they create, and the existing techniques for controlling them; and *they make intuitive judgments about the motivations and capabilities of the enterprises they deal with, namely rating them on the hierarchy of good to bad apples.*

Notwithstanding the importance of enforcement authorities' discretion, wide discretion presents a tangible risk of *arbitrariness*. The empowerment of regulatory actors with wide discretion creates a *monitoring and control*

---

63 See, for instance, Scholz, "Cooperation, Deterrence, and the Ecology of Regulatory Enforcement," p. 213: "the initial model avoids the problem of agency exploitation by assuming that the agency is primarily concerned with the net enforcement benefits, which are maximized by the combined strategies."

64 See Bardach and Kagan, *Going by the Book: The Problem of Regulatory Unreasonableness*, p. 152: "Discretion is the key of flexible enforcement."

65 See *ibid.*, p. 129, showing that the judgments required from the regulatory actors may be complex and difficult: "a good inspector must have not only technical competence but also the tough-mindedness to probe the businessman's explanations and excuses in a polite but critical manner." See also, Braithwaite and Ayres, *Responsive Regulation: Transcending the Deregulation Debate*, p. 56; Scholz, "Voluntary Compliance and Regulatory Enforcement," 385–404; Fenn and Veljanovski, "A Positive Economic Theory of Regulatory Enforcement," 1055–1070.

66 See Scholz, "Enforcement Policy and Corporate Misconduct: The Changing Perspective of Deterrence Theory," p. 260.

67 See Bardach and Kagan, *Going by the Book: The Problem of Regulatory Unreasonableness*, p. 71 (emphasis added). See also, p. 32: "unlike policemen, who ordinarily patrol public places, inspectors regularly enter private buildings, pore over corporate records, and take product samples."

problem between enforcement authorities and the individual agents acting on their behalf.[68] This agency problem, which is characterized by information asymmetry between enforcement authorities and their individual agents, gives rise to serious concerns regarding potential misuse of regulatory discretion.[69] This misuse includes actions aimed at maximizing one's own utility.[70] In addition, given the repeated interactions with industry players, individual enforcement agents may get *captured* or *corrupted*.[71]

---

[68] See Scholz, "Cooperative Regulatory Enforcement and the Politics of Administrative Effectiveness," p. 121: "Inspectors must have the discretion to overlook minor violations and treat some firms less stringently than others. If inspectors are positively oriented toward policy goals and have the ability to make the tradeoffs appropriate for flexible compliance and to recognize flexible compliance in firms, beneficiaries could obtain the benefits of cooperation by providing the required level of discretion. On the other hand, if the agents are negatively oriented or incapable, discretion is likely to increase the likelihood that enforcement will be captured by business interests. Once discretion is provided, the policy decision locus is shifted more fully from the legislative to the administrative arena in which business is likely to have greater influence. *Discretion increases business incentives to influence the 'street-level' inspectors at the same time it decreases the ability of the national office and oversight agencies to monitor and control the behavior of inspectors*" (emphasis added). See also, Scholz, "Voluntary Compliance and Regulatory Enforcement;" Bardach and Kagan, *Going by the Book: The Problem of Regulatory Unreasonableness*, p. 153.

[69] The risk of misuse of regulatory power may be somewhat mitigated by restrictions to actors' discretion and by some requirements of records and detailed checklists. See, for instance, Bardach and Kagan, *Going by the Book: The Problem of Regulatory Unreasonableness*, pp. 32–33, 74. See also, Scholz, "Enforcement Policy and Corporate Misconduct: The Changing Perspective of Deterrence Theory," 266–267, who offers to deal with the accountability of regulatory agencies by using four mechanisms: (1) formal procedural requirements; (2) legislative and executive oversight; (3) independent commissions and external boards; and (4) interest representation. However, it is questionable whether such checklists may eliminate the inherent risks involved with an actors' discretion.

[70] See Bardach and Kagan, *Going by the Book: The Problem of Regulatory Unreasonableness*, p. 32, 129. The later concern is somewhat worrisome in a reality where inspectors are evaluated on the basis of the citations issued. See *ibid.*, p. 73.

[71] See *ibid*, p. 72, for the risk of the corruption of enforcement agencies. See also, Chapter 3, Sections 3.5.2 and 3.5.3. In addition, see Joel F. Handler, "Dependent People, the State, and the Modern/Postmodern Search for the Dialogic Community," *UCLA Law Review* 35 (1988), p. 1027: "Although no enforcement agency can enforce all of the law all of the time, the use of discretion presents real danger of corruption and capture. There is concern that the costs of formal proceedings are used to bargain away regulatory goals, and that the enforcing agency will be able to override procedural requirements designed to protect the weak in formal proceedings." Braithwaite and Ayres, *Responsive Regulation: Transcending the Deregulation Debate*, p. 56; Kenneth C. Davis, *Discretionary*

In extreme cases, individual enforcement agents may engage in *framing*, thereby threatening innocent individuals with severe regulatory responses in order to extort money from them.[72] Indeed, such risks are not unique to regulatory mixed regimes, but are embedded in any governance framework where public authorities are involved.[73] Yet, given the considerable discretion granted to enforcement authorities by the regulatory mixed regimes, it seems that the risk of arbitrariness is magnified in the context of these regimes.

4.5.2.2 Regulatory inconsistency

Individual enforcement agents differ in their style, personal attitude, and capabilities.[74] Such differences influence agents' judgments when undertaking enforcement tasks. Empirical evidence shows that these regimes

---

Justice: A Preliminary Inquiry (Baton Rouge, US: Louisiana State University Press, 1969); Theodore J. Lowi, *The End of Liberalism: Ideology, Policy, and the Crisis of Public Authority* (New York: Norton, 1969); Bardach and Kagan, *Going by the Book: The Problem of Regulatory Unreasonableness*, p. 152

[72] See Polinsky and Shavell, "Corruption and Optimal Law Enforcement," 1–24.

[73] The risk of arbitrariness with the functions of authorities has been thoroughly analyzed in the scholarly literature in various contexts. The traditional proposals to cope with arbitrariness include the accumulation of additional layers of guardianship. See Susan P. Shapiro, "The Social Control of Impersonal Trust," *The American Journal of Sociology* 93(3) (1987), 623–658, who discusses the traditional way of dealing with failures of trust by adding guardians to monitor the existing guardians and, by that, making guardianship contestable. A notable suggestion, known as '*Tripartism*,' implies that non-governmental organizations and public interest groups should play a crucial role in monitoring the regulatory authority. See Braithwaite and Ayres, *Responsive Regulation: Transcending the Deregulation Debate*, Chapter 3, pp. 54–100; Scholz, "Cooperative Regulatory Enforcement and the Politics of Administrative Effectiveness." For additional measures to ensure the accountability of enforcement authorities, see Bardach and Kagan, *Going by the Book: The Problem of Regulatory Unreasonableness*, pp. 152–184.

[74] See Hawkins, "Bargain and Bluff: Compliance Strategy and Deterrence in the Enforcement of Regulation," p. 48: "regulatory actors also have multiple selves: they can be nice guys or tough guys, self-interested or public-spirited, professional or unprofessional, diligent or lazy, intelligent or confused." See also, Braithwaite and Ayres, *Responsive Regulation: Transcending the Deregulation Debate*, p. 31; Bardach and Kagan, *Going by the Book: The Problem of Regulatory Unreasonableness*, p. 124: "[T]he good inspector still would be tough when toughness was required. His effort to seek cooperation would not blind him to the possibility that personnel in the regulated enterprise may seek to evade even reasonable regulatory requirements, provide him with misleading information, or exaggerate the costs or technical difficulties of compliance . . . All this is, of course, somewhat

sometimes result in regulatory inconsistency, *i.e.*, the application of different styles of enforcement in comparable cases.[75] This result is not surprising considering that a single inspector often lacks the ability of seeing the broader picture and may "*miss the forest by looking only for certain kinds of defective trees in the regulated enterprise.*"[76]

4.5.2.3 Misperceived regulatory responses

Mixed strategies are vulnerable to the risk of misperceived regulatory responses, that is, regulatees may incorrectly perceive enforcement styles employed against them.[77] Empirical evidence shows that regulatory measures that were perceived as cooperative by individual enforcement agents (*e.g.*, issuance of a warning instead of fines), were interpreted as deterrence-based measures by regulatees.[78] In that context, the wide discretion conferred upon enforcement authorities by the regulatory mixed regimes may turn out to be counterproductive.

4.6 SUMMARY AND CONCLUDING REMARKS

In spite of the dichotomy between the deterrence-based and the cooperative schools of thought, these paradigms should not be perceived as incompatible. This chapter demonstrated that enforcement strategies developed by the two schools of thought can be reconciled in a harmonized manner. When the heterogeneity of regulatees and the dynamics of their compliance motivations are considered, deterrence-based and cooperative strategies may be integrated into mixed regimes that enable enforcement authorities to treat diversified regulatees with tailored regulatory measures.

Due to their inclusive approach and targeting attitudes, regulatory

---

utopian. Not every regulatory official can be a perfect judge of what is or is not reasonable or an expert in eliciting cooperation."

[75] See, for instance, Peter Mascini and Eelco Van Wijk, "Responsive Regulation at the Dutch Food and Consumer Product Safety Authority: An Empirical Assessment of Assumptions Underlying the Theory," *Regulation & Governance* 3(1) (2009), 27–47; Nielsen, "Are Regulators Responsive?," 395–416.

[76] See Bardach and Kagan, *Going by the Book: The Problem of Regulatory Unreasonableness*, p. 104 (emphasis added).

[77] See *ibid.*, pp. 78–79.

[78] See, for instance, Mascini and Van Wijk, "Responsive Regulation at the Dutch Food and Consumer Product Safety Authority: An Empirical Assessment of Assumptions Underlying the Theory," pp. 39–41, showing that regulatees tend to perceive regulatory reactions as more coercive than intended by the inspectors.

mixed regimes present important improvements over each of the "stand alone" regimes discussed in the previous chapters. Yet these regimes are also fraught with significant pitfalls, namely *information asymmetry* and *arbitrariness*, which require a further development of mixed enforcement regimes in a way that sustains their virtues, while coping with their pitfalls. This will be my goal in the ensuing parts of this book.

PART II

Corporate liability and the incentive apparatus for corporate proactive compliance

INTRODUCTION TO PART II

The spotlight in this part of the book is focused on corporate liability regimes, which comprise a key policy instrument used to induce corporate proactive compliance. Policymakers desiring to induce corporate proactive compliance often seek to motivate corporations to adopt genuine, comprehensive compliance management systems in which misconduct risks can be identified and reduced.[1] To this end, policymakers normally utilize one of the following policy instruments: First, *legal compulsion*. This instrument was adopted, for instance, by the U.S. securities laws with the enactment of the Sarbanes-Oxley Act (SOX) of 2002, which requires that public corporations adopt various measures aimed at preventing financial fraud.[2] A similar approach is often adopted in areas such as privacy data protection, pharmaceutical production, financial services, and health care provision.[3] Second, *liability frameworks*. Such frameworks may be crudely divided into two major groups: (*i*) *managerial*

---

[1] Compliance management systems comprise a wide range of internal corporate control schemes aimed at preventing, deterring, and reporting corporate misconduct, including misconduct of employees conducted within the scope of their employment. These schemes normally include risk evaluation, codes of conduct, manuals and training programs, monitoring and supervisory measures, as well as disciplinary measures against rebellious employees. Compliance management systems are further discussed in Chapter 5, Section 5.7.3.

[2] The SOX Act requires that public corporations implement various self-enforcement measures, including internal controls, independent auditing, internal audit committees, whistle-blowing systems, and periodic reports. In addition, these corporations are required to "disclose whether or not, and if not, the reason therefor," they adopted a code of ethics for senior financial officers (§406, SOX Act).

[3] See Marcos D. Jiménez and Dana E. Foster, "The Importance of Compliance Programs for the Health Care Industry," *University of Miami Business Law Review* 7 (1998), 503–512. In addition see Karl A. Groskaufmanis, "Impact of Corporate Compliance Outside the Criminal Process," in *Compliance Programs and the Corporate Sentencing Guidelines: Preventing Criminal and Civil Liability*, Jeffrey M. Kaplan and Joseph E. Murphy eds., revised edn (U.S.A.: Tompson/West, 2009), p. 24.30, which reviews several U.S. State laws, such as California and Connecticut laws, which compel corporations with more than 50 employees to provide sexual harassment compliance training for their employees. See also, Michael B. Mukasey and Andrew J. Ceresney, "Should Corporations Self-Report Wrongdoing?" *New York Law Journal* (October 1, 2010), which reviews compulsory compliance-related reporting duties that apply to financial institutions and government contractors. For a critical approach of compelling corporations to undertake internal enforcement efforts, see, for instance, Huff, "The Role of Corporate Compliance Programs in Determining Corporate Criminal Liability: A Suggested Approach," pp. 1275–1276. According to Huff, if the minimum thresholds of an effective compliance management system are determined by the

liability frameworks, under which corporate executives are held personally liable for corporate misconduct or for the failure to institute an effective compliance management system;[4] and (*ii*) *corporate liability frameworks*, under which corporations are held liable for violations committed by their employees within the scope of their employment. The latter group of liability frameworks, which is the most salient policy instrument used to encourage the adoption of compliance management systems, is the main focus of this part of this book.

Corporate liability regimes may be structured in different forms, each of which generates a unique incentive scheme for corporate regulatees. My initial goal for this part of the book is to get the reader acquainted with the major structures of corporate liability regimes employed in legal practice. Hence, I begin this journey by exploring the different structures of corporate liability regimes implemented in major legal systems, and then turn to analyzing various policy trends followed in recent years on both sides of the Atlantic. Once the different liability structures are canvassed, my subsequent goal is to identify which of the alternative structures may efficiently induce corporate proactive compliance. Therefore, I evaluate each of the major regimes according to the incentive apparatus it produces for corporate proactive compliance. This analysis reveals that none of the corporate liability regimes recognized thus far presents an optimal liability framework. Hence, building upon the conclusions of Part I of the book, I take on the challenge of developing an innovative corporate liability regime that comprises a workable liability framework that efficiently induces corporate proactive compliance.

Before plunging into a discussion of the alternative structures of corporate

---

regulator, then corporations may focus primarily on satisfying such thresholds, rather than designing a tailored compliance system that actually deters misconduct.

[4] Such frameworks commonly derive from corporate officials' fiduciary duties and the duty of care. For instance, §404 of the SOX Act explicitly requires corporate management to continuously assess corporate internal controls. This section further requires corporations' annual statements to "state the responsibility of management for establishing and maintaining an adequate internal control structure and procedures for financial reporting." Similarly, in the U.S. health care industry, managers' failure to institute a compliance program may constitute a breach of the directors' fiduciary duties. See Jiménez and Foster, "The Importance of Compliance Programs for the Health Care Industry," 503–512. A similar approach is adopted, for instance, by Israeli law, in which the implementation of an effective "Internal Compliance Program" may reduce executives' exposure to personal liability associated with the violation of their fiduciary duties and antitrust laws. See, for instance, Israeli Antitrust Authority, *Model Internal Compliance Program* (1998).

liability regimes, it may be useful to reflect upon the bedrocks of such regimes which are directly linked to the very nature of corporate legal personality. Indeed, corporate personality has long ago been widely established in legal practice to such an extent that no one actually doubts it any longer. Yet, when dealing with corporate liability, one may question the appropriateness of holding corporations – soulless and bodiless fictitious creatures – liable for actions undertaken by flesh-and-blood agents. After all, the legal personality that grants corporations rights, protections, and privileges is essentially a legal fiction.[5] Corporations do not "fix" prices; they also do not "deceive" or "defraud." In actuality, corporations can act only through their agents.[6] That said, *how can corporations be liable? Can one actually say that a corporation is at fault and therefore should be condemned and sanctioned? Do corporations have the capacity for culpable conduct?*

Naturally, the answers to these questions are highly contingent upon the legal ecology in which the inquiry is made. Consider, initially, *civil* ecologies, where the compensation of victims comprises a key objective of laws.[7] In such ecologies holding corporations liable, thereby requiring them to compensate those who suffer damages caused by the corporate activity, seems fairly explicable; after all, corporations are the principal beneficiaries of these activities, as well as the ones "sitting in the driver's seat," determining and directing such activities.[8] By contrast, where the

---

[5] In *Trustees of Dartmouth College v. Woodward*, 17 U.S. (4 Wheat.) 518, 636 (1819), the court defines a corporation as "an artificial being, invisible, intangible, and existing only in contemplation of the law." Another famous quote is attributed to Baron Thurlow, an eighteenth-century British jurist, who described the metaphysic nature of corporations by referring to them as having "no soul to be damned, and no body to be kicked." See also, Coffee, "No Soul to Damn: No Body to Kick: An Unscandalized Inquiry into the Problem of Corporate Punishment," 386–459; Pitt and Groskaufmanis, "Minimizing Corporate Civil and Criminal Liability: A Second Look at Corporate Codes of Conduct," p. 1563; Khanna, "Corporate Liability Standards: When Should Corporations be Held Criminally Liable?," p. 1242.

[6] For a discussion of corporate personality and criminal liability see Eric Colvin, "Corporate Personality and Criminal Liability," *Criminal Law Forum* 6(1) (1995), p. 5.

[7] See, for instance, Philip A. Lacovara and David P. Nicoli, "Vicarious Criminal Liability of Organizations: RICO as an Example of a Flawed Principle in Practice," *St. John's Law Review* 64 (1989), p. 738.

[8] See, for instance, Huff, "The Role of Corporate Compliance Programs in Determining Corporate Criminal Liability: A Suggested Approach," p. 29: "Sanctions against corporations will have an impact upon shareholders who may not themselves be negligent or whose negligence is less than that required for criminal liability. *Shareholders do, however, reap the benefit of corporate operations. It is therefore not unreasonable to make them bear some of the social costs of*

criminal law ecology is concerned, corporations' blameworthiness may be less obvious. Since criminal law does not usually apply to an actor who has acted with the absence of a "mental fault," the key concern in holding corporations criminally liable pertains to the necessary element of "*mens rea*." This concern intensifies when considering *ultra vires* actions, *i.e.*, actions taken by corporate employees beyond their powers. *Can corporations be said to have acted with the required mental fault when employees exceeded their authorized powers? What about corporations that implemented self-enforcement measures, acted diligently to prevent such misconduct, assiduously monitored their employees, and even reported self-detected violations to the relevant authorities? Should such corporations be held liable?*

These questions lie at the heart of this part of this book, which is composed of the two following chapters. In Chapter 5 I canvass various corporate liability policies used in legal practice and explore their ideological roots. Out of a great variety of legal systems that could have been the subject of a close examination, I chose to primarily focus on the U.S. legal system, which – as my investigation reveals – has undergone the most comprehensive and salient perception transformation regarding the optimal structure of corporate liability regimes. The overview of recent developments in the U.S. legal system reveals a clear tendency of replacing "strict" corporate liability frameworks with "softer," more conciliatory ones. This overview is then complemented by comparative insights taken from other legal systems that have undergone similar developments (the United Kingdom, Canadian, and Australian legal systems), as well as by insights from another major system (the EU legal system) which has undergone the completely opposite transformation. After having presented the major corporate liability regimes, I use the law and economics toolkit in Chapter 6 to evaluate the welfare impacts of these contemporary corporate liability regimes. Enriched by the conclusions of Part I of this book, the analysis is attentive to the perils of both "stand-alone" approaches to law enforcement. Therefore, rather than focusing on the choice between a "harsh" and a "conciliatory" corporate liability framework, this analysis proposes an innovative compound liability framework that reconciles both "stand-alone" approaches in a socially desirable manner.

---

corporate negligence and its consequences . . . The *shareholder* who is concerned about the dangers of corporate negligence *can take protective action by seeking to have safety systems implemented* and by selling her shares if appropriate measures are not implemented" (references omitted, emphasis added). See also, Lacovara and Nicoli, "Vicarious Criminal Liability of Organizations: RICO as an Example of a Flawed Principle in Practice," p. 730.

5. Corporate liability and compliance management systems

5.1 INTRODUCTION

Corporations are often held liable for their employees' misbehavior undertaken within the scope of their employment. In this chapter, I provide an overview of the major structures of corporate liability regimes adopted by U.S. law, along with some comparative insights from other major legal systems that may shed some light on contemporary legal tendencies. The overview provided here is neither intended to present a comprehensive portrayal of corporate liability regimes, nor to capture all disparities between civil and criminal liability frameworks. Such overviews are documented elsewhere.[1] Instead, this chapter seeks to provide the reader with the necessary background for understanding alternative incentive schemes produced by different corporate liability regimes and their aptitude for inducing corporate proactive compliance.

This chapter is organized as follows: Section 5.2 presents the traditional "vicarious liability" framework and its expansion from the civil to the criminal arena. Section 5.3 describes the contours of the transformation in perceptions that has appeared in U.S. law in recent decades. Traditional strict liability regimes have been replaced in the U.S. by somewhat softer regimes, collectively referred to as "duty-based regimes." Such a transformation has appeared in both civil and criminal contexts. Hence, Sections 5.4 and 5.5 present two major avenues of the perception transformation which occurred in the context of civil liability, and Sections 5.6 and 5.7 present two parallel avenues of perception transformation which occurred

---

[1] See, for instance, Kraakman, "Vicarious and Corporate Liability," 669–681; Kraakman, "Corporate Liability Strategies and the Costs of Legal Controls," 857–898; Andrew Weissmann and David Newman, "Rethinking Criminal Corporate Liability," *Indiana Law Journal* (Bloomington) 82 (2007), 411–451; Bowles, Faure and Garoupa, "The Scope of Criminal Law and Criminal Sanctions: An Economic View and Policy Implications," 389–416; Faure, "Environmental Crimes," 320–345; Lacovara and Nicoli, "Vicarious Criminal Liability of Organizations: RICO as an Example of a Flawed Principle in Practice," 725–778.

in the context of criminal liability. Section 5.8 offers some comparative insights from other legal systems and Section 5.9 summarizes and concludes this chapter.

5.2 DIRECT AND VICARIOUS CORPORATE LIABILITY

In spite of their metaphysical nature, corporations are engaged in an endless variety of activities, all of which are carried out by real individuals or flesh-and-blood employees who are operating on their behalf.[2] This unique nature of corporate personality has triggered the development of two complementary types of corporate liability frameworks, *direct* and *vicarious* liabilities, which address the misbehavior of corporations and their employees. Both types of corporate liabilities exist within the *civil* and the *criminal* contexts. In what follows, I present the fundamentals of these liability frameworks in civil and criminal contexts.

5.2.1 Corporate Civil Liability

Under U.S. law, corporations are subject to two types of civil liabilities. The first, and the more palpable one, is *direct civil liability*, which is liability imposed on corporations for *their own* tortious conduct even when in actuality this conduct was undertaken by their employees. The particular conditions for corporate direct liability are stated in the Restatement of Law (Third), Agency, §7.03(1), as follows:[3]

> (1) A principal is subject to direct liability to a third party harmed by an agent's conduct when:
> (a) . . . the agent acts with actual authority or the principal ratifies the agent's conduct; and—
> (i) the agent's conduct is tortious, or
> (ii) the agent's conduct, if that of the principal, would subject the principal to tort liability; or
> (b) . . . the principal is negligent in selecting, supervising, or otherwise controlling the agent; or

[2] See, for instance, The American Law Institute, *Restatement of Law (Third), Agency* (Philadelphia, PA: American Law Institute Publishers, 2006), Vol. 2, comment (b) to §7.03 p. 152. According to these conditions for corporate direct liability: "A principal that is not an individual can take action only through its agents, who typically are individuals."

[3] See *ibid.*, §7.03(1).

(c) . . . the principal delegates performance of a duty to use care to protect other persons or their property to an agent who fails to perform the duty.

In order for direct corporate liability to be triggered, the infringing action must involve a fault on the part of the corporation, even if the particular action constitutes no violation on the corporate employee's part. The specific infringement could be of any duty related to the corporation, including duties of selecting, supervising, or otherwise controlling employees, as well as any duty to use care in protecting other persons or their property.

In addition to direct corporate liability, corporations may also be subject to a *secondary* liability scheme. This secondary liability scheme is often referred to as *vicarious liability*. This type of liability is more intriguing in the sense that it is triggered by wrongs committed by corporate employees that do not necessarily constitute a fault on the part of the corporation. Vicarious liability has sprouted from the common law doctrine of *respondeat superior* ("let the master answer"), which is the fundamental vehicle for imposing responsibility for one person's acts upon another.[4] This doctrine originates in ancient customs, in which servants were treated as part of their masters' households and their relations with their masters made their actions their masters' responsibility as the head of the household.[5] The *respondeat superior* doctrine in its contemporary form is found in the Restatement of Law (Third), Agency, §2.04, which states that: "An employer is subject to liability for torts committed by employees while acting within the scope of their employment." In this contemporary evolution of the doctrine, corporate liability expands beyond the boundaries of authorized employees' actions.[6] The particular conditions for vicarious liability are stated in the Restatement of Law (Third), Agency, §2.03(2), as follows:[7]

---

[4] See, for instance, Groskaufmanis, "Impact of Corporate Compliance Outside the Criminal Process," p. 22.4; William K. Perry and Linda S. Dakin, "Compliance Programs and Criminal Law," in *Compliance Programs and the Corporate Sentencing Guidelines: Preventing Criminal and Civil Liability*, Jeffrey M. Kaplan and Joseph E. Murphy eds., revised edn (U.S.A.: Tompson/West, 2009), pp. 22.1–22.16; Khanna, "Corporate Liability Standards: When Should Corporations be Held Criminally Liable?," p. 1243.

[5] See The American Law Institute, *Restatement of Law (Third), Agency*, Vol. 1, comment (b) to §2.04, p. 140.

[6] See *ibid.*, Vol. 1, comment (b) to §2.04, p. 140. See also, Colvin, "Corporate Personality and Criminal Liability," p. 2.

[7] See The American Law Institute, *Restatement of Law (Third), Agency*, Vol. 1, comment (b) to §2.04, p. 141. This concept is repeated also in the restatement

(2) A principal is subject to vicarious liability to a third party harmed by an agent's conduct when
   (a) . . . the agent is an employee who commits a tort while acting within the scope of employment; or
   (b) . . . the agent commits a tort when acting with apparent authority in dealing with a third party on or purportedly on behalf of the principal.

As opposed to direct liability, a vicarious liability scheme does not require that the corporation itself be at fault; it is a derivative liability imposed on a corporation for misconduct on the part of their employees who purportedly acted on behalf of the corporation. The only condition required for the imposition of vicarious liability is that the misconduct was committed by an employee "within the scope of the employment"[8] or by an agent whose actions were taken with "apparent authority" that enabled him/her to commit a tort or to conceal its commission.[9]

The establishment of corporate civil liability has been explained by the scholarly literature using two major lines of reasoning. First, corporate employees function as "organs of the corporate body." Therefore, corporations are the actual *beneficiaries* of their employees' conduct taken within the scope of their employment. Thus, these corporations ought to be made to bear the costs of such actions undertaken on their behalf.[10] Second, as employing entities, corporations are able to *control their employees and monitor their actions*.[11] Hence, by holding corporations

§7.07. Note that this rule is similar to the rule stated in the *Restatement of Law (Second), Agency* §219(1), but replaced the terminology of "*master–servant*" with "*employer – employee*." The definition of employer–employee relations is contained in §7.07 of the *Restatement of Law (Third), Agency*, which repeats the basic concept of the *respondeat superior* doctrine.

[8] See The American Law Institute, *Restatement of Law (Third), Agency*, §7.07. The restatement describes further in §7.07(2) that employees shall be perceived as acting within the scope of the employment when performing work assigned to them by the corporation, or engaging in a course of conduct subject to the corporation's control, rather than an independent course of conduct not intended by the corporation to serve any of its purposes.

[9] See *ibid.*, Vol. 2, comment (a) to §7.08.

[10] See Pitt and Groskaufmanis, "Minimizing Corporate Civil and Criminal Liability: A Second Look at Corporate Codes of Conduct," pp. 1563–1564, who discuss the "distributing loss" rationale of the *respondeat superior* doctrine. See also, Lacovara and Nicoli, "Vicarious Criminal Liability of Organizations: RICO as an Example of a Flawed Principle in Practice," p. 730.

[11] See Patrick S. Atiyah, *Vicarious Liability in the Law of Tort* (London: Butterworths, 1967), p. 15: "the fact the master in some sense controls the activities of his employees has for many years been treated as some justification for imposing

liable for the wrongs committed by their employees, corporations are motivated to take the necessary measures to ensure normative behavior by their employees.[12]

5.2.2 Corporate Criminal Liability

Corporate liability has long ago exceeded the boundaries of the civil ecology. Under current U.S. Federal Law, corporations are subject to two types of criminal liability:[13] first, a *direct* criminal liability, which is imposed on corporations for *their own* criminal conduct. This type of liability, commonly referred to as "regulatory crimes," does not require any personal fault (*mens-rea*) on the actors' part. Direct liability is commonly applied in areas such as environmental law and public health and safety regulations in which policymakers have traditionally determined that the public interest requires absolute criminal liability to be used to promote compliant behavior.[14] Secondly there is a *vicarious* corporate liability, which is imposed on corporations for crimes committed by their

---

vicarious liability." And on p. 16: "[T]he person in control is the person best placed to take precautions against accidents."

[12] This line of reasoning springs, for instance, from §7.03(1)(b) to the *Restatement of Law (Third), Agency*, discussed above, according to which corporations are subject to direct liability if they are "negligent in selecting, supervising, or otherwise controlling the agent." A similar rationale is apparently used to explain the merits of the respondeat superior doctrine, under which vicarious liability is assigned to corporations: "A firm or organization that employs individuals usually structures their work to limit the scope of discretion and individual action, thus limiting the occasions when unreasonable decisions are likely to be made. . . . *Respondeat superior creates an incentive for principals to choose employees and structure work within the organization so as to reduce the incidence of tortious conduct*. This incentive may reduce the incidence of tortious conduct more effectively than doctrines that impose liability solely on an individual tortfeasor" (emphasis added). See The American Law Institute, *Restatement of Law (Third), Agency*, Vol. 1, comment (b) to §2.04, p. 141.

[13] The distinction between the two types of corporate criminal liability was developed by courts at the beginning of the twentieth century. For a detailed historical overview of the evolution of corporate criminal liability see Kathleen F. Brickey, "Corporate Criminal Accountability: A Brief History and an Observation," *Washington University Law Quarterly* 60(2) (1982), 393–423; Lacovara and Nicoli, "Vicarious Criminal Liability of Organizations: RICO as an Example of a Flawed Principle in Practice," 725–778.

[14] See, for instance, Michael E. Tigar, "It Does the Crime but Not the Time: Corporate Criminal Liability in Federal Law," *American Journal of Criminal Law* 17(3) (1990), 211–234; Walsh and Pyrich, "Corporate Compliance Programs as a Defense to Criminal Liability: Can a Corporation Save its Soul?," p. 608.

employees within the scope of their employment, and at least in part with the motive of benefiting the corporation.[15] This branch of corporate liability includes traditional corporate offenses, such as "white collar crimes," and commonly requires both "guilty acts" (*actus-reus*) and "guilty minds" (*mens-rea*).[16]

Criminal corporate liability has been established over the course of the past centuries through a progressive process.[17] The idea of holding corporations criminally liable was initially rejected based on the perception that it would be "unjust to condemn and punish one person for the conduct of another without reference to whether the former was at fault for what occurred."[18] In addition, serious doubts were raised with respect

---

[15] See *infra* notes 34–38 and the related main text. For a general discussion of existing frameworks of criminal corporate liability see Kraakman, "Vicarious and Corporate Liability," 669–681; Weissmann and Newman, "Rethinking Criminal Corporate Liability," pp. 412, 422; Khanna, "Corporate Liability Standards: When Should Corporations be Held Criminally Liable?," p. 1239; Hefendehl, "Corporate Criminal Liability: Model Penal Code Section 2.07 and the Development in Western Legal Systems," 283–300; Huff, "The Role of Corporate Compliance Programs in Determining Corporate Criminal Liability: A Suggested Approach," 1252–1298; Walsh and Pyrich, "Corporate Compliance Programs as a Defense to Criminal Liability: Can a Corporation Save its Soul?," 605–689; Colvin, "Corporate Personality and Criminal Liability," 1–44; William S. Laufer, *Corporate Bodies and Guilty Minds: The Failure of Corporate Criminal Liability* (Chicago and London: The University of Chicago Press, 1994), p. 647; Lacovara and Nicoli, "Vicarious Criminal Liability of Organizations: RICO as an Example of a Flawed Principle in Practice," 725–778. This liability framework has been adopted by several U.S. State laws. See, for instance, Christopher R. Green, "Punishing Corporations: The Food-Chain Schizophrenia in Punitive Damages and Criminal Law," *Nebraska Law Review* 87 (2008), 197–269; Weissmann and Newman, "Rethinking Criminal Corporate Liability," p. 423, footnote 39 and the related main text.

[16] See Kelly Strader, *Understanding White Collar Crime* (U.S.A.: Lexis/Nexis, 2002), pp. 8–9. Strader points out that the government in order to gain a white-collar conviction must prove, with only a few exceptions, both the required mental state (*mens rea*) and the required physical component (*actus reus*), as well as the result of the illegal behavior in those cases where the crime requires a result. See also, Walsh and Pyrich, "Corporate Compliance Programs as a Defense to Criminal Liability: Can a Corporation Save its Soul?," p. 610.

[17] See, for instance, Brickey, "Corporate Criminal Accountability: A Brief History and an Observation," 393–423; Coffee, "No Soul to Damn: No Body to Kick: An Unscandalized Inquiry into the Problem of Corporate Punishment," p. 386.

[18] See Weissmann and Newman, "Rethinking Criminal Corporate Liability," p. 418. See also, Brickey, "Corporate Criminal Accountability: A Brief History and an Observation," p. 417. Brickey points out that the respondeat superior

to the capability of corporations – entities lacking any physical form – to meet the prerequisites of criminal charges directed against physical actions.[19] But before such theoretical doubts were resolved, a handful of pioneering English case laws appeared in the seventeenth century, in which limited forms of corporate criminal liability were acknowledged. Initially the English court limited the applicability of criminal corporate liability only to crimes of *nonfeasance*, *i.e.*, crimes that involved inaction on the corporation's part.[20] At this stage, and for about a century afterwards, corporations were immune from prosecution for crimes requiring *misfeasance*, *i.e.*, affirmative wrongful actions. A similar approach was adopted on the opposite side of the Atlantic. U.S. courts started imposing criminal liability primarily for nuisances violations that were undertaken by publicly-oriented corporations, *i.e.*, corporations that were established chiefly to provide public services.[21] The arguments in favor of the establishment of criminal corporate liability were somewhat similar to the reasoning given earlier for civil corporate liability, being: (a) corporations are the *beneficiaries* of their employees' criminal conduct, and thereby ought to be held responsible for such crimes; (b) from a deterrence point of view, it may be more favorable to hold corporations liable for their employees' actions, rather than pursuing individual employees whose culpability is not always easy to determine.[22] As the argument

---

doctrine was rejected in criminal cases during the eighteenth century; and Colvin, "Corporate Personality and Criminal Liability," p. 6.

[19] See Weissmann and Newman, "Rethinking Criminal Corporate Liability," p. 419. For a comprehensive historical overview of the rise of corporate criminal liability see Brickey, "Corporate Criminal Accountability: A Brief History and an Observation," 393–423; Coffee, "No Soul to Damn: No Body to Kick: An Unscandalized Inquiry into the Problem of Corporate Punishment," p. 386; James R. Elkins, "Corporations and the Criminal Law: An Uneasy Alliance," *Kentucky Law Journal* 65(1) (1977), 73–129; Laufer, *Corporate Bodies and Guilty Minds: The Failure of Corporate Criminal Liability*, pp. 4–43.

[20] See Brickey, "Corporate Criminal Accountability: A Brief History and an Observation," p. 401, who refers to the case of *Langforth Bridge*, 79 Eng. Rep. 919 (K.B. 1635). See also, Laufer, *Corporate Bodies and Guilty Minds: The Failure of Corporate Criminal Liability*, p. 11.

[21] See Henry W. Edgerton, "Corporate Criminal Responsibility," *The Yale Law Journal* 36(6) (1927), p. 827, who refers to *State v. Ohio R. R.*, 23 Ind. 362 (1864), *State Works Co.*, 20 ME, 41 (1841), and *Delaware Canal Co. v. Commonwealth*, 60 Pa. St. 367 (1869). According to the author, the early cases in which corporate liability was imposed involved either incorporated municipalities or corporations chartered to provide and maintain public thoroughfares. See *ibid*, p. 93. See also, Weissmann and Newman, "Rethinking Criminal Corporate Liability," p. 420.

[22] See *ibid.*, p. 420; Brickey, "Corporate Criminal Accountability: A Brief History and an Observation," pp. 409–410. See also, *Commonwealth v. Proprietors*

goes, holding corporations criminally liable for employee misconduct encourages them to adopt *controlling measures* to monitor the conduct of their employees.[23]

The next milestone in the development of corporate criminal liability appeared in late nineteenth century, when English courts started applying the idea of *vicarious liability* to criminal cases.[24] Initially, the court decided to abandon the distinction between nonfeasance and misfeasance, reasoning that "there are cases where it would be difficult to say whether the offense consisted in the doing of an unlawful act, or in the doing of a lawful act in an improper manner."[25] The court began from this point applying vicarious liability to a criminal context; at first, the court expanded the applicability of criminal liability beyond nonfeasance crimes to misfeasance crimes of a strict liability nature, *i.e.*, where intent on the part of the actor was not required.[26] During this phase, two major issues troubled both English and U.S. courts with respect to the expansion of

---

of New Bedford Bridge, 68 Mass. 339 (1854); *State v. Morris & Essex Railroad Co.* 23 N.J.L 360 (1852). This argument was repeated in later judgments, for instance, *United States v. Hilton Hotels Corp.*, 467 F.2d 1000, (9th Cir. 1972), Para 28, which states that the: "identification of the particular agents responsible for a Sherman Act violation is especially difficult, and their conviction and punishment is peculiarly ineffective as a deterrent. At the same time, conviction and punishment of the business entity itself is likely to be both appropriate and effective."

[23] See, for instance, Lacovara and Nicoli, "Vicarious Criminal Liability of Organizations: RICO as an Example of a Flawed Principle in Practice," p. 730; Walsh and Pyrich, "Corporate Compliance Programs as a Defense to Criminal Liability: Can a Corporation Save its Soul?," pp. 620–621; Pitt and Groskaufmanis, "Minimizing Corporate Civil and Criminal Liability: A Second Look at Corporate Codes of Conduct," p. 1573; Huff, "The Role of Corporate Compliance Programs in Determining Corporate Criminal Liability: A Suggested Approach," p. 1263; Perry and Dakin, "Compliance Programs and Criminal Law," p. 22.2.

[24] See Weissmann and Newman, "Rethinking Criminal Corporate Liability," 411–451; Elkins, "Corporations and the Criminal Law: An Uneasy Alliance," 73–129.

[25] See *Commonwealth v. Proprietors of New Bedford Bridge*, 68 Mass. (2 Gray) 339 (1854), p. 346. See also, *State v. Morris & Essex Railroad Co.* 23 N.J.L 360 (1852); and *ibid.*, pp. 94–95.

[26] See *Cumberland & Oxford Canal Corp. v. Portland*, 56 Me. 77 (1868); *United States v. MacAndrews & Forbes Co.*, 149 F. 823 (C.C.S.D.N.Y. 1906), p. 835; *J.S. Young Co. v. United States, 212 U.S. 585 (1908)*; *State v. Morris & Essex Railroad Co., supra* note 25, *23 N.J.L. 360, (1852)*, 370. See also, Elkins, "Corporations and the Criminal Law: An Uneasy Alliance," 73–129; Weissmann and Newman, "Rethinking Criminal Corporate Liability," p. 419; Laufer, Corporate Bodies and Guilty Minds: The Failure of Corporate Criminal Liability, p. 647; Brickey, "Corporate Criminal Accountability: A Brief History and an Observation," p. 410.

criminal corporate liability.[27] First, the courts found it awkward to indict corporations for crimes requiring *mens rea*.[28] And second, even if the mental state of employees could theoretically be imputed to their employing corporations, the court questioned the appropriateness of such imputation where employees acted outside the scope of their actual authority.

All doubts involved in the application of corporate criminal liability were cleared in the 1909 U.S. Supreme Court decision in *New York Central & Hudson River Railroad v. the United States*.[29] In this case, *New York Central* had questioned the constitutional grounds of the Elkins Act, according to which illegal rebates granted by employees might automatically be attributed to their employing carrier corporations. The core question addressed by the court was whether corporations may be held criminally liable. The court initially surveyed the prevailing civil corporate liability scheme in which corporations might be held liable for damages resulting from their employees' actions within the scope of their employment, even if such actions were undertaken wantonly, recklessly, or against the express orders of the corporation.[30] Based on these grounds, the court turned to the criminal context, and stated:[31]

---

27 See *State v. First Nat'l Bank*, 2 S.D. 568, 571 (1892); see also, Weissmann and Newman, "Rethinking Criminal Corporate Liability," p. 420.

28 See Colvin, "Corporate Personality and Criminal Liability," pp. 31–32: "The idea of attributing these subjective mental states to corporations, other then as a fiction, has troubled some analysts. Indeed, there was far more resistance to the idea of corporate intent than to that of corporate negligence. Subjective mental states are often treated as conceivable only to sentient human beings."

29 212 U.S. 481 (1909).

30 The court has referred to *Lake Shore & Michigan Southern R. Co. v. Prentice*, 147 U.S. 101; *Washington Gas Light Co. v. Lansden*, 172 U.S. 534.

31 See *New York Central supra* note 29, p. 495 (emphasis added). See also, Tigar, "It Does the Crime but Not the Time: Corporate Criminal Liability in Federal Law," p. 219. A similar approach was adopted by the British court and explained by the House of Lords in *Tesco Supermarkets, Ltd. v. Nattrass*, 1972 App. Cas. 153, 170 (1971), as follows: "I must start by considering the nature of the personality which by a fiction the law attributes to a corporation. A living person has a mind which can have knowledge or intention or be negligent and he has hands to carry out his intentions. A corporation has none of these: it must act through living persons, though not always one or the same person. Then the person who acts is not speaking or acting for the company. He is acting as the company and his mind which directs his acts is the mind of the company. There is no question of the company being vicariously liable. He is not acting as a servant, representative, agent or delegate. He is an embodiment of the company or, one could say, he hears and speaks through the persona of the company, within his appropriate sphere, and his mind is the mind of the company. If it is a guilty mind then that guilt is the guilt of the company."

> We see no valid objection in law, and every reason in public policy, why the *corporation, which profits by the transaction*, and can only act through its agents and officers, shall be held punishable by fine because of the knowledge and intent of its *agents to whom it has entrusted authority to act* in the subject-matter . . . and *whose knowledge and purposes may well be attributed to the corporation for which the agents act*.

Two central elements embedded in this ruling became the key conditions for corporate criminal liability under U.S. Federal Law: first, the conduct must be *within the scope of the individual employee's employment*.[32] As interpreted by the court, this condition merely required employee activity to fall within the area of operation that had been assigned to the employee, even if outside the scope of the employee's actual authority.[33] Second, *the employee acted at least in part to benefit the corporation*.[34] As interpreted by the court, it was enough if only one of the motivations for employee conduct had been to benefit the corporation,[35] even if such a motivation was not the primary objective.[36] No actual benefit for the corporation was required to satisfy this condition, which might even be met if the criminal conduct actually harmed the corporation.[37] According to

---

[32] See, for instance, *Hellenic Inc v. Bridgeline Gas Distribution Llc.*, 252 F.3d 391, 395 (5th Cir. 2001): "A corporate principal is generally considered to know what its agents discover concerning those matters in which the agents have power to bind the principal. An agent's knowledge is imputed to the corporation where the agent is acting within the scope of his authority and where the knowledge relates to matters within the scope of that authority." See also, *American Standard Credit, Inc. v. Nat'l Cement Co.*, 643 F.2d 248, 270–71 (5th Cir. 1981); *W.R. Grace & Co. v. W. U.S. Indus., Inc.*, 608 F.2d 1214, 1218 (9th Cir. 1979); *Volkswagen of America, Inc. v. Robertson*, 713 F.2d 1151, 1163 (5th Cir. 1983).

[33] See, for instance, *Hilton Hotels Corp. supra* note 22, p. 107.

[34] See *United States v. 7326 Highway 45 N.*, 965 F.2d 311, 316 (7th Cir, 1992); and *United States v. Cincotta*, 689 F.2d 238, 241–242 (1st Cir., 1982).

[35] See, for instance, *United States* v. *Potter*, 463 F.3d 9, 25 (1st Cir. 2006); and *United States v. Automated Medical Laboratories*, 770 F.2d 399 (4th Cir. 1985).

[36] See, for instance, *Cox v. Adm'r U.S. Steel & Carnegie*, 17 F.3d 1386, 1404 (11th Cir. 1994); *United States v. Automated Med. Labs., Inc.*, 770 F.2d 399, 407 (4th Cir.1985).

[37] See, for instance, *Old Monastery Company v. United States*, 147 F.2d, 905 (4th Cir.), cert. denied, 326 U.S. 734, 66 S. Ct. 44, 90 L. Ed. 437 (1945); *United States v. Automated Medical Laboratories*, 110 F.2d 399 (4th Cir. 1985): ". . . whether the agent's actions ultimately redounded to the benefit of the corporation is less significant than whether the agent acted with the intent to benefit the corporation. The basic purpose of requiring that an agent have acted with the intent to benefit the corporation." See also, *Standard Oil Co. v. United States*, 307 F.2d 120, 128–129 (5th Cir. 1962): "The act is no less the principal's if from such intended conduct either no benefit accrues, a benefit is undiscernible, or . . . the result turns

the interpretation of the court, only if the employee's conduct was "inimical to the interests of the corporation" or had been undertaken solely to advance the interests of the employee or of another party other than the corporation, then the corporation might not be subject to criminal liability.[38]

The new practice of imputing employees' actions and mental fault to their employing corporations led to the development of two approaches concerning which employees should be considered for such imputation.[39] One school of thought imputes the actions and the mind-set of *every* corporate employee at any level in the corporate hierarchy to the employing corporation.[40] Another school of thought restricts the identity of those employees whose actions and mind-set might be imputed to the

---

out to be adverse." See, for instance, *United States v. Sun-Diamond Growers of California*, 138 F.3d 961, 969–970 (D.C. Cir. 1998). In this case the corporation argued that its vice-president's crime should not be imputed to it because the conduct itself was meant to defraud the corporation, and in fact, it actually did. Therefore, this behavior should not be treated as aimed at benefiting the corporation. The Court rejected this argument, stating that the fact that the vice-president used the corporation's money to illegally support a political campaign does not necessarily rule out the conclusion that the vice-president was acting "with an intent (however befuddled) to further the interests of his employer."

[38] See *Automated Medical Laboratories supra* note 37.

[39] See, for instance, Khanna, "Corporate Liability Standards: When Should Corporations be Held Criminally Liable?," p. 1247.

[40] See, for instance, *Hilton Hotels Corp. supra* note 22. In which the court ruled that a corporation could be held liable under the Sherman Act for actions undertaken by a purchasing agent. This approach was sometimes taken to imply that corporations may be held criminally liable even if the required knowledge or intent was not possessed by a single employee; instead, the *collective knowledge* of several employees may be aggregated to reflect the corporate knowledge and intent. See, for instance, *United States v. T.I.M.E.-D.C., Inc.*, 381 F. Supp. 730, 738 (W.D. Va. 1974). For a discussion of the "collective knowledge" theory, which is sometimes referred to as the "aggregated knowledge," see Walsh and Pyrich, "Corporate Compliance Programs as a Defense to Criminal Liability: Can a Corporation Save its Soul?," p. 625; Colvin, "Corporate Personality and Criminal Liability," pp. 18–23; Eliezer Lederman, "Criminal Law, Perpetrator and Corporation: Rethinking a Complex Triangle," *Journal of Criminal Law and Criminology* 76(2) (1985), p. 290; Stacey Newmann Vu, "Corporate Criminal Liability: Patchwork Verdicts and the Problem of Locating a Guilty Agent," *Columbia Law Review* 104 (2004), pp. 473–475; Tigar, "It Does the Crime but Not the Time: Corporate Criminal Liability in Federal Law," p. 222; Khanna, "Corporate Liability Standards: When Should Corporations be Held Criminally Liable?," p. 1247.

corporation only to *key personnel* encompassing the "directing mind" of the corporation.[41]

In this context, the common law *respondeat superior* doctrine was expanded in U.S. Federal Law to the criminal law context.[42] Consequently, civil and criminal types of corporate liability became very close to each other. Under both frameworks, corporations are held liable for offenses committed as a result of their employees' misconduct within the scope of their employment.[43] The remaining difference is that only the imposition of criminal liability requires the prosecution to prove that employee actions were taken, at least in part, with the motive to benefit the corporation.[44]

---

[41] This school is often referred to as "the doctrine of identification," the theory of "inner circle," or the theory of "primary organ." According to this school, corporate criminal liability should not rely on the guilty minds of corporate servants that are "nothing more than hands to do the work and cannot be said to represent the mind or will" of the corporation. Instead, only the state of mind of those individuals at the management level within the organization "who represent the directing mind and will of the company and control what it does" should be imputed to the corporation. See *H.L. Bolton (Engineering) Co. v. T.J. Graham & Sons, Ltd.*, [1957] 1 Q.B. 159, 172 (C.A. 1956). See also, *People v. Canadian Fur Trappers' Corp.*, 161 N.E. 455 (N.Y. 1928); *Tesco Supermarkets* see *supra* note 31; Hefendehl, "Corporate Criminal Liability: Model Penal Code Section 2.07 and the Development in Western Legal Systems," p. 291; Walsh and Pyrich, "Corporate Compliance Programs as a Defense to Criminal Liability: Can a Corporation Save its Soul?," p. 639; Colvin, "Corporate Personality and Criminal Liability," pp. 8–15; Howard M. Friedman, "Some Reflections on the Corporation as Criminal Defendant," *Notre Dame Lawyer* 55 (1979), p. 180.

[42] See, for instance, Paul McNulty, Deputy Attorney General, "Memorandum for Heads of Department Components United States Attorneys: Principles of Federal Prosecution of Business Organizations," U.S. Department of Justice, Office of the Deputy Attorney General (December 12, 2006), p. 2, where the adoption of the *respondeat superior* has been explicitly acknowledged: "Corporations are 'legal persons,' capable of suing and being sued, and capable of committing crimes. Under the doctrine of respondeat superior, a corporation may be held criminally liable for the illegal acts of its directors, officers, employees, and agents." See also, Brickey, "Corporate Criminal Accountability: A Brief History and an Observation," p. 415. See also, Pitt and Groskaufmanis, "Minimizing Corporate Civil and Criminal Liability: A Second Look at Corporate Codes of Conduct," p. 1570.

[43] See *Egan v. United States Union Electric Co. of Missouri*, 137 F. 2d 369, 379 (8th Cir. 1943): "there is no longer any distinction in essence between the civil and criminal liability of corporations, based upon the element of intent or wrongful purpose."

[44] See also, *Sun-Diamond Growers of California supra* note 37, pp. 969–970: "In a civil case, there may be no need to show that the agent acted to further the principal's interests – a showing of 'apparent authority' is often

5.3 THE IMPACT OF CORPORATE PROACTIVE COMPLIANCE EFFORTS ON CORPORATE LIABILITY

5.3.1 The Traditional Approach: Corporate Strict Liability

As mentioned above, one central consideration that supported the use of corporate liability both in civil and in criminal ecologies was corporations' aptitude to control their employees.[45] As the argument goes, when corporations are held liable for their employees' misbehavior they are encouraged to adopt meaningful internal controls to monitor their employees. If so, *should a corporation that acted to prevent misconduct be held liable for its errant employee's misconduct?*

This question was answered in a series of U.S. court decisions in which the court established that the efforts of corporations to prevent employees' misbehavior do not shield them from liability for violations that took place in spite of such efforts. A notable example, advanced in the introduction to this book, is the 1939 case *Dollar S.S. Co. v. United States* in which the appellant's employee was observed dumping waste from the appellant's ship while anchored in harbor.[46] Criminal charges were brought against the appellant. As part of its defense, the appellant demonstrated that it undertook extensive efforts to prevent the particular violation and that the violation occurred while none of the appellant's senior officers was aware of it.[47] Interestingly, the court accepted the appellant's factual arguments and announced that "the appellant took precautions to the end that the law be not violated. . . . we assume that the appellant was reasonably careful that the statute be not violated, and did not intend to violate it."[48] Yet the

---

enough." The court referred to the *American Society of Mechanical Engineers v. Hydrolevel Corp.*, 456 U.S. 556, 573–574, 102 S.Ct. 1935, 1946–1947, 72 L.Ed.2d 330 (1982).

[45] See *supra* note 12 with respect to corporate civil liability and *supra* note 23 with respect to corporate criminal liability.

[46] 101 F.2d 638 (9th Cir. 1939).

[47] See *ibid.*, pp. 638–639: "There was testimony on behalf of the claimant that orders had been issued by the company against throwing of refuse from the ship while in harbor; that signs were placed in conspicuous places written in English and Chinese, warning employees not to throw things overboard; that locks were placed upon the slop chutes to prevent their use while in harbor; that the officers of the ship had no knowledge of violation of the law or their orders in this respect and in this instance."

[48] See *ibid.*

court refused to accept these genuine efforts as a defense from liability and convicted the appellant stating that:[49]

> *The appellant failed to prevent the commission of the forbidden act.* Though apparently unintentional there nevertheless was a technical violation of the Act and for this the minimum fine was imposed. *This 'resulting liability is like many others imposed upon an individual, regardless of his personal fault. Having committed his ship to the seas, an owner takes the risk of much which he cannot easily control.'* Any other construction would change the statute from one of prohibition to that requiring merely due care.

In the same vein, in the *Hilton Hotels Corporation* case, the court rejected the corporation's defense argument that relied on the "*ultra vires*" doctrines.[50] In this case, criminal charges were brought against the *Hilton Corporation* for its purchasing agent's participation in an illegal refusal to deal (boycott) agreement. The appellant presented convincing evidence that the agent's actions were in contradiction to corporate policy and that explicit instructions were given to the agent concerning this matter on two different occasions. Notwithstanding, the court rejected the appellant's arguments and ruled that corporations may be criminally liable for their employee's criminal conduct within the scope of their employment, "even though contrary to general corporate policy and express instructions to the agent."[51] The court established with this ruling that the existence of specific policy statements and instructions to employees cannot, by themselves, constitute a defense from corporate liability.[52] Subsequent court decisions have taken an even harder line on the matter and prevented corporations from presenting any evidence regarding internal controls that were held in place at the time the misconduct took place.[53]

---

49 *Ibid.* (emphasis added).

50 See *Hilton Hotels Corp. supra* note 22. See also, Perry and Dakin, "Compliance Programs and Criminal Law," 22.1–22.16.

51 See *ibid.*, para. 30. See also, *United States v. American Radiator & Standard Sanitary Corp.*, 433 F.2d 174, (3rd Cir. 1970), pp. 204–205; *Standard Oil Co, supra* note 37, pp. 127–128; *United States v. Armour & Co.*, 168 F.2d 342 (3rd Cir. 1947), pp. 343–344; *Egan v. United States*, 137 F.2d 369 (8th Cir. 1943).

52 See *Hilton Hotels Corp. supra* note 22, p. 1007: "appellant could not gain exculpation by issuing general instructions without undertaking to enforce those instructions by means commensurate with the obvious risks."

53 See, for instance, *United States v. Twentieth Century Fox Film Corporation and Leila J. Goldstein*, 882 F.2d 656 (2nd Cir. 1989), in which the Court of Appeals upheld the District Court's decision to refuse evidence regarding the corporate compliance program. The court stated that: "[a] compliance program, however extensive, does not immunize the corporation from liability when its employees,

To summarize, the traditional approach to corporate liability hinges on the presumption that holding corporations vicariously liable for their employees' misdeeds "creates a strong incentive for vigilance by those in a position to guard substantially against the evil to be prevented."[54] Hence, under this approach corporations' internal enforcement efforts – by themselves – do not shield corporations from liability.[55] Under this approach, such efforts were deemed "legally irrelevant" to the liability imposed upon corporations.[56]

5.3.2 Perception Transformation: The Rise of Duty-Based Corporate Liability Regimes

The traditional approach concerning corporate internal enforcement efforts has gone through a sea of change in the modern era. The traditional *strict liability* approach described above has been replaced by various *duty-based liability* regimes – all of which recognize corporations' internal enforcement efforts as a relevant determinant of corporate liability. Under contemporary regimes the adoption of compliance management systems may, in certain circumstances, *shield* corporations from civil and criminal liability. In other instances, the adoption of such systems may

---

acting within the scope of their authority, fail to comply with the law and the consent decree." Rulings in the same spirit were issued by the court in numerous subsequent cases, many of which involved antitrust crimes committed by employees against explicit corporate policy and explicit instructions, and nevertheless were imputed to their employing corporations. See, for instance, *United States v. Harry L. Young & Sons, Inc.*, 464 F.2d 1295, 1297 (10th Cir. 1972); *United States v. Cadillac Overall Supply Co.*, 568 F.2d 1078, 1090 (5th Cir. 1978); *United States v. Basic Const. Co.*, 711 F.2d 570, 573, 12 Fed. R. Evid. Serv. 1178 (4th Cir. 1983); *City of Vernon v. Southern California Edison Co.*, 955 F.2d 1361, 1396 (9th Cir. 1992). See also, Tigar, "It Does the Crime but Not the Time: Corporate Criminal Liability in Federal Law," p. 221; Perry and Dakin, "Compliance Programs and Criminal Law," p. 22.2; Weissmann and Newman, "Rethinking Criminal Corporate Liability," pp. 422–423.

[54] See *Pacific Mut. Life Ins. Co. v. Haslip.* 499 U.S. 1, 111 S. Ct. 1032, 1041, 113 L. Ed. 2d 1 (1991).

[55] See Pitt and Groskaufmanis, "Minimizing Corporate Civil and Criminal Liability: A Second Look at Corporate Codes of Conduct," p. 1560.

[56] See John H. Shenefield and Richard J. Favretto, "Compliance Programs as Viewed from the Antitrust Division," *Antitrust Law Journal* 48 (1979), p. 79; Robert E. Bloch, "Compliance Programs and Criminal Antitrust Litigation: A Prosecutor's Perspective," *Antitrust Law Journal* 57 (1988), p. 226. See also, Groskaufmanis, "Impact of Corporate Compliance Outside the Criminal Process," p. 24.52; Pitt and Groskaufmanis, "Minimizing Corporate Civil and Criminal Liability: A Second Look at Corporate Codes of Conduct," p. 1645.

substantially *mitigate the penalties* imposed upon corporations for misconduct that took place while such systems were held in place. Interestingly, the dramatic change in U.S. corporate liability policies was not a product of a centrally planned legal reform. Instead, it has evolved through several parallel avenues and dressed in different legal garments. Before exploring the actual avenues of policy changes, it is worthwhile to consider some of the major theoretical arguments made by legal scholars with respect to such policy changes.

The departure from a strict liability approach to a duty-based one is supported by many legal thinkers. Laufer (1996), Weissmann (2007), and Weissmann and Newman (2007), for instance, provide theoretical support for the establishment of negligence-based corporate liability through the recognition of a "due diligence defense."[57] According to these studies, shielding corporations that engage in internal enforcement activities from corporate liability reinforces corporations' incentives to proactively ensure compliance among their employees. In addition, it allows enforcement agencies to focus their scarce prosecutorial resources on the most recalcitrant corporations.[58] A closely related study by Pitt and Groskaufmanis (1990) proposes a "Modified Due Diligence Standard." According to this standard, a legal defense applies only if a "'high managerial agent' has exercised due diligence in his or her supervisory efforts."[59] A somewhat more moderate approach is offered by Huff (1996) in which the existence of compliance management systems should not be completely ignored, but at the same time, should not automatically provide an affirmative defense for corporations. Instead, the jury should consider the existence of compliance management systems along with all other relevant evidence and

---

[57] See William S. Laufer, "Integrity, Diligence, and the Limits of Good Corporate Citizenship," *American Business Law Journal* 34(2) (1996), 157–182; Weissmann and Newman, "Rethinking Criminal Corporate Liability," 411–451; Andrew Weissmann, "A New Approach to Corporate Criminal Liability," *American Criminal Law Review* 44 (2007), 1319–1342.

[58] See Laufer, "Integrity, Diligence, and the Limits of Good Corporate Citizenship," p. 164: "In virtually all jurisdictions, prosecutors will more likely decline to prosecute organizations that have compliance programs. The reasons for declination include rewarding firms for compliance, as well as focusing scarce prosecutorial resources on the most abusive firms." See also, Weissmann and Newman, "Rethinking Criminal Corporate Liability," p. 451: ". . . a system that ties criminal liability to the lack of an effective compliance program will do what the practical limitations on a prosecutor's time and resources could never permit: create greater incentives for boardrooms around the country to devise, implement, and monitor compliance measures."

[59] See Pitt and Groskaufmanis, "Minimizing Corporate Civil and Criminal Liability: A Second Look at Corporate Codes of Conduct," p. 1647.

release corporations from liability when appropriate only after analyzing the "totality of the circumstances."[60]

The legal scholarly literature embracing the emerging duty-based approach supports the acknowledgement of compliance management systems as a liability determinant based on several key arguments; first, the "*discouragement effect*" of strict liability regimes. Commentators point out that the adoption of a compliance management system may involve substantial costs and therefore if no tangible benefits result for companies that adopt such systems, then not many corporations are likely to be encouraged to do so.[61] Moreover, it has been argued that a "[r]igid adherence to principles of vicarious liability enshrouds even the best compliance program with a sense of futility."[62] As such, a strict corporate liability regime may discourage corporations from adopting effective compliance measures, and thereby may undermine the central objective of the *respondeat superior* doctrine, being the "effective supervision of employees."[63] To support such views, scholars refer to the fact that the promulgation of the Organizational Sentencing Guidelines (OSG) has, in fact, induced corporations to adopt compliance management systems.[64] Another line of argument focuses on the "*illegitimacy of sanctioning*" self-enforcing corporations. As the argument goes, although corporations usually possess the ability to have a substantial impact on their individual employees' behavior, they are not capable of completely controlling "every thought and deed."[65] In actuality, even when a most effective compliance management system is put in place, "rogue" individual employees may still engage in illegal activities. Hence, once a corporation has adopted an effective compliance management system, none of the legitimate concerns animating

---

[60] See Huff, "The Role of Corporate Compliance Programs in Determining Corporate Criminal Liability: A Suggested Approach," p. 1298. As the argument goes, ". . . a legal rule which considers compliance programs at trial – before conviction – would arguably create an even more powerful incentive for self-policing than the incentive provided by the Guidelines alone" *ibid.*, p. 1282.

[61] See Pitt and Groskaufmanis, "Minimizing Corporate Civil and Criminal Liability: A Second Look at Corporate Codes of Conduct," p. 1560.

[62] See *ibid.*, p. 1645.

[63] See, for instance, Weissmann and Newman, "Rethinking Criminal Corporate Liability," 411–451; Weissmann, "A New Approach to Corporate Criminal Liability," 1319–1342; Pitt and Groskaufmanis, "Minimizing Corporate Civil and Criminal Liability: A Second Look at Corporate Codes of Conduct," 1559–1654.

[64] See, for instance, Kim, "Gatekeepers Inside Out," p. 447. For a detailed discussion of the OSG see Section 5.7.

[65] See Walsh and Pyrich, "Corporate Compliance Programs as a Defense to Criminal Liability: Can a Corporation Save its Soul?," pp. 644–645.

criminal corporate liability are implicated, whereby the sanctioning of such corporations will not achieve any deterrence or retribution goals. More particularly, when corporations have already exerted due efforts to ensure compliance and to prevent misconduct by their employees, it would be "questionable whether the potential for criminal sanctions will have any significant additional effects."[66] Moreover, commentators argue that while corporate vicarious liability may promote the compensatory goals of civil liability, such a liability framework may not coincide with the deterrence and retribution goals of criminal law, which normally require a mental fault by the actor.[67] Legal scholars argue that corporations that adopt effective policies to deter and detect their employees' misconduct do not fulfill the *mens rea* requirement for criminal conviction.[68] Some commentators compare the conviction of corporations that have taken all practical measures to prevent misconduct to the conviction of mentally ill defendants and argue that both are similarly ineffective.[69]

Beside the substantial acknowledgement of compliance management systems as liability determinants, legal scholars address the admissibility of internal-enforcement-related evidence as well as the allocation of the burden-of-proof. Huff (1996), for instance, proposes the "Relevant Factor Approach." According to this approach "when appropriate, the court should admit into evidence the existence of an effective corporate compliance program on the issue of whether to hold the corporation vicariously liable for the actions of its employees. The jury should consider this evidence along with all other relevant evidence in determining whether to impute liability to the corporation."[70] Huff further suggests that ". . . once the defendant corporation has presented to the jury its evidence regarding the effectiveness of the compliance program, the government can rebut this evidence by showing that the compliance program is not

---

[66] See *ibid.*, pp. 644–645. See also, Huff, "The Role of Corporate Compliance Programs in Determining Corporate Criminal Liability: A Suggested Approach," p. 1297; Weissmann and Newman, "Rethinking Criminal Corporate Liability," p. 412; Walsh and Pyrich, "Corporate Compliance Programs as a Defense to Criminal Liability: Can a Corporation Save its Soul?," 605–689.

[67] See Weissmann and Newman, "Rethinking Criminal Corporate Liability," p. 412.

[68] See *ibid.*; see also, Walsh and Pyrich, "Corporate Compliance Programs as a Defense to Criminal Liability: Can a Corporation Save its Soul?," p. 640.

[69] See *ibid.*, p. 640; Cyrus C. Y. Chu and Yingyi Qian, "Vicarious Liability Under A Negligence Rule," *International Review of Law And Economics* 15(3) (1995), 305–322.

[70] See Huff, "The Role of Corporate Compliance Programs in Determining Corporate Criminal Liability: A Suggested Approach," p. 1282.

effective or not comprehensive or that the program was not followed in the instant case."[71] Alternatively, Weissmann and Newman (2007) propose a liability rule of corporate liability under which the prosecution "should bear the burden of establishing as an additional criminal element that the corporation failed to have reasonable policies and procedures to prevent the employee's conduct." According to this study, such a policy would "incentivize boardrooms around the country to devise, implement, and monitor compliance measures."[72] And finally, the study by Goldsmith and King (1997) supports the establishment of evidentiary privileges for compliance-related corporate materials. This approach implies that corporate materials produced as part of a corporate compliance management system should not be held against the corporation in legal proceedings.[73]

Having presented the main ideological arguments advanced by the legal literature favoring the departure from strict liability to a duty-based liability approach, the next sections present various avenues of reform through which compliance management systems have gained significant importance in determining corporate civil and criminal liability. As shown below, some of these reforms have commenced through modern judgments departing from established law, while others were promulgated independently by regulatory agencies in specific fields of law.

5.4 CIVIL LIABILITY (1): COMPLIANCE MANAGEMENT SYSTEMS AS A '*SHIELD*' FROM CIVIL LIABILITY

This section presents two notable fields of law, *sexual harassment* violations and *punitive damages*, in which corporate proactive compliance

---

[71] See *ibid.*, pp. 1285–1286.

[72] See Weissmann and Newman, "Rethinking Criminal Corporate Liability," p. 411. The authors argue that "[l]imiting corporate liability to those corporations that have not taken all reasonable measures to prevent criminality by their employees will spur corporate action in precisely the area that is of most interest to the government and public." See also, *ibid.*, p. 414: ". . . by placing the burden on the government to prove that a company's program was inadequate as a prerequisite to criminal corporate liability, this reform will provide a systemic check on prosecutors who seek to institute such actions in the future, helping to ensure that they do so only where the company should be justifiably responsible for the criminal conduct of its employees."

[73] See Michael Goldsmith and Chad W. King, "Policing Corporate Crime: The Dilemma of Internal Compliance Programs," *Vanderbilt Law Review* 50 (1997), 1–47.

efforts were acknowledged by modern U.S. law as *shielding* corporations from corporate civil liability.

5.4.1 Sexual Harassment Violations

The perception transformation concerning the role of corporate proactive compliance enforcement efforts in determining corporate liability is clearly evident in the courts' rulings against sexual harassment violations. A clear deviation from the traditional strict liability approach initially appeared in the companion cases of *Faragher v. City of Boca Raton*[74] and *Burlington Industries Inc. v. Ellerth.*[75] Both of these cases involved violations of sexual harassment in the workplace by supervisors against Title VII of the Civil Rights Act of 1964. In these cases the U.S. Supreme Court has established that the implementation of internal enforcement measures may, under certain circumstances, shield employers from civil liability for sexual harassment conducted by their employees.[76] For instance, the plaintiff Faragher sued the City of Boca Raton and her supervisors alleging that they created a sexually hostile atmosphere at work for the plaintiff and other female lifeguards which included "offensive touching," as well as the use of "lewd remarks" and "offensive terms." In response to these allegations the City of Boca Raton argued that it should not be held liable for the supervisors' conduct because at the relevant time it had in place a compliance management system that was intended to prevent sexual harassment by its employees. The court held that "an employer is vicariously liable for actionable discrimination caused by a supervisor, but subject to an *affirmative defense* looking to the *reasonableness of the employer's conduct* as well as that of a plaintiff victim."[77] The court provided reasoning for its deviation from the traditional vicarious liability approach by stating that the established responsibility of employers to their employees' actions must be accommodated with the objective of encouraging employers to act in order to prevent sexual harassment in their workplaces. In the court's words:[78]

---

[74] 524 U.S. 775, 118 S. Ct. 2275, 141 L. Ed. 2d 662, 157 A.L.R. Fed 663 (1998).

[75] 524 U.S. 742, 118 S. Ct. 2257, 141 L. Ed. 2d 633, 170 A.L.R. Fed 677 (1998).

[76] See, for instance, Melinda Burrows, "The Seven Elements of an Effective Compliance and Ethics Program," *The Practical Lawyer* February (2006), p. 22.

[77] See *Faragher supra* note 74, p. 780 (emphasis added).

[78] See *Faragher supra* note 74, pp. 807–808 (emphasis added). See also, *Burlington Industries Inc. supra* note 75, pp. 764–765. See also, Kathleen A. Lieder and Christopher P. Mazzoli, "Ellerth and Faragher: Applying the Supreme Court's "Delphic Pronouncements" on Employers' Vicarious Liability for Sexual

> An employer is subject to vicarious liability to a victimized employee for an actionable hostile environment created by a supervisor with immediate (or successively higher) authority over the employee. When no tangible employment action is taken [such as firing and demotion], a defending employer may raise an *affirmative defense* to liability or damages . . . The defense comprises two necessary elements: *(a) that the employer exercised reasonable care to prevent and correct promptly any sexually harassing behavior*, and *(b) that the plaintiff employee unreasonably failed to take advantage of any preventive or corrective opportunities provided by the employer or to avoid harm otherwise.*

The conciliatory approach held in the *Faragher* and the *Burlington* cases has been followed by the court in subsequent judgments.[79] As for the first requirement, the court has further clarified that a *reasonable care* by employers entails substantive and meaningful actions, rather than formalistic ones. In *Fierro v. Saks Fifth Avenue*,[80] for instance, the court has clarified that the enactment of an anti-harassment internal policy that includes a complaint procedure is an important but insufficient action for the defense to hold. In *Lancaster v. Sheffler Enterprises*, the court clarified that "[s]imply forcing all new employees to sign a policy does not constitute '*reasonable care*.' The employer must take reasonable steps in preventing, correcting, and enforcing the policy. Reasonableness requires more than issuing a policy.[81] In the same vein, in *EEOC v. V & J Foods Inc.*,[82] the court rejected the anti-harassment policy of the corporation as meeting the "reasonable care" requirement for being written in a way that was beyond the competence of the teenage workers of the corporation. The specific actions that may satisfy the "reasonableness requirement" should be derived from the specific circumstances surrounding the employment relationship.[83]

To summarize, the new approach adopted by the U.S. court recognizes a "reasonable care" defense, which implies that reasonable corporate efforts to prevent sexual harassment by their employees may, under certain circumstances, constitute an affirmative defense from civil corporate

---

Harassment," *Michigan Bar Journal* 78 (1999), 432–434; Weissmann and Newman, "Rethinking Criminal Corporate Liability," pp. 433–437; Groskaufmanis, "Impact of Corporate Compliance Outside the Criminal Process," p. 24.26.

79 See, for instance, *Montero v. AGCO Corp.*, 19 F. Supp. 2d 1143, 1146 (E.D. Cal 1998), judgment aff'd, 192 F.3d 856 (9th Cir. 1999); *Corcoran v. Shoney Colonial, Inc.*, 24 F. Supp. 2d 601 (W.D. Va. 1998).

80 13 F Sup. 2d 481, 491 (SD NY, 1998).

81 19 F Sup. 2d 1000, 1003 (W.D. Mo. 1998).

82 507 F.3d 575 (7th Cir. 2007).

83 See *Faragher supra* note 74, p. 765. See also, *Wilson v. Tulsa Junior College*, 164 F.3d 534, 541–542 (10th Cir. 1998).

liability. This approach clearly deviates from the traditional corporate strict liability approach described in Section 5.3.1 above.

5.4.2 Punitive Damages

The policy under which the U.S. Supreme Court imposes punitive damages provides another striking example for the conceptual change concerning the role of corporate internal enforcement efforts in determining corporate liability.[84] For instance, in *P & E Boat Rentals Inc. v. Ennia General Insurance Co. Inc.*,[85] which involved a tragic collision between two vessels on the Mississippi River, the Court of Appeals held that a corporation that has exerted reasonable efforts in preventing its employees' misbehavior should not be subject to punitive damages. Accordingly, the Court of Appeals reversed the District Court's decision, which originally included an award of $16 million in punitive damages and stated as follows:[86]

> . . . punitive damages may not be imposed against a corporation when one or more of its employees decides on his own to engage in malicious or outrageous conduct. In such a case, the corporation itself cannot be considered the wrongdoer. *If the corporation has formulated policies and directed its employees properly, no purpose would be served by imposing punitive damages against it except to increase the amount of the judgment.*

A similar approach was upheld in *Kolstad v. American Dental Association*,[87] which involved a violation of Title VII of the Civil Rights Act of 1964. In this case *Kolstad* filed a civil rights action against the respondent, arguing that its decision to promote a man instead of promoting her was an act of gender discrimination. The court has acquiescently recognized that

---

[84] Punitive damages are damages imposed on the defendant in civil proceedings beyond the actual losses suffered by the victim due to the defendants' wrongful act. See, for instance, Polinsky, "Punitive Damages: An Economic Analysis," p. 869. Such damages are aimed at punishing the defendant for his/her outrageous conduct as well as deterring similar conduct in the future. See, for instance, The American Law Institute, *Restatement of Law (Second), Torts* (Philadelphia, PA: American Law Institute Publishers, 1979), §908. See also, Robert D. Cooter, "Punitive Damages for Deterrence: When and How Much," *Alabama Law Review* 40 (1988), p. 1146; Polinsky, "Punitive Damages: An Economic Analysis," p. 869; Pitt and Groskaufmanis, "Minimizing Corporate Civil and Criminal Liability: A Second Look at Corporate Codes of Conduct," p. 1566.

[85] 872 F.2d 642 (5th Cir. 1989).

[86] *Ibid.*, p. 652 (emphasis added).

[87] 527 U.S. 526 (1999), 119 S. Ct. 2118, 144 L Ed. 2d 494 (1999).

according to established law "even an employer who made every *good faith effort* to comply with Title VII would be held liable for the discriminatory acts of agents acting in a 'managerial capacity.'"[88] Yet, the court referred to the rationale advanced in *Faragher* and *Burlington*,[89] and stated that the imposition of punitive damages upon employers who acted to educate their employees on Title VII's prohibitions would reduce the incentive for such employers to implement anti-discrimination programs and would in fact contradict Title VII's prophylactic purposes.[90] Similarly to the approach upheld by courts with respect to sexual harassment violations, the *Kolstad* judgment requires "*good faith efforts*," rather than "*cheap talk*," for the defense to hold. In the same vein, in *Deffenbaugh-Williams v. Wal-Mart*, for instance, the court refused to accept the mere encouragement of employees with grievances to contact higher management as sufficient efforts that may constitute a defense from punitive damages.[91] Likewise in *EEOC v. Wal-Mart*, the court refused to accept the mere existence of a written policy as good faith efforts.[92] In *Copley v. Bax Global*,[93] the court has clarified that "[f]or the good faith exception to apply, there must be a nondiscrimination policy both in words and in practice."[94]

Therefore, under modern U.S. Law, the adoption of a meaningful compliance management system may shield corporations from punitive damages.[95]

---

88 *Ibid.*

89 See *supra* notes 74 and 75.

90 See *Kolstad supra* note 87, p. 652.

91 188 F.3d 278 (5th Cir. 1999).

92 187 F.3d 1241 (10th Cir. 1999): "Wal-Mart certainly had a written policy against discrimination, but that alone is not enough. Our review of the record leaves us unconvinced that Wal-Mart made a good faith effort to educate its employees about the ADA's prohibitions." See also, *Lowery v. Circuit City Stores, Inc.*, 206 F.3d 431, 446 (4th Cir. 2000): "While an employer's institution of a written policy against race discrimination may go a long way toward dispelling any claim about the employer's reckless or malicious state of mind . . . such a policy is not automatically a bar to the imposition of sanctions." See also, *Deters v. Equifax Credit Info. Serv., Inc.*, 202 F.3d 1262, 1271 (10th Cir. 2000).

93 97 F. Supp. 2d 1164 (S.D. Fla. 2000).

94 *Ibid.*, p. 1169.

95 For further discussion of corporate exposure to punitive damages see Groskaufmanis, "Impact of Corporate Compliance Outside the Criminal Process," p. 24.18; Weissmann and Newman, "Rethinking Criminal Corporate Liability," pp. 437–439.

5.5 CIVIL LIABILITY (2): COMPLIANCE MANAGEMENT SYSTEMS AS A '*MITIGATING FACTOR*' OF CIVIL PENALTIES

This section presents various modern U.S. Federal policies under which the adoption of compliance management systems by corporations may comprise a *mitigating factor* of civil penalties, rather than a shield from liability.

5.5.1 Environmental Protection Agency (EPA) Audit Policy

On December 22, 1995, the Environmental Protection Agency (EPA) issued its policy "*Incentives for Self Policing: Discovery, Disclosure, Correction, and Prevention of Violations*".[96] This policy, which was slightly revised and reintroduced on April 11, 2000,[97] has been inspired by some policy developments that have taken place in the criminal context (see Section 5.7 below) and promulgated by the EPA with the aim of encouraging corporate compliance with federal environmental laws. The EPA's investigation conducted prior to the promulgation of the audit policy has shown that the strict approach previously applied has led to a massive adoption of voluntary environmental auditing systems by corporations wishing to minimize their expected penalties.[98] In order to reinforce cor-

---

[96] See Environmental Protection Agency (EPA), "Incentives for Self Policing: Discovery, Disclosure, Correction, and Prevention of Violations," *Fed. Reg.* 60 (1995), 66706, available at: http://www.epa.gov/compliance/resources/policies/incentives/auditing/finalpolstate.pdf.

[97] See Environmental Protection Agency (EPA), "Incentives for Self Policing: Discovery, Disclosure, Correction, and Prevention of Violations," *Fed. Reg.* 65 (2000), 19618, available at: http://www.epa.gov/compliance/resources/policies/civil/rcra/revfinaudpol-fr.pdf (hereinafter "audit policy"). For critiques of the audit policy and its ramifications see Virginia Morton Creighton, "Colorado's Environmental Audit Privilege Statute: Striking the Appropriate Balance," *University of Colorado Law Review* 67 (1996), 443–476; Pfaff and Sanchirico, "Big Field, Small Potatoes: An Empirical Assessment of EPA's Self-Audit Policy," 415–432.

[98] The audit policy refers to a 1995 survey conducted by Price Waterhouse LLP (contained in the Docket as document VIII–A–76), according to which: "more than 90% of corporate respondents who conduct audits identified one of the reasons for doing so as the desire to find and correct violations before government inspectors discover them." See also, Creighton, "Colorado's Environmental Audit Privilege Statute: Striking the Appropriate Balance," p. 443: "With the increase on environmental liability, both civil and criminal, many companies have turned to environmental audits as a means of monitoring their own regulated activities."

porations' incentives to adopt such voluntary systems, the EPA decided to establish a new policy, according to which corporations that exerted meaningful compliance efforts would be rewarded by liability mitigation when a violation occurs in spite of such efforts.[99] Accordingly, the audit policy provides corporations with three sets of incentives for self-policing, each of which alleviates corporations' exposure to liability for noncompliance. These incentives are surveyed below.

5.5.1.1 Incentive I: elimination/mitigation of gravity-based penalties

As a general policy, civil penalties for federal environmental violations are composed of two components: (i) the *economic component*, which captures the economic benefits extracted by violators due to the violation; and (ii) the *gravity component*, which represents the punitive portion of the civil sanction that is imposed beyond the economic benefit gained due to the violation to "reflect the egregiousness of the violator's behavior."[100] The audit policy offers a complete *elimination* of the gravity-based penalties for corporations that satisfy all nine conditions described below. However, those corporations that meet all the conditions below except for the first condition (*i.e.*, systematic disclosure) are offered a *75% mitigation* of gravity-based penalties.[101]

(i) ***Systematic discovery*** – The violation must have been discovered through an "environmental audit" or a "compliance management system" held in place by the corporation.[102] This requirement

---

[99] See audit policy *supra* note 97, p. 19619: ". . . because government resources are limited, universal compliance cannot be achieved without active efforts by the regulated community to police themselves. More than half of the respondents to the same 1995 Price Waterhouse survey said that they would expand environmental auditing in exchange for reduced penalties for violations discovered and corrected."

[100] See audit policy *supra* note 97, p. 19620. For a general overview of the structure of civil penalties for environmental violations see Environmental Protection Agency (EPA), "Calculation of the Economic Benefit of Noncompliance in EPA's Civil Penalty Enforcement Cases," *Fed. Reg.* 64 (June 18, 1999), 32948, available at: http://www.epa.gov/compliance/resources/policies/federalfacilities/enforcement/cleanup/econben20.pdf.

[101] See audit policy *supra* note 97, §II.C.1–2. The nine conditions are presented in Section II.D of the audit policy; commentary on these conditions is included in Section I.E of the audit policy.

[102] See audit policy *supra* note 97, §II.B, p. 19625. The audit policy defines an "Environmental Audit" as "a systematic, documented, periodic and objective review by regulated entities of facility operations and practices related to meeting environmental requirements" and a "Compliance Management System"

entails that the report must be accompanied with complete documentation concerning the violation and the compliance system held by the corporation.

(ii) ***Voluntary discovery*** – The violation was discovered voluntarily and not through a legally required monitoring, sampling, or auditing procedure.

(iii) ***Prompt disclosure*** – The incumbent corporation must fully disclose the violation in writing within 21 days of discovery.

(iv) ***Independent discovery and disclosure*** – The violation must be disclosed before the EPA discovers the violation through its own investigation or based on third-party complaints or suits.

(v) ***Correction and remediation*** – The incumbent corporation must correct the violation within 60 days of discovery and take appropriate measures to remediate the harm caused by the violation.

(vi) ***Prevent recurrence*** – The incumbent corporation agrees in writing to take appropriate measures to prevent the recurrence of the violation.

(vii) ***No repeat violations*** – Repeated violations are ineligible for the incentives offered by the audit policy.[103]

(viii) ***Excluded types of violations*** – Some categories of environmental violations are excluded from the benefits offered by the audit policy, including violations that result in serious actual harm, those that may have presented imminent and substantial endangerment, and those that violate the specific terms of an administrative or judicial order or consent agreement.

(ix) ***Cooperation*** – The corporation must cooperate with the EPA's investigation.

This first incentive offered by the audit policy can be seen as providing corporations with two-tiered penalty mitigation. First, corporations that discovered an eligible violation are encouraged to promptly disclose the violation to the EPA, correct and remediate the violation, prevent the recurrence of the violation, and cooperate with the EPA's investigation. For such actions, corporations are granted 75% of the gravity-based

---

as "encompasses the regulated entity's documented systematic efforts, appropriate to the size and nature of its business, to prevent, detect and correct violations . . .".

[103] The audit policy *supra* note 97, §II.D.7, p. 19626, states that the incentives as per the audit policy apply only if "[t]he specific violation (or a closely related violation) has not occurred previously within the past three years at the same facility, and has not occurred within the past five years as part of a pattern at multiple facilities owned or operated by the same entity."

penalties with mitigation. Moreover, corporations that conduct environmental audits or maintain compliance management systems would be eligible for additional penalty mitigation of the remaining gravity penalties for those violations that occurred in spite of their audits or compliance systems. This policy seeks not only to encourage corporations to act responsibly with respect to every self-detected violation, but also to provide corporations with more general motivations to exert continuous efforts in ensuring environmental compliance through audits and compliance systems.

5.5.1.2 Incentive II: declining recommendations for criminal prosecution

Some environmental violations may give rise to both civil and criminal liability.[104] As a second incentive for self-policing and self-reporting of environmental violations, the audit policy establishes that the EPA will not recommend that the DOJ brings criminal charges against corporations that disclose criminal environmental offenses and meet all conditions 2 through 9 of the audit policy.[105] For this incentive to apply, the first condition of "systematic disclosure" is not required to be met.[106]

5.5.1.3 Incentive III: refraining from routine requests for audit reports

The past practices of the EPA have included routine requests for corporations to disclose internal audit reports when the information contained in these reports was not readily available elsewhere and when the EPA has determined that such information was necessary to assess the applicability of the audit policy in specific cases.[107] These reports have included document analysis, conclusions, and recommendations that resulted from an

---

[104] See, for instance, Daniel Riesel, *Environmental Enforcement: Civil and Criminal* (New York: ALM Properties Inc. Law Journal Press, 1997); Faure, "Environmental Crimes," 320–345.

[105] The audit policy further reinforces the general guidelines adopted by the EPA with respect to criminal investigations, according to which as a general rule, the EPA does not utilize criminal enforcement measures against violations that were promptly and voluntary disclosed, and were appropriately corrected by the offender. See Environmental Protection Agency (EPA), *The Exercise of Investigating Discretion* (January 12, 1994). See also, the main text related to *infra* note 138.

[106] Section II.C.3.(a) of the audit policy restricts the application of this incentive to violations that the EPA determined that are not part of a pattern that involves: "(i) A prevalent management philosophy or practice that conceals or condones environmental violations; or (ii) High-level corporate officials' or managers' conscious involvement in, or willful blindness to, violations of Federal environmental law."

[107] See audit policy *supra* note 97, §I.C.9.

environmental audit.[108] Hence, in order to ensure that corporations are not discouraged from conducting environmental audits and documenting them, the audit policy establishes that the EPA will not request or use corporations' audit reports to initiate civil or criminal enforcement actions against these corporations.[109] With respect to this third incentive, it should be noted that under various U.S. state laws environmental audit reports are protected through an evidentiary privilege. According to this privilege, these internal reports are declared inadmissible and therefore may not be used against the corporation in any civil, criminal, and administrative action.[110] Such evidentiary privileges are aimed at encouraging corporations to implement internal audits and compliance management systems.

5.5.2 The Department of Health and Human Services (HHS) Compliance Programs Guidance

Following the EPA's audit policy, the Department of Health and Human Services (HHS) has promulgated several official guidance documents that set forth various models of compliance programs.[111] Such documents

---

[108] See audit policy *supra* note 97, §II.B.

[109] See Arlen, "The Potentially Perverse Effects of Corporate Criminal Liability," 833–867; Arlen and Kraakman, "Controlling Corporate Misconduct: An Analysis of Corporate Liability Regimes," 687–779. The authors analyzed the potentially perverse effects of self-policing on corporations' payoff due to the increased probability of detection. Such perverse effects may, according to the authors, discourage self-policing actions. For a detailed discussion of the perverse effect of self-policing see Chapter 6, Section 6.3.1. Note that the audit policy clarifies that if the EPA has independent evidence of a violation, it may still request the information from the relevant corporations, if such information is needed to establish the extent and nature of the violation and the degree of culpability. See audit policy *supra* note 97, §II.C.4.

[110] See, for instance, Arlen and Kraakman, "Controlling Corporate Misconduct: An Analysis of Corporate Liability Regimes," p. 743, according to which "[i]n the environmental area, at least eighteen states have granted an evidentiary privilege to corporate environmental audit reports. . . . This privilege is generally available only if the firm promptly reported any wrongdoing it detected during its audit and moved promptly to remedy the problem." See also, David A. Dana, "The Perverse Incentives of Environmental Audit Immunity," *Iowa Law Review* 81 (1995), 969–1006; Khanna, "Corporate Liability Standards: When Should Corporations be Held Criminally Liable?," p. 1267.

[111] See Department of Health and Human Services (HHS), Office of Inspector General (OIG), "Publication of OIG Compliance Program Guidance for Clinical Laboratories," *Fed. Reg.* 63(163) (1998), p. 45076, available at: http://oig.hhs.gov/authorities/docs/cpglab.pdf; Department of Health and Human Services (HHS),

contain recommended models of compliance programs tailored to meet sector-specific ethical and legal challenges. The HHS guidance documents follow the EPA's audit policy approach concerning the role of compliance management systems in determining corporate liability, albeit in a less direct way. Without specifying the exact impact of corporate compliance management systems on corporate liability, the HHS's guidelines state: "the OIG [Office Inspector General at the HHS] will consider the existence of an effective compliance program that pre-dated any governmental investigation when addressing the appropriateness of administrative penalties."[112]

5.5.3 Unofficial Regulatory Enforcement Policies

The adoption of compliance management systems by corporations may affect the level of civil penalties imposed, even in the absence of official policies explicitly acknowledging it. Take, for instance, the FTC Bureau of Competition, which is the federal authority responsible for civil enforcement of U.S. antitrust laws. Although the FTC has no official policy that acknowledges corporate internal enforcement efforts as a mitigating factor, it is evident that the FTC has in fact considered such efforts in

---

Office of Inspector General (OIG), "Publication of the OIG Compliance Program Guidance for Hospitals," *Fed. Reg.* 63(35) (1998), p. 8987, available at: http://oig.hhs.gov/authorities/docs/cpghosp.pdf; Department of Health and Human Services (HHS), Office of Inspector General (OIG), "Publication of the OIG Compliance Program Guidance for Third-Party Medical Billing Companies," *Fed. Reg.* 63(243) (1998), p. 70138, available at: http://oig.hhs.gov/fraud/docs/complianceguidance/thirdparty.pdf. Additional HHS/OIG Guidelines for other sectors, such as Nursing Facilities (2008), Recipients of PHS Research Awards (2005), Pharmaceutical Manufacturers (2003), Ambulance Suppliers (2003), and Individual and Small Group Physician Practices, are available at: http://oig.hhs.gov/fraud/complianceguidance.asp.

[112] See Department of Health and Human Services (HHS), Office of Inspector General (OIG), "Publication of the OIG Compliance Program Guidance for Hospitals," footnote 2; Department of Health and Human Services (HHS), Office of Inspector General (OIG), "Publication of the OIG Compliance Program Guidance for Third-Party Medical Billing Companies," footnote 9; See also, Department of Health and Human Services (HHS), Office of Inspector General (OIG), "Publication of OIG Compliance Program Guidance for Clinical Laboratories," p. 45086: "Prompt reporting will demonstrate the clinical laboratory's good faith and willingness to work with governmental authorities to correct and remedy the problem. In addition, reporting such conduct will be considered a mitigating factor by the OIG in determining administrative sanctions (e.g., penalties, assessments, and exclusion), if the reporting provider becomes the target of an OIG investigation."

determining civil penalties.[113] Daniel P. Ducore, an Assistant Director for Compliance with the FTC, has given strong support for the existence of such an unofficial policy. Ducore is quoted as saying: "the more a company can tell the FTC about its efforts to keep its nose clean, the more likely the Commission is to see its actions as being in good faith and the more willing it is to permit mitigation, including mitigation down to zero penalties."[114]

5.6 CRIMINAL LIABILITY (1): COMPLIANCE MANAGEMENT SYSTEMS AS A '*SHIELD*' FROM CRIMINAL LIABILITY

The perception transformation regarding the role that corporate internal enforcement efforts may play in determining corporate liability has affected corporate criminal liability exposure as well. In the modern era, several paths have been paved for the acknowledgment of corporate internal enforcement efforts as constituting a *shield* from corporate criminal liability. Two main avenues of this acknowledgment are the recognition of *affirmative defense* and the establishment of *criteria for prosecution of business corporations*. Both of these avenues are discussed below.

5.6.1 Affirmative Defense

Several recent judgments have acknowledged corporations' internal enforcement efforts as constituting an affirmative defense from corporate criminal liability. The earliest judgment – at least to my knowledge – that deviated from the then-mainstream approach was the 1946 criminal judgment, *Holland Furnace Co. v. United States*.[115] In this case, criminal

---

113 See, for instance, Joseph E. Murphy, "An FTC View of Compliance Programs: Good Faith Efforts can Mean no Penalties," *Corporate Conduct Quarterly* 4(4) (1996): "In cases where companies violate FTC orders the Commission may pursue civil penalties for the violation. It would take into consideration what a company was doing to assure compliance and would make a distinction on that basis regarding a) whether to seek a penalty, and b) how much of a penalty to seek." See also, Groskaufmanis, "Impact of Corporate Compliance Outside the Criminal Process," p. 24.15.

114 Ducore's quote is found in Murphy, "An FTC View of Compliance Programs: Good Faith Efforts can Mean No Penalties;" see also, Groskaufmanis, "Impact of Corporate Compliance Outside the Criminal Process," p. 24.15; Perry and Dakin, "Compliance Programs and Criminal Law," p. 22.6.

115 158 F.2d 2 (C.C.A. 6th Cir. 1946).

charges were brought against *Holland Furnace* for its employee's criminal violation of the War Production Board's order.[116] In its ruling, the U.S. Court of Appeals underscored the fact that the crime occurred "not only without the knowledge of the appellant corporation of his illegal conduct, but also in express violation of its specific instructions to him and to all its agents."[117] Based on these grounds, the court decided to overturn the corporations' conviction stating that: "to hold the corporation, Holland Furnace Company, criminally liable for [an employee]'s unlawful acts on the facts of this case would carry corporate responsibility . . . beyond the boundary to which we think corporate criminal responsibility should be carried."[118]

For many years the *Holland Furnace* judgment has been perceived as an exceptional ruling that should be narrowly applied to its specific facts.[119] Adhering to the traditional approach described in Section 5.3.1 above, U.S. Federal Courts refused to accept corporations' internal enforcement efforts – by themselves – as constituting an affirmative defense from corporate liability. Ironically, the court has adhered to the *respondeat superior* doctrine, even after acknowledging that this doctrine had no longer been adhered to in civil cases, where a "reasonable diligence" defense was established.[120] It took several decades before the court was willing to reconsider

---

[116] The War Production Board's order in this case restricted the delivery of heating furnaces during World War II.

[117] See *ibid.*, p. 8.

[118] See *ibid.*

[119] See Groskaufmanis, "Impact of Corporate Compliance Outside the Criminal Process," p. 24.15; Perry and Dakin, "Compliance Programs and Criminal Law," p. 22.20, who refer to *United States v. Armour & Co.* 168 F.2d 2 (C.C.A. 3rd Cir. 1948); *United States v. Thompson-Powell Drilling Co.*, 196 F. Supp. 571, 574 (N.D. Tex. 1961). See also, Pitt and Groskaufmanis, "Minimizing Corporate Civil and Criminal Liability: A Second Look at Corporate Codes of Conduct," p. 1612.

[120] See, for instance, *Twentieth Century Fox Film Corp. supra* note 53, the court further rejected the corporation's attempt to rely on the "reasonable diligence" civil defense in the criminal context: "The purpose of civil contempt is remedial and coercive; it thus makes sense to say, at least in some contexts, that if a defendant is doing all it can to comply with a court order, there may be little, if any, coercive purpose that civil contempt sanctions could achieve. Criminal contempt, however, serves the much different purpose of vindicating the court's authority. It serves to punish individuals or corporations for past violations of a court order. Because of this different purpose, the focus of criminal contempt is on the willfulness of the violation. Once it is determined that the corporate agent willfully violated a clear contempt order, the corporation must bear responsibility. *It is this rule of vicarious liability that encourages companies to establish compliance programs. Were we to import "reasonable diligence" into the law of criminal contempt, corporations could more easily distance themselves from the wayward acts of*

its approach concerning the relevance of corporate internal enforcement efforts in the determination of corporate criminal liability. In fact, the first signs of a transformation in the court's perception only appeared in the late 1970s and 1980s. In several pioneering judgments, the court has considered corporate internal enforcement efforts when determining corporate criminal liability. Such a perception transformation has gone through three different legal channels that involve the determination of: (a) corporate *mens rea*; (b) employee offender's *intent to benefit the corporation*; and (c) the *scope of the employment*.[121] A brief overview of these channels is provided below.

5.6.1.1 Corporate *mens rea*

As mentioned above, except for strict liability crimes, a criminal conviction requires the prosecution to prove the offender's *mens rea*, or "guilty mind." In the corporate context, this requirement was satisfied under the traditional approach by imputing employees' state of mind to their corporations.[122] This approach, which disregards corporate internal enforcement efforts in determining corporate *mens rea*,[123] has changed in several modern judgments that held that the existence of a corporate management system and the manner in which it was implemented should be taken into consideration when determining a corporation's *mens rea*. A notable example is the explicit instructions given by the court to the jury in the *United States v. International Paper Co.*[124] The judge instructed that:[125]

> One of the factors you may consider *in determining the intent* of each corporation, among other evidence, is *whether or not that corporation had an antitrust compliance policy*. In this regard, you are instructed that the *mere existence of any antitrust compliance policy does not automatically mean that the corporation did not have the necessary intent*. If, however, you find that the corporation acted diligently in the promulgation, dissemination and enforcement of an antitrust compliance program in an active good faith effort to ensure that the

---

their agents – a prospect that threatens the very authority of the court that criminal contempt is designed to preserve" (para 21), http://cases.justia.com/us-court-of-appeals/F2/882/656/207524/-fn2 (emphasis added, references omitted).

[121] See Perry and Dakin, "Compliance Programs and Criminal Law," 22.1–22.16.

[122] See *supra* notes 39–41 and the related main text.

[123] See Section 5.3.1.

[124] See Criminal No. H-78–11 (S.D. Tex Houston 1979).

[125] *Ibid.* (emphasis added). See also, Section of Antitrust Law, American Bar Association (ABA), *Jury Instructions in Criminal Antitrust Cases, 1976–1980* (U.S.A.: American Bar Association (ABA), 1982), p. 190.

> employees would abide by the law, *you may take this fact into account in determining whether or not the corporation has the required intent.*

Similar instructions were given in other cases, where the court instructed the jury to consider the "good faith" in which compliance programs were implemented *de facto*.[126]

5.6.1.2 Employee offender's intent to benefit the corporation

As discussed above, under U.S. Federal Law corporate criminal liability applies only if the criminal conduct was undertaken at least in part with the motivation to *benefit the corporation*.[127] Modern judgments have considered the existence of compliance management systems in determining whether the employee's conduct was actually conducted with the intent to benefit the corporation.[128] In a case in 1970, *American Radiator*, the court held that evidence concerning the authenticity of compliance management systems was admissible and may be used to support the corporate assertion that its employee did not intend to benefit the corporation with his criminal conduct.[129] A more explicit opinion appeared in *United States v. Basic Constructions Co.*,[130] where the Court of Appeals approved the instructions given by the District Court to the jury. According to these instructions:[131]

> A corporation may be responsible for the action of its agents done or made within the scope of their authority, even though the conduct of the agents may be contrary to the corporation's actual instructions, or contrary to the corporation's stated position. However, *the existence of such instructions and policies, if any be shown, may be considered by you in determining whether the agents, in fact, were acting to benefit the corporation.*

5.6.1.3 The scope of the employment

In other cases, the court has considered the existence of compliance management systems in determining whether the offense was committed by an

---

[126] See, for instance, *United States v. Koppers Co., Inc.*, 652 F.2d 290 (2nd Cir. 1981); *In re Corrugated Container Antitrust Litigation v. Alton box Board Co.*, 659 F 2d. 1322 (5th Cir. 1981). See also, Perry and Dakin, "Compliance Programs and Criminal Law," p. 22.24; Shenefield and Favretto, "Compliance Programs as Viewed from the Antitrust Division," p. 79.

[127] See Section 5.2.2.

[128] See Pitt and Groskaufmanis, "Minimizing Corporate Civil and Criminal Liability: A Second Look at Corporate Codes of Conduct," p. 1613.

[129] See *American Radiator & Standard Sanitary Corp. supra* note 51, p. 204.

[130] 711 F.2d 570, 13 Fed. R. Evid. Serv. 1178 (4th Cir. 1983).

[131] 711 F.2d, p. 572 (emphasis added).

employee *within the scope of their employment*. For instance, in the *United States v. Beusch*, the Court of Appeals approved the instructions given to the jury as a proper statement of the law.[132] The court wrote:[133]

> [A] corporation may be liable for acts of its employees done contrary to express instructions and policies, but . . . *the existence of such instructions and policies may be considered in determining whether the employee in fact acted to benefit the corporation. Merely stating or publishing such instructions and policies without* diligently enforcing them is not enough to place the acts of an employee who violates them outside the scope of his employment.

In summation, corporate internal enforcement efforts, including the diligent promulgation and realization of compliance management systems, may constitute an affirmative defense from corporate criminal liability. In that regard, the reliance on compliance management systems requires such systems to be implemented *de facto* in "good faith" as a meaningful compliance mechanism.

5.6.2 Prosecution of Business Corporations

In recent years the DOJ's perceptions concerning the role that internal enforcement efforts may play in determining whether to bring criminal charges against corporations have undergone radical change. The traditional prosecutorial approach in the mid-twentieth century has been that corporate internal enforcement efforts would not shield corporations from criminal charges once a crime was detected.[134] Prosecutors and regulatory officials have strongly opposed the transformation of perceptions

---

[132] 596 F. 2d. 871 (9th Cir. 1972).

[133] See *ibid.*, p. 878.

[134] See, for instance, Robert E. Bloch, "Compliance Programs and Criminal Antitrust Litigation: A Prosecutor's Perspective," pp. 226, 229. The author states: "In my view, the basic question raised about compliance programs and the intent issue is not whether there is an interrelationship between them. Rather, *the basic question is whether the existence of a corporate compliance program is legally relevant in determining corporate liability. In my judgment, the answer is no*. The attempts to carve out an exception from the general rules concerning proof of intent in a criminal antitrust case and the doctrine of vicarious liability for corporate defendants with compliance programs not only confuses both subjects, but distorts their underlying legal premises. . . . The message here is clear. A corporation whose agents acting within the scope of their authority and for its benefit, knowingly participate in a conspiracy to commit an antitrust violation, cannot absolve itself of liability by arguing that its compliance program establishes its lack of intent to violate the antitrust laws" (emphasis added).

appearing in the courts' judgments and have heavily criticized them.[135] However, following the momentum gathered by new perceptions in court judgments, during the late 1980s and 1990s new approaches started to be tolerated by prosecutors and regulators.[136] For instance, the Fraud Division at the DOJ promulgated a Memorandum in 1987 notifying all U.S. attorneys that the implementation of compliance management systems by defense contractors who voluntarily disclosed a crime may be considered as a mitigating factor against prosecution.[137] Similarly, in 1994 the EPA promulgated a Memorandum that set forth guidelines for prosecutors in which "a violation that is voluntarily revealed and fully and promptly remediated as part of a corporation's systematic and comprehensive self-evaluation program generally will not be a candidate for the expenditure of scarce criminal resources."[138] This new approach has gained growing support throughout the 1990s, and voices calling for policy reforms have become increasingly popular.[139]

---

[135] See, for instance, a public statement made by John H. Shenefield, then Assistant Attorney General for the Antitrust Division, delivered by Richard J. Favretto, Deputy Assistant Attorney General for Litigation and Investigation, in Shenefield and Favretto, "Compliance Programs as Viewed from the Antitrust Division," p. 79. Referring to the judgment in *In re Corrugated Container Antitrust Litigation supra* note 127, Shenefield states: "We believe that *this was an erroneous instruction* and *contrary to settled law*. [Corporate criminal liability] may arise even when the corporation has expressly instructed its employees not to undertake the acts that gave rise to criminal liability. Carrying the Corrugated instruction to its logical conclusion would make it virtually impossible to convict a corporation of criminal antitrust violation, a result that is self-evidently nonsensical" (emphasis added). To remove any remaining doubt, Shenefield further expands: "[I]f, despite the best intentions in the world, the corporation should happen to stray into violation of the antitrust laws, *the existence of a corporate compliance program is, as a matter of law, irrelevant*" (emphasis added).

[136] For an extensive exposé of the different approaches within the DOJ see Perry and Dakin, "Compliance Programs and Criminal Law," 22.1–22.16.

[137] See William C. Hendricks III, Fraud Division Chief to the United States Attorneys, Memorandum (1987). See also, Perry and Dakin, "Compliance Programs and Criminal Law," p. 22.7.

[138] See Environmental Protection Agency (EPA), *The Exercise of Investigating Discretion*, p. 6.

[139] See, for instance, the opinion by Michael Chertoff, U.S. Attorney for the District of New Jersey, in Michele Galen, "Keeping the Long Arm of the Law at Arm's Length," *Business Week* (April 22, 1991), p. 104. For the opinion by Michael Baylson, U.S. Attorney for the Eastern District of Pennsylvania, see Michael Baylson, "Getting the Demons into Heaven: A Good Corporate Compliance Program," *Corporate Conduct Quarterly* 2 (1993), p. 33. Similar views were also presented by the antitrust division at the National Symposium sponsored by the U.S. Sentencing Commission: "Corporate Crime in America:

In a nod to the shift in perceptions, Eric Holder, then U.S. Deputy Attorney General, promulgated on June 16, 1999 a Memorandum that laid down unified principles for the federal prosecution of business corporations ("*Holder Memo*").[140] The Holder Memo included eight factors to be considered by prosecutors when deciding to prosecute business corporations. Three of these factors directly consider corporations' internal enforcement and disclosure efforts. These include factors 4–6:[141]

(4) The *corporation's timely and voluntary disclosure of wrongdoing* and its *willingness to cooperate in the investigation* of its agents . . .;
(5) The existence and adequacy of the *corporation's compliance program*;[142]
(6) The *corporation's remedial actions*, including any *efforts to implement an effective corporate compliance program or to improve an existing one*, to replace responsible management, to discipline or terminate wrongdoers, to pay restitution, and to cooperate with the relevant government agencies.

In line with the approach adopted in the recent judgments described above, the Holder Memo clarified that the existence of a compliance program, in itself, is not sufficient to shield corporations from criminal prosecution. To be considered by prosecutors, compliance programs must be adequately designed to achieve maximum effectiveness in preventing and detecting wrongdoing by employees, rather than being merely "paper programs."[143] Hence, prosecutors were guided to look closely at an assortment of elements that may indicate the quality and the authenticity of compliance programs.[144] Additional elements have been

---

Strengthening the 'Good Citizen' Corporation." See Gary R. Spratling, Deputy Assistant Attorney General – Antitrust Division, "The Experience and View of the Antitrust Division" (Speech at the Capitol Hilton Hotel, Washington, DC, 1995).

[140] See Eric Holder, Deputy Attorney General, *Memorandum for Heads of Department Components United States Attorneys: Principles of Federal Prosecution of Corporations*, U.S. Department of Justice, Office of the Deputy Attorney General (June 16, 1999).

[141] *Ibid.*, §II.A (emphasis added). Other factors included the nature and seriousness of the offense; the pervasiveness of wrongdoing within the corporation; the corporation's history of similar conduct; collateral consequences; and the adequacy of non-criminal remedies.

[142] The Holder Memo refers to compliance programs as programs "established by corporate management to prevent and to detect misconduct and to ensure that corporate activities are conducted in accordance with all applicable laws." See *ibid.*, §VII.A.

[143] See *ibid.*, §VI.B.

[144] Such elements include: the comprehensiveness of the compliance program; the extent and pervasiveness of the criminal conduct; the number and level of the

added by the 2003 Memorandum issued by Larry D. Thompson, the then U.S. Attorney General, in the "*Thompson Memo*".[145] This approach was reinforced in a series of subsequent Memoranda promulgated by the DOJ, all of which recognized corporate management systems as a viable factor to be considered before bringing charges against corporations.[146]

---

corporate employees involved; the seriousness, duration, and frequency of the misconduct; any remedial actions taken by the corporation, including restitution, disciplinary action; revisions to corporate compliance programs; the promptness of any disclosure of wrongdoing to the government; the corporation's cooperation in the government's investigation; and whether corporate management is enforcing the program or is tacitly encouraging or pressuring employees to engage in misconduct to achieve business objectives. See *ibid.*, §VI.B.

[145] See Larry D. Thompson, Deputy Attorney General, *Memorandum for Heads of Department Components United States Attorneys: Principles of Federal Prosecution of Business Organizations*, U.S. Department of Justice, Office of the Deputy Attorney General (January 20, 2003). The Thompson Memo reinforced and slightly revised the factors determined in the Holder Memo. One of the major goals of the Thompson Memo was "to address the efficacy of the corporate governance mechanisms in place within a corporation, to ensure that these measures are truly effective rather than mere paper programs." Accordingly, the Thompson Memo further guided prosecutors to consider whether the corporation has established corporate governance mechanisms that can effectively detect and prevent misconduct. More particularly, the Thompson Memo guided prosecutors to explore, for instance, if "the corporation's directors exercise independent review over [the] proposed corporate actions rather than unquestioningly ratifying officers' recommendations; are the directors provided with information sufficient to enable the exercise of independent judgment; are internal audit functions conducted at a level sufficient to ensure their independence and accuracy; have the directors established an information and reporting system in the organization reasonably designed to provide management and the board of directors with timely and accurate information sufficient to allow them to reach an informed decision regarding the organization's compliance with the law" (*ibid.*, §VII).

[146] See, for instance, Paul McNulty, Deputy Attorney General, *Memorandum for Heads of Department Components United States Attorneys: Principles of Federal Prosecution of Business Organizations*, U.S. Department of Justice, Office of the Deputy Attorney General (December 12, 2006); Craig S. Morford, Acting Deputy Attorney General, *Memorandum for Heads of Department Components United States Attorneys: Selection and Use of Monitors in Deferred Prosecution Agreements and Non-Prosecution Agreements with Corporations*, U.S. Department of Justice, Office of the Deputy Attorney General (March 7, 2008); Mark R. Filip, *Memorandum for Heads of Department Components United States Attorneys: Principles of Federal Prosecution of Business Organizations*, U.S. Department of Justice (August 28, 2008); Gary G. Grindler, Acting Deputy Attorney General, *Memorandum for Heads of Department Components United States Attorneys: Additional Guidance on the Use of Monitors in Deferred Prosecution Agreements and Non-Prosecution Agreements with Corporations*, U.S. Department of Justice, Office of the Deputy Attorney General (May 25, 2010). These Memoranda include minor

A similar approach has been adopted by several U.S. state policies.[147]

In summary, the adoption of a genuine, comprehensive compliance management system may, under certain circumstances, militate against the prosecution of corporations. In that respect, corporations that adopt a meaningful compliance management system may be shielded from criminal liability. The determination of compliance management systems' quality and authenticity is a matter of a case-by-case evaluation that ought to be undertaken by the prosecutor in charge.

5.6.3 Amnesty and Leniency Programs

The contemporary approach which seeks to encourage corporations to play an active role in the exposure of criminal conduct has led to the promulgation of numerous *amnesty* and *leniency policies* in various fields of law. A notable example is the '*Corporate Leniency Policy*' promulgated in 1993 by the DOJ Antitrust Division. According to this policy, corporations reporting their illegal antitrust activity at an early stage may, under certain circumstances, face no criminal charges for the activity being reported.[148] Such policies, which are commonly used in antitrust, tax, and immigration laws, are primarily aimed at encouraging offenders to *step forward* and *report* their own violations to the relevant authority. Although this objective is somewhat restricted compared to the broad objective of the other policies described above, amnesty and leniency programs may still be perceived as an additional avenue, albeit a more remote one, in which the transformation of perceptions has played out in policymaking. Similarly to previously discussed policies that shield corporations from criminal

---

amendments to the Thompson Memo wordings; for instance, the Memorandum promulgated by Mark Filip, then Deputy Attorney General, in August 2008. The "Filip Memo" provided that compliance programs should not be treated by prosecutors as a binary factor. According to the Filip Memo, prosecutors may consider a truly effective compliance program as a factor militating to no charges against the corporation at all, or *to mitigate charges or sanctions against the corporation*. See Mark Filip, *Memorandum for Heads of Department Components United States Attorneys: Principles of Federal Prosecution of Business Organizations*, §9–28.800: "a truly effective compliance program that, when consistent with other federal law enforcement policies, may result in a decision to charge only the corporation's employees and agents or *to mitigate charges or sanctions against the corporation*" (emphasis added). For further discussion of the amendments included in the Filip Memo see Perry and Dakin, "Compliance Programs and Criminal Law," p. 22.4.

[147] See *ibid.*, p. 22.17.

[148] See U.S. Federal Department of Justice, Antitrust Division, *Corporate Leniency Policy* (August 10, 1993). This policy has replaced the earlier corporate amnesty policy of 1978.

charges in return for comprehensive compliance management systems, amnesty and leniency programs offer corporations a similar protection, in return for self-reporting, which is one of the components of a comprehensive compliance management system.

5.7 CRIMINAL LIABILITY (2): COMPLIANCE MANAGEMENT SYSTEMS AS A '*MITIGATING FACTOR*' OF CRIMINAL PENALTIES

In a revolutionary guideline promulgated by the U.S. Sentencing Commission (USSC) as Chapter 8 of the U.S. Sentencing Guidelines, U.S. Federal Law has adopted the most explicit and comprehensive policy in which corporate compliance efforts were officially recognized as a mitigating factor for corporate criminal penalties.[149] Such guidelines, known as the Organization Sentencing Guidelines (OSG), have established a detailed definition of compliance management systems and a systematic sentencing policy which is fully attentive to corporations' internal enforcement efforts. The foundations set by the OSG have inspired many of the succeeding policies promulgated in various fields of law.[150] The sentencing policy established by the OSG is surveyed below.

---

[149] For a detailed historical overview of the development of the OSG and for a general analysis of their provisions, see, for instance, Jeffrey M. Kaplan, "Corporate Sentencing Guidelines: Overview," in *Compliance Programs and the Corporate Sentencing Guidelines: Preventing Criminal and Civil Liability*, Jeffrey M. Kaplan and Joseph E. Murphy eds., revised edn (U.S.A.: Tompson/West, 2009); Ronald J. Maurer, "The Federal Sentencing Guidelines for Organizations: How Do They Work and What Are They Supposed to Do?" *Dayton Law Review* (18) (1993), p. 799; Nolan E. Clark, "Corporate Sentencing Guidelines: Drafting History," in *Compliance Programs and the Corporate Sentencing Guidelines: Preventing Criminal and Civil Liability*, Jeffrey M. Kaplan and Joseph E. Murphy eds., revised edn (U.S.A.: Tompson/West, 2009); John R. Steer, "Sentencing Guidelines: In General," in *Compliance Programs and the Corporate Sentencing Guidelines: Preventing Criminal and Civil Liability*, Jeffrey M. Kaplan and Joseph E. Murphy eds., revised edn (U.S.A.: Tompson/West, 2009); Ilene H. Nagel and Winthrop M. Swenson, "The Federal Sentencing Guidelines for Corporations: Their Development, Theoretical Underpinnings, and Some Thoughts about their Future," *Washington University Law Quarterly* 71 (1993), 205–259; Jeffrey S. Parker, "Rules without . . .: Some Critical Reflections in the Federal Corporate Sentencing Guidelines," *Washington University Law Quarterly* 71 (1993), 397–442.

[150] Such policies include the EPA audit policy discussed in Section 5.5.1 above and the HHS guidelines for sector-specific compliance programs discussed in Section 5.5.2 above.

5.7.1 Organizational Sentencing Guidelines (OSG)

After a thorough government investigation and public hearings coordinated by the USSC, the OSG have been promulgated and became effective on November 1, 1991. These guidelines, which have been amended several times over the course of the last two decades, have served as the roadmap for judges in setting the sentence of convicted organizations, including corporations, partnerships, labor unions, pension funds, trusts, non-profit entities, and governmental units.[151] The OSG seek to encourage corporations to adopt meaningful compliance management systems to prevent, deter, and report law-breaking committed by corporate employees. To this end, the OSG set forth a unique sentencing framework that mitigates the criminal penalties imposed upon corporations, if a corporation can demonstrate that it had put in place an effective compliance program at the time the violation took place, and that it promptly reported the violation to the relevant authorities. Such a sentencing framework is believed to "offer incentives to organizations to reduce and ultimately eliminate criminal conduct by providing a structural foundation from which an organization may self-police its own conduct through an effective compliance and ethics program."[152]

5.7.2 The Sentencing Structure under the OSG

The OSG establish an initial distinction between *recalcitrant corporations*, which operated primarily for a criminal purpose or primarily by criminal means, and *normative corporations*, which includes all other legitimate corporations. As for recalcitrant corporations, the OSG states that the penalties should be sufficiently high to "divest the organization of all its

---

[151] Initially, the Federal Sentencing Guidelines were designed as mandatory guidelines. However, the U.S. Supreme Court in 2005 in the *United States v. Booker*, 543 U.S. 220 (2005) stated that the mandatory application of the Federal Sentencing Guidelines violated the right to trial by jury under the sixth amendment, and therefore excised the provisions of the Sentencing Reform Act that made the Federal Sentencing Guidelines mandatory. As a result, the Federal Sentencing Guidelines (including the OSG) lost their mandatory power and became an advisory policy. For a detailed analysis of the impact of the *Booker* case on the Federal Sentencing Guidelines see United States Sentencing Commission (USSC), *Final Report on the Impact of United States v. Booker on Federal Sentencing* [2012], http://www.ussc.gov/Legislative_and_Public_Affairs/Congressional_Testimony_and_Reports/Booker_Reports/2012_Booker/Part_A.pdf.

[152] The United States Sentencing Commission (USSC), "Federal Sentencing Guidelines Manual: Chapter Eight – Sentencing of Organizations," (2012), p. 488.

assets."[153] By contrast, normative corporations are subject to a composite sentencing framework that determines the range of penalties according to two major considerations: (i) the *seriousness* of the offense; and (ii) the *culpability* of the corporation.[154] This sentencing structure is composed as follows:

A. ***Base penalty*** – the base line penalty is determined by the *seriousness* of the offense, which is captured by the greater of: (1) the pecuniary gain of the corporation from the criminal conduct; (2) the pecuniary loss created by the criminal conduct; and (3) the amount specified for the relevant type of violations in a table included in the OSG where violations are classified according to the level of the offense.[155] The idea underlying the determination of the base penalty is to "deter corporations from seeking to obtain financial rewards through criminal conduct," and at the same time to "ensure that organizations will seek to prevent losses intentionally, knowingly, or recklessly caused by their agents."[156]
B. ***Culpability score*** – once the base fine is identified, the relevant range of the actual fine is defined according to the *culpability level* of the corporation. Corporate culpability is determined according to six factors specified in the OSG, four of which reflect incremental culpability and thereby increase the actual penalty.[157] The other two factors present declined culpability and therefore reduce the actual penalties. These mitigating factors are two components of compliance management systems: (i) the existence of an effective compliance and ethics program; and (ii) self-reporting, cooperation, or acceptance of responsibility. Both components are further discussed in Section 5.7.3 below.
C. ***The fine range*** – To determine the range of the actual sanction, the OSG guide courts to start by determining the base line fine. For illustration purposes, suppose that the base line fine is $M1.2. Then, starting with a default level of 5 culpability points (a default provided by the OSG), the court considers the relevant culpability factors and adds and subtracts the applicable culpability points. For example,

---

153 *Ibid.*, p. 488.
154 See *ibid.*, p. 488.
155 See *ibid.*, §8C2.4.
156 *Ibid.*, Commentary to §8C2.4.
157 These factors include: (i) the involvement in or tolerance of criminal activity by "substantial authority personnel" within the corporation; (ii) the prior history of the organization; (iii) the violation of a judicial order or injunction; and (iv) the obstruction of justice.

suppose that after weighting all relevant factors the court found that 4 culpability points should be added to the default 5 points. Hence, the final culpability score is now 9 points. For each final culpability score §8C2.6 to the OSG provides minimum and a maximum multipliers. According to §8C2.7 of the OSG, the range of the applicable fine should be determined by multiplying the base fine by the applicable maximum and minimum multipliers. In our example, the culpability score 9 has 1.8 minimum and 3.6 maximum multipliers, respectively. Therefore, the fine range would be between $M2.16 (*i.e.*, $M1.2 × 1.8) and $M4.32 (*i.e.*, $M1.2 × 3.6).[158] The final determination of the actual fine is made by the court in light of a series of considerations set forth in §8C2.8 of the OSG.

5.7.3 Compliance Management Systems under the OSG

Compliance management systems comprise a wide variety of schemes, most of which share some common components. The OSG is one of the only existing official policies that provide a detailed, comprehensive description of compliance management systems. This description is focused upon two major modules: (1) a *compliance and ethics program*, which involves self-policing activities undertaken by corporations to prevent, deter, detect, and investigate employees' violations; and (2) a *self-reporting mechanism*, which involves corporations self-reporting, cooperating with the investigation, and accepting responsibility for the misconduct. Although more detailed than comparable policies, the OSG still provides wide discretion for corporations in designing their own compliance management systems and tailoring such systems to meet their own propensities. I provide below a brief overview of both modules of compliance management systems as determined by the OSG.

5.7.3.1 Effective compliance and ethics programs

The OSG provides seven 'key criteria' for the establishment of an "effective compliance and ethics program." Such criteria are intended to motivate corporations to self-prevent and self-detect employees' misconduct.[159] To be eligible for any liability mitigation associated with the existence

---

[158] See The United States Sentencing Commission (USSC), "Federal Sentencing Guidelines Manual: Chapter Eight – Sentencing of Organizations," (2012), §8C2.5–6.

[159] All seven criteria are established in *ibid.*, §8B2.1.(b). See also, Nick Ciancio, *The Seven Pillars of an Effective Ethics and Compliance Program*, Global compliance, available at: http://www.globalcompliance.com/pdf/the-seven-pillars-

of compliance and ethics programs, corporations must satisfy *all* seven criteria, cumulatively:

(i) ***Establishment of standards and procedures*** – As an initial step in promulgating a compliance and ethics program a corporation is required to establish the "standards of conduct and internal controls that are reasonably capable of reducing the likelihood of criminal conduct."[160]

(ii) ***Oversight by high-level personnel*** – The second criterion requires the top management to be engaged in the promulgation and implementation of the compliance program. The OSG specify the minimal level of engagement of different members of corporate management. For instance, the Board of Directors is required to be "knowledgeable about the content and operation of the compliance and ethics program and shall exercise reasonable oversight with respect to the implementation and effectiveness of the compliance and ethics program."[161] High-level personnel, such as directors and executive officers, who have substantial control over the corporation or participate in designing its policy, are required to "ensure that the organization has an effective compliance and ethics program."[162] In addition, specific individuals should be assigned with "day-to-day operational responsibility for the compliance and ethics program."[163] These individuals may include the Chief Compliance Officer, members of an Internal Compliance Committee or an Internal Audit Committee. Such individuals must be provided adequate resources, appropriate authority, and direct access to the governing authority to which they are accountable.[164]

(iii) ***Due care in delegating substantial discretionary authority*** – The OSG are aware of the fact that those individuals possessing authority in organizations are sometimes the most likely actors to misbehave. Therefore, the next criterion requires corporations to carefully select their personnel who possess substantial authority within the

---

of-an-effective-ethics-and-compliance-program.pdf (2007); Burrows, "The Seven Elements of an Effective Compliance and Ethics Program," pp. 21–23.

160 See United States Sentencing Commission (USSC), "Federal Sentencing Guidelines Manual: Chapter Eight – Sentencing of Organizations," commentary 1 to §8B2.1.(b), pp. 496–497.

161 *Ibid.*, §8B2.1.(b)(2)(a).

162 *Ibid.*, §8B2.1.(b)(2)(b).

163 *Ibid.*, §8B2.1.(b)(2)(c).

164 See *ibid.*

corporation. More particularly, corporations are required to refrain from delegating substantial authority to individuals who engaged in "illegal activities or other conduct inconsistent with an effective compliance and ethics program."[165]

(iv) ***Effective communication for employees at all levels*** – Corporations' compliance programs must not be merely "paper programs." Therefore, the OSG require corporations to periodically communicate their standards and procedures to their employees at all levels. It is left up to the corporations to determine what particular channels of communication they will employ. Hence, corporations are required to identify and employ effective ways to communicate their codes of conduct for their employees. Such channels may include the dissemination of clearly and practically written codes of conduct; the provisions of compliance and ethics training; the periodic distribution of additional information and updates to the program; and securing available sources of information for their employees.[166]

(v) ***Active monitoring*** – Another criterion focuses on corporations' duty to maintain active monitoring and auditing systems. According to this criterion, corporations are required to evaluate periodically the effectiveness of their compliance and ethics program. This evaluation should include an internal scheme that facilitates the reporting of suspected wrongdoing without fear of reprisal. These "whistle-blowing" schemes may include direct access to the corporate compliance officer, as well as to an external hotline that "allow[s] for anonymity or confidentiality, whereby the corporations' employees and agents may report or seek guidance regarding potential or actual criminal conduct without fear of retaliation."[167]

(vi) ***Incentivizing and disciplinary mechanisms*** – The sixth criterion requires corporations to promote and enforce their compliance and ethics program by using incentives and disciplinary mechanisms. Incentivizing mechanisms include remuneration, bonuses, prizes, awards, and positive citations for employees that are designed to encourage an employee's compliant and ethical behavior. Disciplinary mechanisms include all sorts of sanctions imposed on employees for violating corporate standards and procedures, such as delaying an employees' promotion or discharging them.[168]

---

165 *Ibid.*, §8B2.1.(b)(3).
166 See *ibid.*, §8B2.1.(b)(4).
167 *Ibid.*, §8B2.1.(b)(5)(c).
168 See *ibid.*, §8B2.1.(b)(6).

(vii) ***Preventing recurrence*** – The final criterion pertains to corporate responses to detected misconduct. The OSG requires corporations which have detected criminal conduct to take reasonable steps "to respond appropriately to the criminal conduct and to prevent further similar criminal conduct."[169] Such steps may include, for instance, updates and the revision of standards and procedures.

These criteria comprise the principle requirements that should be implemented by corporations in "good faith." In implementing such principles, corporations are required to consider their specific circumstances and to tailor their actions to meet compliance goals. Among other considerations, corporations should take into account existing industry practices and relevant standards included in applicable regulations. In addition, the size of the corporation may be a relevant factor to consider when determining the level of formality and the scope of corporate compliance activities. Normally, compared to small corporations, large corporations are expected to maintain more formal operations and to invest greater resources in meeting the seven principles above.[170]

5.7.3.2 Self-reporting, cooperation, and acceptance of responsibility

A second module of compliance management systems, which pertains to the post-detection phase, deals with stepping forward, cooperation with the investigation, and acceptance of responsibility. Note that not all three components of this module of compliance management systems are required to be satisfied for a corporation to be eligible for penalty mitigation. Yet only the fulfillment of all these requirements grants corporations with the greatest possible liability mitigation.

(i) ***Reporting*** – This criterion requires corporations to report self-detected violations "within a reasonably prompt time after becoming aware of the offense."[171] In determining the promptness of the report, the OSG allow corporations a reasonable period of time to conduct an internal investigation that would verify the relevant facts and the illegality embedded in the examined conduct.

(ii) ***Cooperation*** – Corporations are required to cooperate with the government's investigation. This requirement pertains to the corporation in its entirety, rather than to cooperation with just specific

---

169 *Ibid.*, §8B2.1.(b)(7).

170 See *ibid.*, commentary 2(c) to §8B2.1.

171 *Ibid.*, §8C2.5(g)(1).

individuals.[172] The OSG requires full cooperation which must begin at a very early stage. The corporation's cooperation is required "at the same time as the organization is officially notified of the criminal investigation."[173] In addition, the cooperation must be thorough, and corporations are required to disclose "all pertinent information known by the organization."[174]

(iii) ***Affirmative acceptance of responsibility*** – The third criterion requires corporations to demonstrate recognition and to explicitly accept responsibility for their employees' criminal conduct. One obvious way of accepting responsibility would be to enter a guilty plea prior to the commencement of a trial.[175]

5.7.4 Compliance Management Systems as Mitigating Factors under the OSG

Each one of the modules of compliance management systems discussed above constitutes an independent mitigating factor of corporate penalties. First, the existence of an *effective compliance and ethics program* is acknowledged in §8C2.5(f)(1) of the OSG as a mitigating factor leading to a subtraction of 3 culpability points.[176] This mitigation is contingent upon the following conditions: (1) all seven factors of compliance and ethics programs described in Section 5.7.3.1 above are satisfied; (2) the mitigation does not apply if after becoming aware of an offense, the corporation "unreasonably delayed reporting the offense to the appropriate governmental authority;"[177] and (3) the mitigation does not apply, under

---

[172] A refusal to cooperate by certain individual employees need not be treated as a lack of cooperation by the entire corporation. See *ibid.*, commentary 13 to §8C2.5(g).

[173] *Ibid.*

[174] *Ibid.*

[175] According to the OSG, a corporation's decision to exercise their constitutional right to a trial, in itself, does not prevent this 'acceptance of responsibility' criterion to be met. This could be the case, for instance, if the corporation goes to trial to argue on issues not related to their factual guilt, such as constitutional and applicability issues. And yet, a corporation that admits guilt and expresses remorse after its conviction, where the prosecution has met its burden of proof, may not benefit from liability mitigation associated with its late acceptance of responsibility. See *ibid.*, commentary 14 to §8B2.5.

[176] See *ibid.*, §8C2.5(f)(1): "[i]f the offense occurred even though the organization had in place at the time of the offense an effective compliance and ethics program . . . subtract **3** points."

[177] According to this condition, as long as the corporation did not detect an offense, it is entitled to a penalty mitigation associated with its compliance and

certain circumstances specified in §8C2.5(f)(3) of the OSG, if "an individual within high-level personnel of the organization . . . participated in, condoned, or was willfully ignorant of the offense."[178]

The second mitigating factor pertains to the *self-reporting, cooperation, and acceptance of responsibility* module. The smallest mitigation (subtraction of 1 culpability point) is granted to a corporation that "clearly demonstrated recognition and affirmative acceptance of responsibility for its criminal conduct."[179] A mid-size mitigation (subtraction of 2 culpability points) is granted to corporations that in addition to accepting responsibility have also "fully cooperated in the investigation."[180] And finally, the greatest mitigation (subtraction of 5 culpability points) is granted to corporations that in addition to accepting responsibility and cooperating in the investigation have reported the offense to appropriate governmental authorities prior to an imminent threat of disclosure or government investigation, and within a reasonably prompt time after becoming aware of the offense.[181]

In summation, the OSG presents one of the most comprehensive modern policies in which corporations' internal enforcement efforts are officially acknowledged as mitigating factors in determining convicted corporations' sentences. These guidelines, along with the other policies surveyed above, present the modern perception adopted by U.S. law, according to which the recognition of corporate internal enforcement efforts through mitigation or elimination of corporate liability may encourage corporations to become an active partner in the battle against law-breaking.

5.7.5 Summing Up

The corporate liability regimes presented in Sections 5.4 through 5.7 comprise an array of parallel avenues in which U.S. corporate liability policies have departed from the traditional strict liability approach that corresponds with the deterrence-based school of thought discussed in

---

ethics program, if the other two conditions are satisfied. However, once the corporation has detected the criminal conduct, it must promptly report this conduct to the relevant authority, subject to a reasonable period of time required to conduct an internal investigation.

[178] This condition was amended in the recent amendment to the OSG in 2010. A reader-friendly version of the recent amendment to the OSG is available at: http://www.ussc.gov/Guidelines/2010_guidelines/ToC_PDF.cfm

[179] See *ibid.*, §8C2.5(g)(3).

[180] See *ibid.*, §8C2.5(g)(2).

[181] See *ibid.*, §8C2.5(g)(1).

Chapter 2. The new regimes, adopted both in civil and criminal contexts, are "duty-based" regimes that attach greater importance to corporate proactive compliance efforts as a liability determinant. As shown above, in some civil and criminal contexts U.S Federal Law has replaced strict liability regimes by negligence regimes, according to which corporations that adopt an effective compliance management system meet their duty of care, and thereby are shielded from liability.[182] Such regimes may be seen as corresponding with the cooperative enforcement school of thought described in Chapter 3. Under such regimes, cooperative corporations, *i.e.*, those acting to prevent employee misconduct, bear no liability even if a violation eventually occurs in spite of their proactive compliance efforts. In other contexts, a somewhat more modest approach is adopted in the form of "mixed regimes." Under these regimes, corporations are held liable for employee misconduct, but they can benefit from powerful privileges, such as sanction mitigation and evidentiary privileges, if they had an effective compliance management system in place.[183]

5.8 COMPARATIVE INSIGHTS

The U.S. legal system is not the only one in which enforcement policies seek to encourage corporate compliance management systems through the use of liability mitigation or elimination. Many policymakers around the globe have considered the recognition of compliance management systems as a liability determinant. A striking example is the recent U.K. Bribery Act of 2010. This Act holds corporations vicariously liable if a person associated with them "bribes another person intending: (a) to obtain or retain business for [the corporation], or (b) to obtain or retain an advantage in the conduct of business for [the corporation]."[184] Section 7(2) of the Act exempts corporations from liability, if they can show that despite a particular case of bribery they nevertheless had in place "adequate procedures designed to prevent persons associated with [the corporation] from undertaking such conduct."[185]

In other areas of the law, such as antitrust/competition law, compliance management systems have been widely acknowledged as a mitigating

---

182 These negligence corporation liability regimes are discussed in Sections 5.4 and 5.6.

183 These mixed corporation liability regimes are discussed in Sections 5.5 and 5.7.

184 See §7(1) of the U.K. Bribery Act 2010.

185 *Ibid.*, §7(2).

factor in determining corporate liability. For instance, the Office of Fair Trading (OFT) in the U.K. promulgated in 2005 its guidelines, *How your Business can Achieve Compliance*. These OFT guidelines provide corporations with practical guidance concerning the recommended structure of compliance management systems.[186] According to the OFT guidelines, "the fact that a compliance programme is in place may be taken into account as a mitigating factor when we calculate the level of a financial penalty."[187] This approach was reinforced in the recent report, *Drivers of Compliance and Non-compliance with Competition Law*, published in May 2010, in which the OFT stated: "Where, in an individual case, we consider that the existence or adoption of a compliance programme should be regarded as a mitigating factor, we will reduce the financial penalty by up to 10 percent."[188] A similar approach has been adopted by the Australian Competition and Consumer Commission (ACCC) in its policy statement of 2005. According to their policy, "if the ACCC institutes proceedings, the verifiable presence of a compliance culture, as demonstrated by a substantial and successfully implemented compliance program, can be scrutinized by the courts when the quantum of penalty is determined."[189] In the same vein, the Canadian Competition Bureau has stated in its 2008 final report, *Corporate Compliance Programs*, that "the presence of a credible and effective [compliance] program may be seen as a mitigating factor warranting a reduction in the penalty that the Commissioner would otherwise recommend to the [Director Public Prosecutor] for submission to the court."[190]

---

[186] Office of Fair Trading (OFT), *How Your Business Can Achieve Compliance with Competition Law: Guidance*, U.K. (2011), available at: http://www.oft.gov.uk/shared_oft/ca-and-cartels/competition-awareness-compliance/oft1341.pdf.

[187] *Ibid.*, p. 15.

[188] Office of Fair Trading (OFT), *Drivers of Compliance and Non-Compliance with Competition Law*, U.K. (2010), p. 79. Several respondent corporations urged the OFT to increase the amount by which penalties are mitigated by as much as 10–30%. The OFT did not accept such suggestions, stating (p. 79): "We consider that larger discounts for compliance programmes would be undesirable for two reasons. First, the availability of a large discount might have an adverse impact on the deterrent effect of the potential financial penalties, perhaps even having an adverse effect on compliance activities. Second, such a policy could encourage the adoption of 'sham' compliance programmes in order to qualify for a discount."

[189] Australian Competition and Consumer Commission (ACCC), *Corporate Trade Practices Compliance Programs* (2005), p. 9: "If the ACCC institutes proceedings, the verifiable presence of a compliance culture, as demonstrated by a substantial and successfully implemented compliance program, can be scrutinised by the courts when the quantum of penalty is determined."

[190] Canada Competition Bureau, *Corporate Compliance Programs* (2008), p. 18.

Yet, the recognition of compliance management systems as a corporate liability determinant is not accepted universally. Several legal systems adhere to what was referred to as the traditional approach to corporate liability, according to which compliance efforts constitute neither a shield from, nor a mitigating factor of corporate liability. In many of these legal systems, compliance management systems are acknowledged as a desirable instrument which may improve corporate compliance and reduce enforcement costs. Yet, at the same time, these legal systems do not perceive liability mitigation/elimination as a desirable policy which may promote the use of such compliance systems. The most prominent jurisdiction in which this issue has arisen in the recent polemic is the EU Competition policy. Initially, the EU Commission held – in line with the modern approach adopted by the U.S. federal authorities – that when a corporation was found infringing upon competition laws, notwithstanding the implementation of a compliance management system, then the existence of a compliance program *would be* considered as a mitigating factor of corporate liability. This approach was stated explicitly in a series of the Commission's decisions in the 1980s and the 1990s.[191] However, in a series of more recent decisions, the EU Commission has rejected this approach and held that although compliance management systems generally represent a desirable mechanism, their implementation *may not* be considered as a mitigating factor that calls for liability reduction.[192] This transition

---

[191] See, for instance, Case T-77/92 *Parker Pen Ltd v. Commission of the European Communities* [July 14, 1994], ECR 1994 p. II-549, para 93: "In this case, the Court considers that the *Commission took into account in point 24 of its decision the mitigating factors in favour of Parker*, in particular the fact that it cooperated from the beginning of the administrative procedure and also that it *implemented a compliance programme intended to ensure compliance* by its distributors and subsidiaries with the competition rules" (emphasis added). See also, *National Panasonic (U.K.) Ltd.*, Decision 82/853 [1982] OJ L354/29, para 67–9; Case No IV/30.778 *Napier Brown – British Sugar*, Commission Decision 88/518/EEC [18 July 1988] OJ L 284, 19.10.1988; Case IV/F-3/33.708 *British Sugar plc*, Commission Decision 1999/210/EC [October 14, 1998], OJ L076/1, 22.3.1999; and Jonathan Faull and Ali Nikpay, eds., *The EC Law of Competition* (New York: Oxford University Press, 2007), pp. 1089–1090; Ivo Van Bael, *Competition Law of the European Community* (The Netherlands: Kluwer Law International, 2005), p. 1139; Kiran Desai and Mayer Brown, "Compliance," *The European Antitrust Review* (2010), Section 2(3).

[192] See, for instance, *Professional Videotape*, Case COMP/38.432 [2007] OJ C 57, para 241: "Whilst the Commission welcomes measures taken by undertakings to avoid the recurrence of cartel infringements in the future, *such measures cannot change the reality of the infringement and the need to sanction it in this Decision* . . ." (emphasis added). See also, *Pre-Insulated Pipes* [1999] OJ L24/1, para. 172;

in the Commission's approach has been approved by the Court of Justice of the European Union. The Court found no valid reason to make the Commission stick to its previous holdings, stating that: "the mere fact that in certain cases the Commission took the implementation of a competition law compliance programme into consideration as a mitigating factor does not mean that it is obliged to act in the same manner in any given case."[193]

In recent years the EU Commission has been called upon by various industry members to reconsider their approach regarding the relevance of compliance management systems in the determination of corporate penalties. One salient call came, for instance, from the International Chamber of Commerce (ICC), in its 2009 report, *The Fining Policy of the European Commission in Competition Cases.*[194] The report states that:

> [the] ICC regrets that the Commission does not take into consideration best practice compliance programs as a mitigating circumstance when determining the level of fines. . . . Recognizing that best practice compliance programs can have a possible mitigating effect on fines would send a very positive signal and

---

Graphite Electrodes [2002] OJ L100/1, para. 194; *Citric Acide* [2002] OJ L239/18, para. 288; *Zinc Phosphate* [2003] OJ L153/1, para. 331; *Food Flavour Enhancers* [2004] OJ L75/1, para. 279; *Choline Chloride* [2005], OJ L190/22, para. 217.

It should be noted that the EU Commission has promulgated a leniency program that rewards undertakings which are or have been party to secret cartels affecting the Community, for their cooperation in the Commission investigation. This program immunizes (and under certain circumstances merely mitigates the sanctions of) corporations that disclosed information and evidence regarding the cartel. See *Commission notice on immunity from fines and reduction of fines in cartel cases*, OJ C 298 [8.12.2006], p. 17, available at: http://eur-lex.europa.eu/LexUriServ/LexUriServ.do?uri=CELEX:52006XC1208(04):EN:NOT. Yet, beside self-reporting, this policy does not consider the existence of comprehensive compliance management systems as a mitigating factor.

193 See *BPB plc v. Commission*, T-53/03, *BPB plc v. Commission* [July 8, 2008], OJ C 209/41, para. 423–4. See also, Case T-13/03, *Nintendo v. Commission* [April 30, 2009], para 211; T-329/01, *Archer Daniels Midland Co. v. Commission* [September 27, 2006], OJ C 294/85, para 299; T-224/00, *Archer Daniels Midland Company and Archer Daniels Midland Ingredients Ltd. v. Commission* [July 9, 2003]; Case T-7/89 *Hercules Chemicals v. Commission* [1991] ECR II-1711, para. 357; Case T-31/99 *ABB Asea Brown Boveri Ltd. v. Commission of the European Communities*, [March 20, 2002], para 216–222. See also, *European Union (EU) Commission, Guidelines on the Method of Setting Fines Imposed Pursuant to Article 23(2)(a) of Regulation (EC) no 1/2003* (OJ C 210/2 [1.9.2006]), in which corporations' compliance efforts are not included as a mitigating factor of corporate liability.

194 See The International Chamber of Commerce (ICC), *The Fining Policy of the European Commission in Competition Cases*, Paris, France (2009).

> encourage companies to set in place such programs, which would contribute to the policy goal of specific and general prevention of infringements.[195]

The EU Commission, in turn, has agreed that corporate internal enforcement efforts are an important instrument for securing corporate compliance. Nevertheless, as stated by Philip Lowe, then Director-General of Competition at the EU Commission, "it will take some time [before] we get to the position where we can say explicitly that a compliance programme gives the company some degree of advantage."[196]

5.9 SUMMARY AND CONCLUDING REMARKS

In this chapter, I have presented the pragmatic implications of the conceptual tension between the harsh style of the deterrence-based approach and the conciliatory style of the cooperative approach to law enforcement, which were both analyzed in Part I of this book. As mentioned above, corporations are the actual beneficiaries of their employees' behavior. Moreover, corporations design and direct their employees' activities, and are thereby usually able to control their conduct. Based on these grounds, corporations – although soulless and bodiless – are subject to civil and criminal liability. These liabilities are believed to motivate corporations not only to comply with the law, but also to proactively ensure compliance among their employees.

The survey of various liability regimes advanced in this chapter has revealed the spectrum of corporate liability frameworks used in practice, as well as the recent developments that have taken place in various legal systems. At one edge of the spectrum, we found *strict liability* structures that hold corporations strictly liable for their employees' misconduct regardless of any internal enforcement efforts exerted by these corporations. Such liability structures correspond with the harsh and uncompro-

---

[195] *Ibid.*, p. 5. Available at http://www.icc.se/policy/statements/2009/EU_fining_policy.pdf.

[196] Lowe's quote is found in Lewis Crofts, "EC's Lowe Still to be Convinced of Effective Compliance Programmes," *MLex Market Intelligence* (January 11, 2010). For a similar approach voiced by Lowe see Lewis Crofts, "EC's Lowe Moots Due-Process Improvements, but Firms' Compliance Rewards Not on Agenda," *MLex Market Intelligence* (November 17, 2009): "we could get to a point where there would be a discussion about the extent to which the behavior of a company in terms of its strict enforcement of a compliance programme could be possibly taken into account in terms of a mitigating factor. . . . We are not there yet."

mising style of the deterrence-based approach, centering upon the threat of legal sanctions in order to promote compliance. At the other end of the spectrum, we found *negligence* corporate liability structures. These structures avoid imposing liability on corporations *unless* it is proven that these corporations have acted irresponsibly and failed to undertake internal enforcement measures.[197] Such liability structures correspond with the conciliatory style of the cooperative enforcement approach that reserves the threat of legal sanctions only as a last resort. Between these two ends of the spectrum, we found a handful of *mixed structures* that follow an intermediate approach. According to this intermediate approach, corporations are held liable for their employees' misconduct, but benefit from penalty mitigation or evidentiary privileges if they exert internal enforcement efforts.[198]

As suggested by this chapter, the departure from the more traditional strict liability regimes towards duty-based regimes is not unique to the U.S. federal legal system. Various other legal systems, including the U.K., Australia, and Canada, have followed a similar pattern of policy development. Yet these new policy trends have been explicitly rejected by other legal systems, including the EU legal system, which has gone through the opposite transformation by rejecting duty-based liability regimes, while adhering to the traditional strict liability ones. The question can be posed then, *how should a corporate liability regime be structured to efficiently induce corporate proactive compliance?* This question is addressed in the following chapter.

---

[197] In this category of regimes, I refer to liability frameworks that shield corporations from civil liability (Section 5.4) and criminal liability (Section 5.6) if they had undertaken effective internal enforcement efforts in good faith.

[198] In this category of regimes, I refer to liability frameworks that recognize compliance management systems as a mitigating factor of civil penalties (Section 5.5) and criminal penalties (Section 5.7).

6. Corporate liability regimes: a law and economics analysis[1]

6.1 INTRODUCTION

Corporate liability may be imposed through a wide spectrum of legal regimes. As shown in Chapter 5, one end of the spectrum consists of "deterrence-oriented" liability regimes that hold corporations "strictly" liable for employee misconduct, regardless of any internal enforcement efforts exerted by these corporations. The other end of the spectrum consists of "cooperation-oriented" liability regimes in which no liability is imposed on cooperative corporations, *i.e.*, corporations that implement due internal enforcement measures aimed at preventing misconduct.[2] The middle of the spectrum is populated by various "mixed regimes" in which corporations are held liable for their employee misconduct, but may benefit from penalty mitigation or evidentiary privileges if they have established and maintained internal enforcement measures.[3] All such regimes, although diverse in structure, share a similar objective that boils down to encouraging corporate proactive compliance at the lowest enforcement cost.

Law and economics thinkers have analyzed different structures of corporate liability regimes according to the incentive scheme they produce for corporate proactive compliance. Thus far, no consensus has been reached regarding the optimal structure of corporate liability regimes. Commentators show that in each particular setting, a specific structure of corporate liability may be superior to others.[4] Yet, none of the existing

---

[1] A substantial portion of this chapter is adopted from Oded, "Inducing Corporate Compliance: A Compound Corporate Liability Regime."

[2] In this category of regimes, I refer to liability frameworks that shield corporations from civil liability (Chapter 5, Section 5.4) and criminal liability (Chapter 5, Section 5.6) if they adopted effective internal enforcement efforts in good faith.

[3] In this category of regimes, I refer to liability frameworks in Chapter 5, Sections 5.5 and 5.7.

[4] Major structures of corporate liability regimes are discussed in Section 6.3 below.

regimes has been widely accepted as producing socially desirable outcomes across a broad range of potential settings. The scholarly polemic outlined below demonstrates the need for an innovative liability framework that may sustain the strengths of the existing regimes, while at the same time coping with their weaknesses. The development of such an efficient liability regime is the key objective of this chapter. Therefore, in what follows I answer the question: *How should a corporate liability regime be structured to efficiently induce corporate proactive compliance?* More particularly, *how should the law structure the responsibility of corporations for crimes and intentional torts of their employees?*[5]

This chapter is organized as follows: Section 6.2 provides the required background for a welfare analysis of corporate liability regimes and focuses on the economic functions of corporate liability regimes in inducing corporate proactive compliance. Section 6.3 evaluates the existing liability frameworks discussed in Chapter 5 according to the incentive apparatus they produce for corporate proactive compliance. The analysis reveals that none of the existing liability regimes discussed in Chapter 5 creates an optimal liability framework. Therefore, I develop in Section 6.4 an innovative corporate liability regime, entitled the "*Compound Corporate Liability Regime*," which may present a workable, socially desirable liability framework in most settings. I summarize and conclude this chapter in Section 6.5.

6.2 THE ECONOMICS OF CORPORATE LIABILITY

The point of departure of the law and economics literature analyzing corporate liability regimes is the deterrence theory that was discussed in detail in Chapter 2. As the reader may recall, the deterrence theory perceives regulatees as utility-maximizing agents, who decide whether to obey the law or to violate it according to a cost–benefit analysis. Agents are assumed to

---

[5] Following the existing law and economics literature in this field, most notably Arlen and Kraakman, "Controlling Corporate Misconduct: An Analysis of Corporate Liability Regimes," 687–779, the current study focuses on intentional wrongdoing. The conclusions of the analysis concerning the structure of an optimal corporate liability regime are applicable to unintentional wrongs when liability for the underlying activity is governed by a strict liability rule. Note that where unintentional misconduct is concerned, the optimal sanctions faced by corporations may differ from those proposed by this study because corporations are likely to bear their employees' expected individual liability for unintentional wrongdoing, either through *ex-ante* payments of higher wages, or through *ex-post* indemnification. See *infra* note 20.

compare their expected compliance utility, *i.e.*, the payoffs they expect to obtain when they obey the law, with their expected violation utility, *i.e.*, the payoffs they expect when they violate the law. Consequently, agents obey the law only when their expected compliance utility is greater than their expected violation utility.[6] Accordingly, as discussed in Chapter 2, regulatory enforcement systems may achieve an optimal level of deterrence by setting the expected liability for misconduct at the level of the total social costs caused by the misconduct, discounted by the probability of detection.[7]

6.2.1 Corporate Liability – Do We Really Need It?

By applying the logic of the deterrence theory to corporate settings, an optimal level of deterrence could, theoretically, be produced by an individual-liability scheme that holds individual primary actors operating on behalf of corporations personally liable.[8] However, the organizational settings of corporations, in which various agents act on the behalf of their corporations, pose some challenges to an ordinary enforcement system tailored to induce the compliance of individual players. These challenges stem from the composite structure of corporate actors.[9] Under the typical corporate setting, the assumption of a single entity conducting a cost–benefit analysis when making behavioral choices is no longer valid.

---

6 See, for instance, Becker, "Crime and Punishment: An Economic Approach," 169–217; Stigler, "The Optimum Enforcement of Laws," 526–536; Heyes, "Making Things Stick: Enforcement and Compliance," 50–63; Polinsky and Shavell, "The Economic Theory of Public Enforcement of Law," 45–76. For a discussion of the deterrence-based theory, see Chapter 2, Section 2.2.

7 See Chapter 2, Section 2.2.4. See also, Stigler, "The Optimum Enforcement of Laws," 526–536; Cooter, "Prices and Sanctions," 1523–1560; Becker, "Make Punishment Fit the Corporate Crime," 22–30; Block, "Optimal Penalties, Criminal Law and the Control of Corporate Behavior," 395–419; Heyes, "Making Things Stick: Enforcement and Compliance," 50–63; Polinsky and Shavell, "The Economic Theory of Public Enforcement of Law," 45–76.

8 See, for instance, Arlen and Kraakman, "Controlling Corporate Misconduct: An Analysis of Corporate Liability Regimes," p. 695; Khanna, "Corporate Liability Standards: When Should Corporations be Held Criminally Liable?," p. 1243.

9 The analysis mainly refers to large corporations, in which a vast amount of business activity is carried out by a large number of employees. Individual liability frameworks may still perform relatively well when small, family-owned corporations are concerned, in which corporate activity is undertaken by a small group of individuals who are personally engaged in corporate decision-making, and who are directly influenced by the corporate performance.

Behavioral choices of large business corporations are taken and executed on two interconnected levels: first, the *central decision-making level*, in which the corporate administration shapes the corporate business activity by determining the sorts of activity engaged in, the technology to be used, and the overall level of activity. Second, the *execution level*, in which employees at different levels in the corporation operate as an integrated team in executing the corporate policy. Given this complex structure, even when corporations decide to obey the law, violations may still be committed at the execution level. Such violations may occur, for instance, due to an imperfect flow of information and commands within corporations; conflicts of interest between corporations and their employees; or simply due to corporations' inability to control their employees at all times.[10]

Considering the composite structure of corporate regulatees, law and economics scholars point to particular deficiencies in the use of an individual-liability scheme in controlling corporate actors. At the outset, as implied above, an individual-liability scheme does not consider the agency relationship between corporations and their employees, and therefore may fail to provide appropriate incentives at both the management and employee levels.[11] *Second*, individual liability alone cannot provide adequate compliance incentives to employees, who are unable to modify procedures exceeding their own discretion. *Third*, corporate activity is normally carried out by a group of individual actors operating as an integrated team. Therefore, it may be difficult for enforcement agencies to detect culpable individuals, as well as to identify their personal level of culpability.[12] *Fourth*, challenges to individual-liability schemes may arise with regards to individual employees' limited wealth, which may not

---

[10] See Alan O. Sykes, "The Economics of Vicarious Liability," *The Yale Law Journal* 93 (1984), p. 1239.

[11] See, for instance, Lewis A. Kornhauser, "An Economic Analysis of the Choice between Enterprise and Personal Liability for Accidents," *California Law Review* 70 (1982), 1345–1392; Sykes, "The Economics of Vicarious Liability," 1231–1280; Alan O. Sykes, "The Boundaries of Vicarious Liability: An Economic Analysis of the Scope of Employment Rule and Related Legal Doctrines," *Harvard Law Review* 101 (1988), 563–609; Kraakman,"Vicarious and Corporate Liability," 669–681.

[12] See, for instance, Kornhauser, "An Economic Analysis of the Choice between Enterprise and Personal Liability for Accidents," pp. 1370–1371; Walsh and Pyrich, "Corporate Compliance Programs as a Defense to Criminal Liability: Can a Corporation Save its Soul?," p. 635. Compare also with Eric Holder, Deputy Attorney General, *Memorandum for Heads of Department Components United States Attorneys: Principles of Federal Prosecution of Corporations*, §VI(B): "It will often be difficult to determine which individual took which action on behalf of the corporation."

suffice to cover the sanctions imposed by the enforcement system.[13] This judgment proof problem may be stringent, for instance, when the optimal sanction is relatively high due to the rigorous harm resulting from the violation.[14] *Fifth*, various scholars have pointed to the "defective rationality of individual agents" as an additional source of concern.[15] These scholars favor the establishment of corporate liability regimes, based on the presumption that corporations, although run by individuals, come closer to the "*rational agent*" or the "*economic man*" than most individuals that are subject to a marketplace of biases.[16] Altogether, an enforcement policy may fail to induce corporate compliance by treating corporations as monoliths, *i.e.*, by simply motivating corporate "brains," the corporate management, to adjust corporate activities to regulatory requirements. A desirable enforcement policy must go a step further to ensure that employees' actions, which are taken within the scope of their employment, are effectively monitored and controlled.

6.2.2 The Economic Functions of Corporate Liability

Corporate liability, in which corporations are held liable for their employees' misconduct, comprises a valuable policy instrument used to induce corporate proactive compliance.[17] Law and economics scholars propose

---

[13] See, for instance, Shavell, "The Judgment Proof Problem," 45–58; Heyes, "Making Things Stick: Enforcement and Compliance," p. 57; Kornhauser, "An Economic Analysis of the Choice between Enterprise and Personal Liability for Accidents," 1345–1392; Sykes, "The Economics of Vicarious Liability," 1231–1280; Shavell, *Economic Analysis of Accident Law*; Khanna, "Corporate Liability Standards: When Should Corporations be Held Criminally Liable?," p. 1243.

[14] See, for instance, Colvin, "Corporate Personality and Criminal Liability," p. 26. Colvin has argued that "the characteristic scale of corporate operations makes the risk of harm resulting from inaction usually much greater than it would be in the case of individuals."

[15] See, for instance, Khanna, "Corporate Liability Standards: When Should Corporations be Held Criminally Liable?," p. 1242; Staw, "Dressing Up Like an Organization: When Psychological Theories can Explain Organizational Action," 805–819; Croley, "Vicarious Liability in Tort: On the Sources and Limits of Employee Reasonableness," 1705–1738; Schwartz, "The Hidden and Fundamental Issue of Employer Vicarious Liability," 1739–1767. See also, Kraakman, "Vicarious and Corporate Liability," p. 672.

[16] See, for instance, Sutherland, *White Collar Crime: The Uncut Version*; Khanna, "Corporate Liability Standards: When Should Corporations be Held Criminally Liable?," p. 1245. For a discussion of the rationality of individual agents and corporations see Chapter 2, Section 2.4.4.

[17] An overview of corporate liability regimes used in practice to control corporate misconduct is provided in Chapter 5.

that this policy instrument has two major economic functions: an *internalization* function and a *self-enforcement* function.[18]

6.2.2.1 Internalization function

The first economic function of corporate liability regimes focuses on the position of corporations as the main beneficiaries of their employees' activities. Applying the wisdom of the deterrence theory to the corporate ecology, law and economics scholars show that an efficient corporate liability regime would induce corporations to *internalize* the social ramifications of their activities, and thereby adjust their activities – carried out by their employees – to socially optimal standards of behavior.[19] As the argument goes, like a rational individual actor, if profit-maximizing corporations incur an optimal expected liability, which is set at the level of the social costs of their employees' misconduct, then such corporations are induced to factor in the social ramifications of their activities when determining the type of their activities (*e.g.*, what should they produce?); the level of their activities (*e.g.*, how much should they produce?); and the technology to be used for their activities (*e.g.*, how should they produce it?).[20]

---

[18] The economic function identified in the law and economics scholarly literature corresponds with the legal justification of corporate liability regimes given by legal scholars and courts. See the discussion in Chapter 5, Section 5.2. For a general discussion of both economic functions of corporate liability see Arlen and Kraakman, "Controlling Corporate Misconduct: An Analysis of Corporate Liability Regimes," p. 697; Khanna, "Corporate Liability Standards: When Should Corporations be Held Criminally Liable?," p. 1261; Walsh and Pyrich, "Corporate Compliance Programs as a Defense to Criminal Liability: Can a Corporation Save its Soul?," p. 635; Huff, "The Role of Corporate Compliance Programs in Determining Corporate Criminal Liability: A Suggested Approach," pp. 1263, 1295; Pitt and Groskaufmanis, "Minimizing Corporate Civil and Criminal Liability: A Second Look at Corporate Codes of Conduct," p. 1573; Gregory D. Miller, "Hypotheses on Reputation: Alliance Choices and the Shadow of the Past," *Security Studies* 12(3) (2003), p. 66; Shavell, "The Optimal Level of Corporate Liability Given the Limited Ability of Corporations to Penalize their Employees," 203–213; Polinsky, "Punitive Damages: An Economic Analysis," p. 869.

[19] See, for instance, Arlen and Kraakman, "Controlling Corporate Misconduct: An Analysis of Corporate Liability Regimes," p. 697; Khanna, "Corporate Liability Standards: When Should Corporations be Held Criminally Liable?," p. 1261.

[20] Note that corporate expected liability for intentional wrongdoing must be set at the level of the total social costs of the wrongdoing, even if corporate employees are also held liable for the same misconduct, since corporations bear their own expected liability for these wrongs. As shown in the existing literature, corpora-

6.2.2.2 Self-enforcement function

The second economic function of corporate liability regimes hinges on corporations' ability to control their employees. Law and economics scholars show that an efficient enforcement policy must utilize corporations' ability to control their employees and ensure that they obey the law, especially when these corporations are able to control their employees more efficiently than government agencies.[21] By holding corporations liable for their employees' misconduct, an enforcement policy may produce incentives for corporations to *self-enforce* the law, that is, to act in order to prevent, deter, and report their own misconduct as committed by their employees within the scope of their employment. In this way, a corporate liability regime motivates corporations to become "active partners" in the battle against law-breaking.[22]

To capture the social gain produced by the participation of corporations in the battle against law-breaking, it is important to consider the superior capabilities of corporations in controlling their employees' behavior. When compared to enforcement authorities, corporations are better acquainted with their own type of activities and have better access to information,

---

tions will not compensate employees for their expected liability from intentional wrongs that the corporations do not want to commit. See Arlen, "The Potentially Perverse Effects of Corporate Criminal Liability," p. 852, footnote. 59; Arlen and Kraakman, "Controlling Corporate Misconduct: An Analysis of Corporate Liability Regimes," p. 698, footnote 27. In contrast, where unintentional wrongdoing is concerned, corporations normally compensate their employees for their expected liability, either *ex-ante* through higher wages, or *ex-post* by indemnifying them. Therefore, for this type of wrongdoing the optimal corporate expected liability should be set at the level of the total social costs of the wrongdoing minus the fine paid by the employee. See Mitchell A. Polinsky and Steven Shavell, "Should Employees be Subject to Fines and Imprisonment Given the Existence of Corporate Liability?" *International Review of Law and Economics* 13(3) (1993), p. 241. See also, Arlen and Kraakman, "Controlling Corporate Misconduct: An Analysis of Corporate Liability Regimes," p. 698, footnote 27.

[21] See, for instance, Khanna, "Corporate Liability Standards: When Should Corporations be Held Criminally Liable?," p. 1245: ". . . corporate liability enlists the corporation as a monitor of its agents' behavior and hence serves a desirable function when individual liability is likely to fail."

[22] See, for instance, Huff, "The Role of Corporate Compliance Programs in Determining Corporate Criminal Liability: A Suggested Approach," p. 1263, 1295; Pitt and Groskaufmanis, "Minimizing Corporate Civil and Criminal Liability: A Second Look at Corporate Codes of Conduct," p. 1573; Walsh and Pyrich, "Corporate Compliance Programs as a Defense to Criminal Liability: Can a Corporation Save its Soul?," pp. 620–621, 636, 678; Shavell, "The Optimal Level of Corporate Liability Given the Limited Ability of Corporations to Penalize their Employees," 203–213.

as well as superior capabilities and resources to efficiently determine internal processes and closely monitor their employees.[23] Furthermore, corporations may rely on their direct past experience and facilitate internal learning processes that may efficiently address compliance-related risks. Hence, corporations' participation in the battle against law-breaking may increase employee compliance and reduce the overall enforcement costs.

Where corporations' self-enforcement actions are concerned, it is possible to distinguish between three types of self-enforcement actions:

(i) ***Ex-ante self-policing*** – this type of action includes all education and prevention activities that may be undertaken by corporations *before* any law-breaking occurs; *e.g.*, the provision of detailed working procedures, guidelines, manuals, ethics codes, employee training, and close monitoring. Given the vast amount of information possessed by corporations regarding the nature of their regulated activities, *ex-ante* self-policing actions may substantially reduce the number of regulatory violations committed by employees, and thereby, increase the social welfare.[24]

---

[23] See, for instance, Arlen and Kraakman, "Controlling Corporate Misconduct: An Analysis of Corporate Liability Regimes," p. 700: ". . . where both the firm and the government can administer a comparable sanction . . . the firm may be the least-cost administrator simply because it can identify and charge culpable agents more cheaply than the government can." See also, Walsh and Pyrich, "Corporate Compliance Programs as a Defense to Criminal Liability: Can a Corporation Save its Soul?," p. 678; Khanna and Dickinson, "The Corporate Monitor: The New Corporate Czar," pp. 1728–1729; Heineman, "Caught in the Middle," p. 89; Kraakman, "Vicarious and Corporate Liability," p. 671; Shavell, *Economic Analysis of Accident Law*, pp. 173–174; Arlen, "The Potentially Perverse Effects of Corporate Criminal Liability," 833–867; Huff, "The Role of Corporate Compliance Programs in Determining Corporate Criminal Liability: A Suggested Approach," p. 1281; Khanna, "Corporate Liability Standards: When Should Corporations be Held Criminally Liable?," p. 1245.

[24] The definitions used in this chapter differ slightly from the definition of 'policing measures' used by Arlen and Kraakman in "Controlling Corporate Misconduct: An Analysis of Corporate Liability Regimes," 687–779. The authors define policing measures as measures taken by corporations before and/or after the wrongdoing occurs, which deter wrongdoing by increasing the probability that culpable agents will be sanctioned. This definition includes measures such as monitoring, investigating, and reporting actions altogether. See Arlen and Kraakman, "Controlling Corporate Misconduct: An Analysis of Corporate Liability Regimes," p. 706. For the sake of isolating the impact of each sort of self-enforcement action on the social costs of regulatory violations, I find the detailed definition presented above useful.

(ii) ***Ex-post self-policing*** – this type of action includes all deterrence activities that may be undertaken by corporations *after* the specific law-breaking has occurred. Within this category of actions we may consider, for instance, active detection and self-investigation of misconduct. As shown in the literature, corporations usually possess greater access to relevant information, and thereby are much more likely to detect employees' misconduct than any enforcement authority.[25] Hence, when such *ex-post* self-policing activity is undertaken by corporations, rather than by enforcement authorities, substantial enforcement costs may be saved.

(iii) ***Self-reporting*** – this type of action includes statements or accounts made by corporations to the relevant enforcement authority disclosing their own misconduct. As shown in the literature, self-reporting may substantially reduce the costs of enforcement associated with the detection of misconduct, the collection of evidence, and the litigation of the detected misconduct.[26]

After having explored the twin economic functions of an efficient corporate liability regime, I begin in the next section to evaluate the different structures of liability regimes presented in Chapter 5.

---

[25] The scholarly literature has specifically pointed out that corporations commonly possess greater access to relevant information, and thereby are more likely to detect employees' misconduct than any government authority. See, for instance, Walsh and Pyrich, "Corporate Compliance Programs as a Defense to Criminal Liability: Can a Corporation Save its Soul?," p. 678; Khanna and Dickinson, "The Corporate Monitor: The New Corporate Czar," pp. 1728–1729; Heineman, "Caught in the Middle," p. 89; Kraakman, "Vicarious and Corporate Liability," p. 671; Shavell, *Economic Analysis of Accident Law*, pp. 173–174; Arlen, "The Potentially Perverse Effects of Corporate Criminal Liability," 833–867; Huff, "The Role of Corporate Compliance Programs in Determining Corporate Criminal Liability: A Suggested Approach," p. 1281; Khanna, "Corporate Liability Standards: When Should Corporations be Held Criminally Liable?," p. 1245.

[26] See, for instance, Louis Kaplow and Steven Shavell, "Optimal Law Enforcement with Self-Reporting of Behavior," *Journal of Political Economy*, University of Chicago Press, 102(3) (1994), 583–606; Malik, "Avoidance, Screening and Optimum Enforcement," 341–353. For a discussion of enforcement costs and the impact of self-reporting on such costs see Section 6.4.1 below.

6.3 MAJOR CORPORATE LIABILITY REGIMES – A COMPARATIVE EVALUATION

The liability regimes discussed in detail in Chapter 5 have been analyzed in the law and economics literature according to their impact on social welfare. This section provides a brief comparative evaluation of such regimes. To allow for a systematic comparative evaluation, the analysis focuses on the capability of each alternative regime to efficiently fulfill the economic functions discussed in Section 6.2.2 above. The conclusions of the analysis are presented in Table 6.1.

6.3.1 Strict Liability

As discussed in Chapter 5, corporations under a strict liability regime are held liable for their employees' wrongdoing which occurs within the scope of their employment. Corporations under a strict liability regime incur sanctions that are equivalent to the total social costs of the wrongdoing, discounted by the probability of detection.[27] This regime corresponds with

Table 6.1 A comparative welfare evaluation of major corporate liability regimes

Economic function of corporate liability	Induced corporate activity	Incentives provided to corporations under the following regimes			
		Strict liability	Negligence	Adjusted strict liability	Composite regime
Internalization	Compliance	Yes	No	Yes	Yes
Self-enforcement	*Ex-ante* self-policing	Yes	No	Yes	No
	Ex-post self-policing	No	No	Yes	No
	Self-reporting	No	Yes	No	Yes

[27] For the discussion of corporate strict liability see Chapter 5, Section 5.3.1. For a comprehensive law and economics analysis of the traditional strict liability frameworks see Guido Calabresi, *The Costs of Accidents: A Legal and Economic Analysis* (New Haven: Yale University Press, 1970); Steven Shavell, "Strict Liability Versus Negligence," *Journal of Legal Studies* 9(1) (1980), 1–25; Hans-Bernd Schäfer and Andreas Schönenberger, *Strict Liability Versus Negligence*, Edward Elgar and the University of Ghent, available at: http://encyclo.findlaw.com/3100book.pdf (1999), 597–624.

the traditional vicarious liability that is based on the *respondeat superior* doctrine.[28] Following the logic of the deterrence theory, provided that sanctions against corporate misconduct are optimally set, a strict liability regime eliminates any firm-level incentive to engage in misconduct. Hence, strict liability is particularly likely to induce corporations to *internalize* the social ramifications of their behavior, as well as to engage in *ex-ante* self-policing.[29] Yet, given that under a strict liability regime self-policing and/or self-reporting actions are not expected to eliminate or even mitigate corporate liability, corporations have an incentive neither to *ex-post* self-police nor to self-report their employee misconduct, especially when such actions may increase the expected liability of the corporation by increasing the probability that corporate misconduct will be detected and sanctioned.[30]

The law and economics literature that analyzes the welfare impact of corporate strict liability regimes suggests that the main drawback of these regimes stems from the "*perverse effects*" of self-enforcement activities that are commonly generated under such regimes. The initial reason for the potential perverse effect of self-enforcement activities is that even when corporations diligently self-police, they are unlikely to prevent all possible wrongdoing.[31] Hence, under a strict liability regime, self-enforcement actions, such as monitoring, investigations, and self-reporting may create two opposite effects.[32] While they may reduce the probability that employee misconduct occurs since employees are more closely monitored, at the same time they may also increase the probability that employee misconduct will be detected, which therefore increases the probability that corporations will be sanctioned for this misconduct.[33]

---

[28] The *respondeat superior* doctrine is discussed in Chapter 5, Section 5.2.1.

[29] See, for instance, Arlen and Kraakman, "Controlling Corporate Misconduct: An Analysis of Corporate Liability Regimes," p. 704; Khanna, "Corporate Liability Standards: When Should Corporations be Held Criminally Liable?," p. 1263.

[30] See Arlen, "The Potentially Perverse Effects of Corporate Criminal Liability," 833–867; Arlen and Kraakman, "Controlling Corporate Misconduct: An Analysis of Corporate Liability Regimes," 687–779.

[31] See Arlen and Kraakman, "Controlling Corporate Misconduct: An Analysis of Corporate Liability Regimes," p. 707.

[32] Note that Arlen in "The Potentially Perverse Effects of Corporate Criminal Liability," 833–867, and Arlen and Kraakman in "Controlling Corporate Misconduct: An Analysis of Corporate Liability Regimes," p. 706, define self-policing actions as measures that "operate by increasing the probability that culpable agents will be sanctioned." This definition slightly differs from the definition used in this chapter. See *supra* note 24.

[33] See Arlen, "The Potentially Perverse Effects of Corporate Criminal Liability," p. 836; Arlen and Kraakman, "Controlling Corporate Misconduct: An

When the latter effect dominates the former, self-enforcement actions may result in an increase in corporations' expected liability.[34] As a result, there is a consensus in the scholarly literature that under a strict liability regime the potentially perverse effects of self-enforcement actions may discourage corporations from engaging in *ex-post* self-policing and self-reporting. Moreover, it has been suggested that under certain circumstances, a corporate strict liability regime may not only provide no incentive for self-policing, but may even induce corporations to reduce the level of self-policing they would have maintained were they not subject to a strict liability regime.[35]

6.3.2 Negligence

A negligence corporate liability regime holds corporations liable for their employees' misconduct undertaken within the scope of their employment only if they failed to take due care, namely, failed to meet a legal duty to act to prevent, police, and report their employee misconduct.[36] This liability regime corresponds with the newly emerged corporate liability

---

Analysis of Corporate Liability Regimes," p. 707; Khanna, "Corporate Liability Standards: When Should Corporations be Held Criminally Liable?," p. 1264; Kraakman, "Vicarious and Corporate Liability," 669–681.

[34] The perverse effect is straightforward when self-reporting is considered. Self-reporting makes detection certain (the probability of detection is 1), and therefore, under a strict liability regime, in which self-reporting does not include sanction elimination or mitigation, it increases a corporation's expected liability. Theoretically, the perverse effect may also result from *ex-post* self-policing actions. Arlen and Kraakman provide an example of a securities firm that records broker phone calls to monitor for securities fraud. This self-policing activity may increase corporations' expected liability if the tapes produced by the firm are used by the public authorities to prove corporate culpability (see Arlen and Kraakman, "Controlling Corporate Misconduct: An Analysis of Corporate Liability Regimes," pp. 708–709). For further discussion of the potentially perverse effects with respect to self-policing activity see *infra* notes 88–90 and the related main text.

[35] See Arlen, "The Potentially Perverse Effects of Corporate Criminal Liability," 833–867. Arlen uses an example of corporations that are exposed to reputational damage from employee misconduct. Arlen points out that (p. 843) holding such corporations strictly liable might deter them from self-policing. A related observation, made in Chu and Qian, "Vicarious Liability Under a Negligence Rule," 305–322, is that strict vicarious liability may motivate corporations to act to withhold information produced by their self-policing activity from the enforcement authorities.

[36] For a comprehensive law and economics analysis of the strict liability and the negligence frameworks see Calabresi, *The Costs of Accidents: A Legal and*

policies that shield corporations from liability if they had in place an effective compliance management system.[37] Although a negligence corporate liability regime may, under certain circumstances, induce corporations to self-report employee wrongdoing (and by that shield themselves from corporate liability), this regime may neither induce corporations to *internalize* the social ramifications of their activities, nor to engage in effective self-policing.

As for the *internalization* goal, negligence corporate liability may fail to induce corporations to internalize the social ramifications of their activities, whereas once a corporation has satisfied the required due level of care, it is no longer incurring any sanction, and therefore has no incentive to factor in the social ramifications of its actions.[38] For example, suppose that certain regulations determine that in order to meet a due level of care, corporations must install a particular filtration system. In that case, by installing and appropriately maintaining the particular filtration system a corporation meets its legal duty and is, therefore, shielded from liability, even if its operation results in a high level of pollution. Under such circumstances, corporations have no incentive to internalize the social ramifications when determining the actual level of their activities.[39]

Regarding the incentives of "*self-policing*," the law and economics literature suggests that one of the main drawbacks of the negligence corporate liability regime stems from the heavy "*information burden*" that is imposed by such regimes on enforcement authorities and courts. At the outset, a negligence corporate liability regime requires enforcement authorities to *ex-ante* determine the due level of care. This determination may involve substantial errors: "the authorities do not have the kind of detailed information about the firm that would generally be needed to make assessments and even if they did, courts might err in

---

Economic Analysis; Shavell, "Strict Liability Versus Negligence," 1–25; Schäfer and Schönenberger, *Strict Liability Versus Negligence*, pp. 597–624.

37 For a discussion of these liability regimes see Chapter 5, Sections 5.4 and 5.6.

38 For the discussion of the welfare impacts of negligence regimes see Shavell, "Strict Liability Versus Negligence," 1–25; Polinsky and Shavell, "Should Employees be Subject to Fines and Imprisonment Given the Existence of Corporate Liability?," p. 239; Sykes, "The Boundaries of Vicarious Liability: An Economic Analysis of the Scope of Employment Rule and Related Legal Doctrines," 563–609.

39 See Arlen and Kraakman, "Controlling Corporate Misconduct: An Analysis of Corporate Liability Regimes," p. 692: ". . . a duty-based regime – under which a firm is liable only if it failed to take appropriate actions to discourage wrongdoing – would distort activity levels by allowing the firm to avoid liability for the full costs of their employees' actions simply by acting reasonably or taking 'due care'."

applying them to specific facts."[40] Hence, negligence corporate liability regimes may fail to induce efficient *ex-ante* self-policing measures.[41] Moreover, negligence corporate liability regimes require enforcement authorities to evaluate corporations' self-enforcement activities *ex-post*, in order to determine whether a corporation satisfied a due level of care in undertaking self-enforcement. Such liability regimes are prone to failure due to *information asymmetry* between the law enforcers and the corporations being regulated. This information asymmetry may be strategically used by corporations in order to escape liability by presenting law enforcers with only "window dressing" in order to protect themselves.[42] Specifically, Laufer (1999) and Krawiec (2003, 2005), for instance, show that self-policing actions can be easily mimicked to present only a "window dressing" which is less costly for corporations.[43] These studies show that courts and agencies do not always possess

---

[40] See Khanna, "Corporate Liability Standards: When Should Corporations be Held Criminally Liable?," p. 1263. See also, Cooter, "Prices and Sanctions," 1523–1560, who examines the impact of the three categories of court-made errors in setting standards, establishing liability, and assessing damage; Arlen and Kraakman, "Controlling Corporate Misconduct: An Analysis of Corporate Liability Regimes," p. 705: ". . . a duty-based regime would face serious problems of judicial error. Reviewing compensation and discharge policies is a difficult task. . . . By comparison, strict liability does not require courts to distinguish legitimate from illegitimate firm behavior."

[41] See also, Arlen and Kraakman, "Controlling Corporate Misconduct: An Analysis of Corporate Liability Regimes," p. 703: "Determining the right mix of screening, security, and gatekeeping measures *ex-ante*, and compensation-based measures *ex-post*, clearly requires detailed knowledge about the firm. For this reason, strict liability ordinarily dominates duty-based liability as a means of inducing preventive measures."

[42] The risk of "window dressing" self-enforcement activities is not merely theoretic. In several cases the court has actually found that the corporate compliance program was merely a "paper program." See, for instance, *United States v. Greyhound Corp.*, 370 F. Supp. 881 (N.D. III. 1974); *United States v. LBS Bank-New York, Inc.* 757 F. Supp. 496 (E.D. Pa. 1990); *Medical Slenderizing, Inc. v. State*, 579 S.W.2d 569 (Tex. Civ. App. Tyler 1979).

[43] William S. Laufer, "Corporate Liability, Risk Shifting, and the Paradox of Compliance," *Vanderbilt Law Review* 52, (1999), 1341–1420; Kimberly D. Krawiec, "Cosmetic Compliance and the Failure of Negotiated Governance," *Wash. U. L. Q.* 81, (2003), 487–544; Kimberly D. Krawiec, "Organization Misconduct: Beyond the Principal Agent Model," *Florida State Law Review* 32, (2005), 571–615. For empirical evidence regarding the existence of ineffective compliance management systems, see, for instance, Marie M. McKendall, Beverly DeMarr and Catherine Jones-Rikkers, "Ethical Compliance Programs and Corporate Illegality: Testing the Assumptions of the Corporate Sentencing Guidelines," *Journal of Business Ethics* 37(4) (2002), 367–383.

sufficient information to adequately distinguish between "effective" and "cosmetic" self-policing actions.[44] As a result, duty-based regimes may encourage corporations to adopt cosmetic self-enforcement actions.[45] Therefore, although negligence liability regimes could, in theory, induce corporations to self-police, they are fraught with the perils of opportunistic behavior and self-policing measures that serve only as mere "window dressing."[46]

---

[44] See, for instance, Senator Edward Kennedy at the Commission-sponsored Second Symposium On Crime and Punishment in the United States, in the *Proceedings*, pp. 115, 119, cited in William S. Laufer, "Corporate Liability, Risk Shifting, and the Paradox of Compliance," p. 1207, footnote 268: "Members of the business community and those who counsel corporate clients must recognize that there will always be skepticism about a policy that gives any break to corporations that have committed crimes, as the guidelines will sometimes do when a corporation demonstrates a solid compliance program. That skepticism will grow if the public comes to believe that companies are approaching the guidelines with a 'window dressing' compliance effort and a clever law firm waiting in the wings at the first sign of trouble."

[45] "Window dressing" compliance programs are a major source of concern of enforcement agencies. For instance, a recent report promulgated by the British Office of Fair Trading (OFT) states: "We consider that larger [penalty] discounts for compliance programmes would be undesirable for two reasons. First, the availability of a large discount might have an adverse impact on the deterrent effect of the potential financial penalties, perhaps even having an adverse effect on compliance activities. Second, such *a policy could encourage the adoption of 'sham' compliance programmes in order to qualify for a discount*" (emphasis added). See Office of Fair Trading (OFT), *Drivers of Compliance and Non-Compliance with Competition Law*, p. 79.

[46] For a similar approach see, for instance, Ronald J. Gilson, "The Devolution of the Legal Profession: A Demand Side Perspective," *Maryland Law Review (1936)* 49 (1990), pp. 880–881: "The problem with a subjective approach is error. Because of the difficulty of fact finding, a subjective approach can be simultaneously over and underinclusive, with costs resulting from error in either direction. But because a strategic plaintiff will have had the opportunity to shape the facts in a favorable manner, the dominant result is, again, underinclusiveness." See also, Perry and Dakin, "Compliance Programs and Criminal Law," p. 22.3. For a different approach, see Amitai Aviram, "In Defense of Imperfect Compliance Programs," *FSU Law Review* 32.2 (2005), 763–780; Khanna, "Corporate Liability Standards: When Should Corporations be Held Criminally Liable?," p. 1272. Note, the problem of opportunistic behavior is diminished in industries where enforcement authorities and business corporations may rely on well-established, verifiable best practices of compliance management systems.

6.3.3 Adjusted Strict Liability

An adjusted strict liability regime holds corporations strictly liable for their employees' misconduct, while insulating their expected liability from the effect of self-policing actions using measures such as immunity and privileges.[47] This regime corresponds with enforcement policies recently adopted by various environmental agencies, in which environmental audit reports are protected through evidentiary privileges and, therefore, become inadmissible in any civil, criminal, and administrative action.[48] Like the pure strict liability regime, the adjusted strict liability regime disregards actions taken by corporations to prevent, deter, or report violations when determining corporate liability. Nevertheless, unlike the traditional strict liability regime, this regime seeks to mitigate the possible perverse effects of self-enforcement actions arising under the pure strict liability regime.[49] Hence, the incentive scheme provided by an adjusted strict liability regime is largely similar to the one provided by the pure strict liability regimes, with the exception that under the adjusted strict liability regimes corporations may have a somewhat greater incentive to engage in *ex-post* self-policing. For instance, given the establishment of evidentiary privileges to compliance-related materials, corporations may be less reluctant to investigate their own violations internally. Nevertheless, as with the pure strict liability regime, under an adjusted strict liability regime corporations' self-reporting constitutes neither an affirmative defense nor a mitigating factor in determining corporate liability. Therefore, under such a regime, corporations have no incentive to step forward and *report* their own violations to the relevant enforcement authorities.[50]

---

[47] See Arlen and Kraakman, "Controlling Corporate Misconduct: An Analysis of Corporate Liability Regimes," pp. 719–726; Khanna, "Corporate Liability Standards: When Should Corporations be Held Criminally Liable?," p. 1267.

[48] For a discussion of these liability regimes see Chapter 5, note 18 and the related main text.

[49] Adjusted strict liability regimes hold the corporations' expected liability insulated from the effects of self-enforcement measures in two alternative ways: (1) using rules of privilege or immunity to ensure that the probability that the corporation is sanctioned stays unchanged whether it self-enforces or not; (2) by adjusting the actual sanction to offset the increase in the probability of detection due to self-enforcement actions. See Arlen and Kraakman, "Controlling Corporate Misconduct: An Analysis of Corporate Liability Regimes," pp. 719–726.

[50] See *ibid.*, p. 726: "This regime can ensure optimal *ex-ante* monitoring, but standing alone, it cannot induce optimal investigation and reporting, nor can it induce optimal monitoring if agents cannot verify their firms' monitoring efforts *ex-ante*."

6.3.4 Composite Liability Regime

A composite liability regime is a liability framework under which sanctions are bifurcated into different levels: one level contains high default sanctions that apply to all detected wrongs committed by corporations with suboptimal policing measures. Other levels include somewhat mitigated sanctions which are imposed on corporations that have satisfied (fully or partially) their self-policing and self-reporting duties.[51] Composite liability regimes correspond with the liability policies adopted by the EPA Audit policy and the Organizational Sentencing Guidelines (OSG) in which the default sanction is mitigated when corporations had effective compliance programs in place.[52] This type of liability regime can be seen as laying a negligence liability layer on top of a strict liability one. Specifically, at the base level corporations are held strictly liable for their employees' misconduct and incur a base sanction that equals the social cost of the misconduct, discounted by the probability of detection when self-policing is optimal.[53] However, corporations may face additional layers of sanctions according to their culpability level, which is determined by the level of care undertaken in preventing, deterring, and reporting violations. With this type of liability regime, corporations that reasonably satisfy all their duties of care incur no additional penalty on top of the base sanction.[54]

Like negligence corporate liability regimes, composite regimes reward corporations for self-reporting violations, and thereby they may, under certain circumstances, induce self-reporting.[55] Unlike negligence corporate liability regimes, under composite regimes corporations that have taken due care in adopting self-enforcement measures are not exempt from liability. Instead, these corporations incur a sanction that equals the social cost of the misconduct, discounted by the probability of detection. Hence, unlike negligence regimes, composite liability regimes provide corporations with the incentive to *internalize* the social ramifications of their activities even when due care is taken. However, like negligence liability regimes, compos-

---

[51] See *ibid.*, pp. 727–735.

[52] For a discussion of these corporate liability regimes see Chapter 5, Sections 5.5 and 5.7.

[53] See Arlen and Kraakman, "Controlling Corporate Misconduct: An Analysis of Corporate Liability Regimes," p. 727: "this residual sanction should equal the social cost of misconduct divided by its probability of detection."

[54] See *ibid.*, p. 727: "it [the composite regime] assigns full mitigation to any firm that monitors and investigates optimally even if it fails to report misconduct, provided that it fails to report because it did not detect misconduct."

[55] See *ibid.*, p. 729. The authors show that when the applicable sanctions are set at particular levels, then composite regimes may induce corporations to self-report.

ite liability regimes rely on corporations' self-enforcement actions when determining corporate liability. Hence, like negligence regimes, composite ones require enforcement authorities to *ex-post* evaluate corporations' self-enforcement activity, in order to determine whether these corporations have satisfied a due level of care in carrying out self-enforcement measures.[56] Therefore, like negligence corporate liability regimes, composite liability regimes may also fail to induce genuine and effective self-policing measures given the heavy "*information burden*" they impose.[57] In that respect, the deficiencies pertaining to judicial errors and "window dressing" discussed in the context of negligence corporate liability regimes are fully applicable when composite liability regimes are concerned.[58]

6.3.5 Summing Up

The choice of a specific liability regime is context-dependent and requires policymakers to weigh the comparative advantages of each regime in every given setting.[59] The law and economics scholarly literature has identified no corporate liability regime that may widely satisfy the twin economic

---

[56] The composite regime does not require the regulatory authority to specify, *ex-ante*, the measures that corporations should take in order to satisfy the threshold of a 'due level of care.' Yet, enforcement authorities and the court are still required to determine: (1) what are the actual measures taken by the corporation; (2) whether these measure satisfy the threshold of a 'due level of care.' See *ibid.*, p. 732: "Under a composite regime, a court must determine whether a firm merits a reduced penalty for having satisfied its monitoring and investigatory duties. But contrary to initial appearances, this negligence-based inquiry does not require the court to identify optimal policing measures as a yardstick for evaluating the firm's actual behavior. Like any negligence rule, the mitigation provision of a composite regime only requires a search for efficient enforcement measures that the firm failed to take."

[57] See *ibid.*, p. 730: "Although increasingly elaborate strict liability regimes meld into composite regimes, composite liability always forces a heavier informational burden on courts, and hence imposes larger administrative costs." For a discussion of the information burden imposed by composite regimes on enforcement authorities see Krawiec, "Cosmetic Compliance and the Failure of Negotiated Governance"; Krawiec, "Organization Misconduct: Beyond the Principal Agent Model"; Gilson, "The Devolution of the Legal Profession: A Demand Side Perspective," pp. 880–881; Office of Fair Trading (OFT), *Drivers of Compliance and Non-Compliance with Competition Law*, p. 79; Perry and Dakin, "Compliance Programs and Criminal Law," p. 22.3; Laufer, "Corporate Liability, Risk Shifting, and the Paradox of Compliance," pp. 1405–1419.

[58] See *supra* notes 40–46 and the related main text.

[59] See Arlen and Kraakman, "Controlling Corporate Misconduct: An Analysis of Corporate Liability Regimes," pp. 730–735.

functions of corporate liability in most settings. The aim of the next section of this book is the development of such a liability regime.

6.4 A COMPOUND CORPORATE LIABILITY REGIME

Based on the conclusions drawn in the previous section regarding the strengths and the weaknesses of existing corporate liability regimes, this section develops an innovative, workable corporate liability regime, referred to as a "Compound Corporate Liability Regime," that sustains the strengths of the existing liability regimes, while coping with their weaknesses. In a nutshell, the proposed framework is a two-tier strict liability regime, which hinges upon sanction mitigation when corporations step forward. Under the compound regime, when corporations self-report their employees' misconduct, the applied sanction is reduced by the variable enforcement cost that the enforcement authority will no longer need to incur. Such a compound regime, I believe, aligns both social considerations and the interests of corporations.

6.4.1 The Analytical Framework

Enforcement systems can achieve an optimal level of deterrence by setting the *expected liability* for misconduct at the level of the *total social costs* caused by the misconduct, discounted by the probability of detection. This way, agents are compelled to bear the social costs of their misconduct.[60] As we have seen in Chapter 2, when considering the total social cost of

[60] See, for instance, Stigler, "The Optimum Enforcement of Laws," 526–536; Cooter, "Prices and Sanctions," 1523–1560; Becker, "Make Punishment Fit the Corporate Crime," 22–30; Block, "Optimal Penalties, Criminal Law and the Control of Corporate Behavior," 395–419; Heyes, "Making Things Stick: Enforcement and Compliance," 50–63; Polinsky and Shavell, "The Economic Theory of Public Enforcement of Law," 45–76. It should be noted that deterrence can also be achieved through a 'gain-based liability' which forces the infringer to disgorge the gains achieved due to the law violation. See Becker, "Crime and Punishment: An Economic Approach," 169–217; Van den Bergh, "Should Consumer Protection Law be Publicly Enforced? An Economic Perspective on EC Regulation 2006/2004 and its Implementation in the Consumer Protection Laws of the Member States," p. 196. However, when considering the possibility of courts' errors in estimating the gain and harm, "harm-based liability" may be superior to a "gain-based liability." For a comparative analysis of a "gain-based liability" and a "harm-based liability" see Polinsky and Shavell, "Should Liability be Based on the Harm to the Victim Or the Gain to the Injurer?," 427–437.

misconduct, one must take into account the relevant enforcement costs, which are the costs of enforcement actions associated with the specific misconduct.[61] To identify the "relevant enforcement cost" it may be useful to resort to the traditional distinction commonly followed by the law and economics literature between *fixed* and *variable* enforcement costs, sometimes referred to as the distinction between *general* and *violation-specific* enforcement costs.[62]

A. ***Fixed/general enforcement costs*** include the costs of enforcement actions that do not depend on the number of individuals who actually commit harmful acts. These fixed costs are associated with ongoing control, monitoring, and detection activities undertaken regularly by enforcement authorities irrespective of any specific violation; for instance, the cost of periodic tests of river water carried out by the Environmental Protection Agency. Such enforcement activities are undertaken to verify that the law is obeyed and to detect any deviation from the law.
B. ***Variable/violation-specific enforcement costs*** are enforcement costs that are contingent upon the number of violations. These variable costs include the costs of enforcement actions normally taken against a specific violation after a suspicion was raised; for instance, the cost of an investigation of specific red flags, evidence collection, litigation, and the imposition of sanctions against culpable actors. These costs are normally associated with enforcement actions undertaken against known suspects and against specific misconducts.

Altogether, to achieve an optimal level of deterrence, the sanction imposed by the public enforcement policy must equal the *total social costs*

---

[61] The importance of enforcement costs as part of the total social costs associated with misconduct was first introduced by George Stigler, who has shown that the goal of the enforcement authority is to minimize the sum of the damages created by the misconduct and the enforcement costs; see Stigler, "The Optimum Enforcement of Laws," p. 533. See also, Malik, "Avoidance, Screening and Optimum Enforcement," p. 397.

[62] See, for instance Mitchell A. Polinsky and Steven Shavell, "Enforcement Costs and the Optimal Magnitude and Probability of Fines," *The Journal of Law & Economics* 35 (1992), 133–148. See also, Gilson, "The Devolution of the Legal Profession: A Demand Side Perspective," 869–916. Gilson distinguishes between "*ex-ante* indirect enforcement" (screening and prevention) and "*ex-post* direct enforcement" (litigation and sanctioning); and Coffee, "The Attorney as Gatekeeper: An Agenda for the SEC," 1293–1316. Coffee distinguishes between *ex-ante* and *ex-post* enforcement costs.

generated by the misconduct, discounted by the probability of detection.[63] To evaluate the "total social costs," one should take into account not only the costs of the *direct harm* generated by the misconduct, *e.g.*, the harm suffered by the direct victims of the pollution caused by the environmental violation, but also the *variable enforcement costs* produced by the misconduct.[64]

6.4.1.1 The general settings

The law and economics literature has conducted an analysis of two major structures of individual-liability schemes, notably *strict liability* and *negligence*, weighing their comparative strengths and weaknesses.[65] The analysis in the individual actor's context focuses on the aptitude of different liability schemes to induce individuals to *internalize* the social ramifications of their behavior. However, as shown above, where the corporate context is concerned, liability systems have an additional goal, that is, to induce corporate proactive compliance by motivating corporations to engage in *self-enforcement* activities.[66] Hence, the analysis of corporate liability regimes is based on a slightly different analytical framework. This section sketches the analytical framework for the development of an innovative corporate liability regime that simultaneously satisfies the twin goals of corporate liability regimes.

The point of departure for the analysis is that a precise standard of behavior is provided by regulations, *e.g.*, a per-se prohibition of

---

[63] The current study deals with regulatory enforcement systems that rely exclusively on public (criminal or administrative) enforcement. The basic structure of an optimal corporate liability regime as proposed in this chapter can apply to enforcement systems in which public enforcement is complemented by private enforcement. Nevertheless, in such cases the optimal sanction may differ, whereas when public and private enforcement mechanisms are used intertwiningly, an optimal corporate liability regime should generate an expected liability that equals the total social costs of the misconduct minus the expected liability generated by the private enforcement mechanism.

[64] See Stigler, "The Optimum Enforcement of Laws," p. 533; Block, "Optimal Penalties, Criminal Law and the Control of Corporate Behavior," p. 397; Polinsky and Shavell, "Enforcement Costs and the Optimal Magnitude and Probability of Fines," 133–148; Polinsky and Shavell, "Should Employees be Subject to Fines and Imprisonment Given the Existence of Corporate Liability?," p. 241.

[65] For a general discussion of the optimal choice between strict liability and negligence standards for an individual liability scheme see Shavell, "Strict Liability Versus Negligence," 1–25.

[66] See Section 6.2.2.

price fixing or precise restrictions on the discharge of pollution.[67] Given such regulations, suppose that a corporation by violating the regulation creates social harm, denoted as H; $(H > 0)$. Suppose that the enforcement authority is likely to detect such violations with a positive probability, denoted as P; $P \in (0,1)$; and that corporations have a private gain generated by engaging in the regulated activity, denoted as G. Within this framework, the analysis relies on the following assumptions.

Assumption 1 – Corporations' *ex-ante* self-policing actions (education and prevention) reduce the probability that a violation occurs within these corporations; meaning that, if a corporation does not self-police *ex-ante*, the probability that a violation occurs is V^H; $V^H \in (0,1)$. Alternatively, if a corporation self-polices *ex-ante* and bears the private costs of these actions, C_{ea} per violation, it reduces the probability that a violation occurs to V^L; $(V^L \in (0,1); V^L < V^H)$.

$$\text{In summary:} \quad \begin{cases} C_{ea} > 0;\ V = V^H \\ C_{ea} = 0;\ V = V^L \end{cases} \qquad (0 < V^L < V^H < 1)$$

Assumption 2 – Corporations' *ex-post* self-policing actions (detection and investigation) increase the probability that corporations detect their own violations.[68] If corporations do not self-police *ex-post*, the probability of self-detection is D^L; $D^L \in (0,1)$. If alternatively, corporations self-police *ex-post*, and bear the private costs of *ex-post* self-policing, C^P_{ep} per violation, the probability of self-detection increases to D^H $(D^H \in (0,1); D^L < D^H)$.

$$\text{In summary:} \quad \begin{cases} C^P_{ep} > 0;\ D = D^L \\ C^P_{ep} = 0;\ D = D^H \end{cases} \qquad (0 < D^L < D^H < 1)$$

67 I overlook vague and ambiguous regulations, including the rule of reason regulations, since when the regulatory standard is unclear corporations only know a probability distribution of being liable at any level of care. See, for instance, Roger Van den Bergh and Hans-Bernd Schäfer, "Member States Liability for Infringement of the Free Movement of Goods in the EC: An Economic Analysis," *Journal of Institutional and Theoretical Economics (JITE)* 156 (2000), 382–403.

68 This assumption is based on the findings of the law and economics literature discussed above. See *supra* note 25 and the related main text.

Assumption 3 – Self-reporting can be undertaken with no significant administrative costs for the corporation.[69]

Assumption 4 – Self-reporting actions reduce the *variable* enforcement costs by saving some of the violation-specific enforcement actions, such as evidence collection and litigation.[70] Given that I am merely interested in the *marginal* impact of self-reporting actions on the total social costs, for simplification purposes, I assume that when a violation is self-reported the variable enforcement costs, denoted C^S_{ep}, are zero $(C^S_{ep} = 0)$, and that when a violation is not self-reported, the variable enforcement costs are positive $(C^S_{ep} > 0)$.[71]

6.4.1.2 Corporate compliance and self-enforcement decisions

To be able to develop a socially desirable incentive scheme that induces corporate proactive compliance, it is valuable to recognize the array of compliance-related decisions corporations typically confront. These decisions are normally taken in a subsequent manner, as sketched in Figure 6.1.

1. ***Compliance decision*** – Corporations have to choose whether to comply with the regulations, taking into account the sanction that would be imposed against violation of the regulations. These decisions often include choices which are related to the sort of activities the corporation is engaged in (*e.g.*, what to produce?); the level of their activity (*e.g.*, how much to produce?); and the technology they use

---

[69] Note that corporate self-reporting increases the probability of detection, and thereby adversely affects employees' expected liability. This effect may generate additional costs for corporations with respect to unintentional wrongdoing, for which employees are normally compensated by the corporation (see *supra* note 20). The same is not true for intentional wrongdoing, which is the main focus of this study. Where intentional wrongdoing is concerned, corporations will not compensate their employees for the increase in their expected liability for intentional misconduct due to self-reporting. Hence, within the analytical scope of this chapter, self-reporting, by itself, does not generate additional costs for the corporation.

[70] This assumption is based on the findings of the law and economics literature discussed above. See *supra* note 26 and the related main text.

[71] I realize that even when violations are self-reported, variable enforcement costs may still be positive. Nevertheless, my focus here is on the marginal impact of self-reporting actions on the variable enforcement costs. Therefore, a similar result is reached if the variable enforcement costs of a self-reported violation have a positive value, say X, and the variable costs of a non-self-reported violation is $X + C^S_{ep}$. The only crucial assumption is that self-reporting actions reduce *variable* enforcement costs.

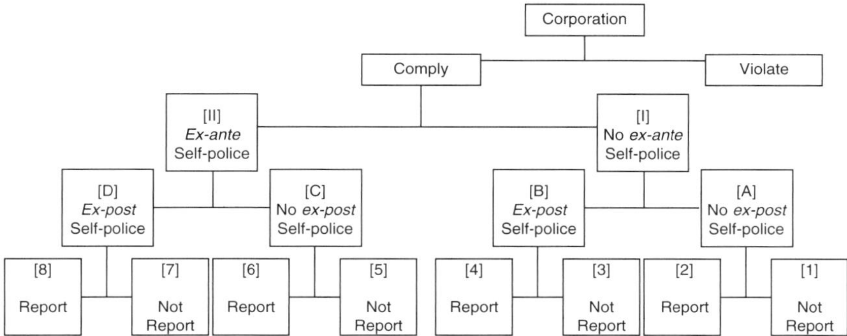

Figure 6.1 Corporate compliance and self-enforcement decisions

(*e.g.*, how should they produce it?). When corporations opt for the compliance option, they have to adjust their activities to regulatory standards, *e.g.*, to secure a certain level of production that would prevent an excessive level of pollution. However, as mentioned in Section 6.2.1 above, even when the corporate management decides to comply with regulations, regulatory violations can still be committed by employees, even if these go against the explicit corporate policy. Therefore, when corporations decide to comply, they face the following subsequent decisions.

2. ***Ex-ante self-policing decision*** (decision: *I–II* in Figure 6.1) – Corporations have to choose whether to self-police *ex-ante*, *i.e.*, whether to act in order to educate their employees and prevent violations. When considering this decision, corporations take into account: (i) the costs involved with *ex-ante* self-policing, $C_{ea} > 0$; and (ii) the benefits which may result from these actions, namely, a reduction in the probability that a violation occurs in spite of the corporations' decision to comply. This reduction, which is attributed to the *ex-ante* self-policing, is captured by the difference between V^H and V^L, denoted as δV.
3. ***Ex-post self-policing*** (decisions: *A–B* / *C–D* in Figure 6.1) – Corporations have to choose whether to undertake *ex-post* self-policing actions, *i.e.*, whether to detect and investigate violations that have taken place within the corporation. When considering this decision, corporations take into account: (i) the costs involved with *ex-post* self-policing, $C^P_{ep} > 0$; and (ii) the additional probability of the self-detection of violations resulting from the *ex-post* self-policing actions. This increase, which is attributed to the *ex-post* self-policing, is captured by the difference between D^H and D^L, denoted as γD. Such an increased probability

of detection facilitates more self-reporting, and therefore may be desirable for corporations that are motivated to self-report violations.

4. ***Self-reporting*** (decisions: *1–2* / *3–4* / *5–6* / *7–8* in Figure 6.1) – Provided that corporations may self-detect their own violations, at a subsequent phase they have to choose whether to self-report these violations to the relevant enforcement authority.[72]

As mentioned above, profit-maximizing corporations make compliance and self-enforcement decisions using a cost–benefit analysis; they compare their net expected payoff under each of the alternative choices and opt for choices that maximize their expected payoff. Given the subsequent nature of corporations' decisions, the analysis that follows is made through a backward induction.

6.4.1.3 Optimal decisions from a social perspective

The question can be posed then under what circumstances is corporate compliance and self-enforcement socially desirable? The answer to this question may be provided by the "golden rule," according to which a certain action is socially desirable whenever the social benefits of this action equal or exceed the associated social costs. In other words, a given action is socially desirable when the net expected social welfare is positive if such an action is taken, rather than not taken. Following this rule, let me now consider corporate compliance and self-enforcement decisions from a social point of view. The results of the analysis are summarized in Table 6.2, which is followed by a detailed explanation.

Self-reporting – Following the "golden rule," it is socially desirable that corporations self-report whenever the social benefit from self-reporting is greater than the social costs of self-reporting. Self-reporting, which can be done with insignificant costs (Assumption 3 above), may generate a social benefit by reducing the variable enforcement costs (Assumption 4 above). Hence, self-reporting is socially desirable, when:

Social benefit of self-reporting $\rightarrow$ $C^S_{ep} > 0$ $\leftarrow$ Social cost of self-reporting

[72] It should be noted that some positive probability of self-detection may exist even when corporations decide not to self-police *ex-post*, for instance, when employees voluntarily report violations to the corporation. Hence, the self-reporting decision remains relevant whether corporations decide to self-police or not.

Table 6.2 The socially optimal corporate compliance and self-enforcement decisions

Economic function of corporate liability	Induced corporate activity	The conditions for a socially desirable action
Self-Enforcement	Self-Reporting	Always (*i.e.*, whenever a violation has been self-detected)
	Ex-Post Self-policing (given self-reporting)	$C^S_{ep} \cdot V \cdot \gamma D \geq C^P_{ep}$ (condition [1])
	Ex-ante Self-policing (given self-reporting)	$(H + C^S_{ep} - DC^S_{ep}) \cdot \delta V \geq C_{ea}$ (condition [2])
Internalization	Compliance (given conditions [1] and [2])	$(H + C^S_{ep})(1 - V^L) + V^L D^H C^S_{ep} \geq C_{ea} + C^P_{ep}$ (condition [3])

Given that by definition whenever the firm does not self-report its own violations the variable enforcement cost, C^S_{ep}, is positive (Assumption 4 above), it is always socially desirable that corporations self-report every self-detected violation.

Ex-post self-policing – As mentioned above (Section 6.4.1.2), *ex-post* self-policing actions (detection and investigation) may increase the probability that corporations detect their own violations. Moving backwards in the corporation decision scheme, given our earlier results, according to which self-reporting is always socially desirable, a social welfare evaluation of *ex-post* self-policing activity assumes that corporations report every self-detected violation. Such reports reduce the variable enforcement costs associated with the reported violations (Assumption 4 above). Hence, *ex-post* self-policing is desirable whenever the costs of such actions are lower than the variable enforcement costs which would have been invested by the enforcement authority had the violation not been self-reported. Meaning that, corporate *ex-post* self-policing is socially desirable if condition [1] below is met, when V represents the relevant probability that a violation takes place:[73]

[73] When corporations self-police *ex-ante*, $V = V^H$; alternatively, when corporations do not self-police *ex-ante*, $V = V^L$ (see Assumption 1 above).

Social benefit of ex-post self-policing → $C^S_{ep} \cdot V \cdot (D^H - D^L) \geq C^P_{ep}$ ← Social cost of ex-post self-policing

Ex-ante self-policing – *Ex-ante* self-policing actions (education and prevention) may reduce the probability that a violation occurs. Hence, sticking to the "golden rule," such actions are socially desirable whenever their costs are lower than the total social costs of a prevented violation, *i.e.*, the social harm and the variable enforcement costs that would have been generated by the regulatory violation had the violation not been prevented. Hence, *ex-ante* self-policing is socially desirable whenever condition [2] below is met:[74]

Social benefit of *ex-ante* self-policing → $(H + C^S_{ep} - DC^S_{ep})(V^H - V^L) \geq C_{ea}$ ← Social cost of *ex-ante* self-policing

Compliance – Compliance with regulations is socially desirable whenever the total social costs caused by a violation are greater than the social costs associated with compliance. Assume, for instance, that conditions [1] and [2] above are met. Under these circumstances, it is socially desirable that corporations comply with the regulations whenever the social *costs* associated with compliance, *i.e.*, the costs of self-enforcement, are lower than the social *benefit* of compliance, *i.e.*, the total social costs saved due to the corporations' decision to comply and self-enforce. Hence, the condition for an efficient compliance is presented by condition [3] below:[75]

---

74 For every violation committed, the society bears a cost which equals the social harm caused by the violation and the variable enforcement costs $(H + C^S_{ep})$. As we have seen, it is socially desirable that corporations report every self-detected violation. Hence, when considering the social condition for *ex-ante* self-policing through backward induction, we should consider that corporations report every violation they detect with a probability$D$, and by that save DC^S_{ep} for every reported violation. Note that $D = D^H$ when corporations self-police *ex-post*; alternatively, when corporations do not self-police *ex-post*, $D = D^L$. As mentioned, *ex-ante* self-policing may reduce the probability that a violation occurs$(\delta V = V^H - V^L)$. Hence, such actions are socially desirable whenever the social costs of the prevented violations $(H + C^S_{ep} - DC^S_{ep})(V^H - V^L)$ are greater than the corporation's cost of *ex-ante* self policing, C_{ea}.

75 For the sake of simplicity, I assume that compliance with regulations is not involved with positive costs except for costs of self-policing. Hence, if conditions [1] and [2] are met, and the corporation decides to comply and self-police, the social benefit from these decisions are represented by the total costs which were saved

Social benefit of self-enforcement	→	$(H + C^S_{ep})(1 - V^L) + V^L D^H C^S_{ep} \geq C_{ea} + C^P_{ep}$	←	Social cost of self-enforcement

The next section relies on the analytical framework presented here in developing the compound liability regime.

6.4.2 Compound Corporate Liability Regime

In this section, I propose an innovative liability regime that may satisfy both economic functions of corporate liability regimes in most settings. To this end, I look at a vital aspect that, in spite of its great importance, has not received enough attention in the previous literature analyzing the various structures of corporate liability regimes, that is, *the impact of corporate self-reporting on the total variable enforcement costs associated with regulatory violations*. This aspect, which is examined in an independent stream of literature, has been incorporated into the analytical framework presented above, which acknowledges that self-reporting actions reduce the variable enforcement costs associated with the reported violations.[76] I argue that when considering the impact of self-reporting actions on the variable enforcement costs, then an alignment of the corporations' incentives with the social interest can be reached if corporations' expected liability is adjusted to the social consequences of self-enforcement actions. More specifically, under the compound liability regime suggested here, sanctions against corporate misconduct are bifurcated into two layers:

---

due to the corporation's compliance $(H + C^S_{ep})(1 - V^L)$, and the variable enforcement costs saved due to the corporation's self-policing $V^L D^H C^S_{ep}$. When such social benefit is equal or greater than the costs of compliance, $C_{ea} + C^P_{ep}$, compliance is socially desirable.

76 See Kaplow and Shavell, "Optimal Law Enforcement with Self-Reporting of Behavior," 583–606; Malik, "Avoidance, Screening and Optimum Enforcement," 341–353. For the purpose of this chapter, I concentrate on the impact of self-reporting actions on the variable enforcement costs and disregard their potential impact on the social harm. In fact, prompt reports of violations may, under certain circumstances, be crucial in restoring the harm and preventing its expansion. See Robert Innes, "Self-Policing and Optimal Law Enforcement when Violator Remediation is Valuable," *Journal of Political Economy* 107(6) (1999), 1305–1325. This, for instance, is the case of drinking-water pollution. It is clear that a prompt detection of the discharges may be crucial in preventing greater social harm.

first, a *default sanction* which equals the sum of the social harm and the variable enforcement costs caused by the violation, discounted by the probability of detection ($L^D = \frac{H + C^S_{ep}}{P}$); and *second*, a *reduced sanction* which is set at the level of the social harm caused by the violation ($L^R = H$). According to the compound regime, a reduced sanction shall be imposed instead of the default sanction against misconduct that has been self-reported.

The compound regime can be seen as a two-layer strict liability regime, which holds corporations strictly liable for two different sorts of wrongs: (i) the regulatory violation committed (*e.g.*, pollution, price fixing); and (ii) corporations' failure to act in order to deter and report the regulatory violation. For each of these wrongs, the compound regime ensures that corporations face an expected liability that equals the social costs generated by the specific wrong.

To recognize the merits of the compound liability regime, it is important to notice that the total social costs associated with a regulatory violation are greater when corporations do not report, rather than when they report. When corporations do not self-report, the total social cost of the violation includes not only the direct harm generated by the violation, but also the variable enforcement costs, such as the cost of detection, evidence collection, and litigation. On the other hand, when corporations step forward and report their own violations, some of these variable enforcement costs are saved and the total social cost of the violation is lower. This variation in the social cost, which was left unrecognized by the liability regimes discussed in the existing literature, is mirrored by the compound regime when determining corporate expected liability. The expected liability of corporations under the compound regime is greater when they do not report than when they report, while in both cases the expected liability equals the total social costs associated with the corporation's course of action.

To clarify the intuition underlying the compound regime, let me use a numerical illustration before turning to a more general model. Suppose that a corporation exceeds the permitted level of the discharge of pollution and thereby causes a social harm of $1,000. Further assume that if the corporation does not report, government agencies have to detect the culpable corporation, collect evidence, bring charges and litigate. Suppose that the variable enforcement costs associated with these actions is $100 per violation. According to the compound regime, if the corporation does not self-report, it is expected to incur an actual sanction which equals the total social cost of the violation, discounted by the probability of detection, *i.e.*, $L^D = 1{,}100/P$. Hence, in that case, the corporation's *expected* liability equals the total social harm caused by the violation, *i.e.*, \$1,100.[77] Accordingly, when deciding whether to violate the regulations, the corporation internalizes the total social costs of the violation. Alternatively, assume that the corporation self-reports the violation, and therefore the \$100 variable enforcement costs are relinquished (*i.e.*, due to the corporate report there is no need for evidence collection, and even possibly no need to engage in complex litigation). Therefore, the cost of evidence collection and litigation is saved. In this case, the total social cost of the violation is the direct harm caused by the violation, *i.e.*, \$1,000. According to the compound liability regime, if the corporation reports the violation, it incurs a reduced actual sanction that equals the social harm caused, \$1,000. This actual sanction also reflects the expected liability, whereas when the corporation self-reports, the probability of detection is one ($P = 1$). Therefore, when deciding whether to self-enforce, corporations internalize the variable enforcement costs; they are expected to undertake self-enforcement actions, *i.e.*, self-policing and self-reporting, whenever the costs of such actions are lower than the variable costs of public enforcement actions.[78]

Having clarified the intuition behind the compound liability regime, let me generalize the analysis of the compound regime by evaluating corporations' expected payoff under each of the decisions they face, using the analytical framework established above.

Self-reporting – As shown in the literature, to induce corporations to self-report an enforcement policy should allow those who report a violation to pay a sanction slightly lower than the certainty equivalent of the sanction they would face if they did not report the violation.[79] Under such circumstances, profit-maximizing corporations find it rational to

[77] The *expected* liability equals the *actual* sanction to be imposed when the violation is detected, multiplied by the probability that the violation is detected.

[78] As mentioned in *supra* note 71, self-reporting actions do not necessarily eliminate all variable enforcement costs. Often, even after a corporation reports a violation, enforcement agencies are required to verify the authenticity and accuracy of the report. The costs of such verification actions obviously are not relinquished due to the self-report and therefore should not be included in the penalty mitigation. Referring to the example above, suppose that a sum of \$20 out of the total \$100 variable enforcement costs is for the cost of verification. In such a case, the correct reduction of variable enforcement costs due to the report is merely \$80, and thus, the reduced sanction would be \$1,100 − \$80, or \$1,020. The crucial aspect of efficient penalty mitigation is that the size of the mitigation is determined by the size of the reduction in variable enforcement costs resulting from the corporation's self-report.

[79] See Kaplow and Shavell, "Optimal Law Enforcement with Self-Reporting of Behavior," p. 584.

self-report their own violations (and bear the mitigated sanction), rather than being exposed to an expected liability, the equivalent certainty of which is greater. This is exactly the bedrock of the compound liability regime. Under the compound liability regime, when corporations self-report their own violations, they incur a reduced sanction that equals the actual social harm caused by the violation which is lower than the full social cost that would have been generated had the violation not been reported. In other words, when corporations self-report a violation they face a lower expected liability ($EL^R = H$) than if they do not report ($EL^D = H + C^S_{ep}$).[80] The expected payoff when corporations self-report, U^R, and when they do not self-report, U^{NR}, is given by the following expressions:[81]

$$U^{NR} = G - V \cdot P \cdot \left(\frac{H + C^S_{ep}}{P} \right) \quad U^R = G - V \left[D \cdot H + (1 - D) \cdot P \cdot \frac{H + C^S_{ep}}{P} \right]$$

U^R is greater than U^{NR}.[82] Hence, under the compound regime, corporations have an incentive to self-report every detected violation. This incentive coincides with the socially optimal condition for self-reporting (see Table 6.2).

Before proceeding, it may be worthwhile to consider the potential reputation impact of corporate self-reporting on corporate payoff, and to elucidate the reason why such potential impacts are excluded from the corporate payoff functions above. The scholarly literature on reputational impacts of corporate self-reporting is highly ambiguous. Two contradicting potential effects of self-reporting have been identified in theoretic and empirical studies. The first stream of literature supports the idea that self-reporting of corporate misconduct may harm a corporation's reputation

---

80 If the corporation does not report, the actual sanction that includes the variable enforcement costs is $L^D = \frac{H + C^S_{ep}}{P}$, and the probability of detection is P. Hence, the expected liability is $EL^D = H + C^S_{ep}$. If, alternatively, the corporation self-reports, the actual sanction is $L^R = H$, and the probability of detection becomes 1 (*i.e.*, certain detection). Hence, the expected liability is ($EL^R = H$).

81 U^{NR} equals the gain of corporations from engaging in their activity, G, minus the expected liability, $P \cdot (H + C^S_{ep})/P$, multiplied by the relevant probability that a violation actually occurs, V. Similarly, U^R equals the gain of corporations from engaging in their activity, G, minus the relevant probability that a violation occurs, V, multiplied by the sum of the expected liability when corporations detect and report, $D \cdot H$, and the expected liability when they do not report and the violation is detected by an enforcement authority $(1 - D) \cdot P \cdot (H + C^S_{ep})/P$.

82 U^R is greater than U^{NR}, when $V^H \cdot D^L \cdot C^H > 0$, which by definition is always the case.

due to the adverse publicity associated with the reported misbehavior.[83] In contrast, a contradicting stream of literature supports the idea that corporate self-reporting may actually signal a corporation's normative commitment, their social responsibility, and their compliant nature expressed by their voluntarily stepping forward, which can improve the public reputation of the corporation.[84] Moreover, scholars have shown that reputation impacts are highly context-dependent and may substantially differ across regulatory environments,[85] markets, and corporations.[86] Taken altogether, the available empirical evidence provides insufficient grounds for the inclusion of potential reputation impacts on the corporate calculus of self-reporting. It is therefore not surprising that reputational impacts have been largely ignored by the law and economics scholarly literature discussing the optimal design of corporate liability.

Ex-post self-policing – As we have seen, under the compound liability regime corporations prefer to self-detect their violations and self-report

---

83 See, for instance, Palmrose, Richardson and Scholz, "Determinants of Market Reactions to Restatement Announcements," 59–89; Akhigbe, Kudla and Madura, "Why are Some Corporate Earnings Restatements More Damaging?," 327–336. These authors explore the loss of reputation corporations experience after admitting errors in their financial statements. Compare with Rupp, "The Attributes of a Costly Recall: Evidence from the Automotive Industry," 21–44; Ahmed, Gardella and Nanda, "Wealth Effect of Drug Withdrawals on Firms and their Competitors," 21–41; Telang and Wattal, "An Empirical Analysis of the Impact of Software Vulnerability Announcements on Firm Stock Price," 544–557. These authors provide strong empirical evidence of reputational losses which are associated with firms that have admitted their products are defective through product recalls.

84 See, for instance, Lee, Peterson and Tiedens, "*Mea Culpa*: Predicting Stock Prices from Organizational Attributions," 1636–1649; Marcus and Goodman, "Victims and Shareholders: The Dilemmas of Presenting Corporate Policy during a Crisis," p. 281. The authors have explored the reputation gains of corporations that have admitted errors in their financial statements. See also, Corona and Randhawa, "The Value of Confession: Admitting Mistakes to Build Reputation," who argue that a corporation's confession may allow it to build a positive reputation in the long term.

85 See, for instance, Karpoff, Lee and Martin, "The Cost to Firms of Cooking the Books," p. 611; Karpoff, Lott and Wehrly, "The Reputational Penalties for Environmental Violations: Empirical Evidence," 653–675. The authors show that in some regulatory fields, such as securities regulation, the disciplinary impact on a corporation's reputation is greater than in other regulatory fields, such as with environmental regulations.

86 See, for instance, Graafland and Smid, "Reputation, Corporate Social Responsibility and Market Regulation," 271–309, who have shown that reputation impacts are weaker for smaller companies and for both highly competitive and monopolistic markets.

them before such violations are detected by any enforcement authority. This way, corporations incur a reduced sanction, which is lower than the expected default sanction. By *ex-post* self-policing (active detection and internal investigation) corporations increase the probability that they self-detect – and thereby increase the probability that they are able to report their own violations – before any enforcement authority detects such violations. Therefore, under the compound regime corporations have an incentive to engage in *ex-post* self-policing. The expected payoff of corporations when they self-police *ex-post*, U_{ep}^{SP}, and when they do not, U_{ep}^{NSP}, are given by the following expressions:[87]

$$U_{ep}^{NSP} = G - V\left[D^{L} \cdot H + (1 - D^{L}) \cdot P \cdot \frac{H + C_{ep}^{S}}{P}\right]$$

$$U_{ep}^{SP} = G - C_{ep}^{L} - V\left[D^{H} \cdot H + (1 - D^{H}) \cdot P \cdot \frac{H + C_{ep}^{S}}{P}\right]$$

U_{ep}^{SP} is greater than U_{ep}^{NSP} whenever $C_{ep}^{S} \cdot V \cdot \gamma D \geq C_{ep}^{P}$. Meaning that, under the compound liability regime, corporations' incentives to *ex-post* self-police coincide with the social interest (condition [1] in Table 6.2).

Skeptics may argue that under the compound liability regime corporations may be discouraged from engaging in *ex-post* self-policing, whereas such actions may, under certain circumstances, have a perverse effect on corporations' expected liability.[88] However, the risk of such a perverse effect does not seem to pose substantial challenges to the compound regime; *first*, *ex-post* self-policing actions, such as the internal investigation of employee misconduct, are a key instrument for corporations to improve and refresh their internal policies, and thereby to prevent recurrence of the misconduct. Therefore, even when facing the risk of a perverse effect in the shortterm, corporations may still be motivated to self-police in order

---

87 U_{ep}^{NSP} equals the gain of corporations from engaging in the regulated activity, G, minus the relevant probability that a violation actually occurs, V, multiplied by the sum of the expected liability when the corporation self-reports, $(D^{L} \cdot H)$, and when it does not report and the violation is detected by an enforcement authority, $(1 - D^{L}) \cdot P \cdot \frac{H + C_{ep}^{S}}{P}$. The U_{ep}^{SP} is calculated in the same way, with two main differences: *first*, it deducts the cost of *ex-post* self-policing born by the corporation from the corporate utility $(-C_{ep}^{L})$; *second*, it considers that when the corporation *ex-post* self-polices, the probability of self-detection is D^{H}, rather than D^{L} (see Assumption 2).

88 See Arlen, "The Potentially Perverse Effects of Corporate Criminal Liability," 833–867.

to minimize their long-term liability exposure. *Second*, when considering the potential impact of *ex-post* self-policing actions on corporate expected liability, one may juxtapose the "*potentially perverse effect*" against the "*potentially positive effect*" of such self-policing actions expressed by a reduction in the probability of erroneous enforcement actions against an innocent corporation.[89] Such a positive effect may outweigh the potentially adverse effect of self-policing. *Third*, the discouraging impact of perverse effects may be overcome by insulating corporations' expected liability from the effect of self-policing actions by using measures such as immunity and privileges, as offered by the adjusted strict liability regime.[90] Moreover, the theory of perverse effect has yet to be supported by empirical evidence. Nevertheless, assuming that such an effect actually exists, it may obviously be relevant to some – but not all – self-policing measures that may be employed by corporations. Hence, choosing from a marketplace of available measures, corporations may decide to employ those measures that are less, if at all, vulnerable to a perverse effect.

Ex-ante self-policing – As discussed in Section 6.2.1 above, by *ex-ante* self-policing (prevention actions, ethics codes, employee training, etc.) corporations may reduce the probability that employee misconduct will take place against corporate policy. Therefore, following the "golden rule," profit-maximizing corporations are motivated to engage in *ex-ante* self-policing to the extent that the marginal benefit of such actions (*i.e.*, the marginal reduction of expected liability resulting from the reduction of the probability that employee misconduct takes place) outweighs their marginal costs (*i.e.*, the costs of an additional unit of self-policing enforcement). Given that, as seen above, under the compound liability

---

[89] Suppose, for instance, that a lake surrounded by several facilities had been polluted, and that one facility initiated a prompt internal investigation to verify its potential involvement in causing the pollution. The internal investigation, which included prompt and extensive examination of the pollutants found in the water, confirmed that the corporate facility is certainly not the source of the pollution. The results of the internal investigation may serve the interests of the corporation in defending itself against any erroneous accusation by enforcement authorities that may rely on less credible evidence. Although generally, reputation effects exceed the scope of this study, one may argue that the "acquittal evidence" produced by corporate internal enforcement actions may protect the corporation from being added to the "list of suspects" at a very early stage of the investigation, and therefore can save severe damage to the corporation's reputation.

[90] See Arlen and Kraakman, "Controlling Corporate Misconduct: An Analysis of Corporate Liability Regimes," pp. 719–726; Goldsmith and King, "Policing Corporate Crime: The Dilemma of Internal Compliance Programs," 1–47.

regime corporations engage in efficient self-reporting and *ex-post* self-policing, the expected payoff of corporations when they *ex-ante* self-police, U_{ea}^{SP}, and when they do not, U_{ea}^{NSP}, are given by the following expressions:

- When corporations engage in *ex-post* self-policing and self-reporting: (*i.e.*, when condition [1], $C_{ep}^{S} \cdot V \cdot \delta D \geq C_{ep}^{P}$ holds):

$$U_{ea}^{NSP} = G - C_{ep}^{P} - V^{H}\left[D^{H}H + (1 - D^{H}) \cdot P \cdot \frac{H + C_{ep}^{S}}{P}\right]$$

$$U_{ea}^{SP} = G - C_{ep}^{P} - C_{ea} - V^{L}\left[D^{H}H + (1 - D^{H}) \cdot P \cdot \frac{H + C_{ep}^{S}}{P}\right]$$

  U_{ea}^{SP} equals (or is greater than) U_{ea}^{NSP} whenever $(H + C_{ep}^{S} - D^{H}C_{ep}^{S}) \cdot \delta V \geq C_{ea}$, *i.e.*, corporations' incentives to engage in *ex-ante* self-policing are aligned with the social interest (see condition [2] in Table 6.2).

- When corporations do not self-police *ex-post*, but self-report (*i.e.*, when condition [1] does not hold, and therefore $C_{ep}^{S} \cdot V \cdot \delta D < C_{ep}^{P}$):

$$U_{ea}^{NSP} = G - V^{H}\left[D^{L}H + (1 - D^{L}) \cdot P \cdot \frac{H + C_{ep}^{S}}{P}\right]$$

$$U_{ea}^{SP} = G - C_{ea} - V^{L}\left[D^{L}H + (1 - D^{L}) \cdot P \cdot \frac{H + C_{ep}^{S}}{P}\right]$$

  U_{ea}^{SP} equals (or is greater than) U_{ea}^{NSP} whenever $(H + C_{ep}^{S} - D^{L}C_{ep}^{S}) \cdot \delta V \geq C_{ea}$, *i.e.*, the corporations' *ex-ante* self-policing are aligned with the social interest (see condition [2] in Table 6.2).

Compliance – Given that corporations under the compound liability regime always face an expected liability which equals the social costs caused by their conduct, then the incentive of corporations to comply with regulations is aligned with the social interest. This result of the compound regime guarantees that corporations internalize the social ramifications of their activities. For instance, assuming that conditions [1] and [2] for *ex-ante* and *ex-post* self-policing are met (*i.e.*, $C_{ep}^{S} \cdot V \cdot \gamma D \geq C_{ep}^{P}$; $(H + C_{ep}^{S} - D^{L}C_{ep}^{S}) \cdot \delta V \geq C_{ea}$), corporations' expected payoff when they comply, U^{C}, and when they violate the regulation, U^{V}, are given by the following expressions:

$$U^V = G - P \cdot \frac{H + C^S_{ep}}{P} \quad U^C = G - C_{ea} - C^P_{ep} - V^L[D^H H + (1 - D^H)(H + C^S_{ep})]$$

Corporations choose to comply whenever $U^C \geq U^V$, *i.e.*, whenever $(H + C^S_{ep})(1 - V^L) + V^L D^H C^S_{ep} \geq C_{ea} + C^P_{ep}$. Meaning that under the compound regime, corporations' incentives to comply coincide with the social interest (condition [3] in Table 6.2). Therefore, corporations under the compound liability regime are expected to comply with regulations whenever compliance is socially desirable.

Using the analytical framework constructed above, it is evident that the compound liability regime aligns corporations' incentives with the social interest. It does so by compelling corporations to internalize the social costs associated with each of the decisions they make. When corporations violate the regulation and appropriately self-enforce, they are compelled to bear an expected liability that equals the social harm caused by the violation. Alternatively, when corporations violate the regulation but do not self-enforce, then they are compelled to incur an expected liability that equals the total social costs of their conduct, *i.e.*, the direct social harm caused by the violations and the variable enforcement costs. Given the complete alignment of incentives, the compound regime attains both of the social goals of a liability regime simultaneously and is likely to induce efficient corporate compliance and self-enforcement measures.

6.5 SUMMARY AND CONCLUDING REMARKS

To induce corporate self-enforcement, the expected liability corporations face when self-enforcing must be lower than the expected liability they face when refraining from doing so; if corporations are not rewarded for self-enforcement actions, then they will have insufficient incentives to self-enforce considering the costs involved with self-enforcement measures. Such a shortage of incentives to self-enforce is the major flaw of the strict liability and adjusted strict liability regimes. On the other hand, if the mitigation of sanctions is determined by corporations' self-policing actions, an information asymmetry problem may result in an inefficient reduction of sanctions, which is triggered by cosmetic self-policing measures. The latter problem is the main failure of duty-based liability regimes, *i.e.*, negligence and composite regimes. The compound liability regime is centered on an idiosyncratic mitigation of the default sanction: (1) the mitigation of the sanction is triggered by verifiable actions, corporations' self-reporting; (2) the amount of the sanction mitigation is determined by the social gain generated by self-enforcement actions, *i.e.*, the reduction in the variable enforcement costs resulting from self-reporting actions. This way, the compound regime induces corporations to internalize the total social costs of their conduct, and at the same time, to self-police and report wrongdoings whenever such actions are socially desirable.

Practically, most regulatory enforcement authorities may apply the compound liability regime simply by using their own enforcement data. Suppose, for instance, that an enforcement authority knows that the average administrative costs of an air pollution investigation and litigation is $50,000, and that only one-third of the pollution cases it examines result in detection and sanctioning. Further suppose that a certain pollution violation caused $500,000 of social harm. Therefore, the default *expected* liability in this case is $550,000, and the default *actual* sanction is $1,650,000.[91] To apply the compound liability regime, the enforcement authority simply has to offer corporations the opportunity to pay a $500,000 fine (instead of a $1,650,000 fine) if they have self-reported the violation. The reduction of the *expected* liability (from $550,000 to $500,000) reflects the reduction of the variable enforcement costs due to the corporation's self-reporting of the misconduct. Such a liability scheme is expected to align corporate and social goals at the same time.

The compound liability regime suggested in this chapter acquires its merits from several sources: *first*, it provides corporations with the appropriate incentives to comply with regulations and to self-enforce them whenever such actions are socially desirable. This outcome is generated due to the fact that the compound regime accounts for the direct impact that self-reporting actions have on the overall social costs associated with regulatory violations; *second*, this regime minimizes the sum of the social harm generated by regulatory violations and the costs of enforcement actions; *third*, unlike duty-based frameworks (negligence and composite regimes), the compound liability regime does not require courts and enforcement authorities to evaluate the effectiveness and the trustworthiness of self-policing actions taken by corporations. Instead, it relies on a *verifiable* action, self-reporting, and therefore is less, if at all, vulnerable to corporate opportunistic behavior; *fourth*, and closely related to the former strength, the compound liability regime provides a workable solution which does not involve substantial administrative and error costs. Under the compound regime, policy-makers are not required to define the proper

---

[91] The *expected* liability equals the total social costs associated with the violation. See Chapter 2, Section 2.2. To set the *actual sanction* the *expected* liability has to be discounted for the probability of detection ($^1/_3$), in this case: $\frac{55{,}000}{1/3}$, or simply $1,650,000.

level of care. Such determination is expected to be done by each corporation when choosing the optimal self-enforcement actions to be employed given its specific circumstances; and *fifth*, the compound liability regime reduces the risk – to the extent it actually exists[92] – of judgment proofness by reducing the "end-sanctions" incurred by corporations.[93]

A question can be posed whether the merits of the compound liability regime will hold even when corporations have a private gain from employee misconduct. One could argue that when corporations benefit from employee violations (*e.g.*, price fixing), then they may be reluctant to engage in self-enforcement. However, in fact, under the compound liability regime, both the corporation's interests and social goals are kept aligned even when corporations may benefit from employee violations. When applying the compound liability regime one must not only consider the effect of additional corporate gains from the misconduct on the private payoff of corporations, but one must also consider the social interest. The net social costs generated by a violation are simply the difference between the total social costs caused by the violation and the gains earned by the corporation due to the violation.[94] Hence, under the compound liability regime, even when additional gains are generated by a violation, corporations' incentives and the social interest remain aligned.

---

[92] Some scholars have argued that the 'judgment proof' problem does not seem realistic: "Individuals are rarely if ever fined an amount approximating their wealth, especially for activities which impose relatively small external costs." See Polinsky and Shavell, "The Optimal Tradeoff between the Probability and Magnitude of Fines," pp. 880–891.

[93] Scholars have shown that the sanctions often imposed upon corporations in reality are based not only on the harm to society, but also on the variable enforcement costs. See Polinsky and Shavell, "Enforcement Costs and the Optimal Magnitude and Probability of Fines," p. 145. The liability framework endorsed by the compound regime recognizes instances that warrant a reduction of end-sanctions, and therefore mitigates the judgment proofness problem.

[94] See Becker, "Crime and Punishment: An Economic Approach," p. 173, which introduces "the social value of the gain to offenders" from their offense. See also, Polinsky, "Punitive Damages: An Economic Analysis," p. 878.

PART III

Corporate monitors: can "swords" turn into "shields"?

INTRODUCTION TO PART III

How should a regulatory monitoring regime be structured to efficiently induce corporate proactive compliance? Scholars, policymakers, and courts around the globe have acknowledged that in many contexts corporations can control their employees more efficiently than public authorities.[1] In Part I of this book, I examined the two major philosophies in law enforcement – deterrence-based and cooperative enforcement approaches – each embracing different styles of enforcement aimed at inducing corporate proactive compliance.[2] The analysis revealed the limited scope of each of these "stand-alone" approaches in producing a socially desirable enforcement policy and explored the virtues of regulatory mixed regimes that reconcile both enforcement styles within a composite framework. Additionally, the analysis revealed that the regulatory mixed regimes proposed in the scholarly literature up to this point are fraught with substantial perils. Therefore, Part I of this book poses the challenge of identifying innovative structures of regulatory enforcement regimes that are able to sustain the advantages of the existing mixed regimes, while overcoming their pitfalls.[3] In Part II of this book, I addressed this challenge with respect to corporate *liability* regimes. In this part of the book, I focus the spotlight on regulatory *monitoring* systems.

In an attempt to improve regulatees' motivations to adopt a proactive approach to regulatory compliance, many regulatory enforcement authorities employ "*targeted monitoring systems*" in which they differentiate monitoring efforts among various regulatees.[4] These systems resemble the regulatory mixed regimes discussed in Part I of this book.[5] Rather

---

1 See, for instance, Arlen and Kraakman, "Controlling Corporate Misconduct: An Analysis of Corporate Liability Regimes," p. 700; Walsh and Pyrich, "Corporate Compliance Programs as a Defense to Criminal Liability: Can a Corporation Save its Soul?," p. 678; Khanna and Dickinson, "The Corporate Monitor: The New Corporate Czar," pp. 1728–1729; Heineman, "Caught in the Middle," p. 89; Kraakman, "Vicarious and Corporate Liability," p. 671; Shavell, *Economic Analysis of Accident Law*, pp. 173–174; Arlen, "The Potentially Perverse Effects of Corporate Criminal Liability," 833–867; Huff, "The Role of Corporate Compliance Programs in Determining Corporate Criminal Liability: A Suggested Approach," p. 1281; Khanna, "Corporate Liability Standards: When Should Corporations be Held Criminally Liable?," p. 1245. See also, Chapter 6, Section 6.2.2.2.

2 See Chapters 2 and 3.

3 See Chapter 4.

4 See *infra* note 5 in Chapter 8 and the related main text.

5 See Chapter 4.

than applying a single enforcement approach – the deterrence-based or the cooperative approach – targeted monitoring systems employ different monitoring styles towards different regulatees; while some regulatees – those identified as recalcitrant – are closely watched, others are subject to less scrutiny.[6] That way, it is believed, enforcement authorities may efficiently achieve a higher level of compliance.[7] *What is the criterion underlying the classification of regulatees into differently monitored groups under a targeted monitoring system? Does this criterion facilitate a targeted monitoring system that may efficiently induce corporate proactive compliance?*

In this part of the book, I argue that existing structures of targeted monitoring systems may fail to overcome the perils of regulatory mixed regimes discussed in Chapter 4. Hence, I am taking on the challenge of developing a structure of regulatory monitoring regimes that efficiently induce corporate proactive compliance, while coping with the perils of the mixed regimes. Specifically, I develop a regulatory monitoring regime, the "Third-Party-Based Targeted Monitoring system," or the "TPTM system," which utilizes corporate monitors as a signaling mechanism that facilitates the creation of a targeted monitoring system. This monitoring system, therefore, sustains the advantages of the mixed enforcement regimes proposed in the existing literature, while overcoming their pitfalls.

This part of the book is composed of two chapters. In Chapter 7, I explore a unique enforcement instrument, known as Deferred Prosecution Agreements (DPAs) and Non-Prosecution Agreements (NPAs), which has been recently incorporated into the U.S. enforcement policy as an alternative enforcement measure against culpable corporations. An intriguing feature of the newly emerged DPA and NPA policies is the use of corporate monitors as "swords" against culpable corporations. While substituting traditional criminal proceedings, DPAs and NPAs often employ corporate monitors as "corporate watchdogs." These corporate watchdogs closely scrutinize corporations' activities and ensure compliance. My major goal in this chapter is to introduce to the reader the contemporary use of corporate monitors in the context of controlling corporate misconduct and to identify the specific challenges that arise with respect to the use of this enforcement mechanism. Accordingly, I describe in this chapter the evolution of corporate monitors as an enforcement instrument within the emerging policies of DPAs and NPAs, and examine scholars' primary criticism of such policies. With this exposition, I wish to

[6] See *infra* note 3 in Chapter 8 and the related main text.
[7] See Chapter 8, Section 8.2.

further the analysis in the following chapter where corporate monitors are used to help facilitate an efficient regulatory monitoring policy.

In Chapter 8, I propose that corporate monitors may be used not only as enforcement "swords," but also as "shields" for corporations adopting a proactive compliance approach. My point of departure in this chapter is the well-established scholarly approach that favors targeted monitoring systems over traditional, non-targeted ones.[8] Yet, a close look into the existing literature reveals that the major targeted monitoring frameworks developed by scholars up to this point face a pivotal challenge pertaining to the criteria they use for the classification of regulatees into different monitored groups. Given the lack of a credible classification mechanism, I develop in the remainder of this chapter a structure of targeted monitoring policy, the TPTM system, which uses the voluntary appointment of corporate monitors as a credible classification mechanism. This system is shown to strengthen corporations' incentive to engage in self-policing, while economizing the overall public enforcement costs.

---

[8] See Chapter 8, Section 8.2.

7. Corporate monitors: the emerging framework of deferred prosecution agreements[1]

7.1 INTRODUCTION

Recent corporate scandals have spurred the development of innovative enforcement mechanisms aimed at inducing corporate proactive compliance. One such mechanism is the newly emerged U.S. Federal enforcement policies of Deferred Prosecution Agreements (DPAs) and Non-Prosecution Agreements (NPAs), which use corporate monitors as "watchdogs" that seek to ensure corporate compliance. Under such agreements, prosecutors agree to defer prosecution of culpable corporations, in return for these corporations' obligation to undertake dictated structural reforms and to comply with certain standards of behavior.[2] These agreements require in many cases that corporations appoint independent corporate monitors to ensure corporate compliance within the terms of the agreements.

Third-party enforcers have been used widely in different contexts as an enforcement instrument aimed at preventing misconduct.[3] Current DPA and NPA policies utilize this invaluable instrument to induce corporate proactive compliance. Such policies replace traditional criminal proceedings against detected misconduct in an attempt to secure future corporate

---

[1] A substantial portion of this chapter is adopted from Oded, "Deferred Prosecution Agreements: Prosecutorial Balance in Times of Economic Meltdown," 65–99.

[2] The definition and specific components of DPAs and NPAs are discussed in Section 7.3 below.

[3] For a general overview of third-party enforcers, see, for instance, Kraakman, "Gatekeepers: The Anatomy of a Third-Party Enforcement Strategy," p. 54; Gilboy, "Compelled Third-Party Participation in the Regulatory Process: Legal Duties, Culture, and Noncompliance," pp. 136–138; Schmidt, *Eyes Half Blind: The Possibilities and Limits of Lawyers as Third Party Enforcers*; Grabosky, "Using Non-Governmental Resources to Foster Regulatory Compliance," 527–550. See also the discussion in Section 7.3 below.

compliance while economizing enforcement costs. In this chapter, I explore the emerging DPA and NPA policies, while paying close attention to the role played by corporate monitors in inducing corporate proactive compliance. The analysis in this chapter provides a necessary backdrop for the development of an efficient targeted monitoring system which is the key objective in the following chapter.

This chapter is structured as follows. In order to put the discussion in context, I briefly survey in Section 7.2 the major prototypes of third-party enforcers identified in the law and economics literature. Once the third-party enforcer prototype that is relevant for the current discussion is clarified, I then explore the newly emerged DPA and NPA policies. In Section 7.3, I present the evolution of the DPAs and the NPAs which have emerged in the past decade. I focus attention in Section 7.4 on corporate monitors that have been appointed by the DPAs and NPAs, and discuss their common roles, responsibilities, and selection. In Section 7.5, I explore the challenges arising with respect to the practical application of DPA and NPA policies, and in Section 7.6, I present the latest policy developments which aim to overcome these challenges. I summarize and conclude in Section 7.7.

7.2 SETTING THE CONTEXT – MAJOR PROTOTYPES OF THIRD-PARTY ENFORCERS

Third-party enforcement systems have become increasingly popular across a broad spectrum of legal areas.[4] Such frameworks are centered upon third parties that although they are not the primary author or beneficiary of the misconduct, their actions may prevent it or at least favorably supplement regulatory agencies' enforcement efforts in combating law-breaking.[5]

---

[4] For the increasing use of third-party enforcers, see, for instance, Kraakman, "Gatekeepers: The Anatomy of a Third-Party Enforcement Strategy," p. 54; Gilboy, "Compelled Third-Party Participation in the Regulatory Process: Legal Duties, Culture, and Noncompliance," pp. 136–138; Schmidt, *Eyes Half Blind: The Possibilities and Limits of Lawyers as Third Party Enforcers*; Grabosky, "Using Non-Governmental Resources to Foster Regulatory Compliance," 527–550.

[5] See Kraakman, "Gatekeepers: The Anatomy of a Third-Party Enforcement Strategy," p. 53; Gilboy, "Compelled Third-Party Participation in the Regulatory Process: Legal Duties, Culture, and Noncompliance," pp. 135–136, 140; Janet A. Gilboy, "Implications of Third-Party Involvement in Enforcement: The INS, Illegal Travelers, and International Airlines," *Law & Society Review* 31 (1997), p. 505; Gilson, "The Devolution of the Legal Profession: A Demand Side Perspective," p. 883.

Table 7.1 Major third-party enforcer prototypes – compared

	Bouncer	Chaperone
Basis for role	Compulsory	Voluntary
Relationship with monitored entity	Occasional	Continuous/recurring monitoring
Roles and functions	Withholding necessary cooperation	Reviewing and monitoring for the purpose of certification, rating, or accreditation
Main motivation to enforce	Duty-based personal liability	Reputation
Compensation for undertaking enforcement roles	No	Yes

Crudely put, the law and economics literature has identified two major prototypes of third-party enforcers: *bouncer* and *chaperone* enforcers. These enforcers differ from one another in their position, duties and motivations. Table 7.1 summarizes the comparison between bouncer and chaperone enforcers.

One prototype of third-party enforcers includes third parties positioned as *bouncers* that are able to disrupt misconduct by withholding necessary cooperation or consent.[6] In order to illustrate this bouncer prototype it is perhaps best to offer actual examples. For instance, this prototype might include pharmacists who are required to refuse to deliver a controlled drug except when given a valid prescription, as well as restaurants, bars, and various shopkeepers which are required to refuse to sell alcohol and cigarettes to underage customers, or international airlines that are required to prevent the landing of travelers in countries in which they are

[6] This type of third-party enforcer was originally defined and analyzed in-depth in Kraakman, "Gatekeepers: The Anatomy of a Third-Party Enforcement Strategy," 53–104. This definition of third-party enforcers was subsequently used in a prolific body of studies. See, for instance, Gilson, "The Devolution of the Legal Profession: A Demand Side Perspective," p. 883, who refers to gatekeepers as "someone in a position to decline when his service will be misused." See also, Hamdani, "Gatekeeper Liability," 53–120; Gilboy, "Compelled Third-Party Participation in the Regulatory Process: Legal Duties, Culture, and Noncompliance," 135–155; Gilboy, "Implications of Third-Party Involvement in Enforcement: The INS, Illegal Travelers, and International Airlines," p. 883; John R. Boatright, "Reluctant Guardians: The Moral Responsibility of Gatekeepers," *Business Ethics Quarterly* 17(4) (2007), 613–632.

unauthorized to be present. In the context of the corporate world, this prototype would include accountants and lawyers who are required to withhold the certification of false or illegal statements, as well as underwriters who are required to withhold the underwriting of fraudulent securities transactions.[7] This type of third-party enforcer is often perceived as a *gatekeeper* who prevents misconduct by refusing to support it.[8]

The law and economics literature has shown that a well-functioning bouncer-type enforcement system requires three basic conditions to be met.[9] *First*, there must be a "gate" and a "gatekeeper;" that is, there must be a service that is unavoidable for the would-be wrongdoer to perform the wrong, and a third party who is in the position to refuse to provide such a service. *Second*, third parties acting as gatekeepers must have the capacity to detect the potential misuse of their services by a would-be wrongdoer. And *third*, these third parties must be adequately incentivized to undertake their duties. As for the last requirement, bouncer-type third-party enforcers commonly receive no direct compensation for undertaking their gatekeeping duties. They are compelled to undertake an enforcement role by law and incur a duty-based liability where if they fail to fulfill their duty then sanctions will be imposed.[10] Therefore, enforcers of this type are sometimes referred to as "*public third-party enforcers*."[11]

The second prototype of third-party enforcers includes those positioned as *chaperones*. Chaperones have the power to control the incen-

---

[7] For an analysis of various examples of third-party enforcers of this prototype, including employers, lawyers, real estate brokers, boat and car dealers, garment manufacturers, doctors, social workers, psychologists, child-care providers, see Gilboy, "Compelled Third-Party Participation in the Regulatory Process: Legal Duties, Culture, and Noncompliance," especially p. 138; Coffee, *Gatekeepers: The Professions and Corporate Governance*, p. 2.

[8] See Kraakman, "Gatekeepers: The Anatomy of a Third-Party Enforcement Strategy," p. 63; Coffee, *Gatekeepers: The Professions and Corporate Governance*, p. 2.

[9] See Gilson, "The Devolution of the Legal Profession: A Demand Side Perspective," pp. 883–884; Kraakman, "Gatekeepers: The Anatomy of a Third-Party Enforcement Strategy," p. 61; Kim, "Gatekeepers Inside Out," p. 415.

[10] See Gilboy, "Compelled Third-Party Participation in the Regulatory Process: Legal Duties, Culture, and Noncompliance," p. 140; Coffee, "Understanding Enron: It's about the Gatekeepers, Stupid," 1403–1420; Schmidt, *Eyes Half Blind: The Possibilities and Limits of Lawyers as Third Party Enforcers*; F. Joseph Warin and Andrew S. Boutros, "Deferred Prosecution Agreements: A View from the Trenches and a Proposal for Reform," *Virginia Law Review* 93 (2007), p. 124.

[11] See Kraakman, "Gatekeepers: The Anatomy of a Third-Party Enforcement Strategy," pp. 61–62.

tives of would-be wrongdoers, and therefore, voluntarily monitor, detect, and disrupt misconduct.[12] Some examples of this prototype might include: accreditation agencies which certify that educational institutions and academic programs provide quality credentials; standardization organizations that certify goods, services or processes as meeting pre-determined standards; ranking institutions that rank academic journals according to impact or quality factors; tourism enterprises that rank hotels, restaurants and tourist attractions; credit rating agencies that evaluate corporations' debt securities; and auditors and in-house counsels that verify corporate compliance with laws and regulations. Such third-party enforcers may function in two different roles: as *gatekeepers*, a role in which they undertake various obstructive deterrence actions short of the disclosure of violations; or as *whistleblowers*, a role under which they disclose crucial misconduct-related information to relevant stakeholders, including potential victims and the relevant regulatory agency.[13]

The law and economics literature has shown that chaperone-type enforcers operate in a different setting than bouncer-type enforcers. Chaperones are normally *repeat players* that serve many clients by acting as "reputational intermediaries" in providing certification or verification services.[14] They use their expertise to investigate and monitor market players according to certain criteria, and form a bridge between these market players and other stakeholders using their reputation. By verifying, ranking, or certifying monitored market players, the chaperone enforcers signal other stakeholders, such as investors and trading partners, of the trustworthiness of the monitored entity. Obviously, the quality of such signals is derived from various determinants, including the frequency and intensity of the monitoring activity, the expertise of the enforcer, and the level of cooperation between the enforcer and the monitored party – all of which determine the market reputation of chaperone enforcers. This reputation and the reward it produces to chaperone enforcers, are the chief motivation for chaperone enforcers to undertake their enforcement

---

[12] See *ibid.*, p. 55. This definition of third-party enforcer is used by Coffee, "The Attorney as Gatekeeper: An Agenda for the SEC," pp. 1296–1297; Coffee, *Gatekeepers: The Professions and Corporate Governance*, p. 2; Kim, "Gatekeepers Inside Out," 411–463; Coffee, "Understanding Enron: It's about the Gatekeepers, Stupid," p. 1405.

[13] See Kraakman, "Gatekeepers: The Anatomy of a Third-Party Enforcement Strategy," pp. 56–58.

[14] See Coffee, *Gatekeepers: The Professions and Corporate Governance*, p. 2; Coffee, "The Attorney as Gatekeeper: An Agenda for the SEC," pp. 1296–1297.

role.[15] Therefore, these enforcers are sometimes referred to as "*market third-party enforcers*."[16]

Obviously, the dichotomy between the twin prototypes of enforcers, presented in Table 7.1, is a simplification of reality. In fact, the differences between actual third-party enforcers are not always obvious. For instance, when the misconduct depends upon the provision of a certification by a third-party enforcer, the refusal to provide misleading certifications may be seen as a disruption of misbehavior (bouncer prototype), as well as a warning signal to potential stakeholders (chaperone prototype).[17] In addition, many actual forms of third-party enforcers are structured as a mix of the various elements of the different prototypes.

Corporate monitors appointed by DPAs and NPAs, which are the main focus of this chapter, are greatly inspired by the chaperone prototype of enforcers. As revealed below, these corporate monitors operate *voluntarily*; they engage in a *continuous relationship* with the monitored corporations; their *reputation* plays an important role in their selection and motivation to perform; and they are *compensated* for their services. Having clarified the theoretical background and the relevant third-party enforcer prototype that corresponds with corporate monitors discussed in this part of the book, in what follows I focus on DPA and NPA policies and the role of the corporate monitors employed by them.

7.3 DEFERRED PROSECUTION AGREEMENTS (DPAs) AND NON-PROSECUTION AGREEMENTS (NPAs)

7.3.1 DPAs and NPAs – What Are They All About?

U.S. prosecutors have had until recently only a single weapon against culpable corporations. If a corporation was suspected of wrongdoing, prosecutors could bring criminal charges against both the corporation and their top functionaries.[18] However, the use of such a powerful weapon by prosecutors has always required them to consider the substantial col-

---

[15] See Coffee, *Gatekeepers: The Professions and Corporate Governance*, p. 3.

[16] See Kraakman, "Gatekeepers: The Anatomy of a Third-Party Enforcement Strategy," pp. 61–62.

[17] See *ibid.*, p. 58.

[18] See James K. Robinson, Phillip E. Urofsky and Christopher R. Pantel, "Deferred Prosecutions and the Independent Monitor," *International Journal of Disclosure and Governance* 2(4) (2005), p. 326; Eugene Illovsky, "Corporate

lateral consequences that such procedures may have on other stakeholders such as shareholders, employees, and consumers.[19] A notable example is the famous case of *Arthur Andersen*, then amongst the world's largest accounting firms (with more than 85,000 employees), which imploded after being convicted for failing to fulfill their professional responsibilities in auditing Enron's financial statements.[20] By the time the Supreme Court overturned their indictment in 2005, the damage to the company was irreversible and the company was driven out of business.[21] Arthur Andersen's case has accentuated the need to consider real-world consequences that corporate indictments may have, and stimulated the further development of an important policy instrument that has been transplanted in some sporadic previous cases to the corporate crime context. These instruments, known as DPAs and NPAs, comprise a wide variety of agreements between the prosecution and culpable corporations, under which prosecutors agree to defer/avoid the prosecution of culpable corporations if these corporations fulfill their obligations to undertake dictated structural reforms and to comply with certain standards of behavior.[22] Although the specific content of DPAs and NPAs may differ substantially, in most cases such agreements include the following components: (a) a corporate commitment to pay a combination of a criminal fine, civil penalty, and

---

Deferred Prosecution Agreements: The Brewing Debate," *Criminal Justice* 21 (2001), p. 36.

[19] See, for instance, Gibson Dunn, *2008 Year-End Update on Corporate Deferred Prosecution and Non-Prosecution Agreements*, available at: http://www.gibsondunn.com/publications/pages/2008Year-EndUpdate-CorporateDPAs.aspx (January 6, 2009): "[the] consequences [of criminal conviction] can be especially harsh for corporations that operate in highly regulated industries. For example, a conviction for certain violations could result in a corporation losing its broker-dealer license, banking license, charter, or deposit insurance; being stripped of eligibility to be a government contractor; or being prohibited from participation in government healthcare programs." See also, Robinson, Urofsky and Pantel, "Deferred Prosecutions and the Independent Monitor," p. 327.

[20] See *United States v. Arthur Andersen LLP*, CRH 02-121 (S.D. Tex. Mar. 7, 2002) (Indictment).

[21] See *Arthur Andersen LLP v. United States*, 544 U.S. 696 (2005).

[22] See Christopher A. Wray and Robert K. Hur, "Corporate Criminal Prosecution in a Post-Enron World: The Thompson Memo in Theory and Practice," *The American Criminal Law Review* 43 (2006), 1095–1188; Robinson, Urofsky and Pantel, "Deferred Prosecutions and the Independent Monitor," p. 325; Scott A. Resnik and Keir N. Dougall, "The Rise of Deferred Prosecution Agreements," *New York Law Journal: Securities Litigation & Regulation* (December 18, 2006); Peter Spivack and Sujit Raman, "Regulating the 'New Regulators': Current Trends in Deferred Prosecution Agreements," *The American Criminal Law Review* 45 (2008), 159–194.

restitution; (b) a corporate obligation to cooperate with ongoing investigations; and (c) a corporate commitment to adopt a preapproved compliance management system that is designed to ensure compliance with the agreement and disrupt misconduct.[23] Moreover, many DPAs and NPAs require corporations to appoint an independent *corporate monitor* that is empowered to oversee the corporate compliance management system and ensure that the corporation follows the agreement.[24]

The key difference between DPAs and NPAs is the stage in which they are concluded: *DPAs* are signed after charges have been brought against a defendant corporation. Thereby, they typically postpone the criminal charges for a set period of time, during which corporations have to fulfill their obligations. *NPAs*, on the other hand, are entered into between prosecutors and *potential* defendant corporations *before* the filing of criminal charges, thereby they typically postpone the *filing* of criminal charges against corporations. The average period of both types of agreements since 2000 is 28 months.[25] If a corporation fulfills its obligations, the prosecutor dismisses all charges (in DPAs), or avoids filing charges (in NPAs) against the corporation for the specific misconduct associated with the agreement. However, if the corporations fail to fulfill their agreements, the prosecutor may request the court to continue with the charges brought (in DPAs), or bring initial charges against the corporation (in NPAs).[26] To avoid the risk

---

23 See, for instance, Gibson Dunn, *2009 Year-End Update on Corporate Deferred Prosecution and Non-Prosecution Agreements* (January 7, 2010).

24 See, for instance, Robinson, Urofsky and Pantel, "Deferred Prosecutions and the Independent Monitor," p. 325; Benjamin M. Greenblum, "What Happens to a Prosecution Deferred? Judicial Oversight of Corporate Deferred Prosecution Agreements," *Columbia Law Review* 105(6) (2005), 1863–1904; Illovsky, "Corporate Deferred Prosecution Agreements: The Brewing Debate," 36–39; Kathleen M. Boozang and Simone Handler-Hutchinson, "'Monitoring' Corporate Corruption: DOJ's use of Deferred Prosecution Agreements in Health Care," *American Journal of Law & Medicine* 35(1) (2009), 89–124.

25 See Gibson Dunn, *2011 Year-End Update on Corporate Deferred Prosecution and Non-Prosecution Agreements*; Khanna and Dickinson, "The Corporate Monitor: The New Corporate Czar," pp. 1713–1756.

26 See Greenblum, "What Happens to a Prosecution Deferred? Judicial Oversight of Corporate Deferred Prosecution Agreements," 1863–1904; Gibson Dunn, *2008 Year-End Update on Corporate Deferred Prosecution and Non-Prosecution Agreements*; Gibson Dunn, *2009 Mid-Year Update on Corporate Deferred Prosecution and Non-Prosecution Agreements* (July 8, 2009). In fact the differences in content between DPAs and NPAs are minor. See *ibid.*, citing James B. Comey, the former DOJ Deputy Attorney General, according to whom: "the lines [between NPAs and DPAs] blur. Talking about DPAs separate from NPAs, . . . I'm not sure there is that meaningful . . . a distinction."

of losing evidence or witnesses due to the postponement of charges, DPAs and NPAs regularly require corporations to admit to substantial facts that may ground a conviction in case they breach such agreements.[27]

7.3.2 The Evolution of Deferred Prosecution in the Corporate Arena

Deferred prosecution is undoubtedly not a new policy instrument. In fact, this instrument is almost a century old. Deferred prosecution was originally created at the beginning of the twentieth century as an alternative arrangement used to rehabilitate juvenile and drug offenders.[28] The idea behind the development of this instrument was to minimize the potentially harsh consequences of criminal convictions. Policymakers sought to avoid the stigmatization of nonviolent first-time offenders who had not yet committed themselves to "criminal careers."[29] Deferred prosecution arrangements were recognized as an official policy instrument by the U.S Congress in 1975, which established special pretrial agencies to assist judges in determining offenders' suitability for the

---

[27] See Robinson, Urofsky and Pantel, "Deferred Prosecutions and the Independent Monitor," 325–347; Illovsky, "Corporate Deferred Prosecution Agreements: The Brewing Debate," p. 37.

[28] The origin of the deferred prosecution arrangement is attributed to the Chicago Boys' Court that initially conceived of deferred prosecution in 1914. See, for instance, David A. Inniss, "Developments in the Law: Alternatives to Incarceration," *Harvard Law Review* 111(7) (1998) 1863–1990; James A. Inciardi, Duane C. McBride and James E. Rivers, *Drug Control and the Courts* (Thousand Oaks, CA: SAGE Publications Inc., 1996); Greenblum, "What Happens to a Prosecution Deferred? Judicial Oversight of Corporate Deferred Prosecution Agreements," 1863–1904; Robinson, Urofsky and Pantel, "Deferred Prosecutions and the Independent Monitor," 325–347. The use of deferred prosecution was extended to drug offenders in 1962 by the Supreme Court's ruling in *Robinson v. California*, 370 U.S. 660, 667 (1962). See Lisa Rosenblum, "Mandating Effective Treatment for Drug Offenders," *The Hastings Law Journal* 53 (2001) 1217–1243; Andrew Armstrong, "Drug Courts and the *De Facto* Legalization of Drug Use for Participants in Residential Treatment Facilities," *The Journal of Criminal Law & Criminology* 94(1) (2003), 133–168; Greenblum, "What Happens to a Prosecution Deferred? Judicial Oversight of Corporate Deferred Prosecution Agreements," p. 1886; Robinson, Urofsky and Pantel, "Deferred Prosecutions and the Independent Monitor," p. 326.

[29] See Robert W. Balch, "Deferred Prosecution: The Juvenilization of the Criminal Justice System," *Federal Probation* 38 (1974), p. 46; Greenblum, "What Happens to a Prosecution Deferred? Judicial Oversight of Corporate Deferred Prosecution Agreements," p. 1886; Gennaro F. Vito and Debora G. Wilson, *The American Juvenile Justice System* (Beverly Hills, CA: Sage Publications, Inc., 1985).

newly created rehabilitation programs and to supervise those offenders during the deferral period.[30] Eventually, the DOJ promulgated unified eligibility criteria and procedures through an official Pretrial Diversion Program as part of the U.S. Attorney's Manual.[31] This program was specifically designed for individual offenders and did not apply to corporate criminals.[32]

The adoption of deferred prosecution arrangements into the corporate arena was a gradual process that started with a handful of cases during the 1990s. The initial step was an NPA reached in the *Salomon Brothers* case in 1992.[33] In this case, a ten-month multi-agency investigation led to several allegations being leveled against the Salomon Brothers. The company was suspected of having submitted false and unauthorized bids in violation of federal forfeiture laws and the False Claims Act. The company and others were also suspected of entering into unlawful agreements with respect to trading in financing and secondary markets in violation of the Sherman Antitrust Act.[34] Nevertheless, the DOJ agreed to seek no criminal charges against the Salomon Brothers with respect to these matters in return for the Salomon Brothers' commitment to pay $290 million in sanctions, forfeitures, and restitution. In addition, the settlement required the Salomon Brothers to continue their cooperation with various government investigations and to institute a compliance management system to prevent

---

[30] See Speedy Trial Act of 1974, Pub. L. No. 93-619, 88 Stat. 2076. (1974). See also, Barry Mahoney *et al.*, *Pretrial Services Programs: Responsibilities and Potential*, U.S. Department of Justice, Office of Justice Programs, National Institute of Justice [2001]; Greenblum, "What Happens to a Prosecution Deferred? Judicial Oversight of Corporate Deferred Prosecution Agreements," p. 1867.

[31] U.S. Attorneys' Manual (1997) ("Attorney's Manual"), available at: http://www.justice.gov/usao/eousa/foia_reading_room/usam/title9/22mcrm.htm, § 9-22.000. The Pretrial Diversion Program is described in § 9-22.010 as: "an alternative to prosecution which seeks to divert certain offenders from traditional criminal justice processing into a program of supervision and services administered by the U.S. Probation Service. In the majority of cases, offenders are diverted at the pre-charge stage. Participants who successfully complete the program will not be charged or, if charged, will have the charges against them dismissed; unsuccessful participants are returned for prosecution."

[32] See F. Joseph Warin and Jason C. Schwartz, "Deferred Prosecution: The Need for Specialized Guidelines for Corporate Defendants," *The Journal of Corporation Law* 23 (1997), pp. 129–130.

[33] See Department of Justice, *Press Release, U.S. Department of Justice and SEC Enter $290 Million Settlement with Salomon Brothers* (May 20, 1992).

[34] See Department of Justice, *Press Release: Department of Justice and SEC Enter $290 Million Settlement with Salomon Brothers in Treasury Securities Case* (May 20, 1992).

the reoccurrence of these violations.[35] In explaining its decision to refrain from criminal charges, the DOJ mainly relied on the Salomon Brothers' "exemplary" cooperation so "there [was] no need for invoking the criminal process."[36]

Shortly after the Salomon Brothers' case, in June 1993, the U.S. Attorney for the Southern District of New York reached an agreement with the *Sequa Corporation*.[37] According to this agreement, the U.S. Attorney agreed to refrain from prosecuting Sequa and its subsidiary for fraud in the manufacture and repair of airplane engine parts, in return for Sequa's commitment to pay $5 million for "scientific testing and expert analysis of airplane parts."[38] In addition, Sequa agreed to managerial changes and guaranteed to continue its cooperation with the investigation.[39] Like with the Salomon Brothers case, the U.S. Attorney considered Sequa's cooperation with the investigation and the harm that may be suffered by Sequa's employees and customers if criminal charges were brought against the corporation.[40]

The next important stepping stone in setting the grounds for deferred prosecution arrangements was the case of *Prudential Securities* in 1994.[41] Prudential was charged with securities fraud related to the sale of some oil and gas limited partnerships. The allegations against Prudential included investor deception regarding the returns and tax status of the

---

35 See *ibid.*; Greenblum, "What Happens to a Prosecution Deferred? Judicial Oversight of Corporate Deferred Prosecution Agreements," p. 1872; Warin and Schwartz, "Deferred Prosecution: The Need for Specialized Guidelines for Corporate Defendants," p. 125; Perry and Dakin, "Compliance Programs and Criminal Law," p. 22.13.

36 See Department of Justice, *Press Release: Department of Justice and SEC Enter $290 Million Settlement with Salomon Brothers in Treasury Securities Case*; Warin and Schwartz, "Deferred Prosecution: The Need for Specialized Guidelines for Corporate Defendants," p. 124; Greenblum, "What Happens to a Prosecution Deferred? Judicial Oversight of Corporate Deferred Prosecution Agreements," p. 1872.

37 See United States Attorney's Office, *Announcement of Decision Not to Prosecute Sequa Corporation* (June 24, 1993); reprinted in Press Releases Issued by United States Attorney, Southern District of New York, 1248 PLI/Corp. 197, 211-14 (2001).

38 See Warin and Schwartz, "Deferred Prosecution: The Need for Specialized Guidelines for Corporate Defendants," p. 125.

39 See *ibid.*, p. 125.

40 See *ibid.*, p. 125.

41 See the Deferred Prosecution Agreement, *United States v. Prudential Securities Incorporated* (S.D.N.Y. Mag. # 94-2189), dated October 27, 1994; available at: http://www.corporatecrimereporter.com/documents/prudential.pdf.

investments.[42] The U.S. Attorney for the Southern District of New York agreed to enter into a DPA with Prudential. According to the DPA, the charges against Prudential would be *deferred* in return for Prudential's commitment to pay $330 million in restitution. Similar to the prior cases, the offender's cooperation with the government's investigation and the concerns of collateral consequences on its employees and investors set the ground for the deferral. Unlike the previous cases, though, Prudential's agreement did not simply *dismiss* the charges against Prudential, but rather *deferred* them for a period of three years, after which, provided that Prudential had complied with the terms of the agreement and avoided additional misconduct, the criminal charges were to be dismissed. Under the specific circumstances of Prudential's agreement, if Prudential failed to comply with the agreed conditions or engaged in wrongdoing during that period, all charges against Prudential would be reinstated.[43] To ensure Prudential's abidance, the agreement further required the company to employ an independent law firm to serve as a corporate monitor to review its regulatory and compliance controls.[44] This "probation period" became an inherent feature of all subsequent DPAs and NPAs.[45]

---

[42] See Greenblum, "What Happens to a Prosecution Deferred? Judicial Oversight of Corporate Deferred Prosecution Agreements," p. 1873; Robinson, Urofsky and Pantel, "Deferred Prosecutions and the Independent Monitor," p. 329; Warin and Schwartz, "Deferred Prosecution: The Need for Specialized Guidelines for Corporate Defendants," pp. 125–126.

[43] See letter from Kenneth J. Vianale and Baruch Weiss, Assistant U.S. Attorneys for the S. Dist. of N.Y., U.S. Department of Justice to Scott W. Muller & Carey R. Dunne, Davis Polk & Wardwell, counsel to Prudential Sec., Inc. (October 17, 1994), p. 3; available at: http://www.corporatecrimereporter.com/documents/prudential.pdf.

[44] See *ibid.*: "It is further understood that [Prudential] shall: . . . (b) comply with all the terms and conditions of the SEC agreement and retain a mutually acceptable outside counsel within 30 days of the filing of this agreement to review [Prudential]'s policies and procedures in order to ensure that [Prudential] has adopted all the compliance-related directives set forth in the SEC agreement." See also, Perry and Dakin, "Compliance Programs and Criminal Law," p. 22.14; Robinson, Urofsky and Pantel, "Deferred Prosecutions and the Independent Monitor," p. 329; Greenblum, "What Happens to a Prosecution Deferred? Judicial Oversight of Corporate Deferred Prosecution Agreements," p. 1873; Warin and Schwartz, "Deferred Prosecution: The Need for Specialized Guidelines for Corporate Defendants," pp. 125–126.

[45] It should be noted that 'corporate probation' was acknowledged even before the *Prudential Securities* case by the OSG as an appropriate measure that can be used against culpable corporations. However, the use of probation measures was meant as part of the sentence, *i.e.*, after the corporation was convicted. See the United States Sentencing Commission (USSC), "Federal Sentencing Guidelines

In 1996, the U.S. Attorney for the Central District of California reached an agreement with *Cooper & Lybrand*.[46] The partnership was accused of concealing essential errors and omissions in the Arizona Governor's financial statements, as well as of receiving inside information regarding a state contract. The U.S. Attorney considered the "*exemplary cooperation*" of Cooper & Lybrand with the investigation and entered into an NPA with the partnership. According to the agreement, the prosecution was to be deferred for a two-year period. In return, the partnership committed to pay an additional $3 million for restitution; to employ an independent corporate monitor to ensure corporate compliance; and to implement a compliance management system that would include training for its professionals nationwide in ethics and integrity.[47] This agreement extended the scope of NPAs further by establishing an *extrajudicial adjudicatory process* in which prosecutors were authorized without any judicial intervention to impose a $100,000 fine for any breach of the agreement that they chose not to prosecute.[48]

As mentioned above, the Pretrial Diversion Program, incorporated into the U.S. Attorneys' Manual (1997), established the criteria that must be met for deferred prosecution with respect to individuals.[49] However, where corporations were concerned, prosecutors who decided to use DPAs or NPAs exercised wide discretion in designing and implementing such agreements.[50] In acknowledgement of the emerging practices, Eric Holder, then U.S. Deputy Attorney General, promulgated a memorandum that laid down unified criteria, composed of eight factors that should be considered when deciding whether to bring charges against corporations ("*Holder*

Manual: Chapter Eight – Sentencing of Organizations," available at: http://www.ussc.gov/Guidelines/Organizational_Guidelines/guidelines_chapter_8.htm: "probation is an appropriate sentence for an organizational defendant when needed to ensure that another sanction will be fully implemented, or to ensure that steps will be taken within the organization to reduce the likelihood of future criminal conduct."

46 See Coopers & Lybrand LLP (C&L), *Settlement Agreement* (C.D. Cal. 1996); see Corporate Crime Reporter, *Crime without Conviction: The Rise of Deferred and Non Prosecution Agreements*, Available at: http://www.corporatecrimereporter.com/deferredreport.htm, Corporate Crime Reporter (December 28, 2005).

47 See Warin and Schwartz, "Deferred Prosecution: The Need for Specialized Guidelines for Corporate Defendants," pp. 126–127.

48 See Greenblum, "What Happens to a Prosecution Deferred? Judicial Oversight of Corporate Deferred Prosecution Agreements," p. 1873; Warin and Schwartz, "Deferred Prosecution: The Need for Specialized Guidelines for Corporate Defendants," p. 127.

49 See *supra* notes 31–32 and the related main text.

50 See Resnik and Dougall, "The Rise of Deferred Prosecution Agreements."

Memo").[51] The factors outlined in the Holder Memo include: (1) the nature and seriousness of the offense; (2) the pervasiveness of wrongdoing within the corporation; (3) the corporation's history of similar conduct; (4) the corporation's timely and voluntary disclosure of wrongdoing and its willingness to cooperate in the investigation; (5) the existence and adequacy of the corporation's compliance program; (6) the corporation's remedial actions; (7) any collateral consequences; and (8) the adequacy of non-criminal remedies. Although the Holder Memo did not explicitly acknowledge DPAs and NPAs as formal instruments, the first signs of such instruments can be seen in the commentary §VI(B) on the Holder Memo:[52] "[A] corporation's cooperation may be critical in identifying the culprits and locating relevant evidence. In some circumstances, therefore, *granting a corporation immunity or amnesty may be considered in the course of the government's investigation.*"

Enron's scandal, which was exposed in 2001, shortly after the promulgation of the Holder Memo, has propelled the issue of corporate controls and the desirability of DPAs to the forefront of the corporate governance polemic.[53] In 2003, DPAs gained substantial support from a new memorandum issued by the U.S. Attorney General, Larry D. Thompson ("*Thompson Memo*").[54] The Thompson Memo reinforced – and slightly revised – the factors established by the Holder Memo for the prosecution

---

[51] See Eric Holder, Deputy Attorney General, *Memorandum for Heads of Department Components United States Attorneys: Principles of Federal Prosecution of Corporations*. The Holder Memo and the principles set forth in this Memo are discussed in Chapter 5, Section 5.6.2.

[52] See *ibid.*, §VI(B) (emphasis added).

[53] Some sources reported that even Arthur Andersen had negotiated a DPA with the DOJ, which eventually failed due to Andersen's refusal to accept the ongoing monitoring requirement of the DOJ. See Alan Vinegrad, "Deferred Prosecution of Corporations," *New York Law Journal* 230(72) (2003); Greenblum, "What Happens to a Prosecution Deferred? Judicial Oversight of Corporate Deferred Prosecution Agreements," p. 1888; Gibson Dunn, *2008 Year-End Update on Corporate Deferred Prosecution and Non-Prosecution Agreements*; Robert L. Bartley, "Andersen: A Pyrrhic Victory," *The Wall Street Journal* (June 24, 2002), A17; Beth A. Wilkinson and Alex Young K. Oh, "The Principles of Federal Prosecution of Business Organizations: A Ten-Year Anniversary Perspective," *NYSBA Inside* 27(2) (2009), 8–11; Blank Rome LLP, "Keeping A Watchful Eye: Corporate Deferred Prosecution Agreements and the Selection of Corporate Monitors," *Mondaq Business Briefing* (July 3, 2008); Corporate Crime Reporter, *Crime without Conviction: The Rise of Deferred and Non Prosecution Agreements* (December 28, 2005).

[54] See Larry D. Thompson, Deputy Attorney General, *Memorandum for Heads of Department Components United States Attorneys: Principles of Federal Prosecution of Business Organizations*.

of business corporations. The major contribution of the Thompson Memo was the greater emphasis it put on the *authenticity of corporations' proffered cooperation* as a major factor in considering the prosecution of corporations.[55] The Thompson Memo explicitly acknowledged the possibility of prosecution deferral in return for genuine corporate cooperation.[56]

Following the Thompson Memo, the use of DPAs and NPAs substantially expanded.[57] This expansion has three key dimensions. *First*, the number of DPAs has substantially increased, from only a handful of DPAs and NPAs that were concluded in the first years of the second millennium to 40 and 32 agreements that were concluded in 2010 and 2011 respectively.[58] Since 2000, the DOJ has entered into more than 230 reported DPAs and NPAs, extracting more than $30 billion in fines, penalties, forfeitures, and civil settlements.[59] Overall, DPAs have continued gaining significance in the past decade and have become an important enforcement instrument used to combat major corporate crimes.[60] *Second*,

---

55 See *ibid.*; Greenblum, "What Happens to a Prosecution Deferred? Judicial Oversight of Corporate Deferred Prosecution Agreements," pp. 1874–1875.

56 See Thompson Memo §VI.A and B.

57 The principles and considerations in the Thompson Memo were highlighted once again in 2006 in a Memorandum issued by Paul McNulty, the Deputy Attorney General, ("*McNulty Memo*"). See Paul McNulty, Deputy Attorney General, *Memorandum for Heads of Department Components United States Attorneys: Principles of Federal Prosecution of Business Organizations*. The McNulty Memo repeats the consideration of the factors from the Thompson Memo and adds new restrictions regarding prosecutors' powers to require privileged information from companies.

58 See Gibson Dunn, *2012 Year-End Update on Corporate Deferred Prosecution and Non-Prosecution Agreements* [July 10, 2012], p. 2. According to this report, in the period between January 1, 2012 through July 10, 2012 the total number of DPAs and NPAs entered into was 21.

59 See *ibid.*

60 See Greenblum, "What Happens to a Prosecution Deferred? Judicial Oversight of Corporate Deferred Prosecution Agreements," p. 1875: "since the dissemination of Thompson [Memorandum], no corporation has been charged in a major corporate fraud investigation outside a deferred agreement." Such agreements involve a wide spectrum of corporations, including American Express Bank International (a former subsidiary of American Express Company), Banco Popular, PNC, Merrill Lynch, Boeing, Bristol-Myers Squibb, British Petroleum, Chevron, Pfizer, Aktiebolaget (AB) Volvo, Wellcare Health Plans, UBS AG, KPMG, WorldCom, Credit Suisse First Boston (CSFB), AOL, Deutsche Bank, Shell Nigeria, ABN Amro Bank N.V., and others. See Gibson Dunn, *2008 Year-End Update on Corporate Deferred Prosecution and Non-Prosecution Agreements*; Gibson Dunn, *2009 Mid-Year Update on Corporate Deferred Prosecution and Non-Prosecution Agreements*; Robinson, Urofsky and Pantel, "Deferred Prosecutions and the Independent Monitor," 325–347; Vinegrad, "Deferred Prosecution

the spectrum in which DPAs have been used has expanded to include a wide range of legal areas, including healthcare, the Foreign Corrupt Practices Act (FCPA), tax, accounting irregularities, mortgage, internet gambling, money laundering, immigration, corrupt sales practices, the False Claims Act, environment, insurance fraud, banking fraud, sexually explicit labeling, and procurement fraud.[61] And *third*, the DOJ is no longer the only enforcement authority that uses DPAs. The U.S. Securities and Exchange Commission (SEC) officially recognized DPAs in 2010 as a valid enforcement practice through the promulgation of the new "Cooperation Initiative" which recognizes a set of enforcement instruments, including DPAs that may be used by the SEC to encourage greater cooperation by individuals and companies in SEC investigations.[62] Accordingly, on May 17, 2011, the SEC entered into the first DPA with Tenaris S.A. which was accused of violating the FCPA.[63] Two additional agreements were reached by the SEC in 2011 to resolve securities fraud allegations.[64]

Altogether, as a result of their gradual recognition as a legitimate

---

of Corporations;" Resnik and Dougall, "The Rise of Deferred Prosecution Agreements;" Corporate Crime Reporter, *Crime without Conviction: The Rise of Deferred and Non Prosecution Agreements*; Gibson Dunn, *2010 Year-End Update on Corporate Deferred Prosecution and Non-Prosecution Agreement*; Melissa Aguilar, "DPA-NPA Tally Marks Decade's Second Highest," *Compliance Week* (January 4, 2011).

[61] See Khanna and Dickinson, "The Corporate Monitor: The New Corporate Czar," 1713–1756; Vikramaditya S. Khanna, "Reforming the Corporate Monitor?" in *Prosecutors in the Board Room: Using Criminal Law to Regulate Corporate Conduct*, Anthony S. Barkow and Rachel E. Barkow eds. (New York: New York University Press, 2011); Boozang and Handler-Hutchinson, "'Monitoring' Corporate Corruption: DOJ's use of Deferred Prosecution Agreements in Health Care," 89–124; Gibson Dunn, *2008 Year-End Update on Corporate Deferred Prosecution and Non-Prosecution Agreements*; Gibson Dunn, *2009 Mid-Year Update on Corporate Deferred Prosecution and Non-Prosecution Agreements*; Gibson Dunn, *2009 Year-End Update on Corporate Deferred Prosecution and Non-Prosecution Agreements.*

[62] See the SEC announcement of the "Cooperation Initiative," at: http://sec.gov/spotlight/enfcoopinitiative.shtml. See also, Gibson Dunn, *2010 Year-End Update on Corporate Deferred Prosecution and Non-Prosecution Agreement*, p. 7; Aguilar, "DPA-NPA Tally Marks Decade's Second Highest."

[63] See United States Attorney's Office, 'The Securities and Exchange Commission today entered into a Deferred Prosecution Agreement (DPA) with Tenaris S.A. in its first-ever use of the approach to facilitate and reward cooperation in SEC investigations' (May 17, 2011), available at: http://www.sec.gov/news/press/2011/2011-112.htm.

[64] Gibson Dunn, *2011 Year-End Update on Corporate Deferred Prosecution and Non-Prosecution Agreements*; Gibson Dunn, *2012 Mid-Year Update on Corporate Deferred Prosecution and Non-Prosecution Agreements.*

enforcement practice, DPAs have become an important tool that expands the prosecutorial toolkit and provides an alternative means of controlling corporate misconduct. To achieve their goals, many DPAs and NPAs rely on *corporate monitors* – a supervisory mechanism that is explored in the following section.

7.4 THE USE OF CORPORATE MONITORS IN DPAs AND NPAs

The use of third-party monitors started long before it was adopted as part of the recently established DPAs. In fact, the roots of third-party monitors can be traced back to the "Special Masters" appointed by the English Chancery in the early sixteenth century.[65] Corporate monitors as they are currently used were developed in the U.S. during the 1980s as a result of the Racketeer Influenced and Corrupt Organizations (RICO) Act.[66] Civil actions under the RICO Act resulted in the appointment of corporate monitors as part of the *remedies* announced by the court.[67] The use of corporate monitors has extended gradually throughout the 1990s. During this period, corporate monitors were appointed *before* any announcement of the court ruling. Corporations, moreover, have agreed to the appointment of third-party experts to monitor their regulatory performance as a substitute for sanctions.[68] In the recent decade, the use of corporate monitors was recognized by the DOJ as valuable in ensuring the optimal functioning of internal corporate governance mechanisms, especially when limited resources or expertise hamper direct supervision by the DOJ.[69]

---

65 See Khanna and Dickinson, "The Corporate Monitor: The New Corporate Czar," p. 1715; Khanna, "Reforming the Corporate Monitor?," 226–248.

66 The RICO Act is a U.S. Federal law that was enacted by section 901(a) of the Organized Crime Control Act of 1970, Pub. L. No. 91-452, 84 Stat. 922 (15 October 1970), codified as Chapter 96 of Title 18 of the United States Code, 18 U.S.C. § 1961 through 18 U.S.C. § 1968. This Act was intended to fight the Mafia by extending criminal penalties and a civil cause of actions for actions carried out as part of an ongoing criminal organization.

67 See Khanna and Dickinson, "The Corporate Monitor: The New Corporate Czar," pp. 1716–1717.

68 Among these cases, corporate monitors were included in the agreements achieved in the *Prudential Securities* and *Cooper & Lybrand* cases discussed above. See the main text related to *supra* notes 42–48. For a historical overview of corporate monitors see *ibid.*, pp. 1715–1720.

69 See United States Government Accountability Office (GAO), *Corporate Crime: Preliminary Observations on DOJ's Use and Oversight of Deferred Prosecution and Non-Prosecution Agreements (Statement of Eileen R. Larence,*

Throughout the last decade, corporate monitors have become a standard feature of many DPAs and NPAs.[70] This feature includes third parties that have been hired based on DPAs or NPAs as a supervisory mechanism used to ensure future corporate compliance. Such monitors are hired by corporations *after* a clear indication of wrongdoing has been detected by enforcement authorities.[71] Therefore, although their appointment stems from an agreement between the corporation and the prosecutor, corporations agree to their appointment only to avoid the consequences of an indictment.[72] According to this approach, if the corporation had a genuine and comprehensive compliance management system in place, corporate monitors would not be required.[73] Hence, from the government's perspective, the appointment of corporate monitors serves as a type of substitute for more complex and costly prosecution proceedings, and may achieve future compliance without using confrontational measures that could result in undesired ends.[74]

Director Homeland Security and Justice), p. 19: "When deciding whether a monitor was needed to help oversee the development or operations of a company's compliance program, DOJ considered factors such as the availability of DOJ resources for this oversight, the level of expertise among DOJ prosecutors to monitor compliance in more technical or complex areas, and existing regulatory oversight."

[70] For an overview of various cases in which the appointment of corporate monitors was required by DPAs and NPAs see Gibson Dunn, *2008 Year-End Update on Corporate Deferred Prosecution and Non-Prosecution Agreements*; Robinson, Urofsky and Pantel, "Deferred Prosecutions and the Independent Monitor," pp. 333–335; Gibson Dunn, *2009 Mid-Year Update on Corporate Deferred Prosecution and Non-Prosecution Agreements.*

[71] See Khanna and Dickinson, "The Corporate Monitor: The New Corporate Czar," pp. 1714, 1727.

[72] See *ibid.*

[73] See Christopher M. Matthews, "Fraud Chief: Effective Compliance Programs can Prevent Monitors," *Main Justice: Politics, Policy and the Law* (May 24, 2010c), quoting Denis McInerney, the Criminal Fraud Section Chief: "If you have already established an excellent compliance program, then it will be less likely that we'll install a compliance monitor, which can come at some cost to the company." See also, Christopher M. Matthews, "Grindler Touts Importance of Compliance, but Doubts Linger," *Main Justice: Politics, Policy and the Law* (May 25, 2010d).

[74] See Khanna, "Reforming the Corporate Monitor?," 226–248; Khanna and Dickinson, "The Corporate Monitor: The New Corporate Czar," p. 1721; Greenblum, "What Happens to a Prosecution Deferred? Judicial Oversight of Corporate Deferred Prosecution Agreements," 1863–1904. For the adverse effects of confrontational strategies of enforcement see Chapter 2, Section 2.4.2.

7.4.1 Roles and Responsibilities

Corporate monitors are usually paid for by the offending corporation.[75] They are appointed to oversee the internal compliance management system of the corporation; to establish new compliance management systems, when such systems do not exist or were proven to be poorly administered; to review the effectiveness of corporate internal controls; and to disrupt misconduct while ensuring that the conditions of the DPAs are fulfilled.[76] The monitor's specific powers are determined and specified in each DPA and NPA. Their responsibilities differ from one case to another and can range from a mere advisory role to significantly more intrusive powers including the restructuring of corporate internal processes and reporting any deviation from appropriate corporate behavior not only to the corporation, but also to the court.[77] For instance, in the case of *AOL*, which faced criminal allegations regarding securities fraud perpetrated by some specific employees, the 2004 DPA specified limited reviewing powers for the corporate monitor.[78] Similarly, in the cases of *InVision*, *Monsanto*, *Titan* and *DPC*, all of which were related to violations of the FCPA, the corporate monitors were entrusted to "evaluate the effectiveness" of the companies' FCPA compliance management

---

[75] See Khanna and Dickinson, "The Corporate Monitor: The New Corporate Czar," p. 1723. Mostly, corporations have to bear the cost of corporate monitors in addition to the monetary payment agreed upon between the parties. An exceptional DPA, in that respect, is Sirchie Acquisition Company, LLC's, entered into in February 2010, according to which Sirchie was allowed to partially offset the cost of its corporate monitor against the fine imposed under the DPAs. See Gibson Dunn, *2010 Mid-Year Update on Corporate Deferred Prosecution and Non-Prosecution Agreements* [August 5, 2010].

[76] See United States Government Accountability Office (GAO), *Corporate Crime: Preliminary Observations on DOJ's Use and Oversight of Deferred Prosecution and Non-Prosecution Agreements (Statement of Eileen R. Larence, Director Homeland Security and Justice)*, p. 19.

[77] See Khanna and Dickinson, "The Corporate Monitor: The New Corporate Czar," pp. 1724–1726; Blank Rome LLP, "Keeping a Watchful Eye: Corporate Deferred Prosecution Agreements and the Selection of Corporate Monitors."

[78] See the Deferred Prosecution Agreement of *America Online, Inc.* (*AOL*), 2004, §13. Available at: http://www.corporatecrimereporter.com/documents/aol.pdf: ". . . The Monitor will undertake a *special review* of: the effectiveness of AOL's internal control measures related to its accounting for advertising and related transactions; the training related to these internal control measures; AOL's deal sign-off and approval procedures; and AOL's corporate code of conduct. AOL agrees to cooperate with the Independent Monitor" (emphasis added).

systems.[79] Conversely, in other cases, the powers of corporate monitors expanded beyond reviewing and evaluation powers. In the *Micrus* case, for instance, which also involved FCPA violations, the DPA stated that "[d]uring the monitor's term, no amendments or changes will be made to the policies and procedures without the prior approval of the monitor."[80] Similarly, in the *KPMG* case, which involved allegations of designing fraudulent tax shelters, the appointed corporate monitor was given extensive powers to review and monitor, not only concerning the compliance management system, but also concerning the "implementation and execution of personnel decisions regarding individuals who engage in or were responsible . . . for the illegal conduct described in the information and may require any personnel action, including termination, regarding any such individuals."[81] Additionally, in this case the corporate monitor was required to actively *investigate*, report any potential misconduct to the corporate compliance officer and to recommend actions needed to secure compliance. In other cases, such as the *CIBC*, *Micrus*, and *InVision*, the corporate monitors were required to file periodic reports to the agencies concerning the corporation's compliance with their agreement and to provide any additional information about the corporations as requested by the agencies.[82] In some cases, corporate monitors are extremely powerful and involved in all critical corporate decisions.[83] For instance, in the *Bristol-Myers Squibb* case, the board removed the Chief Executive Officer (CEO) and the general counsel of the corporation based on the corporate monitor's recommendations.[84]

---

[79] See Robinson, Urofsky and Pantel, "Deferred Prosecutions and the Independent Monitor," p. 333.

[80] See the Non Prosecution Agreement with Micrus S.A. (February 28, 2005). Available at: http://www.justice.gov/criminal/fraud/fcpa/cases/micrus-corp/02-28-05micrus-agree.pdf

[81] See Deferred Prosecution Agreement with *KPMG* (August 26, 2005), §18. Available at: http://www.justice.gov/usao/nys/pressreleases/August05/kpmgdpagmt.pdf.

[82] See Robinson, Urofsky and Pantel, "Deferred Prosecutions and the Independent Monitor," p. 333.

[83] See Jennifer O'Hare, "The Use of the Corporate Monitor in SEC Enforcement Actions," *Brooklyn Journal of Corporate, Financial and Commercial Law* 1 (2006), 89–118. O'Hare describes WorldCom's corporate monitor, who was involved in every important corporate decision, as the most powerful person in WorldCom.

[84] See Deferred Prosecution Agreement with *Bristol-Myers Squibb* (June 13, 2005). Available at: http://lib.law.virginia.edu/Garrett/prosecution_agreements/pdf/bristol-meyers.pdf.

7.4.2 Selection

Corporations, with varying levels of prosecutorial involvement, typically select the corporate monitors.[85] In some cases, such as with *Monsanto* and *Mircus*, the agreements allowed the corporations the chance to choose corporate monitors that would be "acceptable" to the prosecution.[86] In other cases, such as with the *CIBC*, the prosecution itself selected the monitor for the corporation.[87] In most cases, corporate monitors are selected from a small group of former enforcement officials, including former judges, prosecutors and regulatory agents that are perceived as trustworthy by all the parties to the DPA/NPA.[88] Such monitors are not subject to formal market forces and need not meet any level of qualification or special expertise in the relevant regulatory field.[89]

---

[85] See United States Government Accountability Office (GAO), *Corporate Crime: Preliminary Observations on DOJ's Use and Oversight of Deferred Prosecution and Non-Prosecution Agreements (Statement of Eileen R. Larence, Director Homeland Security and Justice)*, pp. 2, 23–27: "For the DPAs and NPAs GAO reviewed, even though DOJ was not a party to the contracts between companies and monitors, DOJ typically selected the monitor, and its decisions were generally made collaboratively among DOJ and company officials." See also, Blank Rome LLP, "Keeping A Watchful Eye: Corporate Deferred Prosecution Agreements and the Selection of Corporate Monitors."

[86] See Deferred Prosecution Agreement, *United States v. Monsanto Company* (January 6, 2005), at §9, available at: http://www.corporatecrimereporter.com/documents/monsantoagreement.pdf; see also, Non Prosecution Agreement between United States and Micrus S.A. (February 28, 2005), *supra* note 80 at §D.11.

[87] See Robinson, Urofsky and Pantel, "Deferred Prosecutions and the Independent Monitor," p. 332; Gibson Dunn, *2008 Year-End Update on Corporate Deferred Prosecution and Non-Prosecution Agreements*.

[88] See Khanna and Dickinson, "The Corporate Monitor: The New Corporate Czar," p. 1722; O'Hare, "The Use of the Corporate Monitor in SEC Enforcement Actions," p. 108. See also, United States Government Accountability Office (GAO), *Corporate Crime: Preliminary Observations on DOJ's Use and Oversight of Deferred Prosecution and Non-Prosecution Agreements (Statement of Eileen R. Larence, Director Homeland Security and Justice)*, p. 2: "Monitor candidates were typically identified through DOJ or company officials' personal knowledge or recommendations from colleagues and associates." See also, Blank Rome LLP, "Keeping A Watchful Eye: Corporate Deferred Prosecution Agreements and the Selection of Corporate Monitors."

[89] See Khanna, "Reforming the Corporate Monitor?," 226–248.

7.5 CHALLENGES TO THE EMERGING POLICIES OF DPAs AND NPAs

Ever since DPAs and NPAs were adapted to the corporate arena, they have been subject to growing criticism in the scholarly literature. Commentators have pointed at the various hurdles that hinder the work of corporate monitors. Some even ascribe the significant decline in the number of DPAs and NPAs entered into in 2008 and 2009 to the growing criticism of the prevailing policies.[90] Here follows the major points of criticism.

7.5.1 Lack of DOJ Guidance

One central point of criticism addresses the lack of guidance from the DOJ.[91] Until 2008, the DOJ issued no specific instructions as to the use of DPAs and NPAs. Therefore, individual prosecutors possessed wide discretion in entering into such agreements.[92] Apparently, as shown by the

---

[90] The number of DPAs and NPAs entered into in 2008–2009 significantly declined, from 41 agreements in 2007, to 19 and 21 agreements in 2008 and 2009 respectively. See the United States Government Accountability Office (GAO), *Corporate Crime: Preliminary Observations on DOJ's Use and Oversight of Deferred Prosecution and Non-Prosecution Agreements (Statement of Eileen R. Larence, Director Homeland Security and Justice)*, p. 1. See also, Gibson Dunn, *2009 Mid-Year Update on Corporate Deferred Prosecution and Non-Prosecution Agreements*; Gibson Dunn, *2008 Year-End Update on Corporate Deferred Prosecution and Non-Prosecution Agreements*. According to these reports, the decline has continued in 2009, during which the DOJ only entered into 18 DPAs/NPAs, which is the smallest number of agreements since 2005. This mid-year update further suggests that the "downturn" in the use of DPAs and NPAs may "reflect the debate surrounding DPAs and the cautious approach that the DOJ took in entering into DPAs while awaiting further legislative guidance." See also, Corporate Crime Reporter, *Crime without Conviction: The Rise of Deferred and Non Prosecution Agreements*.

[91] See, for instance, Wilkinson and Oh, "The Principles of Federal Prosecution of Business Organizations: A Ten-Year Anniversary Perspective," p. 9; Warin and Boutros, "Deferred Prosecution Agreements: A View from the Trenches and a Proposal for Reform," 121–134; Spivack and Raman, "Regulating the 'New Regulators': Current Trends in Deferred Prosecution Agreements," p. 162.

[92] See, for instance, Greenblum, "What Happens to a Prosecution Deferred? Judicial Oversight of Corporate Deferred Prosecution Agreements," 1863–1904; Gibson Dunn, *2008 Year-End Update on Corporate Deferred Prosecution and Non-Prosecution Agreements*; Gibson Dunn, *2009 Mid-Year Update on Corporate Deferred Prosecution and Non-Prosecution Agreements*. See also, Warin and Schwartz, "Deferred Prosecution: The Need for Specialized Guidelines for

United States Government Accountability Office (GAO) Report issued in 2009, the wide prosecutorial discretion led to an inconsistent use of DPAs and NPAs. Not only different U.S. attorneys but also different sections within the DOJ varied substantially in setting the terms and the use of such agreements.[93] A recent example is presented by the *Tenaris* case of 2011, in which the corporation entered into a DPA with the SEC and into an NPA with the DOJ based on the same facts.[94] No particular reason has been advanced by either authority to explain the inconsistency regarding the use of a DPA by one authority and an NPA by the other. Obviously, such inconsistency in the application of DPAs and NPAs may present a major risk of *arbitrariness* and *inequality*, and makes it difficult for corporations to map themselves a path to follow in case of a governmental investigation.[95]

Corporate Defendants," 121–134. The authors underscore the need for guidance with respect to DPAs and NPAs in the corporate context. See also, Greg Burns, "Corporations Avoid Criminal Cases," *Chicago Tribune* (March 20, 2005), p. 5: "Other critics say that putting off a corporate prosecution can be appropriate, but they worry the guidelines are too loose, and judicial oversight too limited." Burns also quotes Prof. John C. Coffee Jr., as saying "This is a major and largely unrecognized gear shift in the law since Arthur Andersen . . . It's probably a sensible thing to do, but it is too unstructured."

[93] United States Government Accountability Office (GAO), *Corporate Crime: Preliminary Observations on DOJ's use and Oversight of Deferred Prosecution and Non-Prosecution Agreements (Statement of Eileen R. Larence, Director Homeland Security and Justice)*, p. 2: "prosecutors differed in their willingness to use DPAs or NPAs. In addition, prosecutors' varying perceptions of what constitutes a DPA or NPA has led to inconsistencies in how the agreements are labeled." See also, Warin and Boutros, "Deferred Prosecution Agreements: A View from the Trenches and a Proposal for Reform," pp. 125, 132, who compare the DPAs reached in *Shell* and *Bristol Mayers-Squibb* cases, and conclude that the appropriate guidance must be provided to prevent future inconsistencies in designing DPAs/NPAs.

[94] For the press release by the SEC see *supra* note 63. For the press release by the DOJ see Department of Justice, *Tenaris S.A. Agrees to Pay $3.5 Million Criminal Penalty to Resolve Violations of the Foreign Corrupt Practices Act* (May 17, 2011). Available at: http://www.justice.gov/opa/pr/2011/May/11-crm-629.html.

[95] See Gibson Dunn, *2008 Year-End Update on Corporate Deferred Prosecution and Non-Prosecution Agreements*: "absent consistent and uniform guidance, a corporation has no way of measuring the consequences of coming forward and self-reporting potential criminal activity." For suggested guidelines, see Warin and Boutros, "Deferred Prosecution Agreements: A View from the Trenches and a Proposal for Reform," 121–134; Spivack and Raman, "Regulating the 'New Regulators': Current Trends in Deferred Prosecution Agreements," 159–194. For a discussion of the risk of arbitrariness in regulatory enforcement see Chapter 4, Section 4.5.2.

7.5.2 Overreach of Prosecutorial Discretion

Another major criticism advanced by the scholarly literature is the overreach of prosecutorial discretion embedded in DPAs/NPAs.[96] Such agreements are usually not a product of true negotiation between equally powered parties. In fact, given the substantial adverse impact that criminal proceedings may have on a corporation's reputation, corporations that are offered a DPA or an NPA are *de facto* compelled to accept the conditions set forth by the prosecution.[97] Such powers may first and foremost raise a concern about the *over-expansion of DPAs and NPAs*, even in cases that would not have triggered prosecution in the past.[98] Furthermore, given their wide discretion, prosecutors are using DPAs and NPAs to induce corporations to undertake *dramatic structural reforms*

---

[96] See, for instance, Brandon L. Garrett, "Structural Reform Prosecution," *Virginia Law Review* 93 (2007), 853–957; Erik Paulsen, "Imposing Limits on Prosecutorial Discretion in Corporate Prosecution Agreements," *New York University Law Review* (1950) 82 (2007), 1434–1469; Warin and Boutros, "Deferred Prosecution Agreements: A View from the Trenches and a Proposal for Reform," 121–134; John C. Coffee Jr., "Deferred Prosecution: Has it Gone Too Far?" *The National Law Journal* (July 25, 2005), p. 13.

[97] See Greenblum, "What Happens to a Prosecution Deferred? Judicial Oversight of Corporate Deferred Prosecution Agreements," p. 1885: "[t]he offender can choose either to agree to the terms of deferral as defined by the prosecutor, or to reject the deferral and face the adverse publicity of a trial and the potential collateral consequences of a felony conviction. The corporation offender's unique vulnerability to adverse publicity and collateral consequences sets the stage for a deferral negotiation that 'stack[s] the deck against the defendant' and calls into question whether the choice to enter into deferral is really a choice at all" (references omitted). See also Weissmann and Newman, "Rethinking Criminal Corporate Liability," p. 414: "In the post-Enron world, it is the rare corporation that will risk indictment by the Department of Justice (DOJ), let alone a trial. The financial risks are simply too great. Knowing this, the government has virtually unfettered discretion to exact a deferred prosecution agreement from a corporation that mandates fines and internal reforms."

[98] See Gibson Dunn, *2009 Mid-Year Update on Corporate Deferred Prosecution and Non-Prosecution Agreements*: "in the past, the DOJ often declined to prosecute cases in which the allegations involved low-level misconduct or there was a lack of sufficient evidence. However, the increased use of DPAs and NPAs raises a question of whether this new prosecutorial tool may be encouraging the government to seek agreements with corporations in instances that previously resulted in declinations." See also, Weissmann and Newman, "Rethinking Criminal Corporate Liability," p. 414: "Contrary to the system of checks and balances that pervades our legal system, including the criminal law with respect to individuals, no systemic checks effectively restrict the government's power to go after blameless corporations."

without being subject to adequate judicial supervision.[99] In the same vein, commentators have pointed to the professional judgments involved in an efficient design of corporate compliance programs and suggested that prosecutors, who often lack the required expertise, should not impose any such structural reforms. Instead, a civil regulatory authority which is more likely to have the required expertise should be responsible for mandating reform.[100] Others have suggested restricting the discretion of individual prosecutors by requiring them to receive the permission of the Deputy Attorney General before entering into any DPA/NPA.[101] An alternative proposal suggests that the judicial system should become more involved in interpreting and applying the terms of DPAs and NPAs.[102]

7.5.3 Over-Expansion of Corporate Monitors' Powers

Scholars have expressed their concerns about the over-expansion of corporate monitors' powers beyond the authority the court orders originally intended to grant. One proposal suggests limiting the use of corporate monitors only to very rare cases.[103] A different proposal recommends that prosecutors and corporations should better specify corporate monitors'

---

[99] See Greenblum, "What Happens to a Prosecution Deferred? Judicial Oversight of Corporate Deferred Prosecution Agreements," p. 1895. See also, Gibson Dunn, *2009 Year-End Update on Corporate Deferred Prosecution and Non-Prosecution Agreements*, which reports that the most recent DPAs/NPAs include a provision that grants the DOJ "sole discretion to determine whether the agreement has been breached by the company."

[100] See Jennifer Arlen, "Removing Prosecutors from the Boardroom: Limiting Prosecutorial Discretion to Impose Structural Reforms," in *Prosecutors in the Board Room: Using Criminal Law to Regulate Corporate Conduct*, Anthony S. Barkow and Rachel E. Barkow eds. (New York: New York University Press, 2011), 62–86.

[101] See Paulsen, "Imposing Limits on Prosecutorial Discretion in Corporate Prosecution Agreements," 1434–1469.

[102] See Greenblum, "What Happens to a Prosecution Deferred? Judicial Oversight of Corporate Deferred Prosecution Agreements," p. 1904. The author suggests reducing the risk of an abuse of prosecutorial discretion by increasing the judicial involvement "not during the negotiation phase of the [agreement], but rather during the implementation of the [agreement], where dissolution of the agreement can result in prosecution and the stakes are highest." See also, Warin and Boutros, "Deferred Prosecution Agreements: A View from the Trenches and a Proposal for Reform," p. 128: "The DOJ should surrender to the courts at the preindictment stage the determination of whether a corporation has materially breached the terms of a DPA."

[103] See, for instance, O'Hare, "The Use of the Corporate Monitor in SEC Enforcement Actions," 89–118.

tasks and powers in the DPA/NPA, leaving little discretion for the monitors to determine their own powers.[104] A related criticism focuses on the position of corporate monitors as surrogate policeman, acting on behalf of the government.[105] As "outsiders," corporate monitors may face substantial difficulties in accessing all kinds of internal, informal relevant information.[106]

7.5.4 Selection of Corporate Monitors

Finally, scholars have also been critical of the selection processes used to employ corporate monitors. In the absence of specific guidelines, corporate monitors were subject to no qualifications or expertise requirements and their appointment was widely influenced by the personal discretion of the individual prosecutors in charge. Interestingly, such monitors were usually selected from a small group of former public officials, rather than through any market mechanism.[107] In 2007, this aspect of the appointment of corporate monitors attracted the media's attention and was subject to intense outside criticism when the New Jersey U.S. Attorney Chris Christie awarded a $52 million contract to a consulting firm – founded by the former Attorney General John Ashcroft – to serve as a corporate monitor.[108] To prevent the tangible risk of abuse of prosecutorial powers, scholars have strongly recommended that the government select corporate monitors in a more transparent process and appoint them only after verifying their background and expertise on the basis of merit.[109] In the same vein, scholars have suggested that corporate monitors, who are not selected by shareholders and are not subject to market forces that could discipline their behavior, should be subject to fiduciary duties to shareholders and therefore be held accountable to them.[110]

---

[104] See Khanna and Dickinson, "The Corporate Monitor: The New Corporate Czar," p. 1737.

[105] See Sue Reisinger, "Designated Drivers," *Corporate Counsel* (October 2004).

[106] See Kim, "Gatekeepers Inside Out," pp. 448–457, 460.

[107] See *supra* notes 88–89 and the related main text.

[108] See, for instance, Neil Gordon, "Checking Up on DPAs, NPAs and Corporate Monitors" (June 26, 2009); Eric Lichtblau and Kitty Bennett, "30 Former Officials Became Corporate Monitors," *The New York Times*, May 23, 2008, available at: http://www.nytimes.com/2008/05/23/washington/23justice.html?_r=2&; Christopher M. Matthews, "Compliance Monitors Are Here to Stay," *Main Justice: Politics, Policy and the Law* (April 8, 2010b).

[109] See Khanna, "Reforming the Corporate Monitor?," 226–248.

[110] See O'Hare, "The Use of the Corporate Monitor in SEC Enforcement Actions," p. 105. O'Hare explains that the corporate monitors' primary responsi-

7.6 EMERGING POLICIES

The cumulative experience gained with respect to the use of DPAs, coupled with the growing criticism of these mechanisms, has led U.S. policymakers to take initial steps to regulate DPAs.

7.6.1 Bills: Accountability in the Deferred Prosecution Act

The first attempts were undertaken in 2008 and 2009, through several bills presented before the U.S. Congress.[111] These bills were aimed at requiring the DOJ to promulgate official guidelines with respect to the appointment and function of corporate monitors. The bills also acknowledged the use of DPAs and corporate monitors, while at the same time attempting to address some of the major criticisms of the prevailing policies by recommending several amendments. Here are the major recommendations for reforming the current policies which were introduced in the bills presented before the U.S. Congress:

(i) ***Clear guidelines*** – The bills require the Attorney General to issue public written guidelines for DPAs and NPAs. Such guidelines should cover: *inter alia*, the criteria under which it would be appropriate for federal prosecutors to enter DPAs/NPAs; the appropriate terms and conditions of DPAs and NPAs; the circumstances in which corporate monitors are warranted; and the duties and powers of such monitors.[112]

---

bility is not to benefit shareholders, but rather to further the court order. See also, Khanna and Dickinson, "The Corporate Monitor: The New Corporate Czar," p. 1742. The authors suggest that a fiduciary duty be established for corporate monitors.

[111] See *Accountability in Deferred Prosecution Act of 2008*, H.R. 6492, 110th Cong. (2d Sess. 2008), available at: http://www.govtrack.us/congress/billtext.xpd?bill=h110-6492. "To require the Attorney General to issue guidelines delineating when to enter into deferred prosecution agreements, to require judicial sanction of deferred prosecution agreements, and to provide for Federal monitors to oversee deferred prosecution agreements," H.R. 5086, 110th Cong. (2d Sess, 2008), available at: http://frwebgate.access.gpo.gov/cgi-bin/getdoc.cgi?dbname=110_cong_bills&docid=f:h5086ih.txt.pdf; and Accountability in Deferred Prosecution Act of 2009, H.R. 1947, 111th Cong. (1st Sess. 2009), available at: http://frwebgate.access.gpo.gov/cgi-bin/getdoc.cgi?dbname=111_cong_bills&docid=f:h1947ih.txt.pdf (hereinafter: "Bill H.R. 1947"). This Bill was referred to the House subcommittee Commercial and Administrative Law on May 26, 2009 (see http://www.washingtonwatch.com/bills/show/111_HR_1947.html).

[112] See Sec. 4 of the Bill H.R. 1947.

(ii) ***A core of corporate monitors*** – The bills require the Attorney General to create a publicly available "national list of possible corporate monitors." Such a list shall include "organizations and individuals who have the expertise and specialized skills necessary to serve as independent monitors."[113]

(iii) ***Selection process and compensation of corporate monitors*** – The bills require the Attorney General to establish rules for the selection of corporate monitors for DPAs and NPAs that will ensure the credibility of the selection process while allowing for an "open, public, and competitive process for the selection of such monitors."[114] In addition, the Attorney General is required to establish a publicly available fee schedule for the compensation of independent monitors.[115] Furthermore, the bills seek to ensure the credibility of the corporate monitor selection process by prohibiting the participation of attorneys who are involved in the prosecution and in the selection process except when suggesting the necessary qualifications for the monitors.[116]

(iv) ***Judicial oversight of DPAs*** – The bills propose a court oversight mechanism for DPAs. DPAs must get court approval before being enacted, and all parties to the agreement, including the corporate monitors, are required to submit quarterly reports to the court regarding the progress made toward the completion of the DPA. These reports to the court are intended to ensure that the implementation or termination of the DPA is consistent with the interests of justice.[117]

Due to the growing interest in DPAs and NPAs and the practical need for official guidelines, while the bills are pending in the U.S. Congress, the DOJ has promulgated its first official guidelines regarding the selection and use of corporate monitors in DPAs and NPAs. These guidelines and the ones that followed are discussed below.

7.6.2 DOJ Memoranda

New guidelines concerning the selection and the utilization of corporate monitors in DPAs and NPAs were issued on March 7, 2008 in a

113 See Sec. 5(a)–(b) of the Bill H.R. 1947.
114 See Sec. 5(b) of the Bill H.R. 1947.
115 See Sec. 5(a), (c)–(d) of the Bill H.R. 1947.
116 See Sec. 6(b) of the Bill H.R. 1947.
117 See Sec. 7 of the Bill H.R. 1947.

memorandum by Craig S. Morford, Deputy Attorney General ("*Morford Memo*"). [118] The Morford Memo mainly covered the following aspects:

(i) ***When corporate monitors should be used*** – The Morford Memo strives to ensure an *efficient* use of corporate monitors in DPAs and NPAs. Therefore, it explicitly states that monitors should be used *only* when appropriate, given the specific circumstances at hand. The Memo sets forth a cost–benefit criterion for the use of corporate monitors; that is, before requiring the appointment of a corporate monitor, the prosecutor is required to consider the "potential benefits that employing a monitor may have for the corporation and the public" against "the cost of a monitor and its impact on the operations of a corporation."[119] The Morford Memo provides specific examples for circumstances in which: (a) a company does not have an effective internal compliance program; and (b) a company needs to establish necessary internal controls.[120]

(ii) ***Criteria for selecting a monitor*** – To ensure that the corporate monitors appointed possess the required expertise and qualifications, the Morford Memo establishes the *criteria* for the appointment of corporate monitors. The criteria requires the monitor, first and foremost, to be "a highly qualified and respected person or entity based on suitability for the assignment and all of the circumstances." In addition, the corporate monitor must be independent so that their appointment avoids any "potential or actual conflicts of interest."[121] Furthermore, the Morford Memo creates a detailed procedure for the *selection of monitors*. The procedure starts with a discussion between the corporation and the government, which is aimed at identifying the qualifications for a monitor in the particular case. Then, the procedure requires the creation of a specialized committee that will consider all corporate monitor candidates. Finally,

---

[118] See Craig S. Morford, Acting Deputy Attorney General, *Memorandum for Heads of Department Components United States Attorneys: Selection and Use of Monitors in Deferred Prosecution Agreements and Non-Prosecution Agreements with Corporations*.

[119] See *ibid.*, Sec. I.

[120] See *ibid.*, Sec. I.

[121] See *ibid.*, Sec. II. According to the Morford Memo, the corporation must commit itself 'not to employ or be affiliated with the monitor' during the period of the agreement and an additional one year after its termination. See also, Sec. III, according to which monitors must be independent third parties, not employees or agents of the corporations or of the government.

the Office of the Deputy Attorney General must approve the appointment.[122]

(iii) ***Role and responsibilities*** – The Morford Memo clarifies that the role of corporate monitors is to "assess and monitor a corporation's compliance with the terms of the agreement specifically designed to address and reduce the risk of reoccurrence of the corporation's misconduct, and not to further punitive goals."[123] To prevent the risk of overreaching powers, the Morford Memo also clarifies that "the monitor's responsibility should be no broader than necessary to address and reduce the risk of recurrence of the corporation's misconduct."[124] In the same vein, it is made clear that the corporate monitor is *not* responsible for the corporation's shareholders, and therefore "the responsibility for designing an ethics and compliance program that will prevent misconduct should remain with the corporation, subject to the monitor's input, evaluation and recommendations."[125] Moreover, according to the Morford Memo, corporate monitors may be required to provide the government and the corporation with periodic written reports regarding their activities, the corporate compliance with the agreement and recommendations for changes required to foster corporate compliance with the agreement. If the corporation chooses not to adopt those recommendations, a report must be submitted to the government along with the corporation's reasoning.[126]

The Morford Memo, which for the first time laid out the basic rules for the use of corporate monitors, substantially contributed to the selection process of corporate monitors for subsequent DPAs and NPAs.[127] For instance, the DPAs reached in the *Willbros Group's* and *AGA Medical's* cases explicitly required the corporate monitors to possess "demonstrated expertise with respect to the FCPA, including experience [in] counseling on FCPA issues" and "experience [in] designing and/or reviewing corporate compliance policies, procedures and internal controls, including FCPA-specific policies, procedures and internal controls."[128] Nevertheless,

---

[122] See *ibid.*, Sec. II.

[123] See *ibid.*, Sec. I and III.B.3.

[124] See *ibid.*, Sec. 1 and III.B.4.

[125] See *ibid.*, Sec. III.B.3.

[126] See *ibid.*, Sec. III.C.5–6.

[127] See Gibson Dunn, *2008 Year-End Update on Corporate Deferred Prosecution and Non-Prosecution Agreements.*

[128] See Deferred Prosecution Agreement of *Willbros Group Inc.*, May 14, 2008, §12. Available at: http://www.techagreements.com/agreement-preview.as

the Morford Memo did not go as far as creating a publicly available "core of corporate monitors" as proposed in the bills discussed above. Hence, the appointment of corporate monitors has remained, thus far, a matter of particular negotiation between the government and the relevant corporation – a process that is still being criticized and may require future re-evaluation.[129]

On May 14, 2008, Mark Filip, the Deputy Attorney General, issued a new Memorandum dealing with the Federal Prosecution of Business Organizations ("*Filip Memo*").[130] The Filip Memo reinforces the factors

---

px?num=585046&title=willbros%20group%20-%20deferred%20prosecution%20 agreement; see also, DOJ Press Release No. 08-417, *Willbros Group Inc. Enters Deferred Prosecution Agreement and Agrees to Pay €22 Million Penalty for FCPA Violations* (May 14, 2008), available at: http://www.foley.com/files/ WillsbrosDOJRelease.pdf. Compare with Deferred Prosecution Agreement of *AGA Medical*, June 3, 2008, §10, available at: http://www.law.virginia.edu/pdf/ faculty/garrett/agamedical.pdf. See also DOJ Press Release No. 08-491, *AGA Medical Corporation Agrees to Pay $2 Million Penalty and Enter Deferred Prosecution Agreement for FCPA Violations* (June 3, 2008), available at: http:// www.justice.gov/opa/pr/2008/June/08-crm-491.html. See also, Blank Rome LLP, "Keeping A Watchful Eye: Corporate Deferred Prosecution Agreements and the Selection of Corporate Monitors."

[129] The issue of corporate monitors' selection seems to comprise a serious source of concern, even after the promulgation of the Morford Memo. See Gordon, "Checking Up on DPAs, NPAs and Corporate Monitors:" "Corporate monitor appointments, which the [Morford Memo] carefully spell out to help U.S. attorneys avoid the appearance of cronyism are still largely a secretive matter because DOJ does not require prosecutors to document the process by which prosecutors are chosen." See also, the findings of the United States Government Accountability Office (GAO), *Corporate Crime: Preliminary Observations on DOJ's Use and Oversight of Deferred Prosecution and Non-Prosecution Agreements (Statement of Eileen R. Larence, Director Homeland Security and Justice)*, p. 1: "In March 2008, DOJ issued guidance stating that for monitor selection to be collaborative and merit-based, committees should consider the candidates and the selection must be approved by the Deputy Attorney General. However, because DOJ does not require documentation of the process used or the reasons for particular monitor selection decisions, it will be difficult for DOJ to validate whether its monitor selection guidance – which, in part, is intended to instill public confidence – is adhered to." See also, Christopher M. Matthews, "Judge Blasts Compliance Monitors at Innospec Plea Hearing," *Main Justice: Politics, Policy and the Law* (March 18, 2010a); Gibson Dunn, *2009 Year-End Update on Corporate Deferred Prosecution and Non-Prosecution Agreements.*

[130] See Filip, *Memorandum for Heads of Department Components United States Attorneys: Principles of Federal Prosecution of Business Organizations*. The Filip Memo was incorporated into the U.S. Attorney's Manual, *supra* note 31, § 9-28.000-1300. Available at: http://www.justice.gov/usao/eousa/foia_reading_ room/usam/title9/28mcrm.htm.

previously established in the Holder and Thompson Memos, with some slight changes and adjustments,[131] and supports the use of DPAs and NPAs as a valuable prosecutorial means of controlling corporate behavior.[132]

> In certain instances, it may be appropriate, upon consideration of the factors set forth herein, to resolve a corporate criminal case by means other than indictment. *Non-prosecution and deferred prosecution agreements, for example, occupy an important middle ground between declining prosecution and obtaining the conviction of a corporation.*

The development of DPAs and NPAs continued in 2010 with a new memorandum being issued on May 25, 2010 by Gary G. Grindler, Deputy Attorney General ("*Grindler Memo*").[133] The Grindler Memo supplements the Morford Memo with an additional principle that guides prosecutors to explicitly explain in future DPAs and NPAs "what role the Department [of Justice] could play in resolving any disputes between the monitor and the corporation, given the facts and circumstances of the case."[134] The Grindler Memo requires prosecutors to consider incorporating the following provision in future DPAs:

> With respect to any Monitor recommendation that the company considers unduly burdensome, impractical, unduly expensive, or otherwise inadvisable, the company need not adopt the recommendation immediately; instead, the company may propose in writing an alternative policy, procedure, or system designed to achieve the same objective or purpose. As to any recommendation on which the company and the Monitor ultimately do not agree, the views of the company and the Monitor shall promptly be brought to the attention of the Department. The Department may consider the Monitor's recommendation and the company's reasons for not adopting the recommendation in determining whether the company has fully complied with its obligations under the Agreement.[135]

Furthermore, the Grindler Memo requires that prosecutors consider incorporating another provision in their agreement which compels

---

131 See U.S. Attorney Manual, § 9-28.300.

132 See U.S. Attorney Manual, § 9-28.200.B. See also, Mark J. Stein and Joshua A. Levine, "The Filip Memorandum: Does it Go Far Enough?" *New York Law Journal* (2008) (emphasis added).

133 See Gary G. Grindler, Acting Deputy Attorney General, *Memorandum for Heads of Department Components United States Attorneys: Additional Guidance on the Use of Monitors in Deferred Prosecution Agreements and Non-Prosecution Agreements with Corporations.*

134 See *ibid.*

135 See *ibid.*, Sec II.

corporations and the DOJ representatives to at least meet annually to discuss "the monitorship and any suggestion, comments, or improvements the company may wish to discuss with or propose to the [DOJ], including with respect to the scope or costs of the monitorship."

7.7 SUMMARY AND CONCLUDING REMARKS

Corporate monitors have become an invaluable enforcement instrument in the battle against corporate misconduct. This chapter explored the recently developed U.S. Federal DPA and NPA policies where corporate monitors are used as "corporate watchdogs" which seek to secure corporate compliance. These policies use corporate monitors as "swords" against culpable corporations. Although corporate monitors are appointed as part of an agreement between corporations and the prosecution, corporations agree to their appointment only to avoid the consequences of an indictment.[136] Once appointed, corporate monitors closely scrutinize corporate activity and thereby provide corporations with a strong incentive to adopt a proactive approach to compliance. If evaluated based on the experience accumulated in the last decade, the emerging policies seem to successfully induce corporate compliance. In actuality, most of the DPAs and NPAs entered into since 2000 were respected and followed by the corporations, and therefore required no further criminal proceedings.[137]

---

[136] See *supra* note 72 and the related main text.

[137] A very few exceptions are known, for instance, in the case of *Wright Medical Group*, the DOJ accused Wright of "knowingly and willfully" breaching the DPA reached with the company in 2010 to resolve allegations of conspiracy to violate the Federal Anti-Kickback statute. Given this accusation, the company conducted a reshuffling of its management and agreed to extend the DPA and the appointment of its corporate monitor for another year. Gibson Dunn, *2011 Year-End Update on Corporate Deferred Prosecution and Non-Prosecution Agreements.* Additionally, in the case of *FirstEnergy Corp.*, all charges for misrepresentations to the Nuclear Regulatory Commission were deferred according to the DPA that was reached with the company. Later on, the DOJ perceived that an insurance claim brought by FirstEnergy violated the DPA. However, the DOJ eventually took no actual action because FirstEnergy dropped the claim. In the *Aibel Group* case, by contrast, the DOJ decided to revoke the DPA it entered into with Aibel in 2007 after it found that Aibel did not follow its commitments. Aibel agreed to a guilty plea and reached a new agreement which resembled the DPA, except for the requirement to employ an external corporate monitor. See Gibson Dunn, *2008 Year-End Update on Corporate Deferred Prosecution and Non-Prosecution Agreements.*

After discussing the evolution of the recently developed policies concerning DPAs and NPAs, the challenges they are currently facing and the latest policy developments aimed at overcoming these challenges will be discussed in the next chapter. In the following chapter, I also propose that the use of corporate monitors in the battle against corporate misconduct may be expanded to facilitate an efficient targeted monitoring system.

8. Corporate monitors: facilitating an efficient targeted monitoring system[1]

8.1 INTRODUCTION

Recent corporate scandals have spurred the development of innovative enforcement mechanisms aimed at inducing corporate proactive compliance. One such mechanism, employed as part of the enforcement policies in the United States in recent years, includes the use of corporate monitors as "watchdogs" which seek to ensure corporate compliance. In Chapter 7, I explored the recently emerged enforcement policies of Deferred Prosecution Agreements (DPAs) and Non-Prosecution Agreements (NPAs) where the appointment of corporate monitors replaces traditional criminal proceedings. The analysis has shown that the evolving DPAs and NPAs policies are not free of practical challenges. Considerable criticism was raised, for instance, regarding corporate monitors' appointment procedures and the need to better secure their independence and qualifications.[2] Yet, as shown in Chapter 7, most points of criticism have been dealt with in the more recent policy developments which seem to prepare the ground for an improved utilization of corporate monitors in the battle against corporate misconduct.

The overview provided in Chapter 7 revealed that corporate monitors are currently used in DPAs and NPAs policies during: (1) the *ex-post* enforcement phase, *i.e.*, after a particular misconduct is detected; and (2) when corporate internal compliance schemes were proven *weak* and *malfunctioning*.[3] In this chapter, I propose that the utilization of corporate

---

[1] A substantial portion of this chapter is adapted from Oded, "Corporate Monitors: Overcoming the Classification of Targeted Monitoring Systems", *Berkeley Business Law Journal* 10: No.2 (forthcoming, 2013).

[2] See Chapter 7, Section 7.5.

[3] See Matthews, "Fraud Chief: Effective Compliance Programs can Prevent Monitors," quoting Denis McInerney, the Criminal Fraud Section Chief: "If you have already established an excellent compliance program, then it will be less likely that we'll install a compliance monitor, which can come at some cost to the company."

monitors may be expanded: (1) to the *ex-ante* enforcement phase, *i.e.*, before a particular misconduct is detected; and (2) when corporate internal compliance schemes are *strong* and *robust*. Specifically, I propose that corporate monitors may be voluntarily appointed by corporations genuinely committed to proactive compliance, and thereby be used as a signaling mechanism that facilitates an efficient targeted monitoring system.

To see how corporate monitors may be useful in facilitating an efficient targeted monitoring system, it is important to consider that corporations differ in a wide range of aspects, including size, structure, area of activity, level of employees' commitment, and the monitoring technology available. Accordingly, both the cost and the effectiveness of corporate self-policing activities may greatly differ across corporate regulatees. It is not surprising, thus, that under enforcement policies presenting a similar liability threat to all corporate regulatees, some regulatees find it desirable to engage in self-policing while others do not. Given the costs involved in self-policing, corporations' motivation to engage in self-policing depends on the gain produced by such activities. Specifically, corporations engage in self-policing only when the private benefit produced by self-policing is greater than the cost thereof. Accordingly, the greater the benefit offered by enforcement policies to self-policing corporations, the greater the portion of the regulatee population that finds it desirable to engage in self-policing.

In an attempt to improve regulatee motivation to adopt a proactive compliance approach, many regulatory enforcement authorities employ "*targeted monitoring systems*" in which regulatory monitoring efforts are differentiated across different groups of regulatees. More particularly, rather than monitoring different regulatees randomly, a targeted monitoring system determines a particular group of regulatees to be scrutinized more closely than others.[4] Compliant corporations representing a low risk of non-compliance would be classified into a group that is subject to a lower level of monitoring than would recalcitrant corporations representing a high risk of non-compliance. That way, it is believed, enforcement authorities are better able to tailor the regulatory enforcement policy to the particular regulatee population, and thereby induce

[4] Such policies are sometimes employed without being officially recognized, and even against the publicly announced policy. See, for instance, Michael W. Toffel and Jodi L. Short, "Coming Clean and Cleaning Up: Does Voluntary Self-Reporting Indicate Effective Self-Policing?". The study provides empirical evidence, according to which, in contrast to its officially stated monitoring policy, the U.S. Environmental Protection Agency (EPA) reduces its scrutiny over facilities that recently stepped forward and self-reported their own regulatory violations.

a greater level of compliance. Such monitoring systems are commonly applied by many European environmental authorities, including some German Länder (states), Portugal, Austria, Finland, and the U.K., which employ such systems by offering a regulatory relief in the form of reduced regulatory inspection frequencies to corporations that adopted a certified Environmental Management System (EMS).[5] In addition, in many European jurisdictions, including Sweden, Austria, Denmark, some German Länder (states), France, Italy, Netherlands, the U.K., and Spain, the adoption of certified EMSs results in reduced monitoring or reporting requirements.[6] Yet, unlike many of the prevalent policies, the proposal

---

[5] See B. Webb, J. Chilvers, and J. Keeble. *"Improving Business Environmental Performance: Corporate Incentives and Drivers in Decision Making." A Report to the Department for Environment, Food and Rural Affairs* (Defra, London: Arthur D. Little Ltd., 2006); K. Dahlström, C. Howes, P. Leinster, and J. Skea. "Environmental Management Systems and Company Performance: Assessing the Case for Extending Risk-Based Regulation," *European Environment* 13 (2003): 187–203; see also, ECORYS, *Study on Incentives Driving Improvement of Environmental Performance of Companies* (2012), available at: http://ec.europa.eu/environment/pubs/pdf/Incentives_Ecorys.pdf.

[6] See K. Dahlström, C. Howes, P. Leinster, and J. Skea. "Environmental Management Systems and Company Performance: Assessing the Case for Extending Risk-Based Regulation," p. 189. See also Nyborg and Telle, "Firms' Compliance to Environmental Regulation: Is There Really a Paradox?, 1–18. This study provides evidence from the Norwegian Pollution Control Authority (NPCA) where enforcement routines are determined responsively depending on the gravity of the violations; Russell, "Game Models for Structuring Monitoring and Enforcement Systems," p. 153. Russell refers to the U.S. Internal Revenue Service (IRS), which is widely believed to use data from past audits to define the probability of the current year audit. In such cases, a stained violation record may lead to a closer scrutiny in the subsequent fiscal year. Scholz, "Voluntary Compliance and Regulatory Enforcement," p. 396. According to this study, in many regulatory contexts the enforcement of minor violations is lax, while violations that are more serious are subject to credible threats of strict sanctions. Similarly, Gray and Deily, "Compliance and Enforcement: Air Pollution Regulation in the U.S. Steel Industry," 96–111. This study used data on individual steel plants to show the link between enforcement actions against pollution violations and the plants' compliance. The study shows that steel plants that were evaluated as compliant players faced fewer enforcement activities than others. For similar results see Eckert, "Inspections, Warnings, and Compliance: The Case of Petroleum Storage Regulation," 232–259. Eckert investigated the use of inspections and warnings for environmental violations. This study shows that warnings are used to classify Canadian petroleum storage sites according to their past performance. See also, Rousseau, "Timing of Environmental Inspections: Survival of the Compliant," 17–36; Stafford, "The Effect of Punishment on Firm Compliance with Hazardous Waste Regulations," 290–308; Hawkins, *Environment and Enforcement: Regulation and the Social*

made in this chapter is designed to account for the risk of under-deterrence that may result from such a regulatory relief. It considers that a reduction in the probability of detection may weaken regulatees' incentive to comply, and therefore secures an optimal level of deterrence by leveraging the severity of fines imposed upon regulatees that opt in to the voluntary program. As such, this chapter offers a scientific analytical framework for the analysis and the further improvement of the prevalent targeted monitoring policies.

On the theoretic frontier, targeted monitoring systems were embraced by law and economics scholars, showing that monitoring systems that prioritize their targets may efficiently increase the level of compliance. In the most influential law and economics study on targeted monitoring, Harrington (1988) analyzes a targeted enforcement framework under which an enforcement authority relies on regulatee violation records to divide a regulated industry into "good apples" and "bad apples."[7] The latter group is subject to more frequent inspections. Over time, depending on the outcomes of audits, regulatees may be transferred from one group to another. This targeted monitoring system is shown to augment regulatees' motivations for compliance beyond the avoidance of immediate sanctions, whereas non-compliance threatens greater scrutiny in the future. Therefore, such a system leverages enforcement resources and produces a higher level of compliance, compared to the one produced by the traditional, non-targeted monitoring systems. Harrington's analytical framework has served as fertile ground for many subsequent scholars that extended the analysis and proposed alternative structures of targeted monitoring systems.[8] Few, however, have paused to consider the criteria,

---

Definition of Pollution; Bardach and Kagan, *Going by the Book: The Problem of Regulatory Unreasonableness*; Scholz, "Cooperation, Deterrence, and the Ecology of Regulatory Enforcement," p. 184.

[7] See Harrington, "Enforcement Leverage when Penalties are Restricted," 29–53.

[8] See, for instance, Greenberg, "Avoiding Tax Avoidance: A (Repeated) Game-Theoretic Approach," 1–13; Harrington, "Enforcement Leverage when Penalties are Restricted," 29–53; Russell, "Game Models for Structuring Monitoring and Enforcement Systems," 143–173; Harford and Harrington, "A Reconsideration of Enforcement Leverage when Penalties are Restricted," 391–395; Harford, "Measurement Error and State-Dependent Pollution Control Enforcement," 67–81; Harford, "Improving on the Steady State in the State-Dependent Enforcement of Pollution Control," 133–138; Raymond, "Enforcement Leverage when Penalties are Restricted: A Reconsideration Under Asymmetric Information," 289–295; Friesen, "Targeting Enforcement to Improve Compliance with Environmental Regulations," 72–85.

based on which enforcement authorities classify regulatees into differently monitored groups. In addition to the criterion originally proposed in Harrington (1988), *i.e.*, *regulatee violation records*, the scholarly literature has also considered two alternative criteria for targeted enforcement schemes: the *implementation of compliance management systems* and the *self-reporting of violations*.[9] A close look into these criteria raises substantial doubts regarding their aptitude to facilitate an efficient targeted monitoring system.

My goal in this chapter, then, is to develop a regulatory monitoring regime that *efficiently* facilitates corporate proactive compliance based on a credible classification criterion. More particularly, in what follows, I develop a targeted regulatory monitoring regime, the "Third-Party-Based Targeted Monitoring system," or the "TPTM system," which introduces a voluntary program, according to which corporations that voluntarily hire an independent corporate monitoring firm ("CM") to implement their self-policing activities earn a reduction in the level of regulatory scrutiny, as well as a "label" that is translated into a reputation asset. This system is shown to increase the private gains which can result from a corporation's self-policing. Consequently, the TPTM system enlists more corporations to become proactive in the battle against misconduct, while economizing the overall public enforcement costs.

This chapter is organized as follows. In Section 8.2 I discuss the major challenges which are involved in the classification of corporate regulatees into differently monitored groups as part of a targeted monitoring system and examine the alternative classification criteria proposed by the existing literature. In Section 8.3 I develop an innovative monitoring policy, the TPTM system, which utilizes both liability threats and reputation concerns in inducing corporate proactive compliance. I then discuss in Section 8.4 the lessons learned from DPAs and NPAs regarding ensuring corporate monitors' capacity, selection, and qualification, and its application in the TPTM system. In Section 8.5 I propose the possible extension of the TPTM system when regulatory fines are set at the level of the value of the corporate assets. Finally, I summarize and conclude in Section 8.6.

---

9 The alternative classification criteria are discussed in Section 8.2.

8.2 TARGETED MONITORING SYSTEMS – THE CHALLENGE OF CLASSIFYING REGULATEES

Regulatees' motivation to comply with legal orders depends on their expected liability, which is composed of the product of the *probability of detection* faced by regulatees and the *sanction* (*e.g.*, fines) imposed on regulatees upon detection of a violation.[10] As the reader may recall from the discussion in Chapter 2, to efficiently induce compliance, regulatees' expected liability should be set at the level of the total social cost generated by the misconduct.[11] Once the applicable sanction is set, enforcement authorities are required to exert monitoring efforts at a level that secures an adequate probability of detection. To this end, traditional monitoring policies employ random monitoring techniques, according to which regulatees are randomly selected for inspections out of the common pool of regulatees. Under such a system, all regulatees face a similar probability of being inspected by the enforcement authorities.

The scholarly literature analyzing regulatory monitoring systems has shown that to improve the overall efficiency of regulatory monitoring systems, enforcement policies may adopt a *targeted monitoring system*, under which different levels of monitoring efforts are employed towards different groups of regulatees.[12] Commentators have shown that a targeted monitoring system, which prioritizes regulatee targets and allocates monitoring resources according to effectiveness considerations, may improve the overall efficiency of the regulatory system.[13] To this end, a targeted monitoring system is required to classify regulatees into different groups, each of which is subject to a particular level of monitoring.

What should be the criteria for such regulatee classification into differently monitored groups? The scholarly literature analyzing targeted monitoring systems has focused attention on a handful of alternative criteria for regulatee classification. One central current of the scholarly literature, which corresponds with the regulatory mixed regimes discussed in Chapter 4, suggests that targeted monitoring systems should be based on *regulatee violation records*.[14] In other words, these studies suggest that

---

[10] See the discussion in Chapter 2, Section 2.2.

[11] See Chapter 2, Section 2.2.4.

[12] See *supra* note 7. See also, Nyborg and Telle, "Firms' Compliance to Environmental Regulation: Is There Really a Paradox?," 1–18; and Scholz, "Voluntary Compliance and Regulatory Enforcement," p. 396.

[13] See *ibid.*

[14] This stream of literature is led by Harrington, "Enforcement Leverage when Penalties are Restricted," 29–53. See also, Scholz, "Cooperation, Deterrence,

enforcement responses should correspond to the regulatees' performance. This means that where monitoring responses are concerned, those regulatees whose violation records are clean should be subject to softer monitoring than regulatees with a history of regulatory violations.[15] As the argument goes, such a regime leverages the benefit of regulatory compliance, while increasing the cost of violations. However, as I argue in Chapter 4, an over-reliance on violation records may be misleading. At the outset, violation records include information only about *detected* violations, and therefore may not provide a good indication of the level of corporate compliance or the overall level of corporate law-breaking.[16] Moreover, violation records usually do not capture crucial differences among the regulatees, including the level of their activities, their risk exposure to regulatory violations, and the monitoring technology available to different regulatees.[17] Consequently, it is doubtful whether such records may facilitate a credible classification of different regulatees.

An alternative criterion for the classification of regulatees could, theoretically, be the implementation by corporations of formal *compliance management systems* or *compliance programs*. According to this criterion, which corresponds with various policy proposals made by legal scholars, corporations that adopt official compliance management systems are subject to softer regulatory scrutiny than corporations that do not adopt such systems.[18] The idea behind this criterion is that the adoption of

---

and the Ecology of Regulatory Enforcement," p. 212; Scholz, "Cooperative Regulatory Enforcement and the Politics of Administrative Effectiveness," p. 119. For a detailed discussion of regulatory mixed regimes see Chapter 4, Section 4.3.

15 See Scholz, "Cooperation, Deterrence, and the Ecology of Regulatory Enforcement," p. 179; Scholz, "Voluntary Compliance and Regulatory Enforcement," 385–404; Scholz, "Cooperative Regulatory Enforcement and the Politics of Administrative Effectiveness," 115–136; Scholz, "Can Government Facilitate Cooperation? An Informational Model of OSHA Enforcement," 693–717; Scholz, "Enforcement Policy and Corporate Misconduct: The Changing Perspective of Deterrence Theory," 253–268.

16 See the discussion in Chapter 4, Section 4.5.1.

17 See Scholz, "Enforcement Policy and Corporate Misconduct: The Changing Perspective of Deterrence Theory," 253–268.

18 Various legal scholars have proposed that the adoption of a compliance management system or other adequate internal enforcement mechanisms should be taken into consideration when applying enforcement measures against corporations. See, for instance, Laufer, "Integrity, Diligence, and the Limits of Good Corporate Citizenship," 157–182; Weissmann and Newman, "Rethinking Criminal Corporate Liability," 411–451; Weissmann, "A New Approach to Corporate Criminal Liability," 1319–1342; Pitt and Groskaufmanis, "Minimizing Corporate Civil and Criminal Liability: A Second Look at Corporate Codes of

compliance management systems may signal the corporations' commitment to compliance. Therefore, it may be desirable that corporations that do not adopt compliance management systems – and thereby do not signal their commitment to compliance – be subject to a closer monitoring than corporations that adopt such programs. However, as revealed in Part II of this book, the adoption of compliance management systems may not always credibly signal corporations' genuine commitment to compliance. The scholarly literature has shown that corporations may adopt "window-dressing" systems, and that enforcement authorities are not always able to distinguish genuine compliance management systems from "sham" ones.[19] Therefore, the mere fact that corporations adopt compliance management systems cannot provide a solid ground for the reduction in the regulatory scrutiny of these corporations.

Lastly, another criterion that has been suggested in the scholarly literature is *corporate self-reporting*. Stafford (2008), for instance, has suggested that self-reporting of regulatory violations could be used in determining regulatory monitoring efforts.[20] In Stafford's model, self-reporting corporations are perceived as part of a "good-corporations group," which is subject to reduced monitoring, while other corporations are perceived as part of a "bad-corporations group," which is subject to closer scrutiny.[21] Support for the self-reporting criterion is provided by a recent empirical study by Toffel and Short (2011), according to which corporations that have voluntarily disclosed regulatory violations were found to improve

---

Conduct," 1559–1654; Huff, "The Role of Corporate Compliance Programs in Determining Corporate Criminal Liability: A Suggested Approach," 1252–1298. See also, the discussion in Chapter 5, Section 5.3.2. These studies chiefly concentrate on the impact of internal enforcement measures on corporations' exposure to liability. Policies of a similar spirit could, theoretically, apply with respect to monitoring systems.

[19] See Oded, "Inducing Corporate Compliance: A Compound Corporate Liability Regime"; Krawiec, "Organization Misconduct: Beyond the Principal Agent Model," 571–615; Krawiec, "Cosmetic Compliance and the Failure of Negotiated Governance," 487–544. See also, the discussion in Chapter 6, Section 6.3.2.

[20] See Stafford, "Self-Policing in a Targeted Enforcement Regime," 934–951. This study resembles the model suggested by Harrington in "Enforcement Leverage when Penalties are Restricted," 29–53, while changing the mechanism of regulatee classification.

[21] See *ibid*. Note that the terminology used by Stafford's study is slightly different than the one used in the current study. Stafford in "Self-Policing in a Targeted Enforcement Regime," 934–951, uses the term "self-policing" to denote "a situation in which a facility voluntarily notifies authorities that it has violated a regulation" – an activity termed "self-reporting" in this study.

their regulatory performance in the subsequent period.[22] Hence, Toffel and Short (2011) propose that self-reporting may be used as a tool for reliably identifying voluntary self-policing efforts of regulatees, based on which regulatees may be classified into differently monitored groups.[23] A closer look at the self-reporting criterion, though, reveals that it is vulnerable to opportunistic behavior by corporations. Research has shown that corporations may manipulate the regulatory agency by "cherry-picking" violations to report.[24] Hence, targeted monitoring systems that reduce the scrutiny of self-reporting regulatees may encourage corporations to report minor violations at present in order to benefit from a reduced scrutiny over severe violations in the near future.[25]

Targeted monitoring systems may leverage enforcement resources and produce a higher level of compliance compared to the one commonly produced by the traditional, non-targeted monitoring systems.[26] Yet the success of a targeted monitoring system is greatly contingent upon the robustness of the classification of regulatees. It seems that the scholarly polemic still misses a sound mechanism for regulatee classification. In what follows, I wish to fill this gap by proposing a new structure of regulatory monitoring regimes that utilizes the appointment of CMs as a credible classification mechanism. Such a regime, I believe may encourage more corporations to become proactive in ensuring their compliance, while at the same time economizing public monitoring expenditures.

---

[22] See Toffel and Short, "Coming Clean and Cleaning Up: Does Voluntary Self-Reporting Indicate Effective Self-Policing?"

[23] See *ibid.*

[24] See Pfaff and Sanchirico, "Big Field, Small Potatoes: An Empirical Assessment of EPA's Self-Audit Policy," 415–432. These authors criticized the audit policy of the EPA by pointing to the possibility of manipulated self-reporting.

[25] It should be noted that the empirical evidence discussed above, according to which corporations that have voluntarily disclosed regulatory violations were found to improve their regulatory compliance in the subsequent period, is related to compliance with environmental regulatory requirements enforced through the U.S. Environmental Protection Agency's (EPA's) Audit Policy. With respect to this regulatory context, the EPA has explicitly clarified that self-reporting actions do not affect future EPA's monitoring of self-reporting corporations. See Toffel and Short, "Coming Clean and Cleaning Up: Does Voluntary Self-Reporting Indicate Effective Self-Policing?," Sec. 4.1. It is questionable whether the findings of this study would hold if the EPA's stated policy explicitly announced a scrutiny reduction of all self-reporting corporations. See also the discussion in Chapter 4, Section 4.5.1.

[26] See Harrington, "Enforcement Leverage when Penalties are Restricted," 29–53.

8.3 THIRD-PARTY-BASED TARGETED MONITORING (TPTM) SYSTEM

After having described the regulatee classification challenge involved in the implementation of regulatory targeted monitoring systems, I propose in this section an alternative structure of a regulatory targeted monitoring system, the TPTM system, which hinges upon the appointment of qualified, stand-alone corporate monitoring firms, CMs, by self-policing corporations. This system, I believe, efficiently induces corporate proactive compliance.

8.3.1 The Building Blocks

The basic idea of the TPTM system follows the logic of the U.S. policies regarding DPAs and NPAs discussed in Chapter 7 by delegating some regulatory monitoring tasks from enforcement authorities to independent professionals that can be trusted as corporate "watchdogs." Rather than delegating such powers through DPAs or NPAs that substitute criminal proceedings, the delegation of monitoring powers under the proposed system is done through a voluntary program that sustains corporate regulatees' expected liability, but changes the default combination of the *probability of detection* and *fines* imposed on participating corporations.[27] Under the proposed system, corporations are given the opportunity to opt-in for a voluntary program under which they are exposed to less certain, but more severe liability threats; in return, a reputational assent is conferred upon the corporations as program participants. Specifically, the TPTM system introduces a voluntary program where participating corporations are required to hire CMs to implement their self-policing activity. In return, these corporations gain a *reduction of regulatory scrutiny*, as well as a *program label*.[28] Such a label may become an important asset to

---

[27] Corporate regulatees are assumed to be risk neutral. The risk neutrality of business corporations is a common assumption in the scholarly literature due to corporations' ability to diversify their risks. See, for instance, Roland Kirstein, "Risk Neutrality and Strategic Insurance," *Geneva Papers on Risk and Insurance. Issues and Practice* 25(2) (2000), 251–261; Russell, "Game Models for Structuring Monitoring and Enforcement Systems," p. 216.

[28] A somewhat similar label is commonly used by voluntary programs aiming at improving corporate environmental performance. A notable example is the "EU Eco-Management and Audit Scheme (EMAS)," which is a voluntary program administered by the European Commission Directorate-General (DG) Environment, to assist corporations in evaluating, reporting, and improving their environmental performance. As a reward for voluntary participation in EMAS,

the corporation's reputation since it shows corporate customers, potential trading partners, investors, and other stakeholders that the incumbent corporation is genuinely committed to proactive compliance.[29] To prevent the voluntary program from resulting in under-deterrence, participation in the program implies that corporate regulatees are subject to higher sanctions that are set at a level that compensates for the reduction in expected corporate liability due to their reduced scrutiny.

A key feature of the TPTM system are CMs. The TPTM system utilizes CMs as a signaling mechanism, which facilitates an efficient targeted monitoring system. Based on the conclusions of the previous chapter, this system promotes the creation of a new market for corporate monitoring services, in which qualified, stand-alone monitoring firms, CMs, compete in providing regulatory monitoring services.[30] To ensure CMs' capacity, proper selection, and credibility, it is proposed that the regulatory authorities establish a public list of CMs, whose qualifications and trustworthiness

---

corporations are entitled to use the "EMAS logo." See http://ec.europa.eu/environment/emas/about/index_en.htm.

[29] For the central role of reputation in inducing proactive compliance see, for instance, Khanna and Dickinson, "The Corporate Monitor: The New Corporate Czar," p. 1721. According to these authors, the wish to avoid reputational losses may be significant enough to motivate corporations and executives to accept a DPA/NPA and the appointment of corporate monitors. See also, Pitt and Groskaufmanis, "Minimizing Corporate Civil and Criminal Liability: A Second Look at Corporate Codes of Conduct," p. 1559: "in recent times, overwhelming numbers of public companies have adopted corporate codes of conduct, often either to stay out of news headlines or to extricate themselves from such headlines."

[30] Such a market in which third-party enforcers compete in providing compliance services was originally developed and theoretically analyzed in Ronald J. Gilson and Reinier Kraakman, "Reinventing the Outside Director: An Agenda for Institutional Investors," *Stanford Law Review* 43 (1991), 863–906. The study tackles the familiar, but nonetheless unsolved, agency problem between institutional investors and the management of companies in which they invest – a problem that results from the institutional investors' lack of expertise in monitoring corporate managers. After exploring the imperfections of contemporary mechanisms used to overcome the agency problem, *i.e.*, market for corporate control, shareholder advisory committees, and outside directors, the authors suggest an innovative mechanism that is centered upon the establishment of a *market of independent expert outside directors* that provides institutional investors with compliance monitoring services. The study shows that such a market may comprise a valuable mechanism that strengthens corporate governance. According to the suggested framework, such experts are not tied to particular companies, but rather monitor the operation of an assortment of corporations to which they were assigned by institutional investors (p. 880).

are verified.[31] Furthermore, to strengthen CMs' independence, the list of CMs should include only corporate monitoring firms set-up to provide services to a diversified portfolio of corporate clients.[32] This list comprises a core of monitoring professionals from which corporations wishing to opt in for the voluntary program may choose their CMs. Practically, the appointment of CMs means that the administration of self-policing operations within corporations is outsourced to independent professionals. Such operations may include continuous risk assessment, the overhaul of the corporation's governance structure, creation and reform of internal standards, manuals and ethical codes, employee training, monitoring, investigation of red flags, and the reporting of material regulatory violations further up the ladder among the corporate clients.

Before illustrating how the TPTM system will function in practice, it is important to note that from a social welfare perspective optimal deterrence is reached when the expected liability faced by regulatees equals the total social costs produced by their misconduct. As the reader may recall from Chapter 2, since the higher probability of detection requires more enforcement expenditures, while the imposition of larger cash fines is not involved with the higher costs of fine collection, a more socially efficient enforcement policy would allocate resources to make sanctions less certain

---

[31] This proposal is inspired by various bills recently presented to the U.S. Congress, dealing with the use of CMs in the context of DPAs and NPAs. See, for instance, the Accountability in Deferred Prosecution Act of 2009, H.R. 1947, 111th Cong. (1st Sess. 2009), available at: http://frwebgate.access.gpo.gov/cgi-bin/getdoc.cgi?dbname=111cong_bills&docid=f:h1947ih.txt.pdf. This bill was referred to the House subcommittee Commercial and Administrative Law on May 26, 2009. (See http://www.washingtonwatch.com/bills/show/111_HR_1947.html). The bill requires the Attorney General to create a publicly available "national list of possible corporate monitors." Such a list shall include "organizations and individuals who have the expertise and specialized skills necessary to serve as independent monitors." The bill is discussed in Chapter 7, Section 7.6.1, especially *supra* note 113 in Chapter 7 and the related main text. The framework suggested here resembles the "market for outside directors" developed in Gilson and Kraakman, "Reinventing the Outside Director: An Agenda for Institutional Investors," 863–906. It proposes the creation of a pool of qualified corporate monitors that paves the way for a new *market for corporate compliance services*. Such a market may be institutionalized through a central clearinghouse – the regulatory agency or a professional association – that is financed through annual fees collected from the corporations that choose to appoint CMs. See *ibid*., pp. 886–888. For similar frameworks in which non-governmental organizations maintain and regulate the core of professionals, such as auditors, securities analysts, and attorneys, see Coffee, "The Attorney as Gatekeeper: An Agenda for the SEC," pp. 1302–1303.

[32] Diversified contracting strengthens CMs' independence. See the discussion in Section 8.4.3.

(*i.e.*, lower the probability of detection), but more severe (*i.e.*, impose larger fines).[33] In determining the severity of fines, though, policymakers must ensure that such fines are just as high as the total value of regulatees' assets, whereas larger fines have no additional deterrence effect.[34] Yet, in reality, the need to secure marginal deterrence requires regulatees to develop an escalating schedule of sanctions that mirrors the severity of violations from a social perspective.[35] Accordingly, in this part of the analysis, the study assumes that the default fine imposed against regulatory violations is smaller than the total value of the regulatees' assets.[36] This assumption is relaxed in Section 8.5 below.

---

[33] See Becker, "Crime and Punishment: An Economic Approach," 169–217; Cooter and Ulen, *Law and Economics*, p. 513; Becker, "Nobel Lecture: The Economic Way of Looking at Behavior," pp. 390–391: "Total public spending on fighting crime can be reduced, while keeping the mathematically expected punishment unchanged, by off-setting a cut in expenditures on catching criminals with a sufficient increase in the punishment of those convicted. However, risk-preferring individuals are more deterred from crime by a higher probability of conviction than by severe punishments. Therefore, optimal behavior by the state would balance the reduced spending on police and courts from lowering the probability of conviction against the preference of risk-preferring criminals for a lesser certainty of punishment. The state should also consider the likelihood of punishing innocent persons." See also, Heyes, "Cutting Environmental Penalties to Protect the Environment," 251–265; Harrington, "Enforcement Leverage when Penalties are Restricted," 29–53.

[34] See Shavell, "The Judgment Proof Problem," 45–58; Heyes, "Making Things Stick: Enforcement and Compliance," p. 50; Shavell, "Criminal Law and the Optimal use of Nonmonetary Sanctions as a Deterrent," p. 1232. See also, Chapter 2, Section 2.4.3.

[35] Marginal deterrence, discussed in Chapter 2, Section 2.2.4, refers to the argument made by Stigler in "The Optimum Enforcement of Laws," 526–536. According to Stigler, imposing similar sanctions against various violations that differ from each other in the resulting social harm may distort would-be offenders' decisions and induce them to commit crimes that may result in an even greater social harm. See also, Shavell, "A Note on Marginal Deterrence," 345–355; Mookherjee and Png, "Marginal Deterrence in Enforcement of Law," 1039–1066; Friedman and Sjostrom, "Hanged for a Sheep: The Economics of Marginal Deterrence," 345–366; Becker, "Crime and Punishment: An Economic Approach," 169–217.

[36] This assumption seems to reasonably capture a realistic state of the world, and it corresponds with the theoretical law and economics literature, according to which various considerations such as marginal deterrence may justify that actual sanctions are set at a level which is lower than the maximum. See *supra* note 35 and the related main text. See also, Polinsky and Shavell, "The Optimal Tradeoff between the Probability and Magnitude of Fines," pp. 880–891: "Individuals are rarely if ever fined an amount approximating their wealth, especially for activities which impose relatively small external costs."

8.3.2 Self-Policing Motivation under the TPTM System

To illustrate the application of the TPTM system, suppose that when corporations take no self-policing actions, the probability that corporate employees engage in regulatory violations (denoted "q") is 0.8.[37] In that case, the total social harm (denoted "h") generated by the misconduct is €500, and the default probability of detection (denoted "p^0") is 0.5. Under these circumstances an optimal fine for a detected violation (denoted "l^0") is €1,000.[38] Hence, the payoff of corporations not engaging in self-policing activities (denoted "U^{NSP}") is presented by the following expression: $U^{NSP} = -(l^0 \cdot p^0 \cdot q^0)$, which is −€400.

For simplification reasons, I assume that the cost of a genuine self-policing scheme (denoted "c") is €200 across all corporations, whether implemented internally or outsourced, and that corporations differ in the productivity of their self-policing schemes. Table 8.1 presents the reduced probability of misconduct resulting from self-policing activities undertaken by three types of corporations and the payoffs expected to be obtained by these corporations if engaged in self-policing (denoted U_i^{SP}). Note, the payoff when corporations do not engage in self-policing activities, $U^{NSP} = -€400$, presents the benchmark payoff for corporations' decisions whether they should self-police. Provided that the payoff when corporations do not self-police is −€400, corporations will engage in self-policing only if by doing so their payoff increases. Put differently, given the cost of self-policing activities, corporations engage in self-policing only if their self-policing activities are productive enough to reduce the probability of misconduct to at least 0.4.[39] Accordingly, as shown in Table 8.1, given these circumstances, only Type-1 corporations engage in self-policing.

When the TPTM system is introduced, corporations are offered the opportunity to hire CMs in return for a reduction in regulatory scrutiny and the program label. Although the reduction in corporate expected liability due to the reduced scrutiny is eventually offset by the higher fines imposed on participating corporations, such corporations benefit from the reputation asset embedded in the program label. Hence, the TPTM system

---

37 An employee violation may be deliberate or inadvertent.

38 The actual sanction is set at the level in which corporate expected liability (€1000 × 0.5) equals the total social harm (€500). For simplification reasons, I assume that the social harm represents the total social costs of the violation.

39 If as a result of self-policing activities the probability of misconduct is reduced to 0.4, corporations' payoff is $U_1^{SP} = -(l^0 \cdot p^0 \cdot q_1 + c) = -(1000 \cdot 0.5 \cdot 0.4 + 200) = -400$. In that case, corporations are indifferent as to whether to undertake self-policing activities.

Table 8.1 Corporations' self-policing decisions

	q (When corporations self-police)	Corporate payoff (when corporations self-police) (€)	Would corporations self-police? (€)
Type-1	$q_1 = 0.3$	$U_1^{SP} = -(l^0 \cdot p^0 \cdot q_1 + c)$ $= -(100 \cdot 0.5 \cdot 0.3 + 200) = -350$	Yes $(-350 > -400)$
Type-2	$q_2 = 0.6$	$U_2^{SP} = -(l^0 \cdot p^0 \cdot q_2 + c)$ $= -(100 \cdot 0.5 \cdot 0.6 + 200) = -500$	No $(-500 < -400)$
Type-3	$q_3 = 0.7$	$U_3^{SP} = -(l^0 \cdot p^0 \cdot q_3 + c)$ $= -(100 \cdot 0.5 \cdot 0.7 + 200) = -550$	No $(-550 < -400)$

Table 8.2 Corporations' self-policing decisions after the TPTM system is introduced

	q (When corporations self-police)	Corporate payoff (when corporations self-police) (€)	Would corporations self-police? (€)
Type-1	$q_1 = 0.3$	$U_1^{SP} = r - (l^h \cdot p^l \cdot q_1 + c)$ $= 125 - (1430 \cdot 0.35 \cdot 0.3 + 200) = -225$	Yes $(-225 > -400)$
Type-2	$q_2 = 0.6$	$U_2^{SP} = r - (l^h \cdot p^l \cdot q_2 + c)$ $= 125 - (1430 \cdot 0.35 \cdot 0.6 + 200) = -375$	Yes $(-375 > -400)$
Type-3	$q_3 = 0.7$	$U_3^{SP} = r - (l^h \cdot p^l \cdot q_3 + c)$ $= 125 - (1430 \cdot 0.35 \cdot 0.7 + 200) = -425$	No $(-425 < -400)$

leverages the benefit gained by corporations engaging in self-policing activities. To refer to the example provided above, suppose that a reduced scrutiny implies that the probability of detection faced by participating corporations (denoted "p^l") is 0.35, and that the reputation value of the conferred label (denoted "r") is €125. Given the reduction of the probability of detection, corporate expected liability would be sustained at its optimal level (*i.e.*, at the level of the total social harm), if the applicable fine increases accordingly. The fine applied to participating corporations (denoted "l^h") is, then, €500/0.35, which is €1,430. Table 8.2 presents corporations' self-policing decisions given that the TPTM system is introduced.

As illustrated in Table 8.2, the TPTM system strengthens corporations' incentives to engage in efficient self-policing activities by reinforcing the benefit gained by self-policing corporations. While sustaining the expected liability at the optimal level, the TPTM system provides self-policing corporations with a reputation asset that motivates them to engage in self-policing. As clearly seen in the example above, when the TPTM system is introduced, Type-2 corporations that previously did not self-police now engage in self-policing activities.

8.3.3 Welfare Evaluation

The TPTM system presents a workable framework for a regulatory targeted monitoring regime that efficiently induces corporate proactive compliance. Such a system sustains the virtues of the regulatory mixed regimes discussed in Chapter 4, by following an inclusive approach, under which monitoring efforts are tailored to the differently motivated regulatees.[40] Under the suggested regime, regulatees that are motivated to engage in self-policing are subject to reduced scrutiny, while other regulatees are more closely watched. If viewed through the lenses of the mixed regimes discussed in Chapter 4, one may say that under the suggested regime *compliant* regulatees are subject to reduced scrutiny, while *recalcitrant* ones are closely watched.[41] Such a targeted method of regulatory monitoring allows enforcement authorities to utilize enforcement resources more efficiently. Moreover, the TPTM system overcomes the pitfalls of the regulatory mixed regimes that were discussed in Chapter 4.[42] This system bases the classification of regulatees into differently monitored groups on a sound criterion that indicates regulatees' engagement in self-policing activities. Such a criterion is clear and transparent, and thereby alleviates *information asymmetry* and *arbitrariness* concerns.[43]

The gains produced by the TPTM from a social welfare perspective are straightforward. *First*, the TPTM system increases the portion of corporate regulatee population that engages in self-policing, thereby it efficiently reduces misconduct and relinquishes the social costs associated with such misconduct.[44] By conferring the program label on corporate

---

[40] For a discussion of the virtues of regulatory mixed regimes, *i.e.*, "inclusiveness" and "targeting attitudes," see Chapter 4, Section 4.4.

[41] For a discussion of the heterogeneity of the regulatory population underlying the regulatory mixed regimes see Chapter 4, Section 4.2.

[42] For a discussion of the pitfalls of regulatory mixed regimes, *i.e.*, "information asymmetry" and "arbitrariness," see Chapter 4, Section 4.5.

[43] See Chapter 4, Section 4.5.

[44] This benefit is presented by Type-2 regulatees in the example used in Section 8.3.2 above. Such regulatees are incentivized to efficiently self-police once the TPTM system is introduced.

regulatees that opt in for the voluntary program, the TPTM system utilizes an important motivating mechanism, *i.e.*, reputation, to increase the gain corporations extract from self-policing activities. The use of such a labeling mechanism normally involves no significant social cost. *Second*, the TPTM system economizes the cost of regulatory monitoring costs by facilitating a reduction of regulatory scrutiny on an additional portion of the regulatee population. Of course, the net social gain of the TPTM system depends on the social costs involved with the establishment of – and the control over – the core of CMs.[45] Therefore, the TPTM system may produce a higher social value when implemented in regulatory areas in which a corporation's reputation for compliance is highly valued. In such contexts, the additional costs associated with the use of CMs may be borne by corporations participating in the voluntary program up to a complete erosion of their reputation gains.[46] *Third*, given that the TPTM system encourages the delegation of some monitoring tasks to corporate monitors who are financed by monitored corporations, some enforcement costs are, in fact, borne by their presumptive beneficiaries, *i.e.*, by regulated corporations and their clients. This transformation of costs is not only a matter of the distribution of wealth, but, in fact, it increases the efficiency in the regulated market by compelling corporations (or their clients to which these costs will eventually be shifted) to bear the true cost of regulatory monitoring embedded in the production of their relevant goods and services.[47]

8.4 CORPORATE MONITORS AS A FACILITATING MECHANISM

The TPTM system hinges upon the use of CMs in facilitating a targeted monitoring mechanism. Given the key role played by CMs under the TPTM system, I find it useful to look at the capacity, selection, and

---

45 For a discussion of authorities' control over CMs see Section 8.4.3 below.

46 Screening and selection costs of CMs to be included in the public list, as well as the cost of controlling CMs, may be financed through an annual fee that may be paid by corporations opting into the voluntary program, or by CMs included in the list of CMs. In the latter case, these costs will be shifted to the CMs' corporate clients through their fees. Given that corporations opting into the voluntary program have a positive reputation gain, they will be willing to bear these costs up to a complete erosion of their net gain.

47 See Kraakman, "Gatekeepers: The Anatomy of a Third-Party Enforcement Strategy," p. 93.

motivations of CMs in performing their tasks. The law and economics literature has thoroughly analyzed the incorporation of third-party enforcers into regulatory enforcement systems. Some of the major insights found in this literature that are applicable to the current context, are described below. However, it should be noted that the ensuing section is not intended to present a comprehensive portrayal of third-party enforcement systems, nor is it able to cope with all potential challenges arising with respect to third-party enforcers. Such a discussion deviates from the boundaries of the current study.[48] My goal in this section is to point out the major conclusions found in the existing literature and to show their application in the current context.

8.4.1 Capacity

The capacity of CMs to serve as "corporate watchdogs" is a key factor of the TPTM system. The polemic literature on third-party enforcers is indecisive with regard to which position of third-party enforcers best ensures their capacity to undertake their role. One major group of scholars favors third-party enforcers who are *external* professional enforcers that provide monitoring services to corporations.[49] These scholars argue that in-house counselors are economically dependent on a "single client," their employing corporation, and therefore tend to be too "captured" to exercise independent judgment in undertaking their role.[50] In contrast, outside

---

[48] For a thorough discussion of third-party enforcement systems, see, for instance, *ibid.*; Hamdani, "Gatekeeper Liability," 53–120; Gilboy, "Compelled Third-Party Participation in the Regulatory Process: Legal Duties, Culture, and Noncompliance," 135–155; Coffee, "The Attorney as Gatekeeper: An Agenda for the SEC," 1293–1316; Coffee, "Understanding Enron: It's about the Gatekeepers, Stupid," 1403–1420; Coffee, *Gatekeepers: The Professions and Corporate Governance*; Schmidt, *Eyes Half Blind: The Possibilities and Limits of Lawyers as Third Party Enforcers*; Kim, "The Banality of Fraud: Re-Situating the Inside Counsel as Gatekeeper," 983–1077; Kim, "Gatekeepers Inside Out," 411–463; Grabosky, "Using Non-Governmental Resources to Foster Regulatory Compliance," 527–550.

[49] See, for instance, Coffee, "The Attorney as Gatekeeper: An Agenda for the SEC," pp. 1305–1306; Deborah A. DeMott, "The Discrete Roles of General Counsel," *Fordham Law Review* 74 (2005), p. 967.

[50] See Coffee, "The Attorney as Gatekeeper: An Agenda for the SEC," pp. 1305–1306; DeMott, "The Discrete Roles of General Counsel," p. 967. See also, Kim, "The Banality of Fraud: Re-Situating the Inside Counsel as Gatekeeper," pp. 1005–1007. Kim explains that besides their risk of losing their entire income from their employing corporation, in-house counsels feel "unremitting pressure" to justify their department as a corporate cost center and may be inclined to

enforcers that serve diversified clients have proportionately less at stake in their relationship with a particular client or customer, and therefore tend to exercise more independent judgment in undertaking their role.[51] As argued by Coffee (2006):

> While the outside attorney has been increasingly relegated to a specialist's role and is seldom sought for statesman-like advice, the in-house general counsel seems even less suited to play a gatekeeping role. . . . [T]he in-house counsel is less an independent professional – indeed he is far more exposed to pressure and reprisals than even the outside audit partner.[52]

Another group of scholars led by Kim (2008), questions the superiority of outside third-party enforcers.[53] According to this approach, *in-house* enforcers have an "overwhelming advantage" over external enforcers in gathering relevant information and detecting misconduct through formal and informal communication channels within the corporation. External enforcers, as the argument goes, have a limited capacity for monitoring the corporation and will encounter substantial hurdles in "getting the facts that might serve as the critical red flags."[54]

The resolution of the fundamental debate over the optimal design of third-party enforcers exceeds the limited boundaries of this study. Yet, it is useful to notice that CMs under the TPTM system are designed as hybrid-type third-party enforcers that are retained by corporations on an ongoing basis as *standing counsels*.[55] As such, it seems that these CMs are likely to get adequate access to relevant information through formal and informal channels within the corporation, while exercising independent judgment in undertaking their role.

---

pleasure their managements to get bonuses, and therefore may "more likely feel pressured to conceal [their] personal ethical values that differ from organizational values" (p. 1006).

51 See Kraakman, "Gatekeepers: The Anatomy of a Third-Party Enforcement Strategy," p. 71. See also, Gilson and Kraakman, "Reinventing the Outside Director: An Agenda for Institutional Investors," pp. 884–886.

52 See Coffee, *Gatekeepers: The Professions and Corporate Governance*, p. 195.

53 See Kim, "Gatekeepers Inside Out," 411–463.

54 See *ibid.*, pp. 448–457, 460.

55 Even Kim in "Gatekeepers Inside Out," 411–463, does not argue that in-house counsels are ultimately superior to external enforcers, mainly because in-house counsels may be seriously compromised in their willingness to interdict misconduct. Nevertheless, given the weaknesses of pure external third-party enforcers, Kim suggests incentivizing corporations "to retain outside counsel on a more ongoing basis, in the role of standing counsel for the independent directors" (p. 461).

8.4.2 Selection

The discussion of DPA and NPA policies in Chapter 7 revealed a major line of scholarly criticism that focuses on the selection process of corporate monitors and their qualifications.[56] Scholars have pointed to the excessive involvement of prosecutors in the selection of corporate monitors, which raises concerns regarding potential conflicts of interest.[57] In contrast to the framework established by DPAs and NPAs, under the TPTM system the appointment of CMs is to be done solely by corporations, with no public authority intervention. The authority is merely required to establish a public list of qualified CMs, from which each corporation may choose its own CM. As mentioned earlier, a similar framework was included in the bills proposed to the U.S. Congress concerning the policies of DPAs and NPAs.[58] Such a framework, I believe, ensures the qualifications of CMs in performing their monitoring tasks.

8.4.3 Credibility

CMs' credibility in performing their monitoring tasks is a crucial prerequisite for their incorporation into regulatory enforcement policies. Although the DPA and NPA policies have been implemented for more than a decade, I am not aware of any study in which the credibility of corporate monitors appointed as part of such agreements was in doubt. Yet, from a theoretical point of view, the issue of CMs' credibility may be worthy of some attention. The scholarly literature has analyzed the credibility of third-party enforcers and potential mechanisms that may secure it. Traditionally, two common mechanisms have been proposed to ensure the credibility of third-party enforcement:[59] (a) *noblesse oblige* – outside professional third-party enforcers are normally chosen from a group of people with prominent characters and widespread social ties to the business community which secures their commitment to adequately fulfilling their role;[60] and

---

56 See the discussion in Chapter 7, Section 7.5.4.

57 See, for instance, Garrett, "Structural Reform Prosecution," 853–957; Paulsen, "Imposing Limits on Prosecutorial Discretion in Corporate Prosecution Agreements," 1434–1469; Warin and Boutros, "Deferred Prosecution Agreements: A View from the Trenches and a Proposal for Reform," 121–134; Coffee, "Deferred Prosecution: Has it Gone Too Far?," p. 13.

58 See *supra* note 31.

59 See Gilson and Kraakman, "Reinventing the Outside Director: An Agenda for Institutional Investors," p. 874. The analysis by Gilson and Kraakman that originally refers to outside directors is equally relevant in the context of CMs.

60 See *ibid.*, p. 881.

(b) *market forces* – the market for external professional enforcers, in which corrupted enforcers are punished, has a disciplinary power on external enforcers that is believed to play a crucial role in ensuring their credibility.[61]

To ensure CMs' credibility, the TPTM system relies on a screening mechanism that is designed to satisfy the *noblesse oblige* mechanism.[62] Accordingly, the risk of being excluded from the list of CMs presents a powerful motivation for CMs' adequate performance. CMs simply stand to lose too little if they are found to be incapable or corrupted.[63] Second, CMs are professional monitoring firms operating in a competitive market in which they provide services to a diversified portfolio of corporate clients. Therefore, such CMs may not be willing to sacrifice their reputation and their future income to satisfy a single client.[64] They will actually lose relatively little by rejecting a bribery offer by one of their clients.[65]

---

[61] See *ibid.*, pp. 886, 890, and Gilson, "The Devolution of the Legal Profession: A Demand Side Perspective," p. 888, according to which the best way of establishing and maintaining such a market would be through an independent clearinghouse.

[62] Similar to existing frameworks in which incumbents are screened and selected according to their qualifications, including lawyers, auditors, notaries, securities analysts, CMs are screened and selected according to their capacity, expertise, and integrity before they are included in the list of CMs. See *supra* note 31 and the related main text.

[63] See Kraakman, "Gatekeepers: The Anatomy of a Third-Party Enforcement Strategy," pp. 67–68: "[w]henever entry to a gatekeeping market requires significant capital, including investment in specific human capital or reputation, simple legal penalties such as civil damages, fines, or license revocations can be powerful deterrents." See also, Bardach and Kagan, *Going by the Book: The Problem of Regulatory Unreasonableness*, pp. 61–62: "Large corporations now have staffs of professionals concerned with regulatory matters – academically trained industrial hygienists, environmental engineers, toxicologists, safety experts, biologists, lawyers, occupational physicians, and specialists in administering affirmative action programs. These specialists are by no means uninterested in their corporation's balance sheet, but they also have some loyalty to the standards of their profession. '*I'm a licensed engineer, I'm not going to risk my license by lying to an agency*,' a corporate environmental engineer told us" (emphasis added).

[64] See Coffee, "The Attorney as Gatekeeper: An Agenda for the SEC," p. 1298. See also, Kraakman, "Gatekeepers: The Anatomy of a Third-Party Enforcement Strategy," p. 70: "diversified gatekeepers who have proportionately less at stake in relationships with particular clients or customers are less likely to receive threats (or corrupt offers) that are large enough to offset their expected costs of corruption." See also, Kraakman, "Corporate Liability Strategies and the Costs of Legal Controls," 857–898.

[65] See Kim, "Gatekeepers Inside Out," p. 423; Kraakman, "Corporate Liability Strategies and the Costs of Legal Controls," 857–898. See also, Coffee, "The Attorney as Gatekeeper: An Agenda for the SEC," pp. 1298, 1305–1306; Gilson

Altogether, the TPTM system is designed so that it produces an incentive scheme that leverages CMs' credibility.[66]

8.5 THE TPTM SYSTEM WHEN FINES EQUAL CORPORATE ASSET VALUE

On rare occasions sanctions imposed against regulatory violations are set at the level of the regulatees' asset value. For the sake of completeness, let me consider the application of the TPTM system in such settings. From a policymaking perspective the practical implication of fines set at the level of corporate asset value is that no larger fines can be imposed on corporations opting into the voluntary program. In such contexts, the TPTM system may require the following adjustment: rather than directly imposing higher fines on corporations opting into the voluntary program, these additional costs may be levied by holding CMs strictly liable for their corporate clients' misconduct, and tuning their expected liability so that it offsets the reduction in expected liability gained by the corporations due to their reduced scrutiny.[67] Under such circumstances, CMs' expected liability is *ex-ante* shifted to their corporate clients through the fees paid to CMs, and offsets the reduction gained by participating corporations due to their reduced scrutiny.[68]

---

and Kraakman, "Reinventing the Outside Director: An Agenda for Institutional Investors," p. 886.

[66] As suggested by Kraakman, "Gatekeepers: The Anatomy of a Third-Party Enforcement Strategy," p. 69, the concern of third-party enforcers' corruption is "not to suggest that every [third-party enforcer] has a price; some will presumably resist corruption at any price. Nevertheless, it is the balance of [third-party enforcer] incentives across the entire market that is critical for enforcement purposes . . .." Compare with Gilson, "The Devolution of the Legal Profession: A Demand Side Perspective," pp. 887–888, who discusses the normative commitment of lawyers as gatekeepers, arguing that lawyers are a group of normatively committed actors who are normally attracted to the legal practice because of their motivation to serve the private interest, rather than profit seeking.

[67] Resorting to the example in Section 8.3.2 above: due to the reduction in regulatory scrutiny, corporations opting into the voluntary program face a lower expected liability, that is $l^0 \cdot p^L$ (or, $1000 \times 0.35 = 350$) rather than $l^0 \cdot p^0$ (or, $1000 \times 0.5 = 500$). Therefore, if CMs are held strictly liable for their clients' misconduct, and their expected liability is set equal to €150, these CMs will shift the cost of their expected liability to their corporate clients, and by that completely offset the reduction in expected liability gained by these corporations.

[68] The above is contingent upon CMs' ability to accurately estimate their corporate clients' liability exposure. Otherwise, CMs may pool the risk of various

8.6 SUMMARY AND CONCLUDING REMARKS

Corporate monitors comprise an invaluable enforcement tool in promoting corporate proactive compliance. Recent U.S. policies have begun utilizing corporate monitors in combating corporate crime. Such policies employ corporate monitors' surveillance as part of the DPAs and the NPAs, which are used as alternatives for traditional criminal sanctions. In this chapter, I propose that corporate monitors may be useful in a different enforcement context, namely, in efficiently facilitating regulatory targeted monitoring systems. The virtues of such systems have been explored in the scholarly literature for more than two decades. Yet, a credible mechanism for regulatee classification into differently monitored groups has not been identified. Based on the lessons learned from the current policies utilizing corporate monitors, in this chapter I developed a targeted monitoring system, the TPTM system, which utilizes a uniquely crafted type of corporate monitor to efficiently induce corporate proactive compliance. The suggested policy induces more corporations to engage in self-policing activities, while economizing public monitoring costs.

clients and distort their compliance motivations. See Hamdani, "Gatekeeper Liability," 53–120.

9. Concluding remarks

How Should a Regulatory Enforcement Policy be Designed to Efficiently Induce Corporate Proactive Compliance?

Despite the recent "free market" global trends, governments in modern societies hold a central position in directing and controlling corporate activity through regulations. To attain socially desirable ends, such regulations must be adequately enforced, while taking into consideration the particularities of the regulatory ecology. This book seeks to identify a structure of enforcement policy that efficiently induces corporate proactive compliance. In pursuing this goal, the analysis considers the following particular factors regarding the regulatory ecology:

Corporate regulatees – The organizational settings of corporations, in which various agents act on behalf of their corporate employers, involve unique aspects that pose certain challenges to the traditional enforcement systems which are directed at individual primary actors.[1] The dispersion of responsibility within corporations, the difficulties involved in controlling incorporated groups of actors, as well as potential conflicts of interest within the corporate "black box," require policymakers to avoid treating corporations as monoliths. Instead, enforcement policies must be attentive to the composite structures of corporate regulatees and produce compliance incentives tailored to such structures.[2]

Proactive compliance – Unlike traditional criminal laws, regulations normally provide detailed standards of behavior; they are frequently updated to meet ever-changing market needs; and they often require a certain level of expertise to be fully grasped and obeyed. Hence, an enforcement policy directed at inducing corporate regulatory compliance must encourage regulatees to move from a "reactive" to a "proactive" compliance approach, that is, to take the required steps to ensure adequate implementation of regulatory

---

1 See Chapter 2, Section 2.2.1.

2 See *ibid.*

requirements.[3] Ultimately, a regulatory enforcement policy encourages corporations: (i) to internalize the social ramifications of their activities, and thereby adjust their activities – carried out by their employees – to socially optimal standards of behavior; and (ii) to proactively self-enforce applicable regulations, that is, to act in order to prevent, deter, and report their own misconduct, including misconduct committed by their employees within the scope of their employment.[4]

Positive externalities – As opposed to the enforcement of traditional crime, *e.g.*, murder and burglary, the enforcement of regulations cannot be blind to potential *positive* externalities of regulated activities. If excessively enforced, regulatees may either avoid socially desirable activities or employ excessive (costly) precautions to the detriment of social welfare.[5] Therefore, rather than applying aggressive, uncompromising enforcement measures, a desirable regulatory enforcement policy must be sensitive to the potentially adverse consequences of its application.[6]

Enforcement costs – Regulations normally seek to overcome market failures that may hamper the efficient functioning of market forces, thereby securing a particular social benefit.[7] Accordingly, when crafting a regulatory enforcement policy, the expected social benefit of regulations should be juxtaposed against the social costs associated with the enforcement of such regulations. Hence, from a social welfare perspective, the employment of regulatory enforcement measures can be justified merely to the extent that the marginal social cost of misconduct reduction clears its marginal social benefit.[8]

---

[3] See *ibid.*

[4] See *ibid.*

[5] See Ogus, "Criminal Law and Regulation," 90–110; Ogus, "Enforcing Regulation: Do We Need the Criminal Law?," 42–55.

[6] The particular legal environment in which enforcement policies are employed is crucial to consider when crafting an enforcement policy. See, for instance, Cooter, "Prices and Sanctions," 1523–1560, who suggests that in legal areas in which a certain behavior needs to be deterred then enforcement should employ punitive measures. In contrast, when the goal of an enforcement policy is to induce the internalization of the ramifications of actions then it is better for enforcement policies to employ a pricing mechanism. See also, Cooter and Ulen, *Law and Economics*, p. 493.

[7] See Ogus, "Criminal Law and Regulation," 90–110; Ogus, "Enforcing Regulation: Do We Need the Criminal Law?," 42–55.

[8] See Cooter and Ulen, *Law and Economics*, p. 511. See also, Stigler, "The Optimum Enforcement of Laws," p. 526; Polinsky, "Punitive Damages: An Economic Analysis," pp. 877–878.

9.1 THE TRADITIONAL SCHOOLS OF THOUGHT REGARDING LAW ENFORCEMENT

In this book I have explored two major schools of thought regarding law enforcement, each of which endorses distinct enforcement regimes: first, the *deterrence-based* enforcement approach, which is rooted in the economic literature.[9] This school perceives regulatees as "rational," "amoral calculators," willing to comply with the law only when – and to the extent in which – it coincides with the goals of maximizing profit.[10] On the basis of agents' rational calculations, the deterrence-based school of thought endorses a confrontational style of enforcement which coerces compliance through "by-the-book" legalistic enforcement regimes.[11] By relying on an optimal combination of detection rates and penalties, the deterrence-based enforcement approach seeks to make would-be wrongdoers realize that misconduct does not pay.[12] The alternative philosophy of law enforcement which is the *cooperative* enforcement approach stems from behavioral literature.[13] This school departs from the "rationality-of-agents" perception and perceives regulatees as "law-abiding creatures," who are motivated to obey the law because of their sense of social responsibility.[14] This approach departs from the penal, accusatory, and adversarial style of the deterrence-based approach and endorses conciliatory and compromising enforcement regimes.[15] Under cooperative regimes, enforcement authorities undertake advisory and educative roles, and thereby promote compliance through cooperation and mutual persuasion, rather than through the threat of penalty.[16]

The analysis in Chapters 2 and 3 reveals the comparative strengths and weaknesses of the enforcement regimes developed by both schools of thought. Deterrence-based enforcement regimes are considered as generating high levels of certainty and credibility.[17] Such regimes are argued to adequately link the goal of enforcement systems with the means of attainment.[18] They reduce the risk of arbitrariness and enhance social pressure

---

9 See Chapter 2.
10 See Chapter 2, Section 2.2.1.
11 See Chapter 2, Section 2.2.2.
12 See *ibid.*
13 See Chapter 3.
14 See Chapter 3, Section 3.2.1.
15 See Chapter 3, Section 3.2.2.
16 See *ibid.*
17 See Chapter 2, Section 2.4.
18 See *ibid.*

to comply, by reinforcing social sentiments of disapproval and stamping errant conduct as unacceptable.[19] However, as revealed in Chapter 2, deterrence-based enforcement regimes are fraught with substantial perils including: the high costs involved in the regulatory "cat-and-mouse" game promoted by these regimes;[20] the potential alienation of regulatory subjects resulting from a rigid style of enforcement;[21] the practical challenges involved in reaching optimal levels of detection and sanctioning;[22] and the bounded rationality of regulatees.[23] Cooperative enforcement regimes, on the other hand, are able to cope with most of the weaknesses of the deterrence-based regimes. By embracing a cooperative attitude toward law enforcement, cooperative regimes seek to encourage compliance by promoting regulatees' personal morality and perceived legitimacy.[24] Yet, as revealed in Chapter 3, cooperative enforcement regimes cannot ensure an optimal social outcome at all times. Under certain circumstances, cooperative enforcement regimes may be abused by opportunistic regulatees and thereby produce a suboptimal social outcome.[25] Such regimes are vulnerable to the pitfalls of credulousness,[26] regulatory capture,[27] and corruption.[28] Furthermore, under certain circumstances, such regimes may undermine regulatees' incentives to comply with legal orders and erode the general deterrence of the regulatory system.[29]

Taken altogether, the analysis reveals that neither deterrence-based enforcement regimes nor cooperative enforcement regimes comprise the most optimal enforcement regime that efficiently induces corporate proactive compliance.

9.2 A RECONCILIATION BETWEEN THE TRADITIONAL SCHOOLS OF THOUGHT

Regulatees greatly differ in their responsiveness to enforcement policies. While some regulatees repeatedly engage in regulatory violations even

---

19 See *ibid.*
20 See Chapter 2, Section 2.4.1.
21 See Chapter 2, Section 2.4.2.
22 See Chapter 2, Section 2.4.3.
23 See Chapter 2, Section 2.4.4.
24 See Chapter 3, Sections 3.2.1 and 3.3.
25 See Chapter 3, Section 3.5.
26 See Chapter 3, Section 3.5.1.
27 See Chapter 3, Section 3.5.2.
28 See Chapter 3, Section 3.5.3.
29 See Chapter 3, Sections 3.5.4 and 3.5.5.

under substantial penalty threats, others tend to comply with regulatory requirements even when penalty threats are relatively mild.[30] This heterogeneity of regulatees may be analyzed through different lenses. The *behavioral* perspective on the matter suggests that regulatees differ in their level of social responsibility and normative commitment.[31] While some regulatees are "compliant" in nature, and comply with the law "just because it is law," others are "recalcitrant," "self-seekers," and behave opportunistically when defying legal orders.[32] The *economic* perspective, on the other hand, explains the heterogeneity of regulatees through objective aspects, such as size, structure, area of activity, level of activity, and the available monitoring technology – all of which cause regulatees to react differently to similar incentives.[33] Following either approach, the heterogeneity of regulatees implies that a uniform enforcement policy treating all regulatees alike may fail to produce desirable ends.[34]

After having considered the imperfections of each of these "stand-alone" enforcement regimes, I propose in this book that regulatory mixed regimes which work to combine different elements from both "stand-alone" regimes may be more socially desirable. In Chapter 4, I show that the game theoretic prisoner's dilemma comprises a robust analytical framework for the reconciliation of deterrence-based and cooperative enforcement strategies.[35] Following the logic of the game theoretic Tit-For-Tat (TFT) strategy, enforcement authorities may be empowered to choose between deterrence-based and cooperative enforcement measures according to the particular circumstances at hand.[36] In this way, enforcement authorities follow an *inclusive* approach, *i.e.*, they acknowledge the heterogeneity among regulatees and tailor enforcement responses to differently motivated regulatees.[37] Consequently, enforcement authorities employ *targeting attitudes* by devoting greater enforcement efforts towards insufficiently motivated regulatees.[38]

A look into the law and economics literature reveals that the idea of combining different elements of the "stand-alone" enforcement regimes within mixed frameworks is neither new nor innovative. The scholarly

---

30 See Chapter 4, Section 4.2.
31 See Chapter 3, Section 3.2.1.
32 See *ibid.*
33 See Chapter 2, Section 2.2.
34 See Chapter 4, Section 4.2.
35 See *ibid.*
36 See Chapter 4, Section 4.3.2.
37 See Chapter 4, Section 4.4.1.
38 See *ibid.*

literature has proposed an array of regulatory mixed regimes that allow enforcement authorities to choose particular enforcement responses based on the *past performance* of the regulatees.[39] Such regimes often treat the determination of monitoring efforts and actual enforcement measures (*i.e.*, persuasion/sanctioning) as a single choice.[40] More specifically, enforcement responses – both with respect to the level of monitoring and the style of regulatory measures employed – are determined based on regulatees' *violation records*.[41] Regulatees whose records are clean are subject to relatively infrequent inspections and treated by guidance and persuasion measures. By contrast, regulatees with a history of violations are closely scrutinized and are subject to stricter punitive measures.[42] These regulatory mixed regimes are not merely theoretical. The scholarly literature has shown that the combination of deterrence-based and cooperative enforcement styles is utilized in practice by various regulatory enforcement authorities, explicitly or implicitly.[43]

Compared with the "stand-alone" enforcement regimes, regulatory mixed regimes undoubtedly present an improved framework of regulatory enforcement. These regimes sustain the major virtues of each of the "stand alone" regimes, while coping with their major pitfalls.[44] For instance, like deterrence-based regimes, mixed regimes convey a clear message to regulatees that law-breaking is intolerable. Such regimes even magnify the adverse effect of non-compliance by linking the choice of enforcement responses to the past performance of the regulatee.[45] At the same time, regulatory mixed regimes restrict the "cat-and-mouse" game associated with deterrence-based regimes to circumstances in which it is truly warranted. However, like the pure cooperative regimes, regulatory mixed regimes promote cooperation, avoid regulatee alienation, and save substantial social costs, while promoting voluntary compliance. Yet, compared with the pure cooperative regimes, the mixed regimes are less prone to credulousness and to opportunistic abuse by regulatees.

Notwithstanding their virtues, the particular structures of regulatory mixed regimes discussed thus far in the scholarly literature are fraught with two major pitfalls that have not received sufficient attention in the

---

39 See Chapter 4, Section 4.3.4.

40 See Chapter 4, Section 4.3.4, especially *supra* note 34 in Chapter 4 and the related main text.

41 See *ibid.*

42 See *ibid.*

43 See *ibid.*

44 See Chapter 4, Section 4.4.1.

45 See Chapter 4, Section 4.3.

polemic literature. The first major pitfall is *information asymmetry*.[46] In Chapter 4, I argue that the over-reliance on violation records in determining the adequate response of enforcement may be misleading. Violation records include information merely on *detected* violations, and thus may not provide a credible indication of corporate compliance levels or the overall level of corporate law-breaking.[47] Moreover, violation records normally do not capture crucial differences between regulatees, including activity levels, risk exposure to regulatory violations, and available monitoring technologies.[48] The second major pitfall of regulatory mixed regimes is their *arbitrariness*.[49] Regulatory mixed regimes, which grant enforcement authorities wide discretion in choosing enforcement responses in particular cases, are vulnerable to the risk of the misuse of such discretion, regulatory inconsistency, as well as regulatees' misperceptions over regulatory responses.[50]

Altogether, the regulatory mixed regimes discussed thus far in the scholarly literature cope with the major flaws of both types of "standalone" regimes, and in that respect, they present an improved enforcement framework; yet, the mixed regimes are fraught with serious perils that must be considered before being implemented in particular contexts. I argue that such regimes must develop further in order to overcome the perils described above. As the analysis reveals, an initial step required to overcome the flaws of recognized structures of regulatory mixed regimes is to unbundle the analysis of *liability regimes* and of *monitoring regimes*. Accordingly, each of these components of the regulatory enforcement policies are analyzed separately in Part II and Part III of this book.

9.3 TOWARD AN OPTIMAL CORPORATE LIABILITY REGIME

Corporate liability may be imposed through a wide spectrum of legal regimes. In Chapter 5, I presented an array of liability regimes used in practice to induce corporate proactive compliance. As shown there, one end of the spectrum consists of "*deterrence-based*" liability regimes, under which corporations are held "strictly" liable for employee misconduct regardless of any internal enforcement efforts exerted by these

---

46 See Chapter 4, Section 4.5.1.
47 See *ibid.*
48 See *ibid.*
49 See Chapter 4, Section 4.5.2.
50 See *ibid.*

corporations.[51] The other end of the spectrum consists of "*cooperative enforcement*" liability regimes, according to which no liability is imposed on cooperative corporations, *i.e.*, corporations that implemented genuine compliance management systems to prevent misconduct.[52] The intermediate range of the spectrum is populated by various "*mixed regimes*," under which corporations are held liable for employee misconduct, but may benefit from penalty mitigation or evidentiary privileges if engaged in internal enforcement activities.[53] All such regimes, although diverse in structure, share a similar objective that boils down to encouraging corporate proactive compliance at the lowest enforcement costs.

In a comparative legal analysis conducted in Chapter 5, I explored two contradicting tendencies followed on both sides of the Atlantic concerning the shape of corporate liability regimes. First, the analysis reveals that U.S. Federal enforcement policies against corporate misconduct have gone through a radical reform, replacing "strict" corporate liability regimes with softer "duty-based" ones. This reform was carried out through various channels and applied in both civil and criminal areas of corporate liability.[54] Consequently, current U.S. Federal enforcement policies against corporate misconduct are more willing to accept corporate internal enforcement efforts, such as the adoption of genuine compliance management systems, as a mitigating factor of – and sometimes even as a shield from – corporate liability.[55] First signs of similar developments have been identified in other legal systems (British, Canadian, and Australian legal systems). However, a glance at the EU legal system reveals that this system has undergone a completely reverse transformation.[56] While in the past EU authorities explicitly recognized corporations' internal enforcement efforts as a liability-mitigating factor, this view has changed in a series of recent decisions in which both the European Commission and the European Court of Justice (ECJ) refused to recognize the impact of corporate internal enforcement efforts on corporate liability once a violation was detected.[57] The multiplicity of corporate liability structures and the inconsistency of approaches followed in different legal systems emphasize the complexity of this field.

Law and economics thinkers have identified two economic functions of corporate liability regimes in inducing corporate proactive compliance:

---

51 See Chapter 5, Section 5.3.1.
52 See Chapter 5, Sections 5.4 and 5.6.
53 See Chapter 5, Sections 5.5 and 5.7.
54 See Chapter 5, Sections 5.4–5.7.
55 See *ibid.*
56 See Chapter 5, Section 5.8.
57 See *ibid.*

Table 9.1 A comparative welfare evaluation of major corporate liability regimes

Economic function of corporate liability	Induced corporate activity	Incentives provided to corporations under the following regimes			
		Strict liability	Negligence	Adjusted strict liability	Composite regime
Internalization	Compliance	Yes	No	Yes	Yes
Self-enforcement	*Ex-ante* self-policing	Yes	No	Yes	No
	Ex-post self-policing	No	No	Yes	No
	Self-reporting	No	Yes	No	Yes

(i) inducing corporations to internalize all social ramifications of their activity; (ii) inducing corporations to proactively prevent, deter, and report their employee misconduct. Based on these goals, I evaluated in Chapter 6 all four major structures of corporate liability regimes according to their aptitude to fulfill the economic functions mentioned above that have been discussed so far in the scholarly polemic, namely, strict liability, negligence, adjusted strict liability, and composite regimes.[58] The analysis reveals that none of these liability regimes is expected to fulfill the twin economic functions of corporate liability regimes in most settings. The conclusions of the analysis are summarized in Table 9.1.

Based on the conclusions drawn from the extensive analysis of existing corporate liability regimes, in Chapter 6 I develop the "Compound Corporate Liability Regime" which comprises a workable framework that fulfills both economic functions of the corporate liability regimes in most settings.[59] In a nutshell, the proposed framework is a two-tier strict liability regime that depends on sanction mitigation when corporations step forward. Under the compound regime, when corporations self-report their employees' misconduct, the applied sanction is reduced by the variable enforcement costs that enforcement authorities now do not need to incur.[60] In this way, the compound regime aligns both social interests and

58 For the definition and structure of each liability regime see Chapter 6, Section 6.3.

59 See Chapter 6, Section 6.4.

60 See *ibid.*

the interests of corporate regulatees. Specifically, it induces corporations to internalize the total social costs of their conduct, and at the same time, to self-police and report misconduct whenever such actions are socially desirable.

The compound regime sustains the promises of the regulatory mixed regimes discussed in Chapter 4, while overcoming their pitfalls. This regime follows an inclusive approach and tailors enforcement reactions to various regulatees which have different motivations. In addition, it establishes a targeted enforcement system in which greater enforcement expenditures are devoted to corporations that are insufficiently motivated to engage in internal enforcement activities. Yet, unlike the mixed corporate liability regimes proposed in the existing literature, it does not require courts and enforcement authorities to evaluate the effectiveness and trustworthiness of self-policing actions taken by corporations. Instead, it relies on verifiable action and self-reporting, and therefore is less, if at all, vulnerable to the pitfalls of corporate opportunistic behavior and information asymmetry. Moreover, the compound regime provides a clear, transparent policy of liability mitigation which leaves minimal discretion for enforcement authorities to choose from when reacting to particular cases. Therefore, the compound regime minimizes the risk of arbitrariness discussed in Chapter 4.[61]

9.4 TOWARD AN OPTIMAL REGULATORY MONITORING REGIME

In many regulatory areas enforcement authorities employ targeted monitoring systems in which regulatory monitoring efforts are differentiated among different types of regulatees.[62] Rather than monitoring regulatees randomly, enforcement authorities maximize the productivity of enforcement expenditures by classifying regulatees into different groups where each group is exposed to a specifically tailored level of regulatory scrutiny.[63] These monitoring regimes correspond with the regulatory mixed regimes discussed in Chapter 4. Targeted monitoring systems, rather than apply one of the "stand-alone" deterrence-based or cooperative enforcement approaches, employ different monitoring styles towards different

---

[61] See Chapter 4, Section 4.5.2.
[62] See Chapter 8, Section 8.2.
[63] See *ibid.*

regulatees. While some regulatees are closely scrutinized, others are subject to reduced regulatory monitoring.

The law and economics scholarly literature widely supports the utilization of targeted monitoring systems. The most influential study in this field, Harrington (1988), shows that monitoring frameworks that prioritize their scrutiny targets may produce a higher level of compliance compared to that produced by traditional, non-targeted monitoring systems.[64] Other scholars, seeking to enhance the social gains of targeted enforcement systems, were enthusiastic in extending Harrington's model, creating sophisticated targeted enforcement structures.[65] However, few have paused to consider the criteria based on which enforcement authorities should classify regulatees into differently monitored groups. In Chapter 8, I analyzed a handful of potential criteria discussed in the scholarly literature, namely regulatee "violation records," the application of "compliance management systems," and voluntary "self-reporting."[66] A close look at these criteria revealed substantial doubts regarding their aptitude to facilitate an efficient targeted monitoring system.[67] Accordingly, I address this gap in the literature in Part III of this book by developing the "Third-Party-Based Targeted Monitoring (TPTM) system" which uses *corporate monitors* as a signaling mechanism in facilitating the establishment of an efficient targeted monitoring system.[68]

Corporate monitors have for a long time played an important role in the battle against law-breaking.[69] Traditionally, monitors' surveillance was imposed as part of the sanction against violators.[70] Recent developments in U.S. Federal enforcement policies have expanded the use of corporate monitors by using them as part of Deferred Prosecution Agreements (DPAs) and Non-Prosecution Agreements (NPAs) which have served as a substitute for traditional criminal proceedings.[71] Contemporary U.S. policies allow prosecutors to enter into DPAs and NPAs and agree to the deferred prosecution of culpable corporations, in return for these corporations' obligation to undertake dictated structural reforms and to comply with certain standards of behavior.[72] Many such agreements

---

[64] See Harrington, "Enforcement Leverage when Penalties are Restricted," 29–53.

[65] See Chapter 8, Section 8.2.

[66] See *ibid.*

[67] See *ibid.*

[68] See Chapter 8, Section 8.3.

[69] See Chapter 7, Section 7.2.

[70] See Chapter 7, Section 7.4.

[71] See Chapter 7, Section 7.3.

[72] See *ibid.*

require corporations to appoint independent corporate monitors to ensure corporate compliance with their terms. The newly emerged DPA and NPA policies, as well as the role of corporate monitors in such agreements, are analyzed in Chapter 7. Particular attention is paid to the criticism of these emerging DPA and NPA policies which have started to appear in the more recent scholarly literature, as well as the ongoing policy developments that have attempted to address these points of criticism.[73] The analysis shows that corporate monitors play an invaluable role in inducing corporate proactive compliance.[74] In this book, I propose that the role of corporate monitors should be expanded even further. Corporate monitors may serve as policy instruments, facilitating an efficient targeted monitoring system.

Acknowledging the potential utilization of corporate monitors as an enforcement instrument, in Chapter 8 I develop the TPTM system. The proposed system follows the idea of delegating some enforcement authorities' monitoring tasks to independent corporate monitoring firms (CMs) that can be trusted as corporate "watchdogs."[75] The delegation of monitoring powers is done through a voluntary program that sustains corporate regulatees' expected liability, but changes the default combination of the *probability of detection* and *fines* imposed on participating corporations.[76] Under the proposed system, corporations are given the opportunity to opt into the voluntary program, in which they are exposed to less certain but more severe liability threats in return for a reputational asset that is conferred upon them as program participants.[77]

The analysis considers that corporations differ in their responsiveness to compliance incentives produced by enforcement policies – be it because of differences in the levels of their subjective normative commitment, or due to objective differences, such as variations in the cost and effectiveness of corporate self-policing activities.[78] Hence, under enforcement policies that present similar liability threats to all corporate regulatees, some regulatees find it desirable to engage in self-policing while others do not.[79] Therefore, the introduction of the TPTM system produces a threefold social gain:[80] (i) compared to other regulatory enforcement systems the TPTM system increases the private gain resulting from self-policing,

---

73 See Chapter 7, Sections 7.5–7.6.
74 See Chapter 7, Section 7.4.
75 See Chapter 8, Section 8.3.1.
76 See *ibid.*
77 See Chapter 8, Section 8.3.2.
78 See Chapter 8, Section 8.2.
79 See *ibid.*
80 See Chapter 8, Section 8.3.3.

and thereby enhances corporate motivation to engage in socially beneficial self-policing; (ii) it economizes the cost of regulatory monitoring by facilitating a targeted monitoring system that is workable; and (iii) it compels corporations (or their clients) to bear the true cost of regulatory monitoring embedded in their activity, thereby facilitating more efficient production and consumption decisions.[81]

The TPTM system is shown to sustain the virtues of the regulatory mixed regimes discussed in Chapter 4, while overcoming their pitfalls.[82] First, the TPTM system follows an *inclusive* approach in which monitoring efforts are specifically tailored to address the different motivations of the regulatees.[83] Second, the TPTM system allows enforcement authorities to efficiently *target* regulatory subjects.[84] And third, the TPTM system classifies regulatees into differently monitored groups based on a more sound criterion which depends upon the regulatees' engagement in self-policing activities. Such a criterion is verifiable and transparent, and thereby alleviates *information asymmetry* and *arbitrariness* concerns.[85]

9.5 A COMPREHENSIVE REGULATORY ENFORCEMENT POLICY

Based on the findings above, it is now possible to present a comprehensive structure of an enforcement policy designed to efficiently induce corporate proactive compliance. The proposed policy bundles the TPTM system with the compound corporate liability regime, and may be considered a composite framework that encompasses primarily two components: a *regulatory monitoring component* and a *corporate liability component*.

(i) ***Regulatory monitoring component*** – The proposed enforcement policy introduces a voluntary program in which corporations that want to opt into the program are required to hire CMs to implement their self-policing activities. In return, these corporations not only obtain a *reduction of regulatory scrutiny*, but also earn a *program label* as well. Such a label can serve as an important reputational asset for corporations since it shows corporate customers, potential trading partners, investors, and other stakeholders that the incumbent

---

81 See *ibid.*
82 See *ibid.*
83 See *ibid.*
84 See *ibid.*
85 See *ibid.*

corporation is genuinely committed to proactive compliance. In order to prevent the program from resulting in under-deterrence, corporations' participation in the voluntary program implies that corporate regulatees are subject to higher penalties set at a level that compensates for the reduction in corporate expected liability due to reduced scrutiny.

(ii) ***Corporate liability component*** – When corporations self-report their employees' misconduct, the applied sanction is reduced by the variable enforcement costs that enforcement authorities now do not need to incur. The proposed regime is centered upon an idiosyncratic mitigation of the default sanction. First, the mitigation of the sanction is triggered by verifiable actions which are the corporations' self-reports of any misconduct or violations. Second, the amount of the sanction mitigation is determined by the social gain generated by these self-enforcement actions, *i.e.*, the reduction in the variable enforcement costs resulting from the self-reporting measures.

The proposed enforcement policy is a comprehensive framework, designed to encourage corporate proactive compliance by tailoring enforcement responses to regulatees that have different motivations. The proposed framework departs from the common feature of most regulatory mixed regimes proposed thus far in the scholarly literature, in which the probability of detection and applicable sanctions are treated as a single choice. Instead, it acknowledges that each phase of the enforcement process – the initial phase of general regulatory monitoring and the final stage in which specific sanctions are imposed – must be treated differently depending on the particular challenges that arise in each phase.

The structure of the proposed policy sustains the advantages of other recognized regulatory mixed regimes, while overcoming their flaws. First, *inclusiveness* – the proposed policy follows an inclusive approach by acknowledging the heterogeneity of regulatees, including their different motivations, and therefore allows for variations in both the probability of detection and the sanctions imposed. Once regulatory responses are well adjusted, all types of regulatees are adequately addressed by the enforcement system and are thereby motivated to act in a socially desirable manner. Second, *targeting attitudes* – the proposed policy allocates enforcement expenditures (both with respect to general monitoring and particular prosecution and sanctioning) in a targeted manner, such that cooperative regulatees, who are motivated to pursue proactive compliance are subject to less stringent enforcement responses than recalcitrant, insufficiently motivated ones. Third, *information asymmetry* – the variations of regulatory scrutiny as well as of the applicable sanctions under the proposed policy are based on verifiable criteria. The proposed framework does not require courts or enforcement authorities to evaluate the authenticity of regulatees' social responsibilities or of their internal enforcement efforts. Instead, it provides corporations with the incentive to reveal their own type by verifiable signals, namely, self-reporting and the appointment of CMs. Fourth, *arbitrariness* – the proposed policy uses transparent, verifiable, and consistent criteria for the variation of applicable regulatory scrutiny and sanctions, thereby addressing concerns regarding the arbitrariness of regulatory enforcement.

The proposed regulatory enforcement policy presents a generic, comprehensive framework that may be applied – subject to context-dependent adjustments – in various regulatory areas, such as environmental, anti-bribery and corruption, tax, and antitrust regulations. It is not necessary that this policy be applied in its entirety. In fact, each of the components of the proposed policy – the compound corporate liability regime and the TPTM system – may be independently applicable in particular contexts. It is important to note that as with all other theoretical frameworks of enforcement policies, the application of the proposed policy requires an empirical investigation of policy components such as "the total social cost of misconduct" and "the probability of detection."[86] In that respect, the proposed policy does not pose exceptional information requirements on policymakers.

Additionally, each of the components of the proposed policy may have broader policy implications in related enforcement contexts. For instance, the bedrocks of the compound corporate liability regime may be used in determining the size of penalty mitigation in *plea bargaining* contexts, considering the reduction in variable enforcement costs resulting from the plea bargaining. Similarly, one can rely on the incentive scheme provided by the compound regime to induce *remediation*, *restitution*, or *restoration* of harm caused by wrongdoers, through liability mitigation that mirrors the reduction in public remediation, restitution, or restoration costs. Moreover, the compound regime may provide a law and economics theoretical basis for the analysis of competition *leniency* policies and be used in evaluating the immunity or the sanction mitigation to be awarded to

[86] Estimating the policy components such as the "total social cost of misconduct" and the "probability of detection" are undertaken in actuality as part of the policymaking process. See, for instance, Centre for European Policy Studies (CEPS), Erasmus University Rotterdam (EUR), Luiss Guido Carli (LUISS), *Final Report: Making Antitrust Damages Actions More Effective in the EU: Welfare Impact and Potential Scenarios*, Brussels, Rome, Rotterdam: European Commission [2007].

self-reporting corporations. In all these contexts it seems socially desirable to link the social impact of proactive compliance actions taken by culpable regulatees to their liability exposure. Similarly, the framework of the TPTM system may be used for the analysis of voluntary legal programs seeking to induce regulatees to improve their regulatory performance beyond regulatory requirements in return for a reputation asset.[87]

[87] See, for instance, the "EU Eco-Management and Audit Scheme (EMAS)" which is a voluntary program administered by the European Commission, DG Environment, to help corporations evaluate, report, and improve their environmental performance beyond regulatory compliance. As a reward for voluntary participation in EMAS, corporations are entitled to use the "EMAS logo." See http://ec.europa.eu/environment/emas/about/index_en.htm

Bibliography

Aguilar, Melissa. "Dpa-Npa Tally Marks Decade's Second Highest." *Compliance Week* (January 4, 2011).

Ahmed, Parvez, John Gardella, and Sudhir Nanda. "Wealth Effect of Drug Withdrawals on Firms and Their Competitors." *Financial Management* 31, No. 3 (2002): 21–41.

Akhigbe, Aigbe, Ronald Kudla, and Jeff Madura. "Why Are Some Corporate Earnings Restatements More Damaging?" *Applied Financial Economics* 15, No. 5 (2005): 327–336.

Aleskerov, Fuad, Denis Bouyssou, and Bernard Monjardet. *Utility Maximization, Choice and Preference*. 2nd Edition. Berlin, Heidelberg, New York: Springer, 2007.

Allingham, Michael. *Rational Choice*. New York: St. Martin's Press Inc., 1999.

Amabile, Teresa M., William Dejong, and Mark R. Lepper. "Effects of Externally Imposed Deadlines on Subsequent Intrinsic Motivation." *Journal of Personality and Social Psychology* 34, No. 1 (1976): 92–98.

Aoki, Kazumasu, Lee Axelrad, and Robert A. Kagan. "Industrial Effluent Control in The United States and Japan." In *Regulatory Encounters*, edited by Robert A. Kagan and Lee Axelrad, 64–95. Berkeley, Los Angeles, London: University of California Press, 2000.

Archer, Margaret S. and Jonathan Q. Tritter. *Rational Choice Theory: Resisting Colonization*. New York: Routledge, 2001.

Arlen, Jennifer. "The Potentially Perverse Effects of Corporate Criminal Liability." *Journal of Legal Studies* 23, No. 2 (1994): 833–867.

Arlen, Jennifer. "Removing Prosecutors from the Boardroom: Limiting Prosecutorial Discretion to Impose Structural Reforms." In *Prosecutors in the Board Room: Using Criminal Law to Regulate Corporate Conduct*, edited by Anthony S. Barkow and Rachel E. Barkow, 62–86. New York: New York University Press, 2011.

Arlen, Jennifer and Reinier Kraakman. "Controlling Corporate Misconduct: An Analysis of Corporate Liability Regimes." *NYU Law Review* 72, No. 4 (1997): 687–779.

Armour, John, Henry Hansmann, and Reinier Kraakman. "Agency Problems and Legal Strategies." In *The Anatomy of Corporate Law: A*

Comparative and Functional Approach, edited by Reinier Kraakman, John Armour, Paul Davies, Luca Enriques, Henry Hansmann, Gerard Hertig, Klaus Hopt, Hideki Kanda and Edward Rock, 35–53. New York: Oxford University Press, 2009a.

Armour, John, Henry Hansmann, and Reinier Kraakman. "Agency Problems, Legal Strategies, and Enforcement." In *The Anatomy of Corporate Law: A Comparative and Functional Approach*, edited by Reinier Kraakman, John Armour, Paul Davies, Luca Enriques, Henry Hansmann, Gerard Hertig, Klaus Hopt, Hideki Kanda, and Edward Rock, 21–32. New York: Oxford University Press, 2009b.

Armstrong, Andrew. "Drug Courts and the De Facto Legalization of Drug Use for Participants in Residential Treatment Facilities." *The Journal of Criminal Law & Criminology* 94, No. 1 (2003): 133–168.

Atiyah, Patrick S. *Vicarious Liability in the Law of Tort*. London: Butterworths, 1967.

Australian Competition and Consumer Commission (ACCC). *Corporate Trade Practices Compliance Programs*, 2005. Available at: http://www.accc.gov.au.

Avio, Kenneth L. "Capital Punishment in Canada: A Time-Series Analysis of the Deterrent Hypothesis." *The Canadian Journal of Economics* 12, No. 4 (1979): 647–676.

Aviram, Amitai. "In Defense of Imperfect Compliance Programs." *FSU Law Review* 32 (2005): 763–780.

Axelrod, Robert. "Effective Choice in the Prisoner's Dilemma." *The Journal of Conflict Resolution* 24, No. 1 (1980): 3–25.

Axelrod, Robert. "More Effective Choice in the Prisoner's Dilemma." *The Journal of Conflict Resolution* 24, No. 3 (1980): 379–403.

Axelrod, Robert. "The Emergence of Cooperation Among Egoists." *The American Political Science Review* 75, No. 2 (1981): 306–318.

Axelrod, Robert. *The Evolution of Cooperation*. New York: Basic Books, 1984.

Baggs, James, Barbara Silverstein, and Michael Foley. "Workplace Health and Safety Regulations: Impact of Enforcement and Consultation on Workers' Compensation Claims Rates in Washington State." *American Journal of Industrial Medicine* 43, No. 5 (2003): 483–494.

Balch, Robert W. "Deferred Prosecution: The Juvenilization of the Criminal Justice System." *Federal Probation* 38 (1974): 46–50.

Baldwin, Robert and Martin Cave. *Understanding Regulation: Theory, Strategy, and Practice*. New York: Oxford University Press, 1999.

Bandura, Albert. *Principles of Behavior Modification*. New York: Holt, Rinehart and Winston, 1969.

Bardach, Eugene and Robert A. Kagan. *Going By The Book: The Problem of Regulatory Unreasonableness*. Philadelphia, PA: Temple University Press, 1982.

Bartley, Robert L. "Andersen: A Pyrrhic Victory." *The Wall Street Journal* (June 24, 2002): A17.

Baylson, Michael. "Getting the Demons into Heaven: A Good Corporate Compliance Program." *Corporate Conduct Quarterly* 2 (1992): 33–34.

Bazerman, Max H. and Don A. Moore. *Judgment in Managerial Decision Making*, 7th Edition. Hoboken, NJ: John Wiley & Sons, Inc., 2008.

Beccaria, Cesare. *On Crime And Punishment, and Other Writings*. Translated by Richard Davies, edited by Richard Bellamy, 1995 Edition. Cambridge: Cambridge University Press, 1767.

Becker, Gary S. "Crime And Punishment: An Economic Approach." *The Journal of Political Economy* 76, No. 2 (1968): 169–217.

Becker, Gary S. *The Economic Approach to Human Behavior*. Chicago, IL: University of Chicago Press, 1978.

Becker, Gary S. "Make Punishment Fit the Corporate Crime." *Business Week* (March 13, 1989): 22–30.

Becker, Gary S. "Nobel Lecture: The Economic Way of Looking at Behavior." *The Journal of Political Economy* 101, No. 3 (June, 1993): 385–409.

Becker, Gary S. and George J. Stigler. "Law Enforcement, Malfeasance, and Compensation of Enforcers." *The Journal of Legal Studies* 3, No. 1 (1974): 1–18.

Bentham, Jeremy. *An Introduction to the Principles of Morals and Legislation*, 1973 Edition. Garden City, NY: Anchor Books, 1789.

Bernstein, Lisa. "Opting Out of the Legal System: Extralegal Contractual Relations in the Diamond Industry." *Journal of Legal Studies* 21, No. 1 (1992): 115–157.

Bernstein, Lisa. "Private Commercial Law in the Cotton Industry: Creating Cooperation Through Rules, Norms, and Institutions." *Michigan Law Review* 99, No. 7 (2001): 1724–1790.

Bierschbach, Richard A. and Alex Stein. "Overenforcement." *The Georgetown Law Journal* 93, No. 6 (2005): 1743–1781.

Bittlingmayer, George. "The Market for Corporate Control (Including Takeovers)." In *Encyclopedia of Law and Economics*, edited by Boudewijn Bouckaert and Gerrit De Geest. Vol. 5640, 725–771. Available at: http://encyclo.findlaw.com/index.html: Edward Elgar and The University of Ghent, 1999.

Black, Julia. "Managing Discretion." *ARLC Conference Papers. Penalties: Policy, Principles and Practice in Government Regulation*. Available at: http://w.lse.ac.uk/collections/law/staff%20publications%20full%20text/black/alrc%20managing%20discretion.pdf (2001).

Blank Rome LLP. "Keeping a Watchful Eye: Corporate Deferred Prosecution Agreements and the Selection of Corporate Monitors." *Mondaq Business Briefing* (July 3, 2008).

Bloch, Robert E. "Compliance Programs and Criminal Antitrust Litigation: A Prosecutor's Perspective." *Antitrust Law Journal* 57 (1988): 223–232.

Block, Michael K. "Optimal Penalties, Criminal Law and the Control of Corporate Behavior." *Boston University Law Review* 71 (1991): 395–419.

Blumenthal, Marsha, Charles Christian, and Joel Slemrod. "The Determinants of Income Tax Compliance: Evidence From a Controlled Experiment in Minnesota." *National Bureau of Economic Research Working Papers No. 6575* (1998): 1–39.

Blumstein, Alfred, Jacqueline Cohen, and Daniel Nagin. *Deterrence and Incapacitation: Estimating the Effects of Criminal Sanctions on Crime Rates*. Washington DC: National Academy of Sciences, 1978.

Boatright, John R. "Reluctant Guardians: The Moral Responsibility of Gatekeepers." *Business Ethics Quarterly* 17, No. 4 (2007): 613–632.

Boozang, Kathleen M. and Simone Handler-Hutchinson. "'Monitoring' Corporate Corruption: DOJ's Use of Deferred Prosecution Agreements in Health Care." *American Journal of Law & Medicine* 35, No. 1 (2009): 89–124.

Bose, Pinaki. "Regulatory Errors, Optimal Fines and the Level of Compliance." *Journal of Public Economics* 56, No. 3 (1995): 475–484.

Bowles, Roger, Michael Faure, and Nuno Garoupa. "The Scope of Criminal Law and Criminal Sanctions: An Economic View and Policy Implications." *Journal of Law And Society* 35, No. 3 (2008): 389–416.

Bowles, Roger and Nuno Garoupa. "Casual Police Corruption and the Economics of Crime." *International Review of Law and Economics* 17, No. 1 (1997): 75–87.

Braithwaite, John. "Enforced Self-Regulation: A New Strategy For Corporate Crime Control." *Michigan Law Review* 80, No. 7 (1982): 1466–1507.

Braithwaite, John. *To Punish or Persuade: Enforcement of Coal Mine Safety*. Albany, NY: State University of New York Press, 1985.

Braithwaite, John. *Restorative Justice & Responsive Regulation*. Studies in Crime and Public Policy. New York: Oxford University Press, 2002.

Braithwaite, John and Ian Ayres. *Responsive Regulation: Transcending the Deregulation Debate*. New York: Oxford University Press, 1992.

Braithwaite, Valerie and John Braithwaite. "An Evolving Compliance Model For Tax Enforcement." In *Crimes of Privilege*, edited by N. Shover and J. P. Wright. Oxford: Oxford University Press, 2001.

Braithwaite, John and Toni Makkai. "Trust And Compliance." *Policing and Society* 4, No. 1 (1994): 1–12.

Brehm, Sharon S. and Jack Williams Brehm. *Psychological Reactance: A Theory of Freedom and Control*. New York: Academic Press, 1981.

Brickey, Kathleen F. "Corporate Criminal Accountability: A Brief History and an Observation." *Washington University Law Quarterly* 60, No. 2 (1982): 393–423.

Burns, Greg. "Corporations Avoid Criminal Cases", *Chicago Tribunal* (March 20, 2005): 5.

Burrows, Melinda. "The Seven Elements of an Effective Compliance and Ethics Program." *The Practical Lawyer* February (2006): 21–23.

Calabresi, Guido. *The Costs of Accidents: A Legal and Economic Analysis*. New Haven, CT: Yale University Press, 1970.

Camerer, Colin and Martin Weber. "Recent Developments in Modeling Preferences: Uncertainty and Ambiguity." *Journal of Risk and Uncertainty* 5, No. 4 (1992): 325–370.

Canada Competition Bureau. *Corporate Compliance Programs*, 2008.

Carr-Hill, Roy A. and Nicholas H. Stern. "An Econometric Model of the Supply and Control of Recorded Offences in England and Wales." *Journal of Public Economics* 2, No. 4 (1973): 289–318.

Casper, Jonathan D., Tom R. Tyler, and Bonnie Fisher. "Procedural Justice in Felony Cases." *Law & Society Review* 22, No. 3 (1988): 483–508.

Centre For European Policy Studies (CEPS), Erasmus University Rotterdam (EUR), Luiss Guido Carli (LUISS). *Final Report: Making Antitrust Damages Actions More Effective in the EU: Welfare Impact and Potential Scenarios*. Brussels, Rome, Rotterdam: European Commission (December 21, 2007).

Chang, Juin-Jen, Ching-Chong Lai, and C. C. Yang. "Casual Police Corruption and the Economics of Crime: Further Results." *International Review of Law and Economics* 20, No. 1 (2000): 35–51.

Chayes, Abram and Antonia H. Chayes. "On Compliance." *International Organization* 47, No. 2 (1993): 175–205.

Chu, Cyrus C. Y. and Yingyi Qian. "Vicarious Liability Under a Negligence Rule." *International Review of Law and Economics* 15, No. 3 (1995): 305–322.

Ciancio, Nick. *The Seven Pillars of an Effective Ethics and Compliance Program* 2007. Available at: http://ethicsline.com/resources/news-articles/

Clark, Nolan E. "No Soul to Damn: No Body to Kick: An Unscandalized Inquiry into the Problem of Corporate Punishment." *Michigan Law Review* 79, No. 3 (1981): 386–459.

Clark, Nolan E. "Understanding Enron: It's About the Gatekeepers, Stupid." *The Business Lawyer* 57 (August 2002): 1403–1420.

Clark, Nolan E. "Deferred Prosecution: Has It Gone Too Far?" *The National Law Journal* (July 25, 2005): 13.

Clark, Nolan E. *Gatekeepers: The Professions and Corporate Governance*. New York: Oxford University Press, 2006.

Clark, Nolan E. "Corporate Sentencing Guidelines: Drafting History." Chapter 2 in *Compliance Programs and the Corporate Sentencing Guidelines: Preventing Criminal and Civil Liability*, edited by Jeffrey M. Kaplan and Joseph E. Murphy. Revised Edition, St. Paul, MN: Thomson/West, 2009.

Coffee, John C. Jr. "The Attorney as Gatekeeper: An Agenda For the SEC." *Columbia Law Review* 103 (2003): 1293–1316.

Colvin, Eric. "Corporate Personality and Criminal Liability." *Criminal Law Forum* 6, No. 1 (1995): 1–44.

Commission of the European Communities. *Green Paper – Damages Actions For Breach of the EC Antitrust Rules*. Brussels: Commission of the European Communities (December 19, 2005).

Cook, Philip J. "Research in Criminal Deterrence: Laying the Groundwork for the Second Decade." *Crime and Justice* 2 (1980): 211–268.

Cooter, Robert D. "Prices and Sanctions." *Columbia Law Review* 84 (1984): 1523–1560.

Cooter, Robert D. "Punitive Damages for Deterrence: When and How Much." *Alabama Law Review* 40 (1988): 1143–1196.

Cooter, Robert and Thomas Ulen. *Law And Economics*. The Addison-Wesley Series in Economics. 5th Edition. Boston: Pearson Addison Wesley, 2007.

Corona, Carlos and Ramandeep S. Randhawa. "The Value of Confession: Admitting Mistakes to Build Reputation." *Working Paper*. Available at: SSRN: http://ssrn.com/abstract=1702444 (2010).

Corporate Crime Reporter. *Crime Without Conviction: The Rise of Deferred and Non Prosecution Agreements*. Available at: http://www.corporatecrimereporter.com/deferredreport.htm (December 28, 2005).

Creighton, Virginia Morton. "Colorado's Environmental Audit Privilege Statute: Striking the Appropriate Balance." *University of Colorado Law Review* 67 (1996): 443–476.

Crofts, Lewis. "EC's Lowe Moots Due-Process Improvements, But Firms' Compliance Rewards Not on Agenda." *MLex Market Intelligence* (November 17, 2009).

Crofts, Lewis. "EC's Lowe Still to be Convinced of Effective Compliance Programmes." *MLex Market Intelligence* (January 11, 2010).

Croley, Steven. "Vicarious Liability in Tort: On the Sources and Limits of

Employee Reasonableness." *Southern California Law Review* 69 (1995): 1705–1738.

Curley, Shawn P., Frank J. Yates, and Richard A. Abrams. "Psychological Sources of Ambiguity Avoidance." *Organizational Behavior and Human Decision Processes* 38, No. 2 (1986): 230–256.

Dahlström, K., C. Howes, P. Leinster, and J. Skea. "Environmental Management Systems and Company Performance: Assessing the Case for Extending Risk-Based Regulation." *European Environment* 13 (2003): 187–203.

Dana, David A. "The Perverse Incentives of Environmental Audit Immunity." *Iowa Law Review* 81 (1996): 969–1006.

Davis, Kenneth C. *Discretionary Justice: A Preliminary Inquiry*. Baton Rouge, LA: Louisiana State University Press, 1969.

Deci, Edward L. "Effects of Externally Mediated Rewards on Intrinsic Motivation." *Journal of Personality and Social Psychology* 18 (1971): 105–115.

Deferred Prosecution Agreement with AGA Medical. Available at: http://www.law.virginia.edu/pdf/faculty/garrett/agamedical.pdf (June 3, 2008).

Deferred Prosecution Agreement with America Online, Inc. (AOL). Available at: http://www.corporatecrimereporter.com/documents/aol.pdf (2004).

Deferred Prosecution Agreement with Bristol-Myers Squibb. Available at: http://lib.law.virginia.edu/Garrett/prosecution_agreements/pdf/bristol-meyers.pdf (June 13, 2005).

Deferred Prosecution Agreement with KPMG. Available at: http://www.justice.gov/usao/nys/pressreleases/August05/kpmgdpagmt.pdf (August 26, 2005)

Deferred Prosecution Agreement with Monsanto Company. Available at: http://www.corporatecrimereporter.com/documents/monsantoagreement.pdf (January 6, 2005).

Deferred Prosecution Agreement with Willbros Group Inc. Available at: http://www.techagreements.com/agreement-preview.aspx?num=585046&title=willbros%20group%20-%20deferred%20prosecution%20agreement (May 14, 2008).

Demott, Deborah A. "The Discrete Roles of General Counsel." *Fordham Law Review* 74 (2005): 955–981.

Department of Health and Human Services (HHS), Office of Inspector General (OIG). "Publication of the OIG Compliance Program Guidance for Clinical Laboratories." *Fed. Reg.* 63, No. 163 (1998a): 45076–45087.

Department of Health and Human Services (HHS), Office of Inspector

General (OIG). "Publication of the OIG Compliance Program Guidance for Hospitals." *Fed. Reg.* 63, No. 35 (1998b): 8987–8998.

Department of Health and Human Services (HHS), Office of Inspector General (OIG). "Publication of the OIG Compliance Program Guidance for Third-Party Medical Billing Companies." *Fed. Reg.* 63, No. 243 (1998c): 70138–70152.

Department of Justice. *Press Release, U.S. Department of Justice and SEC Enter $290 Million Settlement with Salomon Brothers*. Available at: http://www.usdoj.gov/atr/public/press_releases/1992/211182.htm (May 20, 1992a).

Department of Justice. *Press Release: Department of Justice and SEC Enter $290 Million Settlement with Salomon Brothers in Treasury Securities Case*. Available at: http://www.justice.gov/atr/public/press_releases/1992/211182.htm (May 20, 1992b).

Department of Justice. *Press Release* No. 08-417, Willbros Group Inc. Enters Deferred Prosecution Agreement and Agrees to Pay €22 Million Penalty for FCPA Violations. Available at: http://www.foley.com/files/willsbrosdojrelease.pdf (May 14, 2008).

Department of Justice. *Press Release* No. 08-491, AGA Medical Corporation Agrees to Pay $2 Million Penalty and Enter Deferred Prosecution Agreement for FCPA Violations. Available at: http://www.justice.gov/opa/pr/2008/June/08-crm-491.html (June 3, 2008).

Department of Justice. *Tenaris S.A. Agrees to Pay $3.5 Million Criminal Penalty to Resolve Violations of the Foreign Corrupt Practices Act*. Available at: http://www.justice.gov/opa/pr/2011/May/11-crm-629.html (May 17, 2011).

Desai, Kiran and Mayer Brown. "Compliance." *The European Antitrust Review* (2010):15–21.

Downs, George W. "Reputation, Compliance, and International Law." *The Journal of Legal Studies* 31, No. S1 (2002): S95–S114.

Downs, George W., David M. Rocke, and Peter N. Barsoom. "Is the Good News about Compliance Good News about Cooperation?" *International Organization* 50, No. 3 (1996): 379–406.

Easton, David. "The Perception of Authority and Political Change." In *Authority*, edited by Carl J. Friedrich. Cambridge, MA: Harvard University Press, 1958.

Eckert, Heather. "Inspections, Warnings, and Compliance: The Case of Petroleum Storage Regulation." *Journal of Environmental Economics and Management* 47, No. 2 (2004): 232–259.

Ecorys. "Study on Incentives Driving Improvement of Environmental Performance of Companies." Available at: http://ec.europa.eu/environment/pubs/pdf/Incentives_Ecorys.pdf (2012).

Edgerton, Henry W. "Corporate Criminal Responsibility." *The Yale Law Journal* 36, No. 6 (1927): 827–844.

Eger, Thomas and Peter Weise. "Limits to the Private Enforcement of Antitrust Law." *German Working Papers in Law and Economics* 2007, No. 2 (2007): 1–14.

Ehrlich, Isaac. "Participation in Illegitimate Activities: A Theoretical and Empirical Investigation." *The Journal of Political Economy* 81, No. 3 (1973): 521–565.

Ehrlich, Isaac. "The Deterrent Effect of Capital Punishment: A Question of Life and Death." *The American Economic Review* 65, No. 3 (1975): 397–417.

Ehrlich, Isaac. "Crime, Punishment, and the Market for Offenses." *The Journal of Economic Perspectives* 10, No. 1 (1996): 43–67.

Ehrlich, Isaac and Mark Randall. "Fear of Deterrence: A Critical Evaluation of the 'Report of the Panel on Research on Deterrent and Incapacitative Effects'." *The Journal of Legal Studies* 6, No. 2 (1977): 293–316.

Elkins, James R. "Corporations and the Criminal Law: An Uneasy Alliance." *Kentucky Law Journal* 65, No. 1 (1977): 73–129.

Ellickson, Robert C. "A Hypothesis of Wealth-Maximizing Norms: Evidence from the Whaling Industry." *Journal of Law, Economics and Organization* 5, No. 1 (1989): 83–97.

Emmett, Ross B., ed. *The Elgar Companion to the Chicago School of Economics*. Cheltenham U.K. & Northampton, MA: Edward Elgar Publishing Limited, 2010.

Environmental Protection Agency (EPA). *The Exercise of Investigating Discretion*. Available at: http://www.epa.gov/enforcement/criminal/documents/policies/exercise.pdf (January 12, 1994).

Environmental Protection Agency (EPA). "Incentives for Self Policing: Discovery, Disclosure, Correction, and Prevention of Violations." *Fed. Reg.* 60 (1995): 66706–66712.

Environmental Protection Agency (EPA). "Calculation of the Economic Benefit of Noncompliance in EPA's Civil Penalty Enforcement Cases." *Fed. Reg.* 64 (June 18, 1999): 32948–32972.

Environmental Protection Agency (EPA). "Incentives for Self Policing: Discovery, Disclosure, Correction, and Prevention of Violations." *Fed. Reg.* 65 (2000): 19618–19627.

Esgate, Anthony, David Groome, and Kevin Baker. *An Introduction to Applied Cognitive Psychology*. New York: Psychology Press, 2004.

Estes, William K. *An Experimental Study of Punishment*. Evanston, IL: The American Psychological Association, Inc., 1944.

European Union (EU) Commission. *Guidelines on the Method of Setting*

Fines Imposed Pursuant to Article 23(2)(A) of Regulation (EC) No 1/2003 OJ C 210/2 (September 1, 2006).

Faull, Jonathan and Ali Nikpay, eds. *The EC Law of Competition*. New York: Oxford University Press, 2007.

Faure, Michael. "Environmental Crimes." Chapter 165 in *Criminal Law and Economics*, edited by Nuno Garoupa. 2nd Edition, 320–345. Cheltenham, U.K. & Cambridge, MA, U.S.A.: Emerald Group Publishing Limited, 2009a.

Faure, Michael. *The Impact of Behavioral Law and Economics on Accident Law*. The Hague, NL: Boom Juridische Uitgevers, 2009b.

Fenn, Paul and Cento G. Veljanovski. "A Positive Economic Theory of Regulatory Enforcement." *The Economic Journal* 98 (1988): 1055–1070.

Filip, Mark R. *Memorandum For Heads of Department Components United States Attorneys: Principles of Federal Prosecution of Business Organizations*. U.S. Department of Justice. Available at: http://www.usdoj.gov/opa/documents/corp-charging-guidelines.pdf (August 28, 2008).

Fisher, Cynthia D. "The Effects of Personal Control, Competence, and Extrinsic Reward Systems on Intrinsic Motivation." *Organizational Behavior & Human Performance* 21, No. 3 (1978): 273–288.

Franck, Thomas M. *Fairness in International Law and Institutions*. New York: Oxford University Press, 1995.

French, John R. Jr and Bertram Raven. "The Bases of Social Power." In *Studies in Social Power*, edited by Dorwin Cartwright. Ann Arbor, MI: University of Michigan, 1959.

Friedman, David and William Sjostrom. "Hanged for a Sheep: The Economics of Marginal Deterrence." *The Journal of Legal Studies* 22, No. 2 (1993): 345–366.

Friedman, Howard M. "Some Reflections on the Corporation as Criminal Defendant." *Notre Dame Lawyer* 55 (1979): 173–202.

Friedman, Milton. *Essays in Positive Economics*. Chicago, IL: The University of Chicago Press, 1953.

Friesen, Lana L. "Targeting Enforcement to Improve Compliance with Environmental Regulations." *Journal of Environmental Economics and Management* 46, No. 1 (2003): 72–85.

Gagné, Marylène and Edward L. Deci. "Self-Determination Theory and Work Motivation." *Journal of Organizational Behavior* 26 (2005): 331–362.

Galen, Michele. "Keeping the Long Arm of the Law at Arm's Length." *Business Week* (April 22, 1991): 104.

Garoupa, Nuno and Daniel Klerman. "Corruption and the Optimal Use of Nonmonetary Sanctions." *International Review of Law and Economics* 24, No. 2 (2004): 219–225.

Garrett, Brandon L. "Structural Reform Prosecution." *Virginia Law Review* 93 (2007): 853–957.

Gibbs, Jack P. *Crime, Punishment, and Deterrence*. New York: Elsevier, 1975.

Gibson Dunn. *2008 Year-End Update on Corporate Deferred Prosecution and Non-Prosecution Agreements*. Available at: http://www.gibsondunn.com/publications/pages/2008year-endupdate-corporatedpas.aspx (January 6, 2009).

Gibson Dunn. *2009 Mid-Year Update on Corporate Deferred Prosecution and Non-Prosecution Agreements* (July 8, 2009).

Gibson Dunn. *2009 Year-End Update on Corporate Deferred Prosecution and Non-Prosecution Agreements* (January 7, 2010).

Gibson Dunn. *2010 Mid-Year Update on Corporate Deferred Prosecution and Non-Prosecution Agreements* (August 5, 2010).

Gibson Dunn. *2010 Year-End Update on Corporate Deferred Prosecution and Non-Prosecution Agreement* (January 4, 2011).

Gibson Dunn. *2011 Mid-Year Update on Corporate Deferred Prosecution and Non-Prosecution Agreements* (July 12, 2011).

Gibson Dunn. *2011 End-Year Update on Corporate Deferred Prosecution and Non-Prosecution Agreements* (January 4, 2012).

Gibson Dunn. *2012 Mid-Year Update on Corporate Deferred Prosecution and Non-Prosecution Agreements* (July 10, 2011).

Gilboy, Janet A. "Compelled Third-Party Participation in the Regulatory Process: Legal Duties, Culture, and Noncompliance." *Law & Policy* 20, No. 2 (1998): 135–155.

Gilboy, Janet A. "Implications of Third-Party Involvement in Enforcement: The INS, Illegal Travelers, and International Airlines." *Law & Society Review* 31 (1997): 505–530.

Gilson, Ronald J. "The Devolution of the Legal Profession: A Demand Side Perspective." *Maryland Law Review (1936)* 49, No. 4 (1990): 869–916.

Gilson, Ronald J. and Reinier Kraakman. "Reinventing the Outside Director: An Agenda for Institutional Investors." *Stanford Law Review* 43 (1991): 863–906.

Goldsmith, Jack L. and Eric A. Posner. "A Theory of Customary International Law." *The University of Chicago Law Review* 66, No. 4 (1999): 1113–1177.

Goldsmith, Michael and Chad W. King. "Policing Corporate Crime: The Dilemma of Internal Compliance Programs." *Vanderbilt Law Review* 50 (1997): 1–47.

Gordon, Neil. *Checking Up On DPAs, NPAs and Corporate Monitors*. Available at: http://pogoblog.typepad.com/pogo/2009/06/checking-up-on-dpas-npas-and-corporate-monitors.html (June 26, 2009).

Graafland, Johan J. and Hugo Smid. "Reputation, Corporate Social Responsibility and Market Regulation." *Tijdschrift Voor Ėconomie En Management* 49, No. 2 (2004): 271–309.

Grabosky, Peter N. "Using Non-Governmental Resources to Foster Regulatory Compliance." *Governance: An International Journal of Policy and Administration* 8, No. 4 (1995): 527–550.

Gray, Wayne B. and Mary E. Deily. "Compliance and Enforcement: Air Pollution Regulation in the U.S. Steel Industry." *Journal of Environmental Economics and Management* 31, No. 1 (1996): 96–111.

Green, Christopher R. "Punishing Corporations: The Food-Chain Schizophrenia in Punitive Damages and Criminal Law." *Nebraska Law Review* 87 (2008): 197–269.

Greenberg, Joseph. "Avoiding Tax Avoidance: A (Repeated) Game-Theoretic Approach." *Journal Of Economic Theory* 32, No. 1 (1984): 1–13.

Greenblum, Benjamin M. "What Happens to a Prosecution Deferred? Judicial Oversight of Corporate Deferred Prosecution Agreements." *Columbia Law Review* 105, No. 6 (2005): 1863–1904.

Grindler, Gary G., Acting Deputy Attorney General. *Memorandum For Heads of Department Components United States Attorneys: Additional Guidance on The Use of Monitors in Deferred Prosecution Agreements and Non-Prosecution Agreements with Corporations*. U.S. Department of Justice, Office of the Deputy Attorney General. Available at: http://www.justice.gov/dag/dag-memo-guidance-monitors.pdf (May 25, 2010).

Groskaufmanis, Karl A. "Impact of Corporate Compliance Outside the Criminal Process." Chapter 24 in *Compliance Programs and the Corporate Sentencing Guidelines: Preventing Criminal and Civil Liability*, edited by Jefferey M. Kaplan and Joseph E. Murphy. Revised Edition St. Paul, MN: Thomson/West, 2009.

Gunningham, Neil. "Negotiated Non-Compliance: A Case Study of Regulatory Failure." *Law & Policy* 9, No. 1 (1978): 69–96.

Gunningham, Neil, Dorothy Thornton, and Robert A. Kagan. "Motivating Management: Corporate Compliance in Environmental Protection." *Law & Policy* 27, No. 2 (2004): 289–316.

Gunningham, Neil. *Mine Safety: Law, Regulation, Policy*. Sydney: The Federation Press, 2007.

Guzman, Andrew T. *How International Law Works: A Rational Choice Theory*. New York: Oxford University Press, 2008.

Haines, Fiona. *Corporate Regulation: Beyond 'Punish and Persuade'*. Oxford: Clarendon Press, 1997.

Hamdani, Assaf. "Gatekeeper Liability." *Southern California Law Review* 77 (2003): 53–120.

Handler, Joel F. "Dependent People, the State, and the Modern/Postmodern Search for the Dialogic Community." *UCLA Law Review* 35 (1988): 999–1113.

Harford, Jon D. "Measurement Error and State-Dependent Pollution Control Enforcement." *Journal of Environmental Economics and Management* 21, No. 1 (1991): 67–81.

Harford, Jon D. "Improving on the Steady State in the State-Dependent Enforcement of Pollution Control." *Journal of Environmental Economics and Management* 24, No. 2 (1993): 133–138.

Harford, Jon D. and Winston Harrington. "A Reconsideration of Enforcement Leverage When Penalties are Restricted." *Journal of Public Economics* 45, No. 3 (1991): 391–395.

Harrington, Winston. "Enforcement Leverage When Penalties are Restricted." *Journal of Public Economics* 37, No. 1 (1988): 29–53.

Harris, John R. "On the Economics of Law and Order." *The Journal of Political Economy* 78, No. 1 (1970): 165–174.

Hawkins, Keith. "Bargain and Bluff: Compliance Strategy and Deterrence in the Enforcement of Regulation." *Law and Policy Quarterly* 5, No. 1 (1983): 35–73.

Hawkins, Keith. *Environment and Enforcement: Regulation and the Social Definition of Pollution*. Oxford Socio-Legal Studies. Oxford: Clarendon Press, 1984.

Hawkins, Keith. "Compliance Strategy, Prosecution Policy, and Aunt Sally: A Comment on Pearce and Tombs." *British Journal of Criminology* 30, No. 4 (1990): 444–466.

Hawkins, Keith. "Enforcing Regulation: More of the Same from Pearce and Tombs." *British Journal of Criminology* 31, No. 4 (1991): 427–430.

Hayek, Friedrich A. "The Use of Knowledge in Society." *The American Economic Review* 35, No. 4 (1945): 519–530.

Hefendehl, Roland. "Corporate Criminal Liability: Model Penal Code Section 2.07 and the Development in Western Legal Systems." *Buffalo Criminal Law Review* 4 (2000): 283–300.

Heineman, Ben W. Jr. "Caught in the Middle." *Corporate Counsel* (April 2007): 84–89.

Hendricks III, William C., Fraud Division Chief to United States Attorneys. *Memorandum*. Reprinted in *White Collar Crime*. New York: American Bar Association, 1987.

Heyes, Anthony G. "Cutting Environmental Penalties to Protect the Environment." *Journal of Public Economics* 60, No. 2 (1996): 251–265.

Heyes, Anthony G. "Making Things Stick: Enforcement and Compliance." *Oxford Review of Economic Policy* 14 (1998): 50–63.

Heyes, Anthony G. and Neil Rickman. "Regulatory Dealing – Revisiting the Harrington Paradox." *Journal of Public Economics* 72, No. 3 (1999): 361–378.

Hicks, John R. "The Foundations of Welfare Economics." *The Economic Journal* 49 (1939): 696–712.

Hirshleifer, Jack and John G. Riley. "The Analytics of Uncertainty and Information – An Expository Survey." *Journal of Economic Literature* 17, No. 4 (1979): 1375–1421.

Holder, Eric, Deputy Attorney General. *Memorandum For Heads of Department Components United States Attorneys: Principles of Federal Prosecution of Corporations*. U.S. Department of Justice, Office of the Deputy Attorney General. Available at: http://federalevidence.com/pdf/Corp_Prosec/Holder_Memo_6_16_99.pdf (June 16, 1999).

Huff, Kevin B. "The Role of Corporate Compliance Programs in Determining Corporate Criminal Liability: A Suggested Approach." *Columbia Law Review* 96 (1996): 1252–1298.

Huntington, Samuel P. "The Marasmus of the ICC: The Commission, The Railroads, and the Public Interest." *The Yale Law Journal* 61, No. 4 (1952): 467–509.

Illovsky, Eugene. "Corporate Deferred Prosecution Agreements: The Brewing Debate." *Criminal Justice* 21 (2001): 36–39.

Inciardi, James A., Duane C. Mcbride, and James E. Rivers. *Drug Control and the Courts*. Thousand Oaks, CA: Sage Publications, Inc., 1996.

Innes, Robert. "Self-Policing and Optimal Law Enforcement When Violator Remediation is Valuable." *Journal of Political Economy* 107, No. 6 (1999): 1305–1325.

Innes, Robert. "Violator Avoidance Activities and Self-Reporting in Optimal Law Enforcement." *Journal of Law, Economics and Organization* 17, No. 1 (2001): 239–256.

Inniss, David A. "Developments in the Law: Alternatives to Incarceration." *Harvard Law Review* 111, No. 7 (1998): 1863–1990.

Israeli Antitrust Authority (IAA). *Model Internal Compliance Program*. Israel, 1998.

Jiménez, Marcos D. and Dana E. Foster. "The Importance of Compliance Programs for the Health Care Industry." *University of Miami Business Law Review* 7 (1998): 503–512.

Johnstone, Richard. "From Fiction to Fact – Rethinking OHS Enforcement." *National Research Center for Occupational Health and Safety Regulation Working Paper 11*, 2003.

Jolls, Christine. "Behavioral Economics Analysis of Redistributive Legal Rules." *Vanderbilt Law Review* 51, No. 6 (1998): 1653–1677.

Kagan, Robert A. and John T. Scholz. "The 'Criminology of the Corporation' and Regulatory Enforcement Strategies." In *Enforcing*

Regulation, edited by Keith Hawkins and John M. Thomas, 352–377. Boston and The Hague: Kluwer-Nijhoff, 1984.

Kahneman, Daniel and Amos Tversky. "Prospect Theory: An Analysis of Decision Under Risk." *Econometrica* 47, No. 2 (1978): 263–290.

Kaldor, Nicholas. "Welfare Propositions of Economics and Interpersonal Comparisons of Utility." *The Economic Journal* 49 (1939): 549–552.

Kaplan, Jeffrey M. "Corporate Sentencing Guidelines: Overview." Chapter 3 in *Compliance Programs and the Corporate Sentencing Guidelines: Preventing Criminal and Civil Liability*, edited by Jeffrey M. Kaplan and Joseph E. Murphy. Revised Edition. St. Paul, MN: Thomson/West, 2009.

Kaplow, Louis and Steven Shavell. "Optimal Law Enforcement with Self-Reporting of Behavior." *Journal of Political Economy* 102, No. 3 (1994): 583–606.

Karpoff, Jonathan M., D. Scott Lee, and Gerald S. Martin. "The Cost to Firms of Cooking the Books." *Journal of Financial and Quantitative Analysis* 43 (2008): 581–611.

Karpoff, Jonathan M., John R. Lott Jr., and Eric W. Wehrly. "The Reputational Penalties for Environmental Violations: Empirical Evidence." *The Journal of Law & Economics* 48, No. 2 (2005): 653–675.

Keohane, Robert O. *After Hegemony: Cooperation and Discord in the World Political Economy*. Princeton, NJ: Princeton University Press, 1984.

Keren, Gideon and Léonie E. M. Gerritsen. "On the Robustness and Possible Accounts of Ambiguity Aversion." *Acta Psychologica* 103, No. 1–2 (1999): 149–172.

Khanna, Vikramaditya S. "Corporate Liability Standards: When Should Corporations Be Held Criminally Liable?" *American Criminal Law Review* 37 (2002): 1239–1283.

Khanna, Vikramaditya S. "Reforming the Corporate Monitor?" In *Prosecutors in the Board Room: Using Criminal Law to Regulate Corporate Conduct*, edited by Anthony S. Barkow and Rachel E. Barkow, 226–248. New York: New York University Press, 2011.

Khanna, Vikramaditya S. and Timothy L. Dickinson. "The Corporate Monitor: The New Corporate Czar." *Michigan Law Review* 105 (2007): 1713–1756.

Kim, Sung H. "The Banality of Fraud: Re-Situating the Inside Counsel as Gatekeeper." *Fordham Law Review* 74 (2005): 983–1077.

Kim, Sung H. "Gatekeepers Inside Out." *The Georgetown Journal of Legal Ethics* 21 (2008): 411–463.

Kinsey, Karyl. "Deterrence and Alienation Effects of IRS Enforcement: An Analysis of Survey Data." In *Why People Pay Taxes: Tax Compliance and Enforcement*, edited by Joel Slemrod, 259–285. Ann Arbor, MI: University of Michigan Press, 1992.

Kirstein, Roland. "Risk Neutrality and Strategic Insurance." *Geneva Papers on Risk and Insurance: Issues and Practice* 25, No. 2 (2000): 251–261.

Kornhauser, Lewis A. "An Economic Analysis of the Choice Between Enterprise and Personal Liability for Accidents." *California Law Review* 70 (1982): 1345–1392.

Korobkin, Russell B. and Thomas S. Ulen. "Law and Behavioral Science: Removing the Rationality Assumption from Law and Economics." *California Law Review* 88 (2000): 1051–1144.

Kraakman, Reinier. "Corporate Liability Strategies and the Costs of Legal Controls." *Yale Law Journal* 93 (1984): 857–898.

Kraakman, Reinier. "Gatekeepers: The Anatomy of a Third-Party Enforcement Strategy." *Journal of Law, Economics, and Organization* 2, No. 1 (1986): 53–104.

Kraakman, Reinier. "Vicarious and Corporate Liability." In *Tort Law and Economics*, edited by Michael Faure. 2nd Edition, 669–681. Cheltenham, U.K. & Northampton MA: Edward Elgar, 2009.

Krawiec, Kimberly D. "Cosmetic Compliance and the Failure of Negotiated Governance." *Wash. U. L. Q.* 81 (2003): 487–544.

Krawiec, Kimberly D. "Organization Misconduct: Beyond the Principal Agent Model." *Florida State Law Review* 32 (2005): 571–615.

Lacovara, Philip A. and David P. Nicoli. "Vicarious Criminal Liability of Organizations: RICO as an Example of a Flawed Principle in Practice." *St. John's Law Review* 64 (1989): 725–778.

Laffont, Jean-Jacques and Jean Tirole. "The Politics of Government Decision-Making: A Theory of Regulatory Capture." *The Quarterly Journal of Economics* 106, No. 4 (1991): 1089–1127.

Landes, William M. and Richard A. Posner. "The Private Enforcement of Law." *Journal of Legal Studies* 4, No. 1 (1975): 1–46.

Landsberger, Michael and Isaac Meilijson. "Incentive Generating State Dependent Penalty System: The Case of Income Tax Evasion." *Journal of Public Economics* 19, No. 3 (1982): 333–352.

Langbein, Laura and Cornelius M. Kerwin. "Implementation, Negotiation and Compliance in Environmental and Safety Regulation." *The Journal of Politics* 47, No. 3 (1985): 854–880.

Laufer, William S. *Corporate Bodies and Guilty Minds: The Failure of Corporate Criminal Liability*. Chicago and London: The University of Chicago Press, 1994.

Laufer, William S. "Integrity, Diligence, and the Limits of Good Corporate Citizenship." *American Business Law Journal* 34, No. 2 (1996): 157–182.

Laufer, William S. "Corporate Liability, Risk Shifting, and the Paradox of Compliance." *Vanderbilt Law Review* 52 (1999): 1341–1420.

Law Reform Commission of New South Wales. "Sentencing: Corporate Offenders." *Issues Paper* 20 (2001).

Lederman, Eliezer. "Criminal Law, Perpetrator and Corporation: Rethinking a Complex Triangle." *Journal of Criminal Law and Criminology* 76, No. 2 (1985): 285–340.

Lee, Fiona, Christopher Peterson, and Larissa Z. Tiedens. "*Mea Culpa*: Predicting Stock Prices from Organizational Attributions." *Personality & Social Psychology Bulletin* 30, No. 12 (2004): 1636–1649.

Lepper, Mark and David Greene. "Turning Play into Work: Effects of Adult Surveillance and Extrinsic Rewards on Children's Intrinsic Motivation." *Journal of Personality and Social Psychology* 31, No. 3 (1975): 479–486.

Levine, Michael E. and Jennifer L. Forrence. "Regulatory Capture, Public Interest, and the Public Agenda: Toward a Synthesis." *Journal of Law, Economics, & Organization* 6, No. 1 (1990): 167–198.

Lichtblau, Eric and Kitty Bennett. "30 Former Officials Became Corporate Monitors." *The New York Times* (May 23, 2008).

Lieder, Kathleen A. and Christopher P. Mazzoli. "Ellerth and Faragher: Applying the Supreme Court's "Delphic Pronouncements" on Employers' Vicarious Liability for Sexual Harassment." *Michigan Bar Journal* 78 (1999): 432–434.

Lind, Edgar A. and Tom R. Tyler. *The Social Psychology of Procedural Justice*: *Critical Issues in Social Justice*. New York: Plenum, 1988.

Lowi, Theodore J. *The End of Liberalism: Ideology, Policy, and the Crisis of Public Authority*. New York: Norton, 1969.

Mahoney, Barry, Bruce D. Beaudin, John A. Carver, Daniel B. Ryan, and Richard B. Hoffman. *Pretrial Services Programs: Responsibilities and Potential*. U.S. Department of Justice, Office of Justice Programs, National Institute of Justice, 2001.

Malik, Arun S. "Avoidance, Screening and Optimum Enforcement." *Rand Journal of Economics* 21, No. 3 (1990): 341–353.

Marcus, Alfred A. and Robert S. Goodman. "Victims and Shareholders: The Dilemmas of Presenting Corporate Policy During a Crisis." *Academy of Management Journal* 34, No. 2 (1991): 281–305.

Marjit, Sugata and He-Ling Shi. "On Controlling Crime with Corrupt Officials." *Journal of Economic Behavior & Organization* 34, No. 1 (1998): 163–172.

Marks, Stephen G. "The Separation of Ownership and Control." In *Encyclopedia of Law and Economics*, edited by Boudewijn Bouckaert and Gerrit De Geest. Vol. 5630, 692–724. Available at: http://encyclo.

findlaw.com/INDEX.HTML: Edward Elgar and the University of Ghent, 1999.

Mascini, Peter and Eelco Van Wijk. "Responsive Regulation at the Dutch Food and Consumer Product Safety Authority: An Empirical Assessment of Assumptions Underlying the Theory." *Regulation & Governance* 3, No. 1 (2009): 27–47.

Matthews, Christopher M. "Judge Blasts Compliance Monitors At Innospec Plea Hearing." *Main Justice: Politics, Policy and the Law* (March 18, 2010a)

Matthews, Christopher M. "Compliance Monitors Are Here to Stay." *Main Justice: Politics, Policy and the Law* (April 8, 2010b).

Matthews, Christopher M. "Fraud Chief: Effective Compliance Programs Can Prevent Monitors." *Main Justice: Politics, Policy and the Law* (May 24, 2010c).

Matthews, Christopher M. "Grindler Touts Importance of Compliance, but Doubts Linger." *Main Justice: Politics, Policy and the Law* (May 25, 2010d).

Maurer, Ronald J. "The Federal Sentencing Guidelines for Organizations: How Do They Work and What Are They Supposed To Do?" *Dayton Law Review* No. 18 (1993): 799–833.

May, Peter J. and Soren Winter. "Regulatory Enforcement and Compliance: Examining Danish Agro-Environmental Policy." *Journal of Policy Analysis and Management* 18, No. 4 (1999): 625–651.

Mckendall, Marie M., Beverly Demarr, and Catherine Jones-Rikkers. "Ethical Compliance Programs and Corporate Illegality: Testing the Assumptions of the Corporate Sentencing Guidelines." *Journal of Business Ethics* 37, No. 4 (2002): 367–383.

Mcnulty, Paul, Deputy Attorney General. *Memorandum for Heads of Department Components United States Attorneys: Principles of Federal Prosecution of Business Organizations*. U.S. Department of Justice, Office of the Deputy Attorney General. Available at: http://www.justice.gov/dag/speeches/2006/mcnulty_memo.pdf (December 12, 2006).

Mearsheimer, John J. "The False Promise of International Institutions." *International Security* 19, No. 3 (1994): 5–49.

Miller, Gregory D. "Hypotheses on Reputation: Alliance Choices and the Shadow of the Past." *Security Studies* 12, No. 3 (2003): 40–78.

Montesquieu, Charles De Secondat (Baron de). *The Spirit of Laws*. Rept. Edition of 1977. Berkeley, CA: University of California Press, 1748.

Mookherjee, Dilip and Ivan Paak-Liang Png. "Marginal Deterrence in Enforcement of Law." *Journal of Political Economy* 102, No. 5 (1994): 1039–1066.

Morford, Craig S., Acting Deputy Attorney General. *Memorandum for*

Heads of Department Components United States Attorneys: Selection and Use of Monitors in Deferred Prosecution Agreements and Non-Prosecution Agreements with Corporations. U.S. Department of Justice, Office of the Deputy Attorney General. Available at: http://www.justice.gov/dag/readingroom/dag-030708.pdf (March 7, 2008).

Muir, William Ker Jr. *Police: Streetcorner Politicians*. Chicago, IL: University of Chicago Press, 1977.

Mukasey, Michael B. and Andrew J. Ceresney. "Should Corporations Self-Report Wrongdoing?" *New York Law Journal* (October 1, 2010).

Murphy, Joseph E. "An FTC View of Compliance Programs: Good Faith Efforts Can Mean No Penalties." *Corporate Conduct Quarterly* 4 (1996): 53–66.

Murphy, Kristina. "'Trust Me, I'm The Taxman': The Role of Trust in Nurturing Compliance." *Centre for Tax System Integrity Working Paper No. 43* (2002): 1–31.

Murphy, Kristina. "Procedural Justice and Tax Compliance." *Australian Journal of Social Issues* 38, No. 3 (2003): 379–407.

Nagel, Ilene H. and Winthrop M. Swenson. "The Federal Sentencing Guidelines for Corporations: Their Development, Theoretical Underpinnings, and Some Thoughts About their Future." *Washington University Law Quarterly* 71 (1993): 205–259.

Nielsen, Vibeke L. "Are Regulators Responsive?" *Law and Policy* 28, No. 3 (2006): 395–416.

Non Prosecution Agreement with Micrus S.A. Available at: http://www.justice.gov/criminal/fraud/fcpa/cases/micrus-corp/02-28-05micrus-agree.pdf (February 28, 2005).

Nyborg, Karine and Kjetil Telle. "Firms' Compliance to Environmental Regulation: Is There Really a Paradox?" *Environmental & Resource Economics* 35, No. 1 (2006): 1–18.

Oded, Sharon. "Deferred Prosecution Agreements: Prosecutorial Balance in Times of Economic Meltdown." *The Law Journal for Social Justice* 2 (2011): 65–99.

Oded, Sharon. "Inducing Corporate Compliance: A Compound Corporate Liability Regime." *International Review of Law and Economics* 31, No. 4 (2011): 272–283.

Oded, Sharon. "Corporate Monitors: Overcoming the Classification Failure of Targeted Monitoring Systems." *Berkeley Business Law Journal* 10, No. 2: (forthcoming, 2013).

Office of Fair Trading (OFT). *Drivers of Compliance and Non-Compliance with Competition Law*. U.K., 2010. Available at: http://www.oft.gov.uk/shared_oft/reports/comp_policy/oft1227.pdf

Office of Fair Trading (OFT). *How Your Business Can Achieve Compliance with Competition Law: Guidance*. June 2011. Available at: http://www.oft.gov.uk/shared_oft/ca-and-cartels/competition-awareness-compliance/oft1341.pdf

Ogus, Anthony. "Self-Regulation." In *Encyclopedia of Law and Economics*, edited by Boudewijn Bouckaert and Gerrit De Geest. Vol. 9400, 587–602. Available at: http://encyclo.findlaw.com/index.html: Edward Elgar and the University of Ghent, 1999.

Ogus, Anthony. "Enforcing Regulation: Do We Need the Criminal Law?" In *New Perspectives on Economic Crime*, edited by H. Sjögren and G. Skogh, 42–55. Cheltenham, U.K.: Edward Elgar Publishing Limited, 2004.

Ogus, Anthony. "Criminal Law and Regulation." In *Criminal Law and Economics*, edited by Nuno Garoupa. 2nd Edition, 90–110. Cheltenham U.K. and Northampton MA: Edward Elgar Publishing Limited, 2009.

Ogus, Anthony and Carolyn Abbot. "Pollution and Penalties." In *An Introduction to the Law and Economics of Environmental Policy: Issues in Institutional Design, Book Series: Research in Law and Economics*, edited by Timothy Swanson. Vol. 20, 493–516. Bingley, U.K.: Emerald Group Publishing Limited, 2002.

O'Hare, Jennifer. "The Use of the Corporate Monitor in SEC Enforcement Actions." *Brooklyn Journal of Corporate, Financial and Commercial Law* 1 (2006): 89–118.

Palmrose, Zoe-Vonna, Vernon J. Richardson, and Susan Scholz. "Determinants of Market Reactions to Restatement Announcements." *Journal of Accounting & Economics* 37, No. 1 (2004): 59–89.

Parker, Jeffrey S. "Rules Without . . . : Some Critical Reflections in the Federal Corporate Sentencing Guidelines." *Washington University Law Quarterly* 71 (1993): 397–442.

Paternoster, Raymond and Sally Simpson. "Sanction Threats and Appeals to Morality: Testing a Rational Choice Model of Corporate Crime." *Law and Society Review* 30, No. 3 (1996): 549–583.

Paulsen, Erik. "Imposing Limits on Prosecutorial Discretion in Corporate Prosecution Agreements." *New York University Law Review (1950)* 82 (2007): 1434–1469.

Pearce, Frank and Steve Tombs. "Ideology, Hegemony, and Empiricism: Compliance Theories of Regulation." *British Journal of Criminology* 30, No. 4 (1990): 423–443.

Pearce, Frank and Steve Tombs. "Policing Corporate 'Skid Rows': A Reply to Keith Hawkins." *British Journal Of Criminology* 31, No. 4 (1991): 415–426.

Perino, Michael A. "*SEC Enforcement of Attorney Up-The-Ladder*

Reporting Rules: An Analysis of Institutional Constraints, Norms and Biases." *Villanova Law Review* 49, No. 4 (2004): 851–866.

Perry, William K. and Linda S. Dakin. "Compliance Programs and Criminal Law." Chapter 22 in *Compliance Programs and the Corporate Sentencing Guidelines: Preventing Criminal and Civil Liability*, edited by Jeffrey M. Kaplan and Joseph E. Murphy. Revised Edition, St. Paul, MN: Thomson/West, 2009: 22.1–22.16.

Pfaff, Alexander A. and William Sanchirico. "Big Field, Small Potatoes: An Empirical Assessment of EPA's Self-Audit Policy." *Journal of Policy Analysis and Management* 23, No. 3 (2004): 415–432.

Phillips, Llad and Harold L. Votey Jr. "Crime Control in California." *The Journal of Legal Studies* 4, No. 2 (1975): 327–349.

Pitt, Harvey L. and Karl A. Groskaufmanis. "Minimizing Corporate Civil and Criminal Liability: A Second Look at Corporate Codes of Conduct." *Georgetown Law Journal* 78 (1990): 1559–1654.

Polinsky, Mitchell A. "Private Versus Public Enforcement of Fines." *The Journal of Legal Studies* 9, No. 1 (1980): 105–127.

Polinsky, Mitchell A. and Steven Shavell. "The Optimal Tradeoff Between the Probability and Magnitude of Fines." *The American Economic Review* 69, No. 5 (1979): 880–891.

Polinsky, Mitchell A. and Steven Shavell. "Enforcement Costs and the Optimal Magnitude and Probability of Fines." *The Journal of Law & Economics* 35 (1992): 133–148.

Polinsky, Mitchell A. and Steven Shavell. "Should Employees be Subject to Fines and Imprisonment Given the Existence of Corporate Liability?" *International Review of Law and Economics* 13, No. 3 (1993): 239–257.

Polinsky, Mitchell A. and Steven Shavell. "Should Liability Be Based on the Harm to the Victim Or the Gain to the Injurer?" *Journal of Law, Economics and Organization* 10, No. 2 (1994): 427–437.

Polinsky, Mitchell A. and Steven Shavell. "Punitive Damages: An Economic Analysis." *Harvard Law Review* 111, No. 4 (1998): 869–962.

Polinsky, Mitchell A. and Steven Shavell. "The Economic Theory of Public Enforcement of Law." *Journal of Economic Literature, American Economic Association* 38, No. 1 (2000): 45–76.

Polinsky, Mitchell A. and Steven Shavell. "Corruption and Optimal Law Enforcement." *Journal of Public Economics* 81 (2001): 1–24.

Polinsky, Mitchell A. and Steven Shavell. "Public Enforcement of Law." In *Criminal Law and Economics*, edited by Nuno Garoupa. 2nd Edition, 1–59. Cheltenham, U.K. and Northampton, MA: Edward Elgar Publishing Limited, 2009.

Porter, Lyman W. and Edward E. Lawler. *Marginal Attitudes and Performance.* Homewood, IL: Dorsey Press, 1968.

Posner, Richard A. *Economic Analysis of Law*. 6th Edition. New York: Aspan Publications, 2003.

Poundstone, William. *Prisoner's Dilemma*. New York: Doubleday, 1992.

Raymond, Mark. "Enforcement Leverage when Penalties are Restricted: A Reconsideration under Asymmetric Information." *Journal of Public Economics* 73, No. 2 (1999): 289–295.

Reisinger, Sue. "Designated Drivers." *Corporate Counsel* (October 2004).

Resnik, Scott A. and Keir N. Dougall. "The Rise of Deferred Prosecution Agreements." *New York Law Journal: Securities Litigation & Regulation* (December 18, 2006).

Riesel, Daniel. *Environmental Enforcement: Civil and Criminal*. Litigation Series. New York: Alm Properties Inc. Law Journal Press, 1997.

Robinson, James K., Phillip E. Urofsky, and Christopher R. Pantel. "Deferred Prosecutions and the Independent Monitor." *International Journal of Disclosure and Governance* 2, No. 4 (2005): 325–347.

Rosenblum, Lisa. "Mandating Effective Treatment for Drug Offenders." *The Hastings Law Journal* 53 (2001): 1217–1243.

Ross, Huge L. *Deterring the Drinking Driver: Legal Policy and Social Control*. Reviewed and Updated Edition. Lexington, MA: Lexington Books, 1984.

Rousseau, Sandra S. "Timing of Environmental Inspections: Survival of the Compliant." *Journal of Regulatory Economics* 32, No. 1 (2007): 17–36.

Rupp, Nicholas G. "The Attributes of a Costly Recall: Evidence from the Automotive Industry." *Review of Industrial Organization* 25, No. 1 (2004): 21–44.

Russell, Clifford S. "Game Models for Structuring Monitoring and Enforcement Systems." *Natural Resource Modeling* 4, No. 2 (1990): 143–173.

Schäfer, Hans-Bernd and Andreas Schönenberger. *Strict Liability Versus Negligence*. Vol. 3100 Edward Elgar and the University of Ghent. Available at: http://encyclo.findlaw.com/3100book.pdf (1999).

Schmidt, Patrick. *Eyes Half Blind: The Possibilities and Limits of Lawyers as Third Party Enforcers*. Presented to the annual meeting of the Western Political Science Association, Portland, OR. Available at: http://citation.allacademic.com/meta/p_mla_apa_research_citation/0/8/8/1/5/pages88159/p88159-1.php (March 12, 2004).

Scholz, John T. "Voluntary Compliance and Regulatory Enforcement." *Law & Policy* 6, No. 4 (1984a): 385–404.

Scholz, John T. "Cooperation, Deterrence, and the Ecology of Regulatory Enforcement." *Law and Society Review* 18 (1984b): 179–224.

Scholz, John T. "Cooperative Regulatory Enforcement and the Politics of

Administrative Effectiveness." *The American Political Science Review* 85, No. 1 (1991): 115–136.

Scholz, John T. "Can Government Facilitate Cooperation? An Informational Model of OSHA Enforcement." *American Journal of Political Science* 41, No. 3 (1997a): 693–717.

Scholz, John T. "Enforcement Policy and Corporate Misconduct: The Changing Perspective of Deterrence Theory." *Law And Contemporary Problems* 60, No. 3 (1997b): 253–268.

Schwartz, Barry. *Psychology of Learning and Behavior*. New York: Norton, 1989.

Schwartz, Gary T. "The Hidden and Fundamental Issue of Employer Vicarious Liability." *Southern California Law Review* 69 (1995): 1739–1767.

Section of Antitrust Law, American Bar Association (ABA). *Jury Instructions in Criminal Antitrust Cases, 1976–1980*. U.S.A.: American Bar Association (ABA), 1982.

Segal, Ilya R. and Michael D. Whinston. "Public vs. Private Enforcement of Antitrust Law: A Survey." *European Competition Law Review* 28, No. 5 (2007): 306–315.

Selten, Reinhard. "What is Bounded Rationality?" In *Bounded Rationality: The Adaptive Toolbox*, edited by Gerd Gigerenzer and Reinhard Selten, 13–36. Boston, MA: MIT Press, 2002.

Shafir, Eldar and Amos Tversky. "Thinking through Uncertainty: Nonconsequential Reasoning and Choice." *Cognitive Psychology* 24, No. 4 (1992): 449–474.

Shapiro, Sidney A. and Randy S. Rabinowitz. "Punishment Versus Cooperation in Regulatory Enforcement: A Case Study of OSHA." *Administrative Law Review* 49, No. 3 (1997): 713–762.

Shapiro, Susan P. "The Social Control of Impersonal Trust." *The American Journal of Sociology* 93, No. 3 (1987): 623–658.

Shavell, Steven. "Strict Liability versus Negligence." *Journal of Legal Studies* 9, No. 1 (1980): 1–25.

Shavell, Steven. "The Social versus the Private Incentive to Bring Suit in a Costly Legal System." *The Journal of Legal Studies* 11, No. 2 (1982): 333–339.

Shavell, Steven. "Liability for Harm versus Regulation of Safety." *Journal of Legal Studies* 13 (1984a): 357–374.

Shavell, Steven. "A Model of the Optimal Use of Liability and Safety Regulations." *Rand Journal of Economics* 15, No. 2 (1984b): 271–280.

Shavell, Steven. "Criminal Law and the Optimal Use of Nonmonetary Sanctions as a Deterrent." *Columbia Law Review* 85, No. 6 (1985): 1232–1262.

Shavell, Steven. "The Judgment Proof Problem." *International Review of Law and Economics* 6, No. 1 (1986): 45–58.

Shavell, Steven. *Economic Analysis of Accident Law*. Cambridge, MA: Harvard University Press, 1987.

Shavell, Steven. "A Note on Marginal Deterrence." *International Review of Law and Economics* 12, No. 3 (1992): 345–355.

Shavell, Steven. "The Optimal Structure of Law Enforcement." *Journal of Law & Economics* 36, No. 1 (1993): 255–278.

Shavell, Steven. "The Optimal Level of Corporate Liability Given the Limited Ability of Corporations to Penalize their Employees." *International Review of Law and Economics* 17, No. 2 (1997): 203–213.

Shenefield, John H. and Richard J. Favretto. "Compliance Programs as Viewed from the Antitrust Division." *Antitrust Law Journal* 48 (1979): 73–79.

Shover, Neal, Donald Clelland, and John Lynxwiler. *Enforcement or Negotiation: Constructing a Regulatory Bureaucracy*. SUNY Series in Critical Issues. Albany, NY: State University of New York Press, 1986.

Simon, Herbert A. "A Behavioral Model of Rational Choice." *The Quarterly Journal of Economics* 69, No. 1 (1955): 99–113.

Simon, Herbert A. "Rational Decision Making in Business Organizations." *The American Economic Review* 69, No. 4 (1979): 493–513.

Spence, David B. "The Shadow of the Rational Polluter: Rethinking the Role of Rational Actor Models in Environmental Law." *California Law Review* 89, No. 4 (2001): 917–998.

Spivack, Peter and Sujit Raman. "Regulating the 'New Regulators': Current Trends in Deferred Prosecution Agreements." *The American Criminal Law Review* 45 (2008): 159–194.

Spratling, Gary R., Deputy Assistant Attorney General – Antitrust Division. "The Experience and View of the Antitrust Division." Speech at the Capitol Hilton Hotel, Washington, DC. Available at: http://www.justice.gov/atr/public/speeches/0456.htm (1995).

Stafford, Sarah L. "The Effect of Punishment on Firm Compliance with Hazardous Waste Regulations." *Journal of Environmental Economics and Management* 44, No. 2 (2002): 290–308.

Stafford, Sarah L. "Self-Policing in a Targeted Enforcement Regime." *Southern Economic Journal* 74 (2008): 934–951.

Staw, Barry M. "Dressing Up Like an Organization: When Psychological Theories Can Explain Organizational Action." *Journal of Management* 17, No. 4 (1991): 805–819.

Steer, John R. "Sentencing Guidelines: In General." Chapter 1 in *Compliance Programs and the Corporate Sentencing Guidelines: Preventing Criminal and Civil Liability*, edited by Jeffrey M. Kaplan and Joseph E. Murphy. Revised Edition St. Paul, MN: Thomson/West, 2009.

Stein, Mark J. and Joshua A. Levine. "The Filip Memorandum: Does It Go Far Enough?" *New York Law Journal* (September 11, 2008).

Stigler, George J. "The Optimum Enforcement of Laws." *The Journal of Political Economy* 78, No. 3 (1970): 526–536.

Stigler, George J. "The Theory of Economic Regulation." *Bell Journal of Economics and Management Science* No. 3 (1971): 3–18.

Strader, J. Kelly. *Understanding White Collar Crime*. Newark, NJ: Lexisnexis, 2002.

Sunstein, Cass R., ed. *Behavioral Law and Economics*. Cambridge, MA: Cambridge University Press, 2000.

Sutherland, Edwin H. *White Collar Crime: The Uncut Version*. New Haven, CT: Yale University Press, 1983.

Suurmond, Guido. *Enforcing Fire Safety in the Catering Industry: An Economic Analysis*. Leiden, Netherlands: Leiden University Press, 2008.

Swaine, Edward T. "Rational Custom." *Duke Law Journal* 52, No. 3 (2002): 559–627.

Sykes, Alan O. "The Economics of Vicarious Liability." *The Yale Law Journal* 93 (1984): 1231–1280.

Sykes, Alan O. "The Boundaries of Vicarious Liability: An Economic Analysis of the Scope of Employment Rule and Related Legal Doctrines." *Harvard Law Review* 101 (1988): 563–609.

Sykes, Alan O. "The Economics of Public International Law." Unpublished manuscript, *John M. Olin Law & Economics Working Paper, No. 216* (2004). Available at SSRN: http://ssrn.com/abstract=564383

Telang, Rahul and Sunil Wattal. "An Empirical Analysis of the Impact of Software Vulnerability Announcements on Firm Stock Price." *IEEE Transactions on Software Engineering* 33, No. 8 (2007): 544–557.

The American Law Institute. *Restatement of Law (Second), Torts*, edited by the American Law Institute at Philadelphia, Pennsylvania American Law Institute Publishers, 1979.

The American Law Institute. *Restatement of Law (Third), Agency*, edited by the American Law Institute at Philadelphia, Pennsylvania American Law Institute Publishers, 2006.

The International Chamber of Commerce (ICC). *The Fining Policy of the European Commission in Competition Cases*. Paris, France, 2009.

Thibaut, John Walter and Laurens Walker. *Procedural Justice: A Psychological Analysis*. Hillsdale, NJ: Erlbaum, 1975.

Thompson, Larry D., Deputy Attorney General. *Memorandum For Heads of Department Components United States Attorneys: Principles of Federal Prosecution of Business Organizations*. U.S. Department of

Justice, Office of the Deputy Attorney General. Available at: http://www.justice.gov/dag/cftf/corporate_guidelines.htm (January 20, 2003).

Thompson, Victor A. *Decision Theory: Pure and Applied.* New York: General Learning Press, 1971.

Thornton, Dorothy, Neil Gunningham, and Robert A. Kagan. "General Deterrence and Corporate Environmental Behavior." *Law and Policy* 25, No. 2 (2005): 262–288.

Tigar, Michael E. "It Does the Crime But Not the Time: Corporate Criminal Liability in Federal Law." *American Journal of Criminal Law* 17, No. 3 (1990): 211–234.

Toffel, Michael W. and Jodi L. Short. "Coming Clean and Cleaning Up: Does Voluntary Self-Reporting Indicate Effective Self-Policing?" *Journal of Law and Economics* 54 No. 3 (2011): 609–649.

Turner, Jonathan H. *The Structure of Sociological Theory*. 7th Edition. Belmont, CA: Wadsworth Publishing Company, 2003.

Tversky, Amos and Daniel Kahneman. "Judgment Under Uncertainty: Heuristics and Biases." *Science (New York)* 185 (1974): 1124–1131.

Tyler, Tom R. "Justice and Leadership Endorsement." In *Political Cognition*, edited by Richard Lau and David Sears, 257–278. Hillsdale, NJ: Lawrence Erlbaum and Associates, 1986.

Tyler, Tom R. "The Psychology of Legitimacy: A Relational Perspective on Voluntary Deference to Authorities." *Personality and Social Psychology Review* 1, No. 4 (1997): 323–345.

Tyler, Tom R. *Why People Obey the Law*. Princeton, NJ: Princeton University Press, 2006.

Tyler, Tom R. and Steven L. Blader. *Cooperation in Groups: Procedural Justice, Social Identity, and Behavioral Engagement*. Philadelphia, PA: Psychology Press, 2000.

Tyler, Tom R. and Peter Degoey. "Trust in Organizational Authorities: The Influence of Motive Attributions on Willingness to Accept Decisions." In *Trust in Organizational Authorities*, edited by Roderick M. Kramer and Tom R. Tyler, 331.Thousand Oaks, CA: Sage Publications, Inc., 1996.

Tyler, Tom R. and E. Allan Lind. "A Relational Model of Authority in Groups." In *Advances in Experimental Social Psychology*, edited by Mark P. Zanna. Vol. 25, 115–191. New York: Academic Press, 1992.

Tyler, Tom R. and Heather J. Smith. "Social Justice and Social Movements." Chapter 101 in *The Handbook of Social Psychology*, edited by Daniel T. Gilbert, Susan T. Fiske and Gardner Lindzey. 4th Edition. Vol. II, 595–629. New York: Oxford University Press, 1998.

Ulen, Thomas S. "Rational Choice Theory in Law and Economics." In *Encyclopedia of Law and Economics*, edited by Boudewijn Bouckaert and Gerrit De Geest. Vol. 0710, 790–818. Available at: http://encyclo.findlaw.com/0710book.pdf: Edward Elgar and the University of Ghent, 1999.

United States Attorney's Office, Announcement of Decision not to Prosecute Sequa Corporation (June 24, 1993). Reprinted in press releases issued by United States Attorney, Southern District of New York, 1248 PLI/CORP. 197, 211–214 (2001).

United States Attorney's Office. *The Securities and Exchange Commission Today Entered into a Deferred Prosecution Agreement (DPA) with Tenaris S.A. in its First-Ever Use of the Approach to Facilitate and Reward Cooperation in SEC Investigations*. Available at: http://www.sec.gov/news/press/2011/2011-112.htm (May 17, 2011).

United States Federal Department of Justice, Antitrust Division. *Corporate Leniency Policy*. Available at: http://www.justice.gov/atr/public/guidelines/0091.pdf (August 10, 1993).

United States Government Accountability Office (GAO). *Corporate Crime: Preliminary Observations On DOJ's Use and Oversight of Deferred Prosecution and Non-Prosecution Agreements (Statement of Eileen R. Larence, Director Homeland Security and Justice)*. Available at: http://www.gao.gov/new.items/d09636t.pdf (June 25, 2009).

United States Sentencing Commission (USSC). Report on the Continuing Impact of United States v. Booker on Federal Sentencing. Available at: http://www.ussc.gov/Legislative_and_Public_Affairs/Congressional_Testimony_and_Reports/Booker_Reports/2012_Booker/Part_A.pdf.

United States Sentencing Commission (USSC). *Federal Sentencing Guidelines Manual: Chapter Eight – Sentencing of Organizations*. Available at: http://www.ussc.gov/Guidelines/Organizational_Guidelines/guidelines_chapter_8.htm (November 1, 2009).

Van Bael, Ivo. *Competition Law of the European Community*. The Hague, Netherlands: Kluwer Law International, 2005.

Van Den Bergh, Roger. "Should Consumer Protection Law Be Publicly Enforced? An Economic Perspective on EC Regulation 2006/2004 and its Implementation in the Consumer Protection Laws of the Member States." In *Collective Enforcement of Consumer Law: Securing Compliance in Europe Through Private Group Action and Public Authority Intervention*, edited by Willem Van Boom and Marco Loos, 177–203. Groningen, Netherlands: Europa Law Publishing, 2007.

Van Den Bergh, Roger and Hans-Bernd Schäfer. "Member States Liability for Infringement of the Free Movement of Goods in the EC: An Economic Analysis." *Journal of Institutional and Theoretical Economics (JITE)* 156 (2000): 382–403.

Van Dijk, Eric and Marcel Zeelenberg. "The Discounting of Ambiguous

Information in Economic Decision Making." *Journal of Behavioral Decision Making* 16, No. 5 (2003): 341–352.

Vianale, Kenneth J. and Baruch Weiss, Assistant U.S. Attorneys for the S. Dist. of N.Y., U.S. Department of Justice Letter to Scott W. Muller & Carey R. Dunne, Davis Polk & Wardwell, Counsel to Prudential Securites, Inc. Available at: http://www.corporatecrimereporter.com/documents/prudential.pdf (October 17, 1994).

Vinegrad, Alan. "Deferred Prosecution of Corporations." *New York Law Journal* 230, No. 72 (2003).

Vito, Gennaro F. and Debora G. Wilson. *The American Juvenile Justice System*. Beverly Hills, CA: Sage Publications, Inc., 1985.

Vu, Stacey Newmann. "Corporate Criminal Liability: Patchwork Verdicts and the Problem of Locating a Guilty Agent." *Columbia Law Review* 104 (2004): 459–495.

Walsh, Charles J. and Alissa Pyrich. "Corporate Compliance Programs as a Defense to Criminal Liability: Can a Corporation Save its Soul?" *Rutgers Law Review* 47 (1995): 605–692.

Warin, F. Joseph and Andrew S. Boutros. "Deferred Prosecution Agreements: A View from the Trenches and a Proposal for Reform." *Virginia Law Review* 93 (2007): 121–134.

Warin, F. Joseph and Jason C. Schwartz. "Deferred Prosecution: The Need for Specialized Guidelines for Corporate Defendants." *The Journal of Corporation Law* 23 (1997): 121–134.

Webb, B., J. Chilvers, and J. Keeble. "Improving Business Environmental Performance: Corporate Incentives and Drivers in Decision Making." A Report to the Department for Environment, Food and Rural Affairs. Defra, London: Arthur D. Little Ltd, 2006.

Weissmann, Andrew. "A New Approach to Corporate Criminal Liability." *American Criminal Law Review* 44 (2007): 1319–1342.

Weissmann, Andrew and David Newman. "Rethinking Criminal Corporate Liability." *Indiana Law Journal (Bloomington)* 82 (2007): 411–451.

Wenzel, Michael. "The Impact of Outcome Orientation and Justice Concerns on Tax Compliance: The Role of Taxpayers' Identity." *Journal of Applied Psychology* 87, No. 4 (2002): 629–645.

Wenzel, Michael. "Principles of Procedural Fairness in Reminder Letters: A Field-Experiment." *Center for Tax System Integrity Working Paper No. 42* (2002).

Wilkinson, Beth A. and Alex Young K. Oh. "The Principles of Federal Prosecution of Business Organizations: A Ten-Year Anniversary Perspective." *NYSBA Inside* 27, No. 2 (2009): 8–11.

Wils, Wouter P. J. "The Relationship Between Public Antitrust

Enforcement and Private Actions For Damages." *World Competition* 32, No. 1 (2009): 3–26.

Wolpin, Kenneth I. "Capital Punishment and Homicide in England: A Summary of Results." *The American Economic Review* 68, No. 2 (1978a): 422–427.

Wolpin, Kenneth I. "An Economic Analysis of Crime and Punishment in England and Wales." *The Journal of Political Economy* 86, No. 5 (1978b): 815–840.

Wray, Christopher A. and Robert K. Hur. "Corporate Criminal Prosecution in a Post-Enron World: The Thompson Memo in Theory and Practice." *The American Criminal Law Review* 43 (2006): 1095–1188.

Yu, Jiang. "Punishment Certainty and Severity: Testing a Specific Deterrence Model on Drunk Driving Recidivism." *Journal of Criminal Justice* 22, No. 4 (1994): 355–366.

Yu, Jiang and Allen E. Liska. "The Certainty of Punishment: A Reference Group Effect and its Functional Form." *Criminology (Beverly Hills)* 31, No. 3 (1993): 447–464.

Zey, Mary. *Rational Choice Theory and Organizational Theory: A Critique*. Thousand Oaks CA: Sage Publications, Inc., 1998.

Zimring, Franklin E. and Gordon Hawkins. *Deterrence: The Legal Threat in Crime Control*. Chicago, IL: University of Chicago Press, 1973.

Index